UNITED ARAB EMIRATES YEARBOOK

2005

The *UAE Yearbook* project is a multimedia publishing programme undertaken by Trident Press in conjunction with the UAE Ministry of Information and Culture. In addition to this book, the project includes operation of the Ministry's official website: www.uaeinteract.com and production of the annual DVD video/rom.

Editors:
Ibrahim Al Abed
Paula Vine
Peter Hellyer

Additional Contributors:
Gabrielle Warnock
Simon Aspinall
Peter Vine
Daniel Potts

Text copyright ©2005: Trident Press

Photographs ©: Trident Press Ltd, Gulf News, Emirates News Agency (WAM), Getty Images,
UAE Ministry of Information and Culture and credited photographers (see page 351).

English edition design and typesetting: Jane Stark, Trident Press

Yearbook information is, by definition, subject to change. The current volume is based on available information at the time of printing. Whilst every care has been taken to achieve accuracy, the publishers cannot accept any liability for consequences arising from the use of information contained in this book.
Statistics are based on available sources and are not necessarily official or endorsed by the UAE Government.

Enquiries may be addressed to:
Ministry of Information and Culture
PO Box 17, Abu Dhabi, UAE
Tel: (9712) 4453000; Fax (9712) 4450458
E-mail: admin@extinfo.gov.ae
Web site: www.uaeinteract.com

Published by Trident Press Ltd
175 Piccadilly, Mayfair, London W1J 9TB
Tel: 020 7491 8770; Fax: 020 7491 8664
E-mail: admin@tridentpress.com
Website: www.tridentpress.com

British Library Cataloguing in Publication Data:
A CIP catalogue record for this book is available
from the British Library.

ISBN 1-900724-71-5 (hardback); 1-900724-89-8 (paperback)

CONTENTS

FOREWORD

EACH YEAR THIS BOOK PLOTS THE COURSE of progress in the UAE. Since the founding of the nation, in 1971, we have charted the tremendous strides that have been taken. In doing so we have also paid tribute to the founding father of the United Arab Emirates and its much loved President, Sheikh Zayed. Involved in government as far back as 1946, Ruler of Abu Dhabi since 1966, the initiator, in 1968, of plans leading to the federation of the seven emirates and then UAE President, he led the country from underdevelopment and poverty to become the modern, prosperous and stable society that it is today. Sheikh Zayed died on 2 November 2004.

The deep sense of loss felt by so many will remain for a long time, but Sheikh Zayed always looked on the positive side of life and would want, more than anything, that we celebrate his life and all that he achieved. This special edition of the *UAE Yearbook* is dedicated to that very purpose.

Through all the years of his Presidency Sheikh Zayed steered a straight course on this great voyage that we are engaged in, aimed at raising standards of living and creating a stable and free society in which business and creativity would prosper. He also fought against injustice and suffering on the international stage and contributed in a significant way to world peace. In doing so he earned deep respect as a statesman and the response to his death from world leaders, and a large number of ordinary people from all around the world, is testament to his impact.

Among the milestones that were passed in 2004, under Sheikh Zayed's Presidency, were two firsts – the first woman appointed as a member of the Council of Ministers, and the first UAE sportsman to win an Olympic Games medal – most appropriately a gold one! Both achievements reflect Sheikh Zayed's vision of how the country should develop – that women, like men, must contribute to the building of our nation and that each individual has a duty to strive for excellence.

The voyage that Sheikh Zayed began so many years ago continues today. He has charted the waters well and has given us a well-founded vessel in which we can continue to travel safely on the same course, and with the same objectives in mind. We are deeply grateful for his contribution to building our nation and improving our lives. We will continue to work hard to honour his legacy.

ABDULLAH BIN ZAYED AL NAHYAN
MINISTER OF INFORMATION AND CULTURE

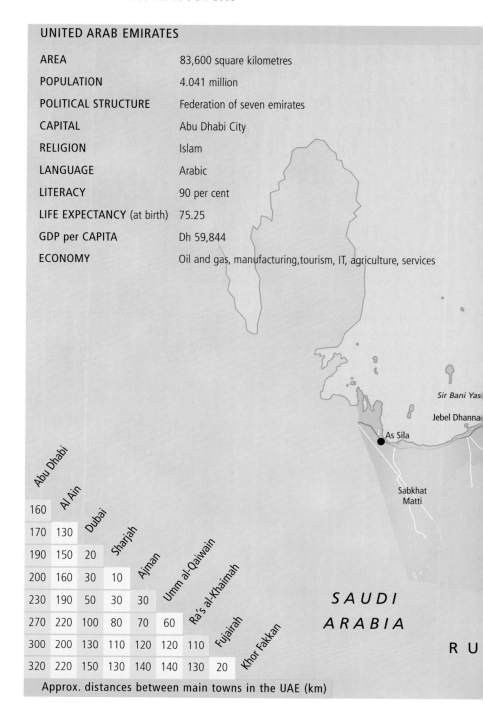

UNITED ARAB EMIRATES

AREA	83,600 square kilometres
POPULATION	4.041 million
POLITICAL STRUCTURE	Federation of seven emirates
CAPITAL	Abu Dhabi City
RELIGION	Islam
LANGUAGE	Arabic
LITERACY	90 per cent
LIFE EXPECTANCY (at birth)	75.25
GDP per CAPITA	Dh 59,844
ECONOMY	Oil and gas, manufacturing, tourism, IT, agriculture, services

Sir Bani Yas

Jebel Dhanna

As Sila

Sabkhat Matti

SAUDI

ARABIA

R U

Abu Dhabi	Al Ain	Dubai	Sharjah	Ajman	Umm al-Qaiwain	Ra's al-Khaimah	Fujairah	Khor Fakkan
160								
170	130							
190	150	20						
200	160	30	10					
230	190	50	30	30				
270	220	100	80	70	60			
300	200	130	110	120	120	110		
320	220	150	130	140	140	130	20	

Approx. distances between main towns in the UAE (km)

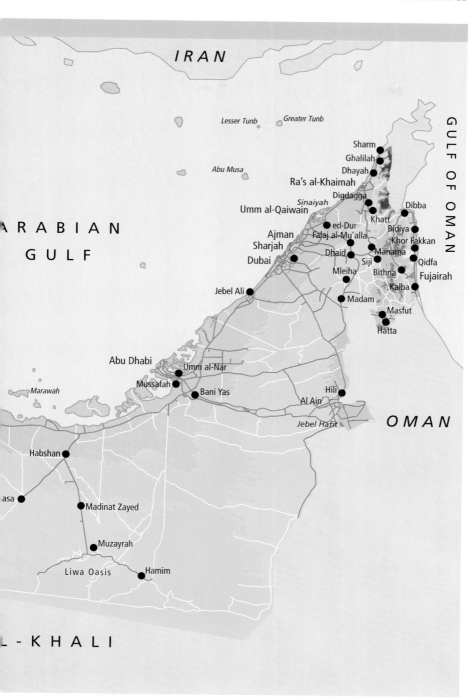

IRAN

GULF OF OMAN

Lesser Tunb   *Greater Tunb*

Sharm
Ghalilah
Abu Musa   Dhayah
Ra's al-Khaimah
Digdagga
ARABIAN   Umm al-Qaiwain   *Sinaiyah*   Dibba
                                                          Khatt
GULF   ed-Dur   Bidiya
                        Ajman   Falaj al-Mu'alla   Khor Fakkan
                     Sharjah   Manama
                     Dubai   Dhaid   Siji   Qidfa
                                          Mleiha Bithna Fujairah
                   Jebel Ali   Kalba
                                         Madam
                                                   Masfut
                                               Hatta

                     Abu Dhabi
                   Umm al-Nar
               Mussafah   Hili
Marawah   Bani Yas   Al Ain
                                    Jebel Hafit   OMAN

                Habshan

asa
            Madinat Zayed

            Muzayrah
        Liwa Oasis   Hamim

L - K H A L I

CLIMATE

Source: UAE Department of Water Resources

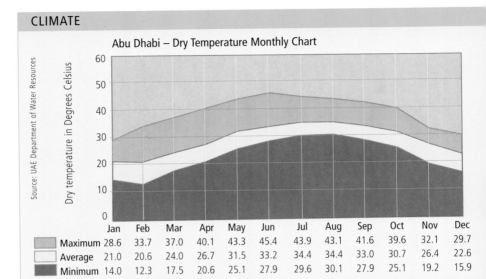

Abu Dhabi – Dry Temperature Monthly Chart

Dry temperature in Degrees Celsius

	Jan	Feb	Mar	Apr	May	Jun	Jul	Aug	Sep	Oct	Nov	Dec
Maximum	28.6	33.7	37.0	40.1	43.3	45.4	43.9	43.1	41.6	39.6	32.1	29.7
Average	21.0	20.6	24.0	26.7	31.5	33.2	34.4	34.4	33.0	30.7	26.4	22.6
Minimum	14.0	12.3	17.5	20.6	25.1	27.9	29.6	30.1	27.9	25.1	19.2	15.9

PHYSICAL FEATURES

The United Arab Emirates (UAE) occupies an area roughly the size of Portugal along the south-eastern tip of the Arabian Peninsula. Qatar lies to the west, Saudi Arabia to the south and west, and Oman to the north and east.

Four-fifths of the UAE is desert, yet it is a country of contrasting landscapes, from awe-inspiring dunes to rich oases, precipitous rocky mountains to fertile plains.

Offshore islands speckle the UAE's Arabian Gulf waters. For the most part seawater depth here is less than 10 metres, with an average overall depth of 31 metres and a very narrow tidal range. Sandy islets, seagrass beds, mangrove stands and *khors* (tidal inlets), as well as white sandy beaches, are scattered along the coast.

Inland from the Arabian Gulf, an extensive area of coastal salt flats (*sabkha*) stretches to the north and west. Isolated *sabkha*, otherwise surrounded by dune and gravel desert, is found further inland (particularly in Abu Dhabi's Western Region).

CLIMATE

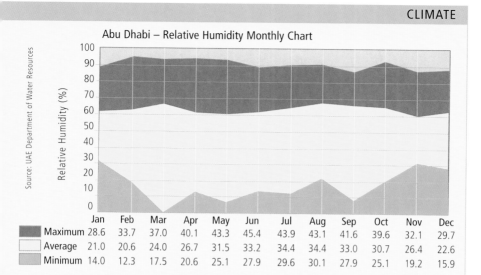

Abu Dhabi – Relative Humidity Monthly Chart

Source: UAE Department of Water Resources

Relative Humidity (%)

	Jan	Feb	Mar	Apr	May	Jun	Jul	Aug	Sep	Oct	Nov	Dec
Maximum	28.6	33.7	37.0	40.1	43.3	45.4	43.9	43.1	41.6	39.6	32.1	29.7
Average	21.0	20.6	24.0	26.7	31.5	33.2	34.4	34.4	33.0	30.7	26.4	22.6
Minimum	14.0	12.3	17.5	20.6	25.1	27.9	29.6	30.1	27.9	25.1	19.2	15.9

PHYSICAL FEATURES

Sandy desert begins behind the coastal *sabkha*, with little white ripples eventually forming an expanse of large orange-red dunes in the south-west. Near Liwa, a series of oasis villages, towering dunes rising to a spectacular 200 metres, form part of the Empty Quarter or Rub al-Khali, a vast desert which extends beyond the UAE's southern border.

Al Ain, another lush oasis, lies to the east in the shade of the solitary mountain Jebel Hafit.

To the north-east a sand and gravel desert

reaches towards the jagged Hajar Mountain chain that splits the UAE from north to south in the Northern Emirates. A fertile plain watered by runoff separates the mountains from the coast around Ra's al-Khaimah. Here rocky slopes rise to 1300 metres within UAE territory, falling steeply to the UAE's East Coast where a fertile gravel plain borders the oceanic waters of the Gulf of Oman. Commercially important fisheries thrive in these nutrient-rich waters and the dramatic shoreline is washed by tides and currents.

SHEIKH ZAYED BIN SULTAN AL NAHYAN

ON 2 NOVEMBER 2004, HIS HIGHNESS SHEIKH ZAYED BIN SULTAN AL NAHYAN, President of the United Arab Emirates and Ruler of the Emirate of Abu Dhabi, died. He was in his late eighties and had been Ruler of Abu Dhabi since 1966, and UAE President since the formation of the Federation on 2 December 1971. He was succeeded as Ruler of Abu Dhabi by his eldest son and Crown Prince, His Highness Sheikh Khalifa bin Zayed Al Nahyan, who, on 3 November, was also elected unanimously by the Supreme Council of Rulers of the UAE as the country's second President.

Sheikh Zayed had been involved in government since 1946, when he became the Representative of the Ruler of Abu Dhabi in the Eastern Region of the emirate, and, upon becoming Ruler in 1966, he took the initiatives that led to the formation of the seven-member UAE Federation five years later. For the citizens of the Emirates, the vast majority of whom were too young to recall any other leader, he was not merely a President and Ruler, but he was also like a father. His passing prompted, as was to be expected, an outpouring of grief throughout the country, both among citizens and amongst the UAE's large expatriate population, many of whom have lived much or all of their lives in the Emirates.

President Sheikh Zayed, however, was not merely a national leader, but a widely-respected Arab and world statesman, as was shown by the fact that many Kings and Heads of State, Crown Princes, Prime Ministers and other senior government figures from around the globe flew in to attend his funeral or to pay their condolences to his successor. Among them were representatives not only from the Arab world, such as the Kings of Bahrain and Jordan, the Sultan of Oman, the Emir of Qatar, the Crown Prince of Saudi Arabia and the Presidents of Yemen, Iraq, Lebanon, Egypt, Sudan and Algeria, but also from Asia, including the Presidents of India, Pakistan and Afghanistan, and from Europe, including the President of France and Britain's Prince Charles, Africa and the Americas. He also received the rare tribute of a special motion of condolences in Britain's House of Commons.

Obituaries in some of the world's leading newspapers, such as *The New York Times* and *The Times*, as well as the many messages of condolence received by President Sheikh Khalifa, from world figures such as Britain's Queen, the US and French presidents, the Emperor of Japan, the Secretary-General of the United Nations and numerous other monarchs, presidents and prime ministers, paid credit both to his achievements in developing the United Arab Emirates into a stable, modern and tolerant state, through a sagacious use of the country's oil and gas revenues, but also to his wisdom in international affairs, holding fast to his own basic principles, while seeking to promote conciliation and peace-making wherever the opportunity arose.

Thus Britain's Queen Elizabeth expressed her condolences to President Sheikh Khalifa 'on the death of your distinguished father . . . who served your country with such dedication and dignity over many years. I am sure that the prosperity of the UAE today will be widely seen as a testimony to Sheikh Zayed's wisdom, skill and devotion to the service of the state'.

US President George W. Bush commented: 'The United States mourns the passing of a great friend of our country . . . Sheikh Zayed was . . . a pioneer, an elder statesman and a close ally. He and his fellow rulers built their federation into a prosperous, tolerant and well-governed state'.

France's President Jacques Chirac, expressing 'deep sorrow and emotion', described Sheikh Zayed as 'a man of peace and vision'. In a message to Sheikh Khalifa, he added: 'The work accomplished by Sheikh Zayed is huge . . . Man of peace and vision, he kept promoting the virtues of compromise, reason and dialogue in a region troubled by crises and conflicts. His name will remain closely associated with the cause of peace and development in the Middle East to which he devoted his life'.

United Nations Secretary-General Kofi Annan noted in a statement that Sheikh Zayed had 'devoted tireless efforts to building the state and nation and, in so doing, earned the respect of the population for his wisdom, generosity and his achievements in building a prosperous economy. Sheikh Zayed's wisdom, strong belief in diplomacy and generous assistance to developing countries also won him wide renown outside his own country – in the Islamic world and even further afield. And he was a friend of the United Nations, who always sought to strengthen relations between the Organisation and his country'.

He was honoured in a special commemorative session of the UN General Assembly, a rare mark of appreciation.

Insofar as it was possible to detect a single thread running through the statements and messages, as well as through the response of UAE residents, it was that the life and achievements of President Sheikh Zayed were characterised by his deep religious faith, his vision, his determination and hard work, his generosity, both at home and abroad, and the way in which he devoted his life to the service of his people and to the pursuit, at home and elsewhere, to helping those in need and to the creation of a better world.

The United Arab Emirates today is his memorial – not just the physical infrastructure but, more importantly, its people – while the international response to his passing is testimony to the way in which he gave to his country a voice listened to, with respect, around the world.

In a statement on the election of Sheikh Khalifa as the new President, the members of the UAE Supreme Council noted their 'keen desire to be loyal to the principles of leadership and the values of justice and right laid down by His Highness Sheikh Zayed' and pledged to follow his path. In their view, such is the best way of honouring his memory.

Born around 1918 in Abu Dhabi, Sheikh Zayed was the youngest of the four sons of Sheikh Sultan bin Zayed Al Nahyan, Ruler of Abu Dhabi from 1922 to 1926. He was named after his grandfather, Sheikh Zayed bin Khalifa, who ruled the emirate from 1855 to 1909, the longest reign in the three and a half centuries since the Al Nahyan family emerged as leaders of the Emirate of Abu Dhabi.

Abu Dhabi, like the other emirates of the southern Arabian Gulf formerly known as the Trucial States, was then in treaty relations with Britain. At the time Sheikh Zayed was born, the emirate was poor and undeveloped, with an economy based primarily on fishing and pearl diving along the coast and offshore and on simple agriculture in scattered oases inland. Part of the population was nomadic, ranging across a wide area of south-eastern Arabia in search of pasture.

Life, even for members of the ruling family, was simple. Education was generally confined to lessons in reading and writing, along with instruction in Islam from the local preacher, while modern facilities such as roads, communications and health care were conspicuous only by their absence. Transport was by camel or boat, and the harshness of the arid climate meant that survival itself was often a major concern.

In early 1928, following the death of Sheikh Sultan's successor, his brother Sheikh Saqr, a family conclave selected as Ruler Sheikh Shakhbut, Sheikh Sultan's eldest son. He was to hold the post until August 1966, when he stepped down in favour of his brother Zayed.

Throughout the late 1920s and 1930s, as Sheikh Zayed grew to manhood, he displayed an early thirst for knowledge that took him out into the desert with the *bedu* tribesmen to learn all he could about the way of life of the people and the environment in which they lived. He later recalled with pleasure his experience of desert life and his initiation into the sport of falconry, which became a lifelong passion.

In his book, *Falconry: Our Arab Heritage*, published in 1977, Sheikh Zayed noted that the companionship of a hunting party

. . . permits each and every member of the expedition to speak freely and express his ideas and viewpoints without inhibition and restraint, and allows the one responsible to acquaint himself with the wishes of his people, to know their problems and perceive their views accurately, and thus to be in a position to help and improve their situation.

From his desert journeys, Sheikh Zayed developed an understanding of the relationship between man and his environment and, in particular, the need to ensure that sustainable use was made of natural resources. Once an avid shot, he abandoned the gun for falconry at the age of 25, aware that hunting with a gun could lead rapidly to extinction of the native wildlife.

He learned, too, about the coastal fishing communities, and the age-old offshore pearling industry, which had begun as long ago as 5000BC, and involved diving without artificial aids to the seabed to harvest the pearls that were to be found there in profusion. By the 1930s, as a result of the world economic depression and of the Japanese invention of the cultured pearl, the industry was dying, and, besides gaining an insight into the hardships faced by those involved, he also saw the urgent need for alternative sources of income to be found. His recognition of the dangers of dependence on one single source of income, linked to the vagaries of international markets, was a lesson that he carried forward into later life, when he insisted, with considerable success, that the United Arab Emirates needed to diversify its economy beyond the lucrative exploitation of oil and gas.

His travels in the remoter areas of Abu Dhabi and his voyages offshore provided Sheikh Zayed with a deep understanding both of the country and of its people. In the early 1930s, when the first oil company teams arrived to carry out preliminary surface geological surveys, he was assigned by his brother the task of guiding them around the desert. At the same time, he obtained his first exposure to the industry that was later to have such a great impact upon the country.

In the year 1946, Sheikh Zayed was chosen to fill a vacancy as Ruler's Representative in the Eastern Region of Abu Dhabi, centred on the oasis of Al Ain, approximately 160 kilometres east of the island of Abu Dhabi itself. Inhabited continuously for over 5000 years, the oasis had nine villages, six of which belonged to Abu Dhabi and three, including Buraimi, by which name the oasis was also known, which belonged to the Sultanate of Oman. The job involved not only the task of administering the six villages but also the whole of the adjacent desert region, enabling Sheikh Zayed to learn the techniques of government as well as deepening his knowledge of the tribes. In the late 1940s and early 1950s, Saudi Arabia's territorial claims to Buraimi provided him with the opportunity to gain experience of politics on a broader scale.

Sheikh Zayed brought to his new task a firm belief in the values of consultation and consensus, in contrast to confrontation. Foreign visitors, such as the British

explorer Sir Wilfred Thesiger, who first met him at this time, noted with approbation that his judgements 'were distinguished by their acute insights, wisdom and fairness'.

Sheikh Zayed swiftly established himself not only as someone who had a clear vision of what he wished to achieve for the people of Al Ain, but also as someone who led by example.

A key task in the early years in Al Ain was that of stimulating the local economy, which was largely based on agriculture. To do this, he ensured that the ancient subterranean water channels or falajes (*aflaj*) were cleaned out, and personally financed the construction of a new one, taking part in the strenuous labour that was involved.

He also ordered a revision of local water ownership rights to ensure a more equitable distribution, surrendering the rights of his own family as an example to others. The consequent expansion of the area under cultivation in turn generated more income for the residents of Al Ain, helping to re-establish the oasis as the predominant market centre for a wide area.

With development gradually beginning to get under way, Sheikh Zayed commenced the laying out of a visionary city plan, and, in a foretaste of the massive afforestation programme of today, he also ordered the planting of ornamental trees that, now grown to maturity, have made Al Ain one of the greenest cities in Arabia.

In 1953, Sheikh Zayed made his first visit to Europe, accompanying his brother Shakhbut to Britain and France and attending an international arbitration tribunal on the legality of offshore oil concessions in the emirate. He recalled later how impressed he had been by the schools and hospitals he visited, becoming determined that his own people should have the benefit of similar facilities:

There were a lot of dreams I was dreaming about our land catching up with the modern world, but I was not able to do anything because I did not have the wherewithal in my hands to achieve these dreams. I was sure, however, that one day they would become true.

Despite the lack of government revenues, Sheikh Zayed succeeded in bringing progress to Al Ain, establishing the rudiments of an administrative machinery, personally funding the first modern school in the emirate and coaxing relatives and friends to contribute towards small-scale development programmes.

Oil production was to provide Sheikh Zayed with the means to fund his dreams, with the export of the first cargo of Abu Dhabi crude in 1962. Although oil prices were then far lower than they are today, the rapidly growing volume of exports, from both onshore and offshore, revolutionised the economy of Abu Dhabi and its people began to look forward eagerly to receiving similar benefits

to those already being enjoyed by their neighbours in Qatar, Bahrain, Kuwait and Saudi Arabia. The pearling industry had finally come to an end shortly after the Second World War, and little had emerged to take its place. Indeed, during the late 1950s and early 1960s, many people had left Abu Dhabi for other, oil-producing, Gulf states where there were opportunities for employment.

The economic hardships experienced by Abu Dhabi since the 1930s had accustomed the Ruler, Sheikh Shakhbut, to a cautious frugality. Despite the growing aspiration of his people for progress, he was reluctant to invest the new oil revenues in development. Attempts by members of his family, including Sheikh Zayed, and by the leaders of the other tribes in the emirate to persuade him to move with the times were unsuccessful, and eventually the Al Nahyan family decided that the time had come for him to step down. The record of Sheikh Zayed over the previous 20 years in Al Ain and his popularity among the people made him the obvious choice as successor.

On 6 August 1966, Sheikh Zayed became Ruler, with a mandate from his family to press ahead as fast as possible with the development of Abu Dhabi. He was a man in a hurry. His years in Al Ain had not only given him valuable experience in government, but had also provided him with the time to develop a vision of how the emirate could progress. With revenues growing year by year as oil production increased, he was determined to use them in the service of the people, and a massive programme of construction of schools, housing, hospitals and roads got rapidly under way.

Of his first few weeks, Sheikh Zayed later said:

All the picture was prepared. It was not a matter of fresh thinking, but of simply putting into effect the thoughts of years and years. First I knew we had to concentrate on Abu Dhabi and public welfare. In short, we had to obey the circumstances: the needs of the people as a whole. Second, I wanted to approach other emirates to work with us. In harmony, in some sort of federation, we could follow the example of other developing countries.

One of Sheikh Zayed's early steps was to increase contributions to the Trucial States Development Fund, established a few years earlier. Abu Dhabi soon became its largest donor. At the beginning of 1968, when the British announced their intention of withdrawing from the Arabian Gulf by the end of 1971, Sheikh Zayed acted rapidly to initiate moves towards establishing closer ties with the emirates.

Along with the late Ruler of Dubai, Sheikh Rashid bin Saeed Al Maktoum, who was to become Vice-President and Prime Minister of the UAE, Sheikh Zayed took the lead in calling for a federation that would include not only the seven emirates that together made up the Trucial States, but also Qatar and Bahrain. When early hopes of a federation of nine states eventually foundered, Sheikh

Zayed led his fellow rulers in achieving agreement on the establishment of the UAE, which formally emerged on the international stage on 2 December 1971.

While his enthusiasm for federation was a key factor in the formation of the UAE, Sheikh Zayed also won support for the way in which he sought consensus and agreement among his fellow rulers:

I am not imposing change on anyone. That is tyranny. All of us have our opinions, and these opinions can change. Sometimes we put all opinions together, and then extract from them a single point of view. This is our democracy.

Sheikh Zayed was elected by his fellow rulers as the first President of the UAE, a post to which he was successively re-elected at five-year intervals.

The new state came into being at a time of political turmoil in the region. A couple of days earlier, on the night of 30 November and the early morning of 1 December, Iran had seized the islands of Greater and Lesser Tunb, part of Ra's al-Khaimah, and had landed troops on Abu Musa, part of Sharjah (see section on Foreign Policy).

On land, demarcation of the borders between the individual emirates and with the Federation's neighbours had not been completed, although a preliminary agreement had been reached between Abu Dhabi and Oman (a final agreement on the UAE border with Oman was ratified in 2003).

Foreign observers, who lacked an understanding of the importance of a common history and heritage in bringing together the people of the UAE, predicted that the new state would survive only with difficulty, pointing to disputes with its neighbours and to the wide disparity in the size, population and level of development of the seven emirates.

Better informed about the character of the country, Sheikh Zayed was naturally more optimistic. Looking back a quarter of a century later he noted:

Our experiment in federation, in the first instance, arose from a desire to increase the ties that bind us, as well as from the conviction of all that they were part of one family, and that they must gather together under one leadership.

We had never (previously) had an experience in federation, but our proximity to each other and the ties of blood relationship between us are factors which led us to believe that we must establish a federation that should compensate for the disunity and fragmentation that earlier prevailed.

That which has been accomplished has exceeded all our expectations, and that, with the help of God and a sincere will, confirms that there is nothing that cannot be achieved in the service of the people if determination is firm and intentions are sincere.

The predictions of those early pessimists were overwhelmingly shown to be unfounded. In the 33 years that have followed, the UAE has not only survived, but has developed at a rate that is almost without parallel. The country has been utterly transformed. Its population has risen from around 250,000 in 1971 to an estimate of around 4.3 million by late 2004. Progress, in terms of the provision of social services, health and education, as well as in sectors such as communications and the oil and non-oil economy, has brought a high standard of living that has spread throughout the seven emirates, from the ultra-modern cities to the remotest areas of desert and mountains. The change has, moreover, occurred against a backdrop of enviable political and social stability, despite the insecurity and conflict that has dogged much of the rest of the Gulf region.

The country has also established itself firmly on the international scene, both within the Arab region and in the broader community of nations. Its pursuit of dialogue and consensus and its firm adherence to the tenets of the Charter of the United Nations, in particular those dealing with the principle of non-interference in the affairs of other states, have been coupled with a quiet but extensive involvement in the provision of development assistance and humanitarian aid that, in per capita terms, has few parallels.

There is no doubt that the experiment in federation has been a success and the undoubted key to the achievements of the UAE has been the central role played by Sheikh Zayed during his years of leadership.

During his years in Al Ain he was able to develop a vision of how the country should progress, and, after becoming first Ruler of Abu Dhabi and then President of the UAE, he devoted over three and a half decades to making that vision a reality.

One foundation of his philosophy as a leader and statesman was that the resources of the country should be fully used to the benefit of the people. The UAE is fortunate to have been blessed with massive reserves of oil and gas and it is through careful utilisation of these, including the decision in 1973 that the government of Abu Dhabi, the emirate with the lion's share of reserves, should take a controlling share of the oil reserves. Together with its total ownership of the associated and non-associated gas reserves, agreed with the oil concession holders several years earlier, this ensured that the new state would have the financial resources necessary to underpin the development programme. Indeed there has been sufficient to permit the setting aside of large amounts for investment on behalf of future generations, now largely managed through the Abu Dhabi Investment Authority.

The financial resources, however, were always regarded by Sheikh Zayed not as a means unto themselves, but as a tool to facilitate the development of what he believed to be the real wealth of the country – its people, and, in particular, the younger generation. As he stated:

Wealth is not money. Wealth lies in men. This is where true power lies, the power that we value. They are the shield behind which we seek protection. This is what has convinced us to direct all our resources to building the individual, and to using the wealth with which God has provided us in the service of the nation, so that it may grow and prosper.

Unless wealth is used in conjunction with knowledge to plan for its use, and unless there are enlightened intellects to direct it, its fate is to diminish and to disappear. The greatest use that can be made of wealth is to invest it in creating generations of educated and trained people.

Addressing the graduation ceremony of the first class of students from the Emirates University in 1982, Sheikh Zayed said:

The building of mankind is difficult and hard. It represents, however, the real wealth [of the country]. This is not found in material wealth. It is made up of men, of children, and of future generations. It is this which constitutes the real treasure.

Within this framework, Sheikh Zayed believed that all of the country's citizens have a role to play in its development. Indeed he defined it not simply as a right, but as a duty. In one address to his colleagues in the Federal Supreme Council, he noted:

The most important of our duties as Rulers is to raise the standard of living of our people. To carry out one's duty is a responsibility given by God, and to follow up on work is the responsibility of everyone, both the old and the young.

Both men and women, he believed, should play their part. Recognising that in the past a lack of education and development had prevented women from playing a full role in much of the activity of society, he took action to ensure that this situation was addressed rapidly. Although women's advocates might argue that there is still much to be done, the achievements have been remarkable, and the country's women are now increasingly playing their part in political and economic life by taking up positions at all levels in the public and private sectors, with the first woman being appointed to the Cabinet late in 2004, the day before he died. In so doing, they enjoyed Sheikh Zayed's full support:

Women have the right to work everywhere. Islam affords to women their rightful status, and encourages them to work in all sectors, as long as they are afforded the appropriate respect. The basic role of women is the upbringing of children, but, over and above that, we must offer opportunities to a woman who chooses to perform other functions. What women have achieved in the Emirates in only a short space of time makes me both happy and content. We sowed our seeds yesterday, and today the fruit has already begun to appear. We praise God for the role that women play in our society. It is clear that this role is beneficial for both present and future generations.

Remarkable progress has now been achieved by the women of the Emirates, due in no small measure to initiatives taken by Sheikh Zayed and by his wife, HH Sheikha Fatima bint Mubarak, who is the President of the country's General Women's Union. Already playing a prominent role in the civil service, health, education and business, and even in the police and armed forces, the UAE's women are now increasingly active in the political process, through membership in the various consultative and legislative bodies, and, as noted above, in the Cabinet.

In an interview in October 2002, Sheikh Zayed noted that:

The Woman is the mother, sister, aunt and wife of Man, and we should not, therefore, deprive women of their rights, which God has instructed us to respect and observe. Women should be respected and encouraged in whatever work they might do.

'The UAE General Women's Union has contributed actively to the enhancement of the role of and contribution of women,' he noted, 'while at the same time, together with this contribution, UAE women have maintained and preserved the values of our society'.

Sheikh Zayed long, and emphatically, made it clear that he believed that the younger generation, those who have enjoyed the fruits of the UAE's development programme throughout their lives, must take up the burden once carried by their parents. Within his immediate family, he ensured that his sons took up posts in government at which they were expected to work, and not simply enjoy as sinecures. Besides his heir as Abu Dhabi Ruler and successor as UAE President, Sheikh Khalifa, most hold senior positions in the federal or local governments. When in the early 1990s, some young UAE men complained about the perceived lack of employment opportunities at a salary level that met their expectations, he bluntly offered them positions as agricultural labourers, so that they might learn the dignity of work:

Work is of great importance, and of great value in building both individuals and societies. The size of a salary is not a measure of the worth of an individual. What is important is an individual's sense of dignity and self-respect. It is my duty as the leader of the young people of this country to encourage them to work and to exert themselves in order to raise their own standards and to be of service to the country. The individual who is healthy and of a sound mind and body but who does not work commits a crime against himself and against society.

We look forward in the future to seeing our sons and daughters playing a more active role broadening their participation in the process of development and shouldering their share of the responsibilities, especially in the private sector, so as to lay the foundations for the success of this participation and effectiveness. At the same time, we are greatly concerned to raise the standard and dignity of the work ethic in our society, and to increase the percentage of citizens in the labour force. This can be achieved by following a realistic and well-planned approach that will improve performance and productivity, moving towards the long-term goal of secure and comprehensive development.

In this sphere, as in other areas, Sheikh Zayed was long concerned about the possible adverse impact upon the younger generation of the easy life they enjoy, so far removed from the resilient, resourceful lifestyle of their parents. One key feature of Sheikh Zayed's strategy of government, therefore, was the encouragement of initiatives designed to conserve and cherish features of the traditional culture of the people, in order to familiarise the younger generation with the ways of their ancestors. In his view, it was of crucial importance that the lessons and heritage of the past were remembered. They provide, he believed, an essential foundation upon which real progress can be achieved:

History is a continuous chain of events. The present is only an extension of the past. He who does not know his past cannot make the best of his present and future, for it is from the past that we learn. We gain experience and we take advantage of the lessons and results [of the past]. Then we adopt the best and that which suits our present needs, while avoiding the mistakes made by our fathers and grandfathers. The new generation should have a proper appreciation of the role played by their forefathers. They should adopt their model, and the supreme ideal of patience, fortitude, hard work and dedication to doing their duty.

Once believed to have been little more than a backwater in the history of the Middle East, the UAE is now known to have been a country which has played a vital role in the development of civilisation in the region for thousands of years.

The first archaeological excavations in the UAE took place 46 years ago, in 1959, with the archaeologists benefiting extensively from the interest shown in their work by Sheikh Zayed. Indeed, he himself invited them to visit the Al Ain area to examine remains in and around the oasis that proved to be some of the most important yet found in south-eastern Arabia. In the decades that followed, Sheikh Zayed continued to support archaeological studies throughout the country, eager to ensure that the achievements of the past became known to the people of today.

Appropriately, one of the UAE's most important archaeological sites has been discovered on Abu Dhabi's western island of Sir Bani Yas, which for over 25 years has been a private wildlife reserve created by Sheikh Zayed to ensure the survival of some of Arabia's most endangered species.

If the heritage of the people of the UAE was important to Sheikh Zayed, so too was the conservation of its natural environment and wildlife. He believed

that the strength of character of the Emirati people derives, in part, from the struggle that they were obliged to wage in order to survive in the harsh and arid local environment.

His belief in conservation of the environment owed nothing to modern fashions. Acknowledged by the presentation to him of the prestigious Gold Panda award of the Worldwide Fund for Nature, and by the inauguration, early in 2001, of the Zayed International Prize for the Environment (whose first recipient was former US President and Nobel Peace Prize winner Jimmy Carter), it derived, instead, from his own upbringing, where a sustainable use of resources required man to live in harmony with nature. This led him to ensure that conservation of wildlife and the environment is a key part of government policy. At the same time he has stimulated and personally supervised a massive programme of afforestation that has now seen over 150 million trees planted.

In a speech given on the occasion of the UAE's first Environment Day in February 1998, Sheikh Zayed spelt out his beliefs:

We cherish our environment because it is an integral part of our country, our history and our heritage. On land and in the sea, our forefathers lived and survived in this environment. They were able to do so only because they recognised the need to conserve it, to take from it only what they needed to live, and to preserve it for succeeding generations.

With God's will, we shall continue to work to protect our environment and our wildlife, as did our forefathers before us. It is a duty, and, if we fail, our children, rightly, will reproach us for squandering an essential part of their inheritance, and of our heritage.

Like most conservationists, Sheikh Zayed was concerned wherever possible to remedy the damage done by man to wildlife. His programme on the island of Sir Bani Yas for the captive breeding of endangered native animals such as the Arabian oryx and the Arabian gazelle achieved impressive results, so much so that not only is the survival of both species now assured, but animals are also being carefully reintroduced to the wild.

As in other areas of national life, Sheikh Zayed made it clear that conservation is not simply the task of government. Despite the creation of official institutions like the Federal Environment Agency and Abu Dhabi's Environmental Research and Wildlife Development Agency, the UAE's President believed firmly that there was also a role for the individual and for non-governmental organisations, both of citizens and expatriates.

He believed that society can only develop and flourish if all of its members acknowledge their responsibilities. This applies not only to concerns such as environmental conservation, but to other areas of national life as well.

Members of the Al Nahyan family have been rulers of Abu Dhabi since at least the beginning of the eighteenth century, longer than any other ruling dynasty in Arabia. In Arabian *bedu* society, however, the legitimacy of a ruler, and of a ruling family, derives essentially from consensus and from consent and the legitimacy of the political system today derives from the support it draws from the people of the UAE. The principle of consultation (*shura*) is an essential part of that system.

At an informal level, that principle has long been practiced through the institution of the *majlis* (council) where a leading member of society holds an 'open-house' discussion forum, at which any individual may put forward views for discussion and consideration. While the *majlis* system – the UAE's form of direct democracy – still continues, it is, naturally, best suited to a relatively small community.

In 1970, recognising that Abu Dhabi was embarking on a process of rapid change and development, Sheikh Zayed established the emirate's National Consultative Council, bringing together the leaders of each of the main tribes and families which comprised the population. A similar body was created in 1971 for the entire UAE, the Federal National Council, the state's parliament.

Both institutions represent the formalisation of the traditional process of consultation and discussion, and Sheikh Zayed frequently urged their members to express their views openly, without fear or favour.

At present members of both Councils, as well as lower-level Municipal Councils, continue to be selected by the rulers, in consultation with leading members of the community in each emirate. In the future, Sheikh Zayed predicted, however, a formula for elected representatives would be devised. He noted, though, that, as in so many other fields, it would be necessary to move ahead with care in order to ensure that only such institutions as are appropriate for Emirati society are adopted.

Questioned in 1998 by *The New York Times* on the topic of the possible introduction of an elected parliamentary democracy, Sheikh Zayed replied:

Why should we abandon a system that satisfied our people in order to introduce a system that seems to engender dissent and confrontation? Our system of government is based upon our religion, and is what our people want. Should they seek alternatives, we are ready to listen to them. We have always said that our people should voice their demands openly. We are all in the same boat, and they are both captain and crew.

Our doors here are open for any opinion to be expressed, and this is well known by all our citizens. It is our deep conviction that God the Creator has created people free, and has prescribed that each individual must enjoy freedom of choice. No-one should act as if he owns others. Those in a position of leadership should deal with their subjects with compassion and understanding, because this is the duty enjoined upon them by God Almighty; who enjoins us to treat all living creatures with dignity.

How can there be anything less for man, created as God's vice-gerent on earth? Our system of government does not derive its authority from man, but is enshrined in our religion, and is based on God's book, the Holy Quran. What need have we of what others have conjured up? Its teachings are eternal and complete, while the systems conjured up by man are transitory and incomplete.

Sheikh Zayed imbibed the principles of Islam in his childhood and they remained the foundation of his beliefs and principles throughout his life. Indeed, the ability with which he and the people of the UAE were able to absorb and adjust to the remarkable changes of recent decades can be ascribed largely to the fact that Islam has provided an immutable and steadfast core of their lives. Today, it provides the inspiration for the UAE judicial system and its place as the ultimate source of legislation is enshrined in the country's Constitution.

Islam, like other divinely-revealed religions, has those among its claimed adherents who purport to interpret its message as justifying harsh dogmas and intolerance. In Sheikh Zayed's view, however, such an approach was not merely a perversion of the message but is in direct contradiction of it. Extremism, he believed, has no place in Islam. In contrast, he stressed that:

Islam is a civilising religion that gives mankind dignity. A Muslim is he who does not inflict evil upon others. Islam is the religion of tolerance and forgiveness, and not of war, of dialogue and understanding. It is Islamic social justice which has asked every Muslim to respect the other. To treat every person, no matter what his creed or race, as a special soul is a mark of Islam. It is just that point, embodied in the humanitarian tenets of Islam, that makes us so proud of it.

Within that context, Sheikh Zayed set his face firmly against those who preach intolerance and hatred:

In these times, we see around us violent men who claim to talk on behalf of Islam. Islam is far removed from their talk. If such people really wish for recognition from Muslims and the world, they should themselves first heed the words of God and His Prophet. Regrettably, however, these people have nothing whatsoever that connects them to Islam. They are apostates and criminals. We see them slaughtering children and the innocent. They kill people, spill their blood and destroy their property, and then claim to be Muslims.

'Muslims stand against any person of Muslim faith who will try to commit any terror act against a fellow human being,' he said in his interview with *Al Ahram* in October 2002. 'A terrorist is an enemy of Islam and of humanity, while the true Muslim is friendly to all human beings and a brother to other Muslims and non-Muslims alike. This is because Islam is a religion of mercy and tolerance.' In accordance with that belief, Sheikh Zayed firmly condemned the wave of terror attacks that have taken place around the world in recent years.

In September 2001, following the attacks against the United States, he noted in a message to Heads of Government of the members of the North Atlantic Treaty Organisation (NATO) as well as to the leaders of Russia and China that:

the UAE clearly and unequivocally condemns the criminal acts that took place last week in New York and Washington, resulting in the deaths and injuries of thousands. There should be a direct move and a strong international alliance to eradicate terrorism, and all those who provide assistance to, or harbour it.

He recognised, however, the necessity not only of eradicating terrorism, but of tackling its fundamental causes, and, in particular, what he described as 'the daily and continuous acts of terrorism being committed by Israeli occupation forces in the occupied Palestinian territories against the unarmed Palestinian people'.

Besides the international campaign against the types of terrorism, there should be, he said, a strong international alliance that worked, in parallel, to exert real and sincere efforts to bring about a just and lasting solution to the Middle East conflict. 'The Arabs and the Islamic world cannot accept what is happening in the occupied Palestinian territories – the daily killings, deportations and destruction. All of this is politically and morally unacceptable'.

'We can work closely together at this critical and dangerous time through which we are passing,' Sheikh Zayed told the foreign leaders in September 2001:

We are confident that we can deal with the situation that we face. But we require, too, that your Governments should work in a parallel and effective way to ensure a just and lasting peace in the Middle East.

We request all leaders to work in full frankness on the two tasks in parallel and at the same time, thus working for the achievement of a just and lasting solution to the Middle East conflict, based upon the application of international legitimacy and enabling the Palestinian people to exercise their right to self-determination, to an end of occupation, and to establish their own independent state on their territory with Jerusalem as its capital.

'There will be no permanent peace,' Sheikh Zayed had noted, 'unless this is done. For the eradication of one or more individuals will not end the problems (of terrorism) in a permanent way when hundreds or thousands of others may step forward to replace them.'

In a paper delivered on his behalf to an international conference on terrorism held in Abu Dhabi in January 2003, he added: 'We cannot accept any link between terrorism and a specific religion or race . . . Terrorism is an international phenomenon that has no religion or race . . . We categorically reject the deliberate attempts to link terrorism with the right of a people to resist occupation'.

Sheikh Zayed was an eager advocate of tolerance, discussion and a better understanding between those of different faiths, and in particular, has been an ardent advocate of dialogue between Muslims and Christians, recognising that this is essential if mankind is ever to move forward in harmony. His faith was well summed up by a statement explaining the essential basis of his own beliefs: 'My religion is based neither on hope, nor on fear. I worship my God because I love Him.'

That faith, with its belief in the brotherhood of man and in the duty incumbent upon the strong to provide assistance to those less fortunate than themselves, was fundamental to Sheikh Zayed's vision of how his country and people should develop. It is, too, a key to the foreign policy of the UAE, which he devised and guided since the establishment of the state until his death.

The UAE itself has been able to progress only because of the way in which its component parts have successfully been able to come together in a relationship of harmony, working together for common goals. That approach has also been applied in the sphere of foreign policy. Within the Arabian Gulf region, and in the broader Arab world, the UAE has sought to enhance cooperation and to resolve disagreement through a calm pursuit of dialogue and consensus. Thus one of the central features of the country's foreign policy has been the development of closer ties with its neighbours in the Arabian Peninsula. The Arab Gulf Cooperation Council, (AGCC) grouping the UAE, Kuwait, Saudi Arabia, Bahrain, Qatar and Oman, was founded at a summit conference held in Abu Dhabi in May 1981, following an initiative by Sheikh Zayed, and has since become, with strong UAE support, an effective and widely-respected grouping. Intended to facilitate the development of closer ties between its members and to enable them to work together to ensure their security, the AGCC has faced three major external challenges during its short lifetime, first the long and costly conflict in the 1980s between Iraq and Iran, which itself prompted the Council's formation, followed by the August 1990 invasion by Iraq of one of its members, Kuwait, and then by the US-led invasion of Iraq in early 2003. Following the 1990 invasion of Kuwait, units from the UAE played a significant role in the alliance that liberated the Gulf state in early 1991. Subsequently, while supporting the international condemnation of the policies of the Iraqi regime and the sanctions imposed on Iraq by the United Nations during and after the conflict, the UAE expressed its serious concern about the impact that the sanctions had upon the country's people. And, as the impending invasion of Iraq loomed in late 2002, President Sheikh Zayed also reaffirmed his belief that 'War never solves a problem. Listening to the sense of reason is the right way to resolve differences between countries . . . This must be based on the principles of justice and the rule of law.'

In the run-up to the war, Sheikh Zayed tried hard to persuade Iraq's leadership to go voluntarily into exile, so as to prevent their country suffering from a third catastrophic conflict in just over two decades.

Later, once the war had taken place, he expressed his disappointment:

Our position on rejecting the war was clear and frank, and we had tried with all our efforts to prevent the war . . . Now, as the catastrophe has taken place, . . . we will not fall behind in supporting our Iraqi brethren, and assisting them with any technical expertise they may need . . . and helping them with all that we can afford.

In that process, the UAE has emerged as one of the major international donors to Iraq's reconstruction programme. It has, at the same time, welcomed the restoration of sovereignty to Iraq that took place in mid-2004, and has offered the hand of friendship, and assistance, to the new Iraqi Government.

Another key focus of the UAE's foreign policy in an Arab context has been the provision of support to the Palestinian people in their efforts to regain their legitimate rights to self-determination and to the establishment of their own state. As early as 1968, before the formation of the United Arab Emirates, Sheikh Zayed extended assistance to Palestinian organisations, and continued to do so, although he always believed that it was for the Palestinians themselves to determine their own policies. Since the establishment of the Palestinian Authority in Gaza and on parts of the occupied West Bank, the UAE has provided substantial help for the building of a national infrastructure and for the refurbishment of Muslim and Christian sites in the Holy Land. While much of the aid has been bilateral, the UAE has also taken part in multilateral development programmes funded by multilateral agencies and groupings and has long been a major contributor to the United Nations Relief Works Agency, UNRWA. With the outbreak of the second Palestinian *Intifada* (Uprising) in September 2000, the UAE, acting on the instructions of Sheikh Zayed, stepped up its assistance to the Palestine Authority, and has also been a forceful critic not only of the repressive policies of the Israeli Government, but also of the failure of the international community, in particular the United States, to force the Israelis to desist. In Sheikh Zayed's view, a solution to the issue could come about only with an end to Israeli occupation of the West Bank and the Gaza Strip, coupled with an implementation of the relevant international resolutions, of the agreed road-map to peace and of the agreements signed by both sides, so that a Palestinian state can be established in the West Bank and Gaza.

Substantial amounts of aid have also been given to a number of other countries in the Arab world. In Lebanon, for example, and on Sheikh Zayed's personal initiative, the UAE has funded a major programme of clearing the many hundreds of thousands of land mines left behind by the Israelis when they were forced to withdraw in 2000, so that the Lebanese civilian population may return to their homes and land. Other countries like Egypt, Syria, Jordan, Yemen and Morocco have received substantial loans and other aid for their infrastructural development programmes.

Sheikh Zayed had a deeply held belief in the cherished objective of greater political and economic unity within the Arab world. At the same time, however, he long adopted a realistic approach on the issue, recognising that any unity, to be effective, must grow slowly, and with the support of the people. Arab unity, he believed, is not something that can simply be created through decrees of governments that may be simply temporary political phenomena. That approach has been tried and tested both at the level of the UAE itself, which is the longest-lived experiment in recent times in Arab unity, and at the level of the Arabian Gulf Cooperation Council.

On a broader plane, Sheikh Zayed sought consistently to promote greater understanding and consensus between Arab countries and to reinvigorate the League of Arab States. 'Relations between the Arab leaders,' he believed, 'should be based on openness and frankness':

They must make it clear to each other that each one of them needs the other, and they should understand that only through mutual support can they survive in times of need. A brother should tell his brother: you support me, and I will support you, when you are in the right. But not when you are in the wrong. If I am in the right, you should support and help me, and help to remove the results of any injustice that has been imposed on me.

'Wise and mature leaders,' he felt, 'should listen to sound advice, and should take the necessary action to correct their mistakes. As for those leaders who are unwise or immature, they can be brought to the right path through advice from their sincere friends'.

Within that context, Sheikh Zayed consistently argued throughout the 1990s for the holding of an Arab summit conference, at which the leaders could honestly and frankly address the disputes between them. Only thus, he believed, could the Arab world as a whole move forward to tackle the challenges that face it, both internally and on the broader international plane:

I believe that an all-inclusive Arab summit must be held, but before attending it, the Arabs must open their hearts to each other and be frank with each other about the rifts between them and their wounds. They should then come to the summit, to make the necessary corrections to their policies, to address the issues, to heal their wounds and to affirm that the destiny of the Arabs is one, both for the weak and the strong. At the same time, they should not concede their rights, or ask for what is not rightfully theirs.

Welcoming the holding of the first of the annual summits, in Jordan in March 2001, Sheikh Zayed noted that:

The spirit of understanding and brotherhood which has prevailed during [the] sessions and discussions has brought me great satisfaction. [The] serious deliberations on the key issues . . . have proved that sincere intentions and frankness are the way for us to achieve success . . . Dialogue is essential between brothers, and we are happy because the Arabs recognise the correct path to follow towards reconciliation and solidarity, and to surmount the negative elements and mistakes of the past, in order to move away from divisions and rifts.

That positive beginning in 2001, however, came to naught in late 2002 and early 2003, as the majority of the leaders of the Arab world failed, in Sheikh Zayed's view, to address themselves sufficiently to the looming crisis in Iraq that preceded the 2003 invasion, and then to the threats to stability throughout the region that subsequently emerged, not only in Iraq.

The UAE President acknowledged readily that unanimity among the Arab leaders, although desirable, cannot always be achieved. He was, therefore, the only leader openly to advocate a revision of the Charter of the League of Arab States to permit decisions to be taken on the basis of the will of the majority. Such has been the experience of the society from which he came, and such has been one of the foundations of the success of the federal experiment in the United Arab Emirates. It was time, he believed, for a similar approach to be adopted within the broader Arab world. That did not mean in his view, however, that essential rights and principles should be set aside. These included, of course, the principle of the inviolability of the integrity of Arab territories. This principle has been a matter of major concern to the United Arab Emirates since its formation, because of the Iranian occupation in 1971 of the UAE islands of Abu Musa and Greater and Lesser Tunb. President Sheikh Zayed and other senior UAE government officials made repeated calls for the occupation to be brought to an end peacefully, either through direct negotiations, or by referral to the International Court of Justice or to international arbitration.

Sheikh Zayed believed:

Our relations with Iran are based on the best interests of the people of the two countries . . . Apart from the issue of the occupied islands, our relations have not been subjected to any kind of difficulties, and it is against this background that we have repeatedly urged Iran to join us in finding a peaceful solution to this problem through mediation and understanding.

Here, as on other foreign policy issues, Sheikh Zayed consistently adopted a firm but calmly worded approach, eschewing rhetoric that could make the search for a solution to problems more difficult.

In the 1990s, the conflicts in the former Yugoslavia were the cause of considerable concern to the UAE President. The time had come, he recognised, for the UAE itself to play a more pro-active role in international peacekeeping operations. The UAE Armed Forces had already begun to establish a record in such peacekeeping activities, first as part of the joint Arab Deterrent Force that sought for a few years to bring to an end the civil strife in Lebanon, and then through participation in UNISOM TWO, the United Nations peacekeeping and reconstruction force in Somalia.

In early 1999, Sheikh Zayed was among the first world leaders to express support for the decision by the North Atlantic Treaty Organisation (NATO) to launch its aerial campaign to force Serbia to halt its genocidal activities against the people of Kosovo. Recognising that there would be a need for an international peacekeeping force once the NATO campaign ended, Sheikh Zayed ordered that the UAE Armed Forces should be a part of any such force operating under the aegis of the United Nations. From late 1999 to 2001, the UAE contingent serving with the UN's KFOR force was the largest from any of the non-NATO states, and the only one from an Arab or Muslim country.

While ensuring that the UAE should increasingly come to shoulder such international responsibilities, however, Sheikh Zayed also made it clear that the UAE's role is one that is focused on relief and rehabilitation.

In the Balkans, and Iraq and Afghanistan and in other countries, the policy adopted by the United Arab Emirates clearly reflects the desire of Sheikh Zayed to utilise the good fortune of his country to provide assistance to those less fortunate. Through bodies like the Zayed Charitable and Humanitarian Foundation and the Abu Dhabi Fund for Development, established by Sheikh Zayed before the foundation of the UAE, as well as through institutions like the Red Crescent Society, the country now plays a major role in the provision of relief and development assistance worldwide.

The UAE itself has been able to progress only because of the way in which its component parts have successfully been able to come together in a relationship of harmony, working together for common goals.

Within the Arabian Gulf region, and in the broader Arab world, the UAE has sought to enhance cooperation and to resolve disagreement through a calm pursuit of dialogue and consensus. However, the pursuit of agreement and consensus did not, in Sheikh Zayed's view, justify the setting aside of essential rights and principles. These include not only support for the basic fundamentals of human and civil rights but also the principle of the inviolability of the territorial integrity of states, whether Arab or others.

Pursuit of these rights and principles has characterised the foreign policy of the state, bringing Sheikh Zayed's own philosophy and humanitarianism to bear far from the boundaries of the state itself. In essence, the philosophy of Sheikh Zayed, derived from his deeply held Muslim faith, was that it is the duty of man to seek to improve the lot of his fellow man.

His record in over half a century of government, from local to international level, is an indication of the dedication and seriousness with which he sought to carry out that belief.

PRESIDENT OF THE UAE

HH SHEIKH KHALIFA BIN ZAYED AL NAHYAN, Ruler of Abu Dhabi, was elected as the new President of the United Arab Emirates on 3 November, to succeed his father, the late HH Sheikh Zayed bin Sultan Al Nahyan. Sheikh Khalifa has committed himself to continue in the footsteps of his late father, a task that he has set himself for nearly 30 years. Sheikh Khalifa has described Sheikh Zayed as his teacher and commented that he learnt something new from him every day, absorbing his values, 'and the need for patience and prudence in all things'.

Born in the inland oasis-city of Al Ain in 1948, Sheikh Khalifa was educated in the local school. On 18 September 1966, following his father's assumption of the post of Ruler of Abu Dhabi, Sheikh Khalifa was appointed as Ruler's Representative in the Eastern Region of Abu Dhabi and as Head of the Courts Department in Al Ain.

On 1 February 1969, Sheikh Khalifa was nominated as the Crown Prince of Abu Dhabi. This was followed on 2 February 1969 by his appointment as the Head of the Abu Dhabi Department of Defence, in which post he oversaw the development of the Abu Dhabi Defence Force (ADDF), which later became the nucleus of the UAE Armed Forces.

On 1 July 1971, as part of the restructuring of the government of the emirate, Sheikh Khalifa was appointed as Prime Minister of Abu Dhabi and Minister of Defence and Finance. On 23 December 1973, Sheikh Khalifa became Deputy Prime Minister in the second UAE Federal Cabinet.

Shortly afterwards, when the Cabinet of Abu Dhabi Emirate was dissolved, as part of the process of strengthening the institutions of the UAE Federation, Sheikh Khalifa was appointed, on 20 January 1974, as the first Chairman of the Abu Dhabi Executive Council, which replaced the emirate's Cabinet.

Under his direction, and in accordance with the instructions of Sheikh Zayed, the Executive Council oversaw the implementation of a wide-ranging development programme in Abu Dhabi, including the construction of housing, water supplies and other essential services, roads and the general infrastructure that led to the emergence of the city of Abu Dhabi as the modern metropolis that it is today.

Of particular importance in terms of ensuring that citizens were able to benefit from the country's increasing wealth was the establishment by Sheikh Khalifa in 1981 of the Abu Dhabi Department of Social Services and Commercial Buildings, charged with the provision of loans to citizens for construction. Over Dh35billion have so far been lent by this Department, with over 6000 multi-storey buildings being constructed throughout the emirate.

The establishment of the Department, popularly known as the 'Khalifa Committee', followed another decision taken by Sheikh Khalifa in 1979 to alleviate the burden on citizens of the repayment of loans from the commercial banks. This involved a fixing of the interest rate payable by citizens of loans for construction at 0.5 per cent, with the balance of the interest being charged by the banks being paid by government.

A further step to ensure that citizens were able to build the properties that they needed, both for residential and for investment purposes, came with the creation by Sheikh Khalifa of the Private Loans Authority, early in 1991. By July of that year, only a few months after the Authority was created, 11,034 citizens had received loans amounting to Dh11.15 billion.

The continuing growth of the population, and rising costs, led to a further step in September 2000, when Sheikh Khalifa instructed that the total amount of individual house-building loans should be raised from Dh900,000 to Dh1.2 million.

President HH Sheikh Khalifa has also been involved extensively in other areas of the country's development. In May 1976, following the unification of the armed forces of the emirates, Sheikh Khalifa was nominated as Deputy Supreme Commander of the UAE Armed Forces. In this capacity, he devoted much attention to the building up of the country's defensive capability, through the establishment of many military training institutions and through the procurement of the latest military equipment and training.

He recently noted, 'the United Arab Emirates is keen that its armed forces are on a par with developments in the military sphere elsewhere in the world, in particular in terms of planning, organisation, weaponry and training. We shall continue to strive for this, so that our armed forces attain the maximum efficiency possible.'

Sheikh Khalifa has held a number of other top posts in the Abu Dhabi government. Since the late 1980s, for example, he has been Chairman of the Supreme Petroleum Council, in which capacity he has also sought to ensure that the country diversifies its economy away from reliance on oil and gas production. In particular, he has worked to develop the UAE's downstream petrochemicals and industrial complex at Ruwais.

He is also Chairman of the Abu Dhabi Fund for Development (ADFD), which oversees the country's international aid programme, from which over 40 countries have now benefited; the Abu Dhabi Investment Authority (ADIA), which manages the financial reserves and investment; and the Environmental Research and Wildlife Development Agency (ERWDA).

Externally, Sheikh Khalifa is a strong supporter of the six-member Gulf Cooperation Council, believing that the success and achievements of this body reflect the depth of understanding reached amongst its leaders. A keen supporter of the regional policy of HH Sheikh Zayed, in particular in terms of promoting solidarity between the Arab states, Sheikh Khalifa is firmly committed to support of the Palestinian people and also of moves designed to promote and restore stability in Iraq.

His key objectives as the new President of the United Arab Emirates, he says, will be to continue on the path laid down by his father. In particular, he says, he will continue with the 'open door' policy and with the practice of holding regular consultations with the country's citizens, so that he may become aware of, and follow up on, their needs and concerns.

HISTORY AND TRADITIONS

HISTORY

EARLY INHABITANTS

MANKIND HAS EXPLOITED THE LAND now known as the United Arab Emirates (UAE) since the Late Stone Age (5500 BC) when the climate was wetter and more humid than it is today. Game such as gazelle and Arabian oryx would have been abundant on the savannah and neighbouring grasslands and even in the deep sands the basic necessities of life would have been available. So, far from being an inhospitable desert, the land and waters of the region presented its ancient inhabitants with an enormous variety of exploitable, economically important resources. At this time the sea level in the Gulf was about half a metre higher than it is today.

The earliest known inhabitants of the UAE were probably skilled herders who would have used finely made stone tools. More than likely, they lived along the coasts and offshore islands in the winter, when fishing and shellfish gathering (including the harvesting of pearls) would have been the main pursuits, and moved to the interior in summer, where pastoralism and, eventually, horticulture, were practiced. This was a pattern of seasonal resource utilisation that was to be repeated throughout the history of the region. These were not an isolated people as there is ample evidence of contacts with the outside world, especially with civilisations to the north such as Mesopotamia (southern Iraq), indicated by finds of painted pottery ('Ubaid type) which originated in these areas.

While the stone tools of the UAE's early inhabitants have been found at dozens of sites from Ghagha' in the west to Khatt in the north, few settlements are known. Of these, undoubtedly the most impressive is a village on the island of Marawah, currently under excavation.

HAFIT TOMBS

At the end of the fourth millennium (c. 3100–3000 BC), the earliest in the form of above-ground tombs built of unworked stone (Hafit tombs) appear at two sites in the UAE: Jebel Hafit (including Mazyad) near Al Ain and Jebel al-Emalah south of Dhaid. These collective tombs contain pottery (Jamdat Nasr type) imported from south-central Iraq. Other imported finds also point to foreign contact and it is thought that trade in copper from the Hajar Mountains was the likely motivation for communication with the outside world. Certainly early 'Archaic texts' (3400–3000 BC) from Uruk in southern Mesopotamia refer to copper from Dilmun, later identified with Bahrain, but as there is no copper in this area it is usually assumed that the precious metal came from further afield, i.e. the copper source which stretches from Fujairah in the north to lower Oman in the south. To date the settlements of the population buried in the Hafit tombs of south-eastern Arabia have yet to be discovered.

UMM AL-NAR

Around 3000 BC the arid climate that is evident today set in. The following era, known as the Umm al-Nar period (2500–2000 BC), was characterised by numerous oasis towns (e.g. at Hili, Tell Abraq, Bidiya, Kalba) dominated by imposing large, circular fortresses. These agriculturally based settlements were possible because of the domestication of the date palm (*Phoenix dactylifera*). Without this blessed tree, the shade necessary for the growth of other less hardy plants, including cereals, vegetables and fruits, would have been lacking. Water was available from the many wells that tapped the relatively abundant, shallow lenses of fresh water found throughout much of the UAE.

During this period, the dead were buried in round communal tombs of finely masoned stone blocks (there is a particularly fine reconstruction at Hili). Finds from these graves point to wide-ranging trade contacts with Mesopotamia, Iran, the Indus Valley, Baluchistan, and Bactria (Afghanistan). Significantly, textual sources from Mesopotamia referred to the area as *Magan* around this time, and the towers of the Umm al-Nar period may have been the power centres for the 'lords of Magan' against whom several of the Old Akkadian emperors (from southern Mesopotamia) campaigned in the twenty-third century BC. There is also ample evidence from this period of the first intensive use of the copper resources found in the Hajar Mountains. Certainly, by 2300 BC, bronze (an alloy of copper and tin) was becoming increasingly popular as a material for manufacturing tools.

In the late third millennium a distinctive industry arose in the manufacture of soft-stone vessels – generally bowls, beakers and compartmented boxes – decorated with dotted circles made using a bow drill.

WADI SUQ AND LATE BRONZE AGE

The Wadi Suq and Late Bronze Age periods (2000–1300 BC) were characterised by fewer towns, although those that continued to be inhabited on a full-time basis (such as Tell Abraq) showed no signs of a cultural decline. It seems, however, that marine resources (fish and shellfish) became more important than they had been in the late third millennium. In addition, there was a change in burial customs to long, generally narrow collective tombs (as at Shimal, Ghalilah and Dhayah).

The hundreds of weapons found in these tombs are particularly interesting. In contrast to the daggers and spears characteristic of the Umm al-Nar period, the appearance of the long sword and bow and arrow, along with hundreds of cast bronze, lanceolate arrowheads with a raised flattened midrib, suggest an evolution in the technology of warfare during these periods.

Other finds, such as gold and electrum plaques in the form of two animals, standing back to back, often with their tails curled up in a spiral, are indications of the accumulation of wealth, some of which may have been earned by long-distance trade in copper through Dilmun (Bahrain). At the same time, the number of soft-stone vessels deposited in tombs increased vastly and new shapes and decorations were developed.

IRON AGE

Domestication of the camel in the late second millennium BC revolutionised the economies of south-eastern Arabia, opening up new possibilities for transport. At the same time, the discovery of the principles of using sub-surface channels to transport water from mountain aquifers to lower-lying gardens (*falaj* irrigation) made possible the extensive irrigation of gardens and agricultural plots that resulted in a veritable explosion of settlement across the Oman Peninsula. This era (1300–300 BC) is termed the Iron Age, although iron was not widely used in this region.

Fish and shellfish continued to be important in the diet of Iron Age inhabitants, although domesticated sheep, goat and cattle were kept, and gazelle, oryx, dugong, turtle and cormorant were exploited as well. Domesticated wheat and barley were cultivated and the date palm remained as important as ever.

There seems to have been some form of centralised power during this period. A cuneiform inscription from Nineveh in Assyria (northern Mesopotamia) speaks of the existence of at least one 'king' in the area, an individual named Pade, king of Qade, who lived at Is-ki-e (modern Izki in Oman) and sent tribute to the Assyrian emperor Assurbanipal in or around this time. Political and economic control by central bodies may also be implied by the appearance at this time of a tradition of stamp seal manufacture. There is also strong evidence of foreign contacts and a pendant found at Tell Abraq, the earliest depiction of a boat with a lateen sail yet discovered, gives us some indication of how such contacts took place.

MLEIHA PERIOD

We know that in the late sixth century BC, the Persian Empire, under Darius the Great, extended its influence to the area, then known as Maka. However, by the third century BC south-eastern Arabia was free of foreign political influence. Alexander the Great's conquests never touched the Arabian side of the Gulf and

IMPORTANT DATES

c.5500 BC	Earliest evidence of Man in UAE, on Marawah Island.
5500–3000 BC	Occupation by skilled groups of herders using finely made stone tools (so-called 'Arabian bifacial tradition').
3000–2500 BC	Hafit period – era of earliest collective burials first noted on the lower slopes of Jebel Hafit in the interior of Abu Dhabi.
2500–2000 BC	Umm al-Nar period – era of first oasis towns (e.g. at Hili, Tell Abraq, Bidya, Kalba) dominated by large, circular fortresses; burial of the dead in round communal tombs; wide-ranging trade contact with Mesopotamia, Iran, Indus Valley, Baluchistan, Bactria (Afghanistan); first intensive use of copper resources of Hajar Mountains; area referred to as *Magan* in Mesopotamian sources.
2000–1300 BC	Wadi Suq period and Late Bronze Age – an era which is characterised by fewer towns; change in burial customs to long, generally narrow collective tombs; close ties to Dilmun (Bahrain).
1300–300 BC	Iron Age – introduction of new irrigation technology in the form of *falaj* (pl. *aflaj*), subterranean galleries which led water from mountain aquifers to lower-lying oases and gardens; explosion of settlement; first use of iron; first writing, using South Arabian alphabet; contacts with Assyrian and Persian empires.
300 BC–0	Mleiha period (or Late Pre-Islamic A–B) – flourishing town at Mleiha; beginnings of local coinage; far-flung imports from Greece (black-glazed pottery), South Arabia (alabaster unguent jars); first use of the horse.
0–250 AD	Ed-Dur period (or late Pre-Islamic C–D) – flourishing towns at ed-Dur and Mleiha; extensive trade network along the Gulf linking up the Mediterranean, Syria and Mesopotamia with India; imports include Roman glass, coinage, brass; massive production of coinage by a ruler called Abi'el; first use of Aramaic in inscriptions from ed-Dur and Mleiha.
240 AD	Rise of the Sasanian dynasty in south-western Iran, conquest of most of eastern Arabia.
6th/7th cent. AD	Introduction of Christianity via contacts with south-western Iran and southern Mesopotamia; establishment of monastery on Sir Bani Yas by Nestorian Christian community; Sasanian garrisons in inner Oman and evidence for contact in the UAE shown by coins and ceramics from Kush (Ra's al-Khaimah), Umm al-Qaiwain and Fujairah.
630 AD	Arrival of envoys from the Prophet Muhammad; conversion of the people to Islam

632 AD	Death of the Prophet Muhammad; outbreak of the *ridda* movement, a widespread rebellion against the teachings of Islam; dispatch of Hudhayfah b. Mihsan by the Caliph Abu Bakr to quell rebellion of Laqit b. Malik Dhu at-Tag at Dibba; major battle at Dibba, collapse of the rebels.
637 AD	Julfar used as staging post for Islamic invasion of Iran.
892 AD	Julfar used as staging post for Abbasid invasion of Oman.
963 AD	Buyids (Buwayhids) conquer south-eastern Arabia.
c. 1220	Geographer Yaqut mentions Julfar as a fertile town.
14th–15th cent.	Close commercial contact between Northern Emirates and kingdom of Hormuz, based on Jarun island in the Straits of Hormuz.
1498	Portuguese circumnavigation of Cape of Good Hope by Vasco da Gama using Arab navigational information.
16th cent.	Portuguese–Ottoman rivalry in the Gulf.
1580	Venetian traveller Gasparo Balbi's description of coast of UAE from Qatar to Ra's al-Khaimah; mention of Portuguese fortress at Kalba; first mention of Bani Yas in Abu Dhabi.
1666	Description of the East Coast of the UAE by a Dutch mariner sailing in the *Meerkat*.
1720s	Growth of English trade in the Gulf; increasing Anglo–Dutch rivalry.
1764	Sharjah and most of Musandam and the UAE East Coast, all the way to Khor Fakkan, under control of Qawasim according to Carsten Niebuhr, German surveyor working with the King of Denmark's scientific expedition.
1800–1819	Repeated English East India Company attacks on Qawasim navy.
1820	General Treaty of Peace between British Government and sheikhs of Ra's al-Khaimah, Umm al-Qaiwain, Ajman, Sharjah, Dubai and Abu Dhabi.
1820–1864	Survey of the Gulf resulting in the publication of the first accurate charts and maps of the area.
1930s	Collapse of the natural pearl market; first agreements signed by rulers of Dubai, Sharjah and Abu Dhabi for oil exploration.
1945–1951	Agreements for oil exploration finalised in Ra's al-Khaimah, Umm al-Qaiwain and Ajman.
1962	First export of oil from Abu Dhabi.
1968	British Government announced its intention to withdraw from the Gulf region; discussions begin on formation of a federation of the emirates.
1969	First export of oil from Dubai.
10 July 1971	Agreement reached amongst rulers of the emirates to form a union.
2 Dec 1971	Formation of the State of the United Arab Emirates.

none of his Seleucid successors were able to establish any sort of Greek dominance in the region. This era has been designated the Mleiha period (300 BC–0 BC) after a flourishing town at Mleiha, a sprawling settlement on the gravel plain south of Dhaid in the interior of Sharjah. To date, there are no other known settlements in the region attributable to this time span. At Mleiha the earliest post-Iron Age settlement probably consisted of *'arish*, palm-frond houses, eminently suited to the hot climate of south-eastern Arabia. Dates were grown and wheat was harvested. Mleiha's dead were buried in mudbrick cists surmounted by a solid tower of brick and capped by crenellated stone ornaments, similar to the funerary towers of Palmyra (Syria) and the early periods at Petra (Jordan).

Some of the most interesting finds include far-flung imports from Greece (black-glazed pottery and Rhodian amphorae), and South Arabia (alabaster unguent jars). Several items (stone stelae, bronze bowls) are inscribed in South Arabian characters and several coins found at Mleiha are also of South Arabian origin, pointing to cultural links with this region. These were important finds in the light of stories of the Azd migration from Yemen to the region. The Mleiha period also witnessed the appearance of iron in large quantities for the first time in the archaeological record of this region.

ED-DUR PERIOD

The first century AD (ed-Dur period 0–250 AD) heralded a time for which considerably more literary documentation exists. The Roman writer Pliny the Younger (23/24–79 AD) completed his *Natural History* in 77 AD and to judge from his account of the peoples and places of south-eastern Arabia, combined with information from the second century AD map by Ptolemy, the area of the UAE was full of settlements, tribes and physical features. The town of Omana, at that time the most important port in the lower Gulf, has been linked with the ancient settlement of ed-Dur in Umm al-Qaiwain, a vast area containing private houses, graves, a fort and a temple (built of beach rock), along with areas of *'arish* habitation. Overland caravan traffic between Syria and cities in southern Iraq, followed by seaborne travel to Omana and thence to India, was an alternative to the Red Sea route used by the Romans, as is clear from finds of Roman glass, brass and coinage.

While ed-Dur was the prime settlement, other minor sites have been found on the islands of Abu Dhabi, and in the interior Mleiha prospered. There was also a massive production of local coinage by a ruler called Abi'el, who appears to have been an important figure in the region during this era. That Aramaic was the language of the populations of Mleiha and ed-Dur at this time is confirmed not only by its use on coinage, but also by the discovery of other inscribed objects.

The *Periplus of the Erythraean Sea*, composed around 60–75 AD, tells us that pearls, purple dye, clothing, wine, a great quantity of dates, gold and slaves were exported from Omana.

Pearls were already in use in the prehistoric era, but it was during the Roman era that the trade reached new heights. Pearling was certainly practiced at ed-Dur, as the recovery of a bell-shaped, lead pearl-diver's weight, complete with iron ring attachment for a rope, attests. Moreover, stacks of pearl oyster shells were found outside the entrance to one of the monumental graves.

PRE-ISLAMIC ERA

The rise of the Sasanian dynasty in south-western Iran in 240 AD brought Sasanian influence to most of eastern Arabia, including the UAE, as is indicated by finds of coins and ceramics at Kush (Ra's al-Khaimah), Umm al-Qaiwain and Fujairah. Indian Ocean trade and communications with the Near East continued during this period. Contact with the outside world was reflected in the spread of religious influences at this time, influences that would have varied from Arab paganism to Sasanian Zoroastrianism and Nestorian Christianity. Certainly by the fourth or fifth centuries AD at least one Nestorian monastery, complete with carved stucco ornamentation, including several crosses, was established on Sir Bani Yas – an island off the coast of Abu Dhabi.

Sea faring and trading were still a mainstay of the coastal areas during this period. Ibn Habib in his *Kitab al-Muhabbar* records the staging of a 'fair' at Dibba, a major port now situated on the UAE's East Coast. Ibn Habib recounts that Dibba was 'one of the two ports of the Arabs [the other being Sohar] merchants from Sind, China, people of the East and West came to it. This fair was held on the last day of Tagab. Merchants traded here by bargaining'.

COMING OF ISLAM

The arrival of envoys from the Prophet Muhammad in 630 AD heralded the conversion of the region to Islam, but the death of the Holy Prophet in 632 AD was followed by a widespread revolt that was subsequently quashed by the army of the first Caliph, Abu Bakr. During this time, a battle at Dibba, on the UAE's East Coast, is said to have resulted in the deaths of over 10,000 rebels. Their graves can still be seen on the outskirts of the town.

By 637 AD, the Islamic armies were using Julfar (Ra's al-Khaimah) as a staging post for the conquest of Iran. Indeed well known historians of early Islam, such as al-Tabari, and local sources indicate that this area was of considerable interest to successive Umayyad and Abbasid rulers. In 892 AD we find Julfar being used again, this time as an entry point for the Abbasid invasion of Oman. In the tenth century the area of Oman and the UAE came under the control of the Buyid

We use 32 rhumbs and we have tirfa, zam and qiyas (measurement of star altitude) but they are not able to do these things nor can they understand the things which we do although we can understand what they do and we can use their knowledge and travel in either ships. We can easily travel in their ships and upon their sea so some have magnified us in this business and look up to us for it.

They acknowledge that we have the better knowledge of the sea and its sciences and the wisdom of the stars in the high roads of the sea, and the knowledge of the division of the ship in length and breadth.

For we divide the ship in length and breadth according to the compass rose and we have measurements of star altitudes. They have no similar division or any means of dividing from the prow of the ship to guide themselves; neither do they use star altitude measurements to guide them when they incline to the right or left. Hence they have to acknowledge that we know best in that.

Ibn Majid, the 'Lion of the Sea' and a legendary figure in UAE history, wrote the verse on the preceding page long before Vasco da Gama ever rounded the Cape of Good Hope or set foot in the Arabian lands from which Ibn Majid, his equally skilled father, grandfather and other forebears had been sailing and exploring throughout their working lives. The 'they' of whom he wrote were, of course, Europeans, and it is true to say that the Arabs had sailed into European waters long before the Europeans had mastered the art of crossing the Indian Ocean. Born in Julfar, close to present day Ra's al-Khaimah, in around 1432–37, Ibn Majid came from a long line of intrepid sailors. His reputation as a navigator is based upon 40 surviving works, 39 of which are in verse. Some are brief, others, such as the 805-verse *al-Sofaliya* describing the sea route from India to Sofala on the Mozambique coast, are considerably longer. One treatise (the *Fawa'id*) is a lengthy opus that not only summarises all of Ibn Majid's own knowledge of navigation, but also draws extensively on the work of early Arab astronomers. His last known poem was written in 1500 AD and it is believed that he died soon after, at a little over 70 years of age.

dynasty (reflected in the discovery of a hoard of Buyid coins in Ra's al-Khaimah in 1965). Julfar continued to be a port and pearling centre of considerable importance, mentioned by al-Maqdisi in the tenth, al-Idrisi in the twelfth and Yaqut in the thirteenth centuries. From here, perpetuating a 5000-year-old tradition, great wooden dhows ranged far and wide across the Indian Ocean, trading as far away as Mombasa in Kenya, Sri Lanka, Vietnam and China.

The growth of Sohar, an important trade emporium on the Batinah coast of Oman, resulted in a proliferation of domestic trade routes leading to Julfar in the north and Tu'am (Al Ain/Buraimi) in the west. By the fourteenth and fifteenth centuries, the UAE had established close commercial contact with the Kingdom of Hormuz based on Jarun Island in the Straits of Hormuz. But this relationship was upset in 1498 following the Portuguese circumnavigation of the Cape of Good Hope by Vasco da Gama using Arab navigational information.

PORTUGUESE PRESENCE

The Portuguese arrival in the Gulf had bloody consequences for the Arab populations of Julfar and East Coast ports like Dibba, Bidiya, Khor Fakkan and Kalba. A string of forts established in these town, often described as 'Portuguese', are in fact better considered strongholds of local Arab sheikhs, allies of the Portuguese.

The Portuguese author Duarte Barbosa, writing in 1517, noted that the people of Julfar were 'persons of worth, great navigators and wholesale dealers. Here is a very great fishery as well, of seed pearls as well as large pearls'. The Portuguese traveller Pedro Teixeira mentions that a fleet of 50 terradas sailed from Julfar every year to the pearl beds. There was even a kind of pearl found near Julfar named after the latter, and it was the growing interest of the Europeans in 'Gulf pearls' that led to the tour of the Venetian state jeweller, Gasparo Balbi in 1580. Interestingly, his description of the UAE coast from Qatar to Ra's al-Khaimah includes the first European record of the Bani Yas tribe in Abu Dhabi.

BANI YAS

The ancestors of the bedouin, who made the sandy deserts of Abu Dhabi and Dubai their home, created date gardens and built themselves date-frond houses in the hollows of the dunes where adequate water was found. The *'arish* habitations eventually formed about 40 settlements, some of which were inhabited all the year round. This arc of villages at Liwa was the focus of economic and social life for the Bani Yas, at least since the sixteenth century. By the early 1790s however, the town of Abu Dhabi had become so important a centre of activity that the political leader of all the Bani Yas groups transferred his residence there from the Liwa. Early in the nineteenth century, members of the Al Bu Falasah, a branch of the Bani Yas, settled by the Creek in Dubai and established Maktoum rule in that emirate.

QAWASIM

While European powers like Portugal, Holland and eventually Britain competed for regional supremacy, a local power, the Qawasim, were gathering strength and at the beginning of the nineteenth century had built up a fleet of over 60 large vessels and could put nearly 20,000 sailors to sea. Their strength posed a serious challenge to the British, then emerging as the dominant power in the Indian Ocean, and in the first two decades of the nineteenth century a series of clashes between the two sides ended in the virtual destruction of the Qasimi fleet and the consolidation of British influence in the Gulf. Based on British claims that the Qasimi vessels had engaged in piracy, the area gained the name 'The Pirate Coast'. However, HH Dr Sheikh Sultan bin Mohammed Al Qasimi, Ruler of Sharjah, has shown in his book *The Myth of Arab Piracy in the Gulf* that the British offensive was based on a desire to control the maritime trade routes between the Gulf and India.

THE TRUCIAL STATES

Following the defeat of the Qawasim, the British signed a series of agreements with the sheikhs of the individual emirates that, later augmented with treaties on preserving a maritime truce, resulted in the area becoming known as 'The Trucial States'. The treaties with Britain meant that the sheikhs could not engage in independent relations with foreign powers, and were obliged to accept the advice of Britain in certain defined areas.

However, peace at sea facilitated uninterrupted exploitation of the ancient pearl fisheries in the lower Gulf, and once again fine pearls from the emirates were exported not only to India, but also to the growing market in Europe. The pearling industry thrived during the nineteenth and early twentieth centuries, providing both income and employment to the people of the Arabian Gulf coast.

On land, freed from the damaging effects of warfare at sea, but lacking any real economic resources, the emirates developed slowly. One of the greatest figures of the period was Sheikh Zayed bin Khalifa of Abu Dhabi, who ruled that emirate for over 50 years from 1855 to 1909, earning the title 'Zayed the Great'.

HARD TIMES

The First World War had already dealt a heavy blow to the pearl fishery, but it was the world economic depression of the late 1920s and early 1930s, coupled with the Japanese invention of the cultured pearl, that eventually finished it off. This was a catastrophic blow to the area.

The population was resourceful and hardy; nevertheless, there is no denying the difficulties that they faced. Opportunities for education were generally confined to lessons in reading and writing, along with instruction in Islam from the local preacher, while modern facilities such as roads, communications and health care

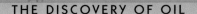

THE DISCOVERY OF OIL

It is now over four decades since oil production first began in the United Arab Emirates. The story of oil however, goes back much further. In the 1930s, the consortium of what became BP, Shell, Total, ExxonMobil and Partex, operating in Iraq as the Iraq Petroleum Company, turned their eyes to the Lower Gulf. Over the next few years, several concession agreements were signed, of which the most important was that with Abu Dhabi in January 1939. To handle those in the Trucial States, as the UAE was then known, IPC established a subsidiary, Petroleum Development (Trucial Coast), PD(TC), which drilled its first well at Ra's Sadr, north-east of Abu Dhabi, in 1951. Although dry, it was, at the time, the deepest well ever drilled in the Middle East.

PD(TC) drilled several other wells before finding traces of hydrocarbons at Murban, (now known as Bab), south-east of Abu Dhabi, in 1954. With its third well on this structure, completed in 1960, PD(TC) declared the field commercially viable and it went into production in 1963. The company was later renamed the Abu Dhabi Petroleum Company (ADPC).

Meanwhile, in 1953, BP had negotiated an offshore concession, assigned to a specially-created subsidiary, Abu Dhabi Marine Areas Ltd (ADMA). Surveys were carried out with the assistance of the famous French underwater explorer, Jacques Cousteau. The first well was drilled on a structure called Umm Shaif in 1958, and struck oil in massive quantities. With Das Island as the export terminal, Umm Shaif went into production in 1962.

Since then, many more important fields have been identified, while the Abu Dhabi National Oil Company (ADNOC), established in 1971, has now taken controlling shares in the concessions, with ADMA being replaced as operator by the Abu Dhabi Marine Operating Company (ADMA-OPCO) and ADPC by the Abu Dhabi Company for Onshore Oil Operations (ADCO) although foreign shareholders retain a share.

Memories of the early days of exploration are now fading fast. The results of the efforts of those, both UAE nationals and expatriates, who took part, however, continue to define the economy of the United Arab Emirates today.

were conspicuous only by their absence. Transport was by camel or boat, and the harshness of the arid climate meant that survival itself was often a major concern.

Zayed the Great's son, Sheikh Sultan, father of the former Ruler, Sheikh Zayed, was in power in Abu Dhabi from 1922 to 1926, and then, after a brief reign by a brother, one of Sheikh Sultan's sons, Sheikh Shakhbut, came to the throne at the beginning of 1928.

NEW BEGINNINGS

In the early 1930s the first oil company teams arrived to carry out preliminary surface geological surveys and the first cargo of crude was exported from Abu Dhabi in 1962. With revenues growing year by year as oil production increased, Sheikh Zayed, who was chosen as Ruler of Abu Dhabi on 6 August 1966, undertook a massive programme of construction of schools, housing, hospitals and roads. One of Sheikh Zayed's early steps was to increase contributions to the Trucial States Development Fund, established a few years earlier by the British. Abu Dhabi soon became its largest donor.

In the meantime, Sheikh Rashid bin Saeed Al Maktoum, *de facto* ruler of Dubai since 1939, had developed facilities for shipping along the Creek in a determined effort to replace pearling revenues. When Dubai's oil exports commenced in 1969 Sheikh Rashid was also able to use oil revenues to improve the quality of life of his people.

FEDERATION

At the beginning of 1968, when the British announced their intention of withdrawing from the Arabian Gulf by the end of 1971, Sheikh Zayed acted rapidly to initiate moves towards establishing closer ties with the emirates. Along with Sheikh Rashid, who was to become Vice-President and Prime Minister of the newly formed state, Sheikh Zayed took the lead in calling for a federation that would include not only the seven emirates that together made up the Trucial States, but also Qatar and Bahrain. Following a period of negotiation however, agreement was reached between the rulers of six of the emirates (Abu Dhabi, Dubai, Sharjah, Umm al-Qaiwain, Fujairah and Ajman) and the Federation to be known as the United Arab Emirates (UAE) was formally established on 2 December 1971. The seventh emirate, Ra's al-Khaimah, formally acceded to the new Federation on 10 February 1972.

ARCHAEOLOGY REVIEW

The winter archaeological season in the UAE, from October 2003 until April 2004, once again saw major discoveries being made throughout the country. As usual, work was undertaken by the local Departments of Archaeology and Antiquities and by visiting foreign teams, a mutually-profitable collaboration that has led to the country becoming one of the top centres today for Arabian archaeology.

In Abu Dhabi, surveys and excavations took place both on offshore islands and along the coast, and inland, both in the desert and in the oasis-city of Al Ain.

On the western island of Marawah, excavations in March 2004 by the Abu Dhabi Islands Archaeological Survey (ADIAS) uncovered the best-preserved and most sophisticated buildings of Neolithic (Late Stone Age) date yet found anywhere in Eastern Arabia. Radiocarbon dating results from charcoal and ash found at the site suggest that it dates to around 5000 BC, or 7000 years ago. ADIAS also collaborated with the Department of Antiquities and Tourism in the Eastern Region on the investigation of a group of Neolithic sites in the deep desert, north of Umm az-Zamul. These sites produced extensive scatters of finely-made flint tools, as well as the remains of several small and simple buildings, the first time that buildings of this date have been discovered in the sands. The sites provide evidence, for the first time, of extensive use of the desert during the Neolithic period, the earliest period for which human occupation of the Emirates has been proved.

In Al Ain itself, a joint team from the Eastern Region Department and France's Centre Nationale des Recherches Scientifiques carried out a sixth season of work in January and February at Hili, focusing on a subterranean grave originally discovered and excavated by the Department in 1984. Around one fifth of the skeletal remains identified by the Department were then left *in situ* and the joint team, including both archaeologists and anthropologists, has been carrying out further studies since 1998. The collective grave was used almost continuously for up to two centuries and dates back to the end of the third millennium BC. Although not yet fully excavated, it contains more than 550 adults and children. Analysis of the skeletons has shown that half of the burials were of new-born babies or children under the age of five, and that most of the population died before they reach 35–40 years of age, a high rate of mortality, but normal for a population of this type. Among finds have been soft-stone vessels and ornaments such as carnelian beads imported from the Indus Valley, silver and lapis lazuli beads from Afghanistan and local bronze rings, while more than 850 pottery vessels have been discovered. The majority of these were locally made, though some were imported from the Indus Valley, Baluchistan and Makran, as well as from southern Mesopotamia.

During the season, a geophysical survey was carried out in and outside the boundaries of Hili Archaeological Park to see if other subterranean graves could be identified. As a result of this survey, trenches will be opened close to one or two of the traditional Umm al-Nar tombs. The only other known similar grave in the UAE is one at Moweihat, in Ajman.

The Eastern Region Department also carried out excavations at the ruins of al-Naqfa fort, at the eastern tip of Jebel Hafit, adjacent to Al Ain. Prior to excavation, only some remains of walls, built of a mixture of stones and mud bricks, were visible on the surface, along with pottery scatters. Although the remains of the fort are badly eroded, its strategic location is significant, while the pottery, a mixture of Late Islamic and Iron Age material, indicates that the site was used at two distinct periods. It is not yet possible to determine whether the Late Islamic fort was built on the remains of an earlier Iron Age one. It is clear already, however, that the surface finds from al-Naqfa and the excavation results obtained so far indicate that it predates the oldest known fort in Al Ain by several centuries.

In Dubai, a team from the University of Munich, working in association with the Department of Tourism and Commerce Marketing, carried out a sixth and final season of excavations at the Bronze Age site of al-Sufouh 2, adjacent to Dubai Internet City. The site, on an old shoreline, is of significance because of the discovery of a large number of camel (dromedary) bones, which show evidence of having been deliberately butchered by Man.

The focus of work was on the recovery of well-preserved bones and related small finds and their full documentation. Again, the active role played by Man was proven by cut and chop marks on the bones themselves, as well as the presence of pottery fragments amongst the bones and fireplaces or cooking pits containing bones. The pottery has been dated to the Late Bronze Age. Evidence from other sites of the same period in south-eastern Arabia suggests that the wild camel became extinct around this time with the domesticated camel first appearing a few hundred years later, during the early Iron Age. The material from al-Sufouh may help to shed light on this process.

The Munich team also carried out further investigations of the climatic and geomorphological conditions of the site. This will help in the interpretation and dating of the two layers of bones found at the site, and also in reconstructing the Late Bronze Age environment.

A team from the Dubai Department, working in association with archaeologists from Jordan, also continued work in the inland deserts of Dubai. During surveys carried out over the last couple of years, a number of previously-unrecorded sites, dating to the Neolithic period, the Bronze and Iron Ages and the Islamic period, have been discovered, adding much new information to the picture of occupation in the UAE's desert areas. A group of Iron Age sites, at Saruq al-Hadeed, has proved to be of particular interest, with evidence of metal-working on the site, and with pottery similar to material from other sites at Qusais, (Dubai), Rumeilah (Al Ain) and Bithna (Fujairah). There is also evidence of old water wells at the site.

In Sharjah, a team from Germany's University of Tubingen, working in association with the local Directorate of Antiquities, carried out a ninth season of excavations at the Neolithic site at Jebel Buhais, south of Dhaid, and also carried out survey work in the surrounding plain, finding evidence of short-term campsites throughout the area. This may have been associated with intensive herding of domestic animals: an evaluation of animal bones found at a midden close to the Buhais cemetery indicates that sheep were the most important domestic animals, closely followed by goats and cattle. Bones of wild animals, presumably killed as a result of hunting, accounted for only around 10 per cent of the total, including, in declining order of frequency, wild ass, wild dromedary, gazelle, Arabian oryx and wild goat. All of these, with the exception of gazelle, are now extinct in the UAE. The dromedary, as noted above, was the first to disappear, in the Late Bronze Age.

The Buhais cemetery appears to have been used only in spring. Examination of the flint tools from nearby sites suggests that around 5000 BC, or 7000 years ago, there may have been a change in the nature of Neolithic land exploitation, from the open plains, now covered by small dunes, towards the mountains and their immediate vicinity. Over 500 individuals, and perhaps as many as 1000, were buried in the Buhais cemetery, which was clearly an important centre of the Neolithic period. Many of the people buried appear to have died elsewhere, and to have then been brought later to Buhais as skeletons, in order to lie with their ancestors. Burial customs indicate some sort of belief in the sun, for most of the burials are orientated trowards the east, towards the rising sun.

Excavations were also carried out at Muwailah, near Sharjah International Airport, by an Australian-American team, working in association with the Sharjah Directorate. Situated 15 kilometres west of Sharjah City, Muwailah is an important Iron Age settlement, and one of the largest of its period in the whole of the UAE. Previous finds from the site have included the oldest writing yet found in the country, as well as the oldest evidence for the use of iron.

The December 2003–January 2004 season identified a number of new buildings within the fortification wall around the site, as well as a major gateway on the eastern side, built of stone, which may have had large wooden doors.

Throughout the Muwailah site, there is evidence that the settlement was completely destroyed by fire around 750 BC. Thanks to this single phase of sudden destruction, much archaeological material has been preserved that will, once analysed, provide an unparalleled degree of information on the lifestyle in the area during the Iron Age.

Other work undertaken in Sharjah has included an evaluation of a small number of stamp seals, dating to the second and first millennia BC, that have been discovered by the Sharjah Directorate of Archaeology during excavations of tombs in the Jebel Buhais area. Bronze Age seals include examples that can be compared with seals from the Dilmun civilisation, in Bahrain, and the Harappan civilisation, in the Indus Valley, providing further evidence of the commercial links of the UAE in the early Bronze Age. The Iron Age seals, in contrast, made of both lead and stone, have parallels from other UAE sites, and may have been made locally. One is very similar to another seal found at Qarn bint Saud, near Al Ain, and may have been made by the same artist. While stamp seals are common in Bahrain and Kuwait, few are known from the Emirates, and the Jebel Buhais assemblage adds considerably to knowledge of this aspect of UAE prehistoric cultures.

The focus of work by the National Museum of Ra's al-Khaimah was a detailed examination of the 'Wadi Sur', a large fortification that was initially thought to be a dam or floodwater barrier, stretching from the edge of the Hajar Mountains, at Shimal, across the coastal plain to Khor Ra's al-Khaimah.

This construction, 7 kilometres long, has now been shown to have been a defensive rampart made of gravel and with a mudbrick wall on top. It is still preserved in some parts to a height of around 2 metres, and was topped by at least 50 round towers, 150 metres from each other, with a ditch, now infilled, that was once at least 2.5 metres deep.

Study of the remains of the wall suggests that it was probably built between the thirteenth and sixteenth centuries AD, to protect the port-city of Julfar and nearby palm-gardens from raiding parties from the interior.

The 'Wadi Sur' is the largest surviving fortification in the Emirates, and must have required major effort both to build and to maintain – evidence of the prosperity of Julfar itself. It is believed to have fallen into disrepair around the end of the sixteenth century, perhaps as a result of the changing political structure of the country at that time.

Finally, two important surveys have been undertaken of surviving Late Islamic buildings in Ra's al-Khaimah and Fujairah. In the former, a team from the National Museum of Ra's al-Khaimah recorded domestic houses from the nineteenth and early twentieth centuries in the towns of Ra's al-Khaimah itself, Ma'arid, Jazirat al-Hamra and Rams, and simpler structures in the palm gardens between Shimal and Falayah, built for use during the summer. Many of these are now abandoned and in disrepair, and the local government is planning to schedule some of the finer examples for restoration and protection, to preserve the architectural heritage from the pre-oil era.

In Fujairah, a similar study was undertaken by locally-based archaeologists on the old fort of Fujairah and its adjacent settlement. The fort itself has played a key role in the history of Fujairah for over 200 years, and has recently been restored. The study, based on archaeological, historical and ethnographic information, provides an insight into the material culture of the late Islamic period.

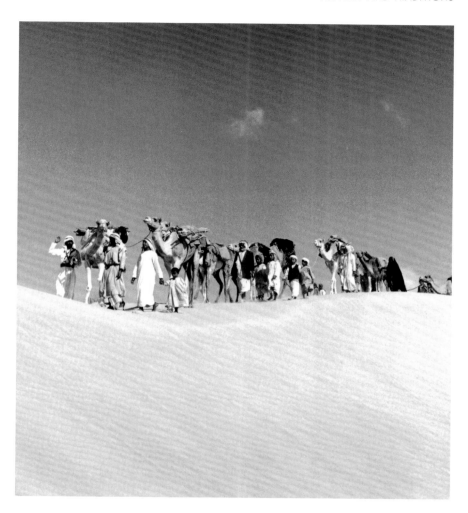

TRADITIONS

Life for the people of the UAE has changed beyond recognition since oil supplanted pearls as the primary economic resource. For most of the country's inhabitants, a traditional lifestyle is but a distant memory. Nevertheless, despite the social transformation that has take place in the UAE, with all its positive and negative implications, the very essence of traditional society, religion, language, family and tribal affiliations, remain constants. In addition, traditions are cherished and nurtured today by heritage groups and societies so that younger generations of UAE nationals can fully appreciate and learn from the resilience and ingenuity of their forefathers.

THE CAMEL

Uniquely adapted to the desert, the camel was the mainstay of the semi-nomadic lifestyle that was practiced by many of the UAE's inhabitants. The largest tribe in the UAE, the Bani Yas, roamed the vast sandy areas that cover almost all of the emirates of Abu Dhabi and Dubai. Other tribes, too, such as the Awamir and Manasir, shared this challenging environment for numerous generations, guarding their valuable knowledge of where to obtain water in the harsh terrain. The camel was both the reason for these lengthy excursions and the means by which they were carried out. Long periods were spent wandering great distances in search of winter grazing provided by dormant vegetation brought to life by intermittent rainfall. Once the arid summer approached, almost all the Bani Yas families, with the exception of fishing groups like the Al Rumaithat, returned to a home in one of the oasis settlements, many to tend and harvest their date gardens. Camel owners who had sufficient summer grazing close to their date-palms were particularly fortunate as they could harvest whilst watering their livestock at the wells that supplied the local communities.

The camel was not just a useful mount and means of transporting possessions and goods on long treks across inhospitable terrain; it also provided food, clothing, household items and recreation, and at the end of the day was a primary source of wealth. In many cases camel milk and the products derived from it were the only protein available to *bedu* families for months on end. The camels were capable of surviving for long periods without water, but it was camels' milk that quenched the herders' thirst. Young male camels were slaughtered on special occasions to provide meat for feasts and informal camel races were held during the festivities. Camel hide was used to make bags and other useful utensils, while tents, rugs and items such as fine cloaks (*bisht*) were woven from camel hair.

FISHING

Although modern fishing methods are employed in the fishing industry of today, traditional techniques remain popular with artisanal fishermen.

Extensive tidal shallows, which are characteristic of much of the Gulf coast, are ideal for fishing with traps or cast nets. Fish traps are of two types – the fixed, v-shaped *hadra* by which fish are guided along a stake-fence and into a small enclosure where they are harvested at low tide; or the small moveable *gargour* traps woven from palm fronds, weighted down by stones and baited to entice fish to enter through a narrow hole. In addition to fish, turtles and dugongs traditionally provided valuable protein – they are protected today. The latter were stalked through the shallows, generally from a canoe, but catching them depended ultimately on the hunter's ability to dive in and grapple physically with his prey. Turtle and bird eggs were also collected from well-known nesting beaches.

Sardines were the most profitable catch along the East Coast. Wooden boats manned by about 20 people were traditionally used to set a weighted net of about 100 metres in length parallel to the beach. For larger fish such as tuna or shark, heavier tangle nets and landlines were used. Fishermen on the East Coast also fished from palm-frond *shashah*.

Dhow construction remains very much a living tradition in the Emirates with at least as many traditional craft being built now as at the beginning of the last century. Dhows with inboard motors are still used for regional trade and fishing, but it is the hugely popular traditional sailing and rowing races that continue to foster the traditional craft.

The construction methods by which these elegant vessels are fashioned have remained the same for centuries. Shell construction involving the fitting of planks first and ribs later contrasts with the European method of forming a skeleton of ribs prior to planking. Boats are all carvel-built with planks laid edge to edge. Hundreds, sometimes thousands, of holes are hand-drilled to avoid splitting the wood and long thin nails wrapped in oiled fibre are driven through to secure the planks to the frames. All the construction work is carried out without the aid of plans and drawings, measurements being made solely by eye and experience. A highly experienced master-craftsman (*ustadh*) usually oversees the calculations. The tools used in building boats are very simple: hammer, saw, adze, bow-drill, chisel, plane and caulking iron. The building of a large vessel could take anything up to ten months, while a smaller one, a *shu'i* for instance, would be finished in one to four months.

Pearling has been an important economic activity in the region since ancient times but the trade fluctuated throughout the centuries. At the end of the nineteenth century pearling was flourishing yet again and an increasing number of able-bodied men participated in diving expeditions (*ghaus*) during four months in the summer, those of the Liwa-based subtribes of the Bani Yas migrating 'home' to tend their date gardens further inland in the winter. By the beginning of the twentieth century there were, according to one calculation, over 1200 pearling boats operating out of the area now known as the UAE, each carrying an average crew of 18 men. The pearling fleet leaving harbour must have been a wonderful sight, but this level of participation meant that during the summer more than 22,000 men were absent on the pearl banks. Long periods away from home placed enormous responsibility on the women of the family, both economically and socially.

For the men, conditions on board the pearling boats were tough and the work was arduous. The profits from a good season's harvest made it all worthwhile, but bad seasons were followed by spiralling debt. Many of the Bani Yas men formed cooperatives, all the crew jointly owning a boat and sharing the proceeds of the sale of the pearls according to an established arrangement: the biggest share to the captain (*nakhuda*), a larger share to the divers than the haulers, and some money left aside to finance preparations for the following year. Over several generations, some tribes involved in pearling became tied to particular locations, and coastal towns such as Abu Dhabi, Dubai and Ra's al-Khaimah thrived. All were badly affected by the collapse of pearl markets in the 1940s,

FALCONRY

Falconry, once an important way of supplementing the diet of the UAE's desert inhabitants, is now enjoyed as a traditional pastime. The most popular hunting birds remain the saker falcon and the peregrine falcon. These were traditionally trapped along the coast during their autumn migration, trained, used for hunting, and then released in the spring.

Once the falconers managed to capture one of the highly prized birds, they had only two to three weeks to train it before the migrating houbara bustards started to arrive. This was done by developing a strong bond of trust between a wild captured bird and its handler, a unique skill that commands the respect of falconers worldwide. Ideally, the training of the falcon was completed by the day when the first houbara arrived and the bedouin would hunt the bustards with his falcon throughout the winter months. Although houbara were the favoured quarry, falcons were also used in the past to take stone curlews and hares, and sometimes with salukis to hunt gazelle.

Today, many birds are caught abroad and imported. In fact, most falconry now takes place outside the Emirates, and the UAE is a leader in research into conservation of falcons.

Ancestor of today's racing thoroughbreds, the Arabian horse has played a noble part in the history of Arabia. Excavations at Mleiha in Sharjah show that over 2000 years ago prized stallions, decorated with gold trappings, were buried close to their owners, evidence of their place in local society. The loyal, gentle and stout heart of the Arabian horse has been the inspiration of much of the finest Arab poetry. Today, the UAE is one of the world's top breeding centres for the breed, and is playing a major role in its preservation. The UAE also sponsors special races for Arabian horses in many countries, including Britain, Germany and Australia. Lacking the speed of the thoroughbred, the Arabian horse is noted for its ability to endure hardship and to be ridden over long distances. Some endurance races last over a distance of 100 kilometres or more. Riders from the Emirates are among the world's top practitioners of this sport, which tests both man and horse to the limits (see the section on Sport and Leisure).

MUSIC, DANCE AND POETRY

Songs were composed to accompany different tasks, from hauling water at the well, to diving for pearl oysters out in the Gulf. In the latter case, a professional song-leader *(naha'an)* would launch into song and all the divers and haulers joined in as they worked. Each song had a rhythm for a particular task and became an inspiration for good team work.

Evening campfires were an occasion for exchanging news, for story telling and for reciting poetry, especially vernacular or *nabati* poetry. The spoken word has always been the superior art form of the tribal people, who lacked the raw materials used elsewhere for more tangible forms of artistic expression. Today, although life has changed utterly, *nabati* poetry remains a popular mode of expression and the poet a much-revered figure in UAE society.

During festival celebrations singing and dancing also took place and many of the songs and dances, handed down from generation to generation, have survived to the present time. Young girls would swing their long black hair, swaying in time to the strong beat of the music. Men would re-enact battles fought or successful hunting expeditions, often symbolically using sticks, swords or rifles.

TRADITIONAL USES OF PLANTS

At one with the desert and its wildlife, the *bedu* of the UAE were familiar with the medicinal properties of many plants. Seeds of *Cassia italica*, the senna plant, are used as a laxative and the *bedu* claim it will heal any kind of stomach pain. Seeds of the desert squash, *Citrullus colocynthis*, are highly acclaimed as a cure for diabetes. The bitter sap of the milkweed, *Calotropis procera*, was even dried and used to fill aching hollow teeth, while the woody parts of this plant were burned to make charcoal, which was an ingredient for gunpowder in the old days. Poultices made of the leaves were applied to joints to heal rheumatism. The leaves also served as fertiliser – dug into the ground around the roots of an ailing palm tree, they help to make the tree more vigorous. *Salsola imbricata* and several *Suaeda* species were dried and powdered to be used as snuff to clear sinuses.

The best known cosmetic use of a plant is that of henna to dye hair and to decorate hands and feet on special days like weddings and Eid celebrations. To make the henna paste, crushed dried berries and leaves are mixed with medicinal herbs, including one containing a blue dye, and applied to the skin in intricate designs. Poultices of the henna plant leaves are also used to calm headaches. The poisonous plant *Rhazya stricta* is used in small quantities to settle gastro-intestinal problems. An important plant for combating fevers is *Teucrium stocksianum*, a most fragrant herb, similar to a sage. The seeds of garat, *Acacia nilotica*, are ground to a powder to dry out second-degree burns.

GOVERNMENT

POLITICAL SYSTEM

SINCE THE ESTABLISHMENT OF THE FEDERATION in 1971, the seven emirates that comprise the United Arab Emirates (UAE) have forged a distinct national identity through consolidation of their federal status and now enjoy an enviable degree of political stability. The UAE's political system, which is a unique combination of the traditional and the modern, has underpinned this political success, enabling the country to develop a modern administrative structure while, at the same time, ensuring that the best of the traditions of the past are maintained, adapted and preserved.

Known until 1971 as the Trucial States, which had separate treaty relationships with Britain, the seven emirates came together to establish a federal state officially entitled *Dawlat al Imarat al Arabiyya al Muttahida* (State of the United Arab Emirates).

The philosophy behind the UAE was explained in a statement that was released on 2 December 1971 as the new state was formally established:

The United Arab Emirates has been established as an independent state, possessing sovereignty. It is part of the greater Arab nation. Its aim is to maintain its independence, its sovereignty, its security and its stability, in defence against any attack on its entity or on the entity of any of its member Emirates. It also seeks to protect the freedoms and rights of its people and to achieve trustworthy co-operation between the Emirates for the common good. Among its aims, in addition to the purposes above described, is to work for the sake of the progress of the country in all fields, for the sake of providing a better life for its citizens, to give assistance and support to Arab causes and interests, and to support the charter of the United Nations and international morals.

Each of the component emirates of the Federation already had its own existing institutions of government prior to 1971 and, to provide for the effective governing of the new state, the rulers agreed to draw up a provisional Constitution specifying the powers that were to be allocated to new federal institutions, all others remaining the prerogative of the individual emirates.

Assigned to the federal authorities, under Articles 120 and 121 of the Constitution, were the areas of responsibility for foreign affairs, security and defence, nationality and immigration issues, education, public health, currency, postal, telephone and other communications services, air traffic control and licensing of aircraft, in addition to a number of other topics specifically prescribed, including labour relations, banking, delimitation of territorial waters and extradition of criminals.

In parallel, the Constitution also stated in Article 116 that 'the Emirates shall exercise all powers not assigned to the Federation by this Constitution'. This was reaffirmed in Article 122, which stated that 'the Emirates shall have jurisdiction in all matters not assigned to the exclusive jurisdiction of the Federation, in accordance with the provision of the preceding two Articles'.

The new federal system of government included a Supreme Council, a Cabinet, or Council of Ministers, a parliamentary body, the Federal National Council, and an independent judiciary, at the apex of which is the Federal Supreme Court.

In a spirit of consensus and collaboration, the rulers of the seven emirates agreed during the process of federation that each of them would be a member of a Supreme Council, the top policy-making body in the new state. They also agreed that they would elect a President and a Vice-President from amongst their number, to serve for a five-year term of office. The Ruler of Abu Dhabi, Sheikh Zayed bin Sultan Al Nahyan, was elected as the first President, a post which he held until his death on 2 November 2004. Sheikh Zayed was succeeded as Ruler of Abu Dhabi by his Crown Prince, Sheikh Khalifa bin Zayed Al Nahyan, who was elected as the new President at a Supreme Council meeting on 3 November 2004. The Ruler of Dubai, Sheikh Rashid bin Saeed Al Maktoum, was elected as first Vice-President in 1971, a post he continued to hold until his death in 1990, at which point his eldest son and heir, Sheikh Maktoum bin Rashid Al Maktoum, was elected to succeed him.

SUPREME COUNCIL MEMBERS

HH President Sheikh Khalifa bin Zayed Al Nahyan, Ruler of Abu Dhabi
HH Vice-President and Prime Minister Sheikh Maktoum bin Rashid Al Maktoum, Ruler of Dubai
HH Dr Sheikh Sultan bin Mohammed Al Qasimi, Ruler of Sharjah
HH Sheikh Saqr bin Mohammed Al Qasimi, Ruler of Ra's al-Khaimah
HH Sheikh Hamad bin Mohammed Al Sharqi, Ruler of Fujairah
HH Sheikh Rashid bin Ahmed Al Mu'alla, Ruler of Umm al-Qaiwain
HH Sheikh Humaid bin Rashid Al Nuaimi, Ruler of Ajman

CROWN PRINCES

Lt.-General HH Sheikh Mohammed bin Zayed Al Nahyan, Crown Prince of Abu Dhabi and Chief of Staff of the UAE Armed Forces
General HE Sheikh Mohammed bin Rashid Al Maktoum, Crown Prince of Dubai and Minister of Defence
HE Sheikh Sultan bin Mohammed Al Qasimi, Crown Prince and Deputy Ruler of Sharjah, Chairman of the Sharjah Executive Council

HE Sheikh Saud bin Saqr Al Qasimi, Crown Prince and Deputy Ruler of Ra's
al-Khaimah
HE Sheikh Saud bin Rashid Al Mu'alla, Crown Prince of Umm al-Qaiwain
HE Sheikh Ammar bin Humaid Al Nuaimi, Crown Prince of Ajman

DEPUTIES OF THE RULERS

HE Sheikh Hamdan bin Rashid Al Maktoum, Deputy Ruler of Dubai, Minister
of Finance and Industry
HE Sheikh Ahmed bin Sultan Al Qasimi, Deputy Ruler of Sharjah
HE Sheikh Khalid bin Saqr Al Qasimi, Deputy Ruler of Ra's al-Khaimah
HE Sheikh Sultan bin Saqr Al Qasimi, Deputy Ruler of Ra's al-Khaimah
HE Sheikh Hamad bin Saif Al Sharqi, Deputy Ruler of Fujairah

The Federal Supreme Council is vested with legislative as well as executive powers.
It ratifies federal laws and decrees, plans general policy, approves the nomination
of the Prime Minister and accepts his resignation. It also relieves him from his
post upon the recommendation of the President. The Supreme Council elects
the President and his deputy for five-year terms; both may be re-elected.

At an historic meeting on 20 May 1996 the Federal Supreme Council approved
a draft amendment to the country's provisional Constitution, making it the
permanent Constitution of the UAE. The amendment also named Abu Dhabi as
the capital of the state.

The Council of Ministers or Cabinet, described in the Constitution as 'the
executive authority' for the Federation, includes the usual complement of
ministerial portfolios and is headed by a Prime Minister, chosen by the President
in consultation with his colleagues on the Supreme Council. The Prime Minister,
currently the Vice-President (although this has not always been the case), then
selects the ministers, who may be drawn from any of the Federation's component
emirates, although, naturally, the more populous emirates have generally provided
more members of each Cabinet.

The current Cabinet was appointed on 1 November 2004 under the terms of
a decree issued by President HH Sheikh Zayed bin Sultan Al Nahyan and according
to the proposal of Vice-President HH Sheikh Maktoum bin Rashid Al Maktoum,
who was requested by the President to restructure the Cabinet. The reshuffle
created a new portfolio of Ministry of Presidential Affairs, while other ministries
have been merged.

MEMBERS OF THE CABINET

The new Cabinet, nominated by President HH Sheikh Zayed bin Sultan Al Nahyan
on 1 November 2004, the day before his death, contains the UAE's first woman
Minister. Membership of the Cabinet is as follows:

Prime Minister: Vice-President HH Sheikh Maktoum bin Rashid Al Maktoum

Deputy Prime Minister: Sheikh Sultan bin Zayed Al Nahyan

Minister of Finance and Industry: Sheikh Hamdan bin Rashid Al Maktoum

Minister of Defence: Gen. Sheikh Mohammed bin Rashid Al Maktoum

Deputy Prime Minister and Minister of State for Foreign Affairs: Sheikh Hamdan bin Zayed Al Nahyan

Minister of Interior: Maj. Gen. Sheikh Saif bin Zayed Al Nahyan

Minister of Presidential Affairs: Sheikh Mansour bin Zayed Al Nahyan

Minister of Information and Culture: Sheikh Abdullah bin Zayed Al Nahyan

Minister of Education: Sheikh Nahyan bin Mubarak Al Nahyan

Minister of Public Works: Sheikh Hamdan bin Mubarak Al Nahyan

Minister of Supreme Council and GCC Affairs: Sheikh Fahim bin Sultan Al Qasimi

Minister of Foreign Affairs: Rashid Abdullah Al Nuaimi

Minister of Health: Hamad Abdul Rahman Al Midfa

Minister of State for Cabinet Affairs: Saif Khalfan Al Ghaith

Minister of Agriculture and Fisheries: Saeed Mohammed Al Raqbani

Minister of Justice, Islamic Affairs and Awqaf: Mohammed Nukhaira Al Dhahiri

Minister of State for Financial and Industrial Affairs: Mohammed Khalfan bin Kharbash

Minister of Economy and Planning: Sheikha Lubna Al Qasimi

Minister of Energy: Mohammed bin Dha'en Al Hamili

Minister of Communications: Sultan bin Saeed Al Mansouri

Minister of Labour and Social Affairs: Dr Ali bin Abdullah Al Ka'abi

FEDERAL NATIONAL COUNCIL

The Federal National Council (FNC) has 40 members drawn from the emirates on the basis of their population, with eight for each of Abu Dhabi and Dubai, six each for Sharjah and Ra's al-Khaimah, and four each for Fujairah, Umm al-Qaiwain and Ajman. The selection of representative members is left to the discretion of each emirate and the members' legislative term is deemed to be two calendar years.

Day-to-day operation of the FNC is governed by standing orders based on the provisions of Article 85 of the Constitution. These orders were first issued in 1972 and subsequently amended by Federal Decree No. 97 of 1977.

The FNC plays an important role in serving the people and the nation and consolidating the principles of *shura* (consultation) in the country. Presided over by a speaker, or either of two deputy speakers, elected from amongst its members, the FNC has both a legislative and supervisory role under the Constitution. This means that it is responsible for examining, and, if it so requires, amending, all

proposed federal legislation, and is empowered to summon and to question any federal minister regarding ministry performance. One of the main duties of the FNC is to discuss the annual budget. Specialised sub-committees and a Research and Studies Unit have been formed to assist FNC members to cope with the increasing demands of modern government.

Since its inception the Council has been successively chaired by the following Speakers:

Thani bin Abdulla
Taryam bin Omran Taryam
Hilal bin Ahmed bin Lootah
Al-Haj bin Abdullah Al Muhairbi
Mohammed Khalifa Al Habtoor
Saeed Mohammed Al Kindi (elected 2003)

At an international level, the FNC is a member of the International Parliamentary Union (IPU) as well as the Arab Parliamentary Union (APU) and participates actively in these bodies.

FEDERAL JUDICIARY

The federal judiciary, whose total independence is guaranteed under the Constitution, includes the Federal Supreme Court and Courts of First Instance. The Federal Supreme Court consists of five judges appointed by the Supreme Council of Rulers. The judges decide on the constitutionality of federal laws and arbitrate on inter-emirate disputes and disputes between the Federal Government and the emirates.

LOCAL GOVERNMENT

Parallel to, and, on occasion, interlocking with, the federal institutions, each of the seven emirates also has its own local government. Although all have expanded significantly as a result of the country's growth over the last 33 years, these differ in size and complexity from emirate to emirate, depending on a variety of factors such as population, area, and degree of development.

Thus the largest and most populous emirate, Abu Dhabi, has its own central governing organ, the Executive Council, chaired by the Crown Prince, Sheikh Khalifa bin Zayed Al Nahyan, until he succeeded as Ruler of Abu Dhabi. He was succeeded as Crown Prince by Sheikh Mohammed bin Zayed, who had been appointed Deputy Crown Prince in November 2003. Announcements of changes in Abu Dhabi's Government were awaited as this *Yearbook* went to press. The Eastern and Western Regions are headed by an official with the title of Ruler's Representative. There is also a Ruler's Representative on the important oil terminal island of Das. The main cities, Abu Dhabi and Al Ain, the latter also the capital of the Eastern Region, are administered by municipalities, each of which has a nominated municipal council. Abu Dhabi's National Consultative Council, chaired by a Speaker, and with 60 members selected from among the emirate's main tribes and families, undertakes a role similar to that of the FNC on a country-wide level, questioning officials and examining and endorsing local legislation. It is also a source of vocal suggestion for the introduction or revision of federal legislation. Administration in the emirate is implemented by a number of local departments, covering topics such as public works, finance, customs and management. Some have a responsibility for the whole of the emirate, although in certain spheres there are also departments covering only the Eastern Region.

A similar pattern of municipalities and departments can be found in each of the other emirates, while Sharjah, with its three enclaves on the country's East Coast, has also adopted the practice of devolving some authority on a local basis, with branches of the Sharjah Emiri Diwan (Court), headed by deputy chairmen, in both Kalba and Khor Fakkan. Sharjah has also created an Executive Council and a Consultative Council to cover the whole emirate.

In smaller or more remote settlements, the ruler and government of each emirate may choose a local representative, an emir or wali, to act as a conduit through which the concerns of inhabitants may be directed to government. In most cases, these are the leading local tribal figures, whose influence and authority derive both from their fellow tribesmen and from the confidence placed in them by the ruler, an example of the way in which local leaders within the traditional system have become involved with, and lend legitimacy to, the new structures of government.

FEDERAL AND LOCAL GOVERNMENT

The powers of the various federal institutions and their relationship with the separate institutions in each emirate, laid down in the Constitution, have evolved and changed since the establishment of the state. Under the terms of the Constitution, rulers may, if they wish, relinquish certain areas of authority, prescribed as being the responsibility of individual emirates, to the Federal Government, one significant such decision being that to unify the armed forces in the mid-1970s. The 1971 Constitution also permitted each emirate to retain, or to take up, membership in the Organisation of Petroleum Exporting Countries (OPEC) and the Organisation of Arab Petroleum Exporting Countries (OAPEC), although none have done so; the only emirate to be a member in 1971, Abu Dhabi, having chosen to relinquish its memberships in favour of the Federation.

In line with the dramatic social and economic development that has taken place since the foundation of the state, the organs of government, both federal and local, have also developed impressively, and their influence now affects almost all aspects of life, for both UAE citizens and expatriates. As with other relatively young states, new institutions that were created for the first time have derived their legitimacy and status from the extent of their activities and achievements, and from acknowledgement and appreciation of their role by the people.

The relationship between the new systems of government, federal and local, has itself evolved in a highly constructive manner. As the smaller emirates have benefited from significant development in terms of, for example, education and vocational training, so they have been able to provide from their own local governments the personnel to extend the variety of services (e.g. tourism) which had once been handled on their behalf by federal institutions. At the same time, in other areas, such as the judiciary, there has been an evolving trend towards a further voluntary relinquishment of local authority to the federal institutions. These new systems of government have not, however, replaced the traditional forms which coexist and evolve alongside them.

TRADITIONAL GOVERNMENT

Traditionally, the ruler of an emirate, the sheikh, was the leader of the most powerful, though not necessarily the most populous, tribe, while each individual tribe, and often its various sub-sections, also generally had a chief or sheikh. Such rulers and chiefs maintained their authority only insofar as they were able to retain the loyalty and support of their people, in essence a form of direct democracy, though without the paraphernalia of western forms of suffrage. Part of that democracy was the unwritten but strong principle that the people should have free access to their sheikh, and that he should hold a frequent and open *majlis*, or council, in which his fellow tribesmen could voice their opinions.

Such a direct democracy, which may be ideally suited to small and relatively uncomplicated societies, becomes steadily more difficult to maintain as populations grow, while the increasing sophistication of government administration means that on a day-to-day basis many of the inhabitants of the emirates now find it more appropriate to deal directly with these institutions on most matters, rather than to seek to meet personally with their ruler or sheikh.

Nevertheless, a fascinating aspect of life in the UAE today, and one that is essential to an understanding of its political system, is the way in which the institution of the *majlis* has continued to maintain its relevance. In larger emirates, not only the ruler, but also a number of other senior members of his family, continue to hold open majlises (or *majalis*), in which participants may raise a wide range of topics, from a request for a piece of land, or a scholarship for a son or daughter to go abroad, to more weighty subjects such as the impact of large-scale foreign immigration upon society or complaints about perceived flaws in the practices of various ministries and departments.

In smaller emirates, the *majlis* of the ruler himself, or of the crown prince or deputy ruler, remains the main focus. The Ruler of Fujairah, for example, holds an open *majlis* at least once a week (daily during the Muslim holy fasting month of Ramadan), which may be attended by both citizens and expatriates. To these majlises come traditionally-minded tribesmen who may have waited several months for the opportunity to discuss with their ruler directly, rather than choose to pursue their requests or complaints through a modern governmental structure.

In modern society, of course, it is naturally easier for a ruler to go to meet his people than for them to come to meet him. The rulers frequently travel around their emirates to inspect projects, providing opportunities for them to meet with citizens away from the formal surroundings of an office or palace. During these regular inspection tours of projects, they also take pains to ensure that citizens living nearby are guaranteed easy access to them.

Just as the modern institutions have developed in response to public need and demand, however, so the traditional forms of tribal administration have adapted. With many relatively routine matters now being dealt with by the modern institutions, traditional institutions, like the *majlis*, have been able to focus on more complex issues rather than on the routine matters with which they were once heavily involved.

In the majlises, for example, it is possible to hear detailed, and often heated, discussions between sheikhs and other citizens on questions such as the policy that should be adopted towards the evolution of the machinery of government, or the nature of relations with neighbouring countries. On matters more directly affecting the individual, such as the highly relevant topic of unemployment among young UAE graduates, debates often tend to begin in the majlises, where discussion can be fast and furious, before a consensus approach evolves that is subsequently reflected in changes in government policy.

Through such means, the well-tested traditional methods of government in the United Arab Emirates have been able to retain both their essential relevance and unique vitality, and they continue to play an important, although often unpublicised, role in the evolution of the state today.

A BALANCED APPROACH

When the rulers of the seven emirates met 33 years ago to agree on the forms of government for their new federal state, they deliberately chose not simply to copy from others. They chose, instead, to work towards a society that would offer the best of modern administration, while at the same time retaining the traditional forms of government, that, with their inherent commitment to consensus, discussion and direct democracy, offered the best features of the past.

With the benefit of hindsight, it is evident that they made the correct choice, for, despite the massive economic growth and the social dislocation caused by an explosion in the population, the state has enjoyed political stability. During the last few decades there have been numerous attempts to create federal states, both in the Arab world and elsewhere. The UAE is the only one in the Arab world to have stood the test of time.

FOREIGN AFFAIRS

FOREIGN POLICY

Two regional issues, of international significance, occupied the centre stage in terms of the UAE's foreign affairs from mid-2003 until late 2004 – the evolving situation in Iraq and the continuing conflict between Israel and the Palestinians. On both issues, the Government of the United Arab Emirates gave its support to those seeking to bring about peaceful resolutions and supported efforts to involve international organisations, such as the United Nations.

A key focus of attention was, naturally, on the situation in Iraq in the aftermath of the invasion in early 2003 and the removal of President Saddam Hussein. The UAE has been consistent, and forthright, both in its support for Iraq's people and their sovereignty, and in its advocacy of a swift re-establishment of an Iraqi Government. Commenting on the situation in Iraq in his December 2003 National Day statement, President Sheikh Zayed noted:

We would like to reaffirm and to emphasise the UAE's support for the people of Iraq. We shall support them with all of the resources at our disposal, so as to help them to regain their dignity, their welfare and their stability. We are fully confident that, with the blessings of Almighty God, the future will be one that is for the good of the Iraqi people, through the efforts of all Iraqi citizens and with the unified support of their Arab brethren. I call upon our brethren in Iraq to put the past behind them, and to work together, hand in hand, and in a spirit of national consensus, patience and wisdom, so that they may achieve a better future, and pass through and beyond these difficult times.

At the same time, the UAE has firmly condemned terrorist acts in Iraq. Following the assassination of the Chairman of Iraq's Governing Council in May 2004, an official source at the Ministry of Foreign Affairs described it as 'a heinous assassination . . . a vicious, criminal act.'

The handover of power at the end of June to the new Iraqi Government, headed by President Sheikh Ghazi al-Yawar, was welcomed, with the UAE President reaffirming the UAE's 'keen desire to strengthen fraternal ties and co-operation with Iraq.'

In November 2004, following heavy fighting in the Iraqi city of Fallujah, President HH Sheikh Khalifa bin Zayed ordered a prompt dispatch of relief supplies by the UAE Red Crescent to help civilians displaced by the fighting.

A key part of the UAE's approach to affairs within the broader Arab region is that of support for the Palestinian people, and their desire to exercise their legitimate rights, to end occupation of their land and to establish their own independent state on their own land, with Jerusalem as its capital. Support for the second Palestinian Uprising (*Intifada*) and for the resistance of the Palestinian people to Israeli violence has, naturally, been an important component of this policy.

Sadly, the conflict between the Palestinians and occupying Israeli forces continued throughout the year, with the Israeli Government continuing to engage in targeted assassinations of Palestinians, the destruction of property, the imposition of curfews and the expansion of settlements on occupied land, as well as the construction of its illegal wall running through the occupied territories on the West Bank.

The death of Yasser Arafat, the President of the Palestine National Authority, in mid-November, concluded a depressing year for the Palestinian people.

In a statement issued in April, Sheikh Hamdan bin Zayed Al Nahyan, UAE Deputy Prime Minister and Minister of State for Foreign Affairs, noted that any solution to the conflict must be based 'on the international and legitimate resolutions that call for an end to the Israeli occupation of the Palestinian and Arab territories and the establishment of a Palestinian state, with Jerusalem as its capital.'

'Security (for Israeli) cannot be maintained through guns and assassinations,' he said. 'It can, however, be maintained through political negotiations and through a willingness to co-exist, and through restoration of the legitimate rights of the Palestinian people, including that most basic of human rights enjoyed by all of the peoples of the planet, that of the right to lead a dignified and stable life and the right to self-determination.'

The UAE condemned in particularly strong terms the killing in March by Israeli forces of the wheelchair-bound founder of the Islamic Hamas movement, Sheikh Ahmed Yassin, Minister of Information and Culture Sheikh Abdullah bin Zayed Al Nahyan describing this as a 'hideous massacre.' 'The murder of Sheikh Yassin is a reflection of the state terrorism espoused by the Israeli government,' he said.

The large-scale demolition of property and associated killings of Palestinians that occurred in Rafah, Gaza, in May, came in for equally strong condemnation. A Foreign Ministry statement noted that 'the UAE regards such a crime by Israeli occupation forces as a disdainful and flagrant violation of international laws and norms and as an escalation of violence in the region, as Israel, under the leadership of (Israeli Prime Minister Ariel) Sharon, and those behind him, is grossly defiant (of such laws and norms), and threatens to escalate tension in the whole region.'

While continuing to express its support for the Palestinians and for efforts designed to revitalise the peace process, the UAE also expressed its frustration with the apparent unwillingness of the international community to take decisive steps on the issue. A statement from the Foreign Ministry in May appealed to the international community, 'particularly member countries of the Quartet, to make a firm and effective move to ensure international protection of the Palestinians against Israeli practices, to help them secure their legitimate rights and to help find a political solution to the current situation in accordance with international resolutions.'

Addressing a special meeting of the United Nations Security Council in May, the UAE's Permanent Ambassador to the UN commented that: 'we are in urgent need for the political will of the international community to put an end to the savage and immoral practices undertaken by the Israeli Government against the Palestinian people for more than five decades, in an unceasing display of arrogance and defiance of international and humanitarian laws.'

In June, senior Government officials denied claims from Israeli sources that approval had been given for the opening of an Israeli office in Abu Dhabi, with Sheikh Mohammed bin Rashid Al Maktoum, Crown Prince of Dubai and Minister of Defence, saying that the UAE had no plans 'to normalise ties with the Jewish entity until the Palestinian issue is totally resolved in a just and comprehensive way.'

Throughout the year, the United Arab Emirates continued to extend all possible support to the international fight against terrorism, while emphasising the necessity both of a clear definition of terrorism and of ensuring that terrorism perpetrated by states, such as Israel, should not be overlooked.

In a statement in May following a series of terrorist attacks in Saudi Arabia, the Deputy Prime Minister and Minister of State for Foreign Affairs, Sheikh Hamdan bin Zayed Al Nahyan, noted that: 'the President, Government and the people of the UAE put their resources at the disposal of the Kingdom of Saudi Arabia, and further affirm their readiness to work alongside the Saudi leadership to eliminate those thugs who are bent on destruction, blood-letting, terrorism and wreaking havoc without any iota of conscience.'

In earlier conversations with German Foreign Minister Josckha Fischer, during his visit to Berlin, Sheikh Hamdan stated that 'terrorism has no religion and no country,' going on to note that 'it is a gross mistake to make a link between this aberrant phenomenon and Islam. Islam is a faith of tolerance and peace, and denounces all forms of extremism, hatred, violence and aggression.'

'We firmly believe,' he said, 'that fighting terrorism requires, above all, decisive measures to eradicate it, the deepening of a culture of dialogue, tolerance and co-operation between nations and joint efforts to promote justice and to encourage all to abide by international law, as well as an enhancing of the role of the United Nations.'

Reiterating the UAE's condemnation of terrorism, President Sheikh Zayed noted in June, in a cable to the South Korean President following the murder of a Korean citizen in Iraq, that the UAE 'categorically denounces terrorism in all its forms and manifestations, and strongly rejects this savage and inhumane crime.' Similar cables were sent to other countries whose citizens were murdered in Iraq.

During the year, despite continued efforts by the UAE to develop the positive environment that now prevails in relations with its neighbour, the Islamic Republic of Iran, no progress was made on what former UAE President Sheikh Zayed described as 'the elimination of the obstacles that stand in the way in achieving a real breakthrough in these relations.'

The UAE continued to receive support in international meetings, and from within the Arab world, for its call for Iran to commence serious negotiations on its occupation of the three UAE islands of Greater and Lesser Tunb and Abu Musa, or to refer the issue to international arbitration or to the International Court of Justice.

At the broader level of the Arab world, the UAE participated actively in the May Arab summit conference in Tunis. Following the summit, the UAE delegation leader, Supreme Council member and Ruler of Fujairah HH Sheikh Hamad bin Mohammed Al Sharqi, noted that the Emirates supported all the resolutions adopted, 'in particular those concerning the Palestinian cause and Arab solidarity.'

Elsewhere, the UAE has continued to promote the development of its political and economic relations with both developed and developing countries.

Of particular note was a series of visits made in April to China, South Korea and Japan, and then to Germany, by a top-level official delegation led by Sheikh Hamdan bin Zayed Al Nahyan, UAE Deputy Prime Minister and Minister of State for Foreign Affairs.

On the Far East trip, Sheikh Hamdan was accompanied by the then Ministers of Higher Education and Scientific Research, of Economy and Commerce, of Justice, Islamic Affairs and Awqaf, and of Communications, as well as by the Under-Secretary of the Ministry of Interior and the Chairman of the Abu Dhabi Economic Department. Senior officials of the Abu Dhabi Chamber of Commerce and of the Abu Dhabi Water and Electricity Authority, as well as leading businessmen from Abu Dhabi and Dubai also took part. Among commercial agreements signed was one between the Dubai Ports Authority and a Chinese manufacturer for the supply of cranes worth nearly US$220 million and one between UAE satellite telecommunications firm Thuraya and a Korean company that will manufacture their second generation of mobile phones.

The importance attached to the visit by the host countries was shown by the high-level talks held with the visitors from the Emirates, as well as by the signing of a number of bilateral agreements, including one on higher education and scientific research with Japan.

In a statement before his departure for the Far East, Sheikh Hamdan noted economic and commercial ties between the UAE and the three states were already very close, but that his visit meant that a new phase of cooperation was beginning. Of particular significance were the detailed discussions held with businessmen in all three countries about the possibility of industrial joint ventures in the UAE, part of plans to continue the process of diversifying the economy.

The visit to Germany was of equal significance, with the delegation again including three ministers, besides Sheikh Hamdan, and other top officials.

This followed the ground-breaking visit to the UAE in October 2003 by the German Chancellor, Helmut Schroeder.

Once again, issues discussed during the visit ranged widely over political, economic, educational, cultural and other topics, with a number of bilateral agreements and Memoranda of Understanding being signed. Sheikh Hamdan also held lengthy talks with Schroeder and other senior German officials during the visit.

Another important visit overseas by an Emirati delegation was to Australia, whose economic and commercial links with the UAE have been developing rapidly in recent years. The UAE delegation was led by Lt-General Sheikh Mohammed bin Zayed Al Nahyan, then Deputy Crown Prince of Abu Dhabi and Chief of Staff of the UAE Armed Forces.

There were also many visits to the UAE by senior ministers from abroad, including officials from the United States and several member countries of the European Union, while the importance attached to the UAE's role in world affairs, and to its former President, Sheikh Zayed, was also well shown by the number of major world leaders who arrived in Abu Dhabi in November to pay their condolences on his death (see Zayed Profile).

Since the establishment of the United Arab Emirates in 1971, it has enjoyed a marked consistency in its foreign policy, this being due to a very large extent to the leadership of Sheikh Zayed. Over the past year, as in previous years, this has helped to consolidate the country's reputation within the international community as a responsible state that seeks to promote dialogue and consensus as a tool for the resolution of disputes and which endeavours to strengthen the legitimacy and authority of international organisations and institutions.

At the end of 2003, the UAE had diplomatic relations with 146 countries and hosts 73 embassies, compared to three in 1971. There are 35 non-resident ambassadors and 54 consulates in Dubai. The UAE has 46 embassies and seven consulates abroad and two Permanent Missions to the United Nations in New York and Geneva.

The country is a member of more than 25 regional and international organisations, and has signed 45 international treaties and conventions, apart from numerous bilateral agreements, including over 60 investment protection agreements, 65 civil aviation agreements and over 50 cultural agreements.

FOREIGN AID

The United Arab Emirates has continued during 2004 to play an active role in the provision of external aid to developing countries and to be a major contributor of emergency relief to countries and areas affected by conflict and natural disasters. Overseas aid is a key feature of the country's foreign policy, as noted

ECONOMIC DEVELOPMENT

THE ECONOMY

DURING LATE 2003 AND THE FIRST HALF of 2004, the UAE economy continued to grow rapidly, due both to high oil prices and to the success of other sectors, including manufacturing, other industries and tourism. This chapter reviews the economic data for 2003 and preliminary data for 2004. It also reports on economic projections for 2005 and beyond. Information is primarily based on figures and reports provided by the UAE Central Bank and the Ministry of Planning.

The 2004 *Yearbook* stated that preliminary data for 2002 indicated a gross domestic product (GDP) based on constant 1995 prices of Dh225.724 billion. Subsequent data has become available that raises this figure to Dh226.011 billion and pegs the 2003 value at Dh241.828 billion (i.e. a 7 per cent growth rate at constant prices). Unless otherwise stated, the following discussion is based on constant price comparisons rather than current prices.

The non-oil sector, amounting to Dh187,250 million in 2003 (preliminary data), grew at a rate of 5.2 per cent on its value for 2002 (Dh178,055 million). Oil and gas output increased by almost 14 per cent in 2003 compared with its value in 2002 (i.e. Dh54.6 billion in 2003 against Dh48.0 billion in 2002). Overall, the hydrocarbon sector contributed 22.6 per cent of GDP in 2003.

Continued development of the non-oil sectors (increasing by 5.2 per cent in 2003) reflects the focus on economic diversification. The non-oil sectors' slight drop in overall contribution to GDP (77.4 per cent in 2003, down from 78.8 per cent in 2002), despite the actual rise in value mentioned above, is accounted for by the larger than usual increase in value of the oil and gas sector during 2003. Meanwhile, the UAE's population has also continued to rise (4,041,000 in 2003 compared with 3,754,000 in 2002) and this has resulted in a slight reduction in per capita GDP, from Dh60,205 in 2002 to Dh59,844 in 2003.

Balance of payments figures improved significantly in 2003 with preliminary analysis indicating an increase in the trade surplus of 37.5 per cent, while the current account surplus rose by 84.6 per cent above the levels achieved in 2002. The overall balance reflected a surplus of Dh4.7 billion in 2003 compared with a deficit of Dh1.5 billion in 2002.

Gross Domestic Product at Base Price by Economic Sectors

(In millions of Dh at constant 1995 prices)

Sectors	2002	2003*
☐ (1) Non-Financial Enterprises Sector	185,770	200,532
☐ - Agriculture, Livestock, Fishery	8,738	8,956
▨ - Mining	48,653	55,311
A. Crude Oil & Natural Gas	47,956	54,578
B. Quarries	697	733
■ - Manufacturing	34,630	38,010
■ - Electricity, Gas and Water	5,115	5,347
▨ - Construction	16,970	17,661
▨ - Wholesale / Retail Trade and Maintenance	22,500	23,495
▨ - Restaurants and Hotels	5,492	5,767
▨ - Transportation, Storage and Communication	20,131	21,692
☐ - Real Estate and Business Services	19,420	20,004
☐ - Social and Private Services	4,121	4,289
☐ (2) Financial Enterprises Sector	16,875	17,808
☐ (3) Government Services Sector	26,895	27,280
- Household Services	1,952	1,981
(Less): Imputed Bank Services Charges	5,481	5,773
TOTAL	226,011	241,828
Total Non-Oil Sectors	178,055	187,250

Source : Central Bank Annual Report 2003 and Ministry of Planning   * Preliminary Data

Gross Domestic Product by Sectors (Percentages of Total GDP)

Sectors	Gross Domestic Product			Non-Mining GDP*		
	2001	2002	2003	2001	2002	2003
A. Goods Production Sectors	52.3	50.5	51.8	37.4	36.9	37.5
☐ Agriculture, Livestock & Fisheries	3.8	3.9	3.7	5.0	4.9	4.8
☐ Mining	23.8	21.5	22.9	-	-	-
■ Manufacturing	15.0	15.3	15.7	19.8	19.5	20.4
☐ Construction	7.4	7.5	7.3	9.8	9.6	9.5
■ Electricity, Gas and Water	2.1	2.2	2.2	2.8	2.9	2.9
B. Services Sectors	47.7	49.5	48.2	62.6	63.1	62.5

* Percentage of GDP at factor cost after excluding mining sector.
Source: Central Bank Annual Report 2003

Gross Domestic Product at Base Price by Economic Sectors

(3) Government Services
26,895

(2) Financial Enterprises
16,875

(1) Non-Financial Services
185,770

				8,738
				48,653
				34,630
				5,115
				16,970
				22,500
				5,492
				20,131
				19,420
				4,121

02

(3) Government Services
27,280

(2) Financial Enterprises
17,808

(1) Non-Financial Services
200,532

				8,956
				55,311
				38,010
				5,347
				17,661
				23,495
				5,767
				21,692
				20,004
				4,289

03*

- Non-Financial Enterprises
- Financial Enterprises
- Government Services

- Agriculture, Livestock and Fishery
- Mining
- Manufacturing
- Electricity, Gas and Water
- Building and Construction

- Wholesale/Retail Trade and Maintenance
- Restaurants and Hotels
- Transportation, Storage and Communications
- Real Estate and Business Services
- Social and Private Services

Gross Domestic Product by Sectors (Percentages of Total GDP)

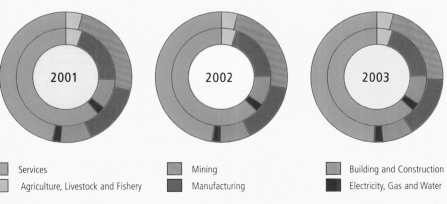

2001   2002   2003

- Services
- Agriculture, Livestock and Fishery
- Mining
- Manufacturing
- Building and Construction
- Electricity, Gas and Water

Source: Central Bank and Ministry of Planning

Source: Ministry of Planning

Per Capita Gross Domestic Product

*at constant 1995 prices

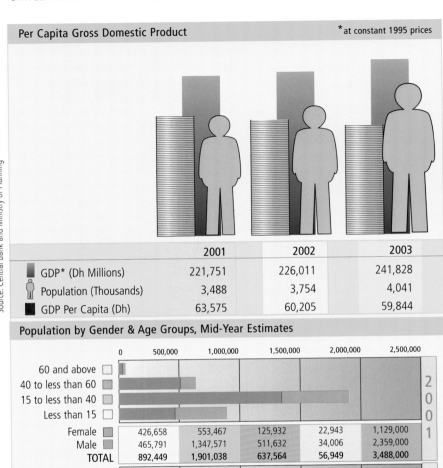

	2001	2002	2003
GDP* (Dh Millions)	221,751	226,011	241,828
Population (Thousands)	3,488	3,754	4,041
GDP Per Capita (Dh)	63,575	60,205	59,844

Population by Gender & Age Groups, Mid-Year Estimates

2001

60 and above
40 to less than 60
15 to less than 40
Less than 15

Female	426,658	553,467	125,932	22,943	1,129,000
Male	465,791	1,347,571	511,632	34,006	2,359,000
TOTAL	892,449	1,901,038	637,564	56,949	3,488,000

2002

60 and above
40 to less than 60
15 to less than 40
Less than 15

Female	456,679	594,729	135,181	24,411	1,211,000
Male	499,132	1,454,816	552,802	36,250	2,543,000
TOTAL	955,811	2,049,545	687,983	60,661	3,754,000

2003

60 and above
40 to less than 60
15 to less than 40
Less than 15

Female	487,560	637,758	144,798	25,884	1,296,000
Male	535,414	1,572,762	598,155	38,669	2,745,000
TOTAL	1,022,974	2,210,520	742,953	64,533	4,041,000

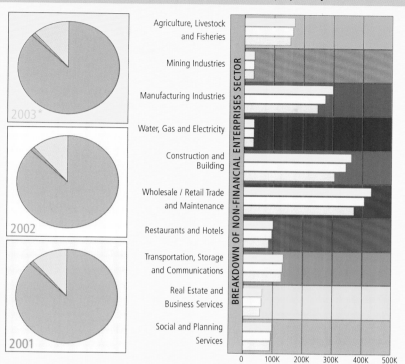

Employees by Economic Sector

SECTORS	2001	2002	2003*
Non-Financial Enterprises Sector	1,497,125	1,629,673	1,716,771
– Agriculture, Livestock and Fisheries	154,043	163,192	168,262
– Mining Industries	30,248	31,702	32,911
A. Crude Oil & Natural Gas	25,945	27,197	28,073
B. Quarries	4,303	4,505	4,838
– Manufacturing Industries	246,910	273,022	297,834
– Water, Gas and Electricity	31,370	32,363	33,140
– Construction and Building	305,477	343,840	362,251
– Wholesale / Retail Trade and Maintenance	370,827	405,874	429,098
– Restaurants and Hotels	84,001	94,930	98,509
– Transportation, Storage and Communication	127,243	130,923	133,913
– Real Estate and Business Services	56,495	60,760	63,065
– Social and Private Services	90,511	93,067	97,788
Financial Enterprises Sector	24,825	25,724	26,214
Government Services Sector	214,226	237,368	248,592
Household	192,846	197,825	199,721
Total	1,929,022	2,090,590	2,191,298

Source: Central Bank Annual Report 2003 and Ministry of Planning.

* Preliminary Data.

The manufacturing sector showed the highest growth rate among the non-oil sectors, rising from Dh34.6 billion in 2002 to Dh38.0 billion in 2003, a 9.8 per cent increase, and this was also reflected by a rise in its overall contribution to GDP from 15.3 per cent in 2002 to 15.7 per cent in 2003. The manufacturing sector is closely linked to the oil and gas sector since a key element is liquified gas and petroleum products. Thus the increase in refining capacity made a vital contribution to the manufacturing sector.

Other sectors grew by varying amounts and more or less kept pace with the overall increase in GDP. The transport, storage and communications sector increased by 7.8 per cent (from Dh20.1 billion in 2002 to Dh21.7 billion in 2003), reflecting the continued development of the UAE as a financial and economic centre and re-export hub where advanced facilities for transportation, communications and storage are given high priority. The financial enterprises sector also reflected this strong activity, rising from Dh16.9 billion in 2002 to Dh17.8 billion in 2003 (a 5.5 per cent growth rate). The government services sector increased by 1.5 per cent (from Dh26.9 billion in 2002 to Dh27.3 billion in 2003), the electricity, gas and water sector output rose 4.5 per cent (from Dh5.1 billion in 2002 to Dh5.3 billion in 2003), while agriculture, livestock and fisheries was up 2.5 per cent (from Dh8.7 billion in 2002 to Dh9.0 billion in 2003), but saw its contribution to GDP drop slightly, from 3.9 per cent in 2002 to 3.7 per cent in 2003. Tourism remains a high profile economic activity in the UAE and looks set to continue to provide strong growth. The hotels and restaurants sector, which is a key element in the equation but by no means the only one, contributed Dh5.8 billion in 2003, compared with Dh5.5 billion in 2002. Meanwhile, the wholesale/retail trade and maintenance sector contributed Dh23.5 billion in 2003 (up from Dh22.5 billion in 2002) and the construction sector rose by 4.1 per cent to reach Dh17.7 billion (compared with Dh17.0 in 2002).

Population and GDP

The UAE's strong economy, healthy social development and its political stability have continued to support a steady rise in population, which has grown from just over 1 million in 1980 to an estimated 4.3 million at the end of 2004. The rapid increase, one of the fastest in the world, is due to an influx of foreign workers, a sharp drop in infant mortality and a comparatively higher birth rate. The average growth rate around 6.4 per cent between 1980 and 1985. It picked up to 7.7 per cent from 1986 to 1995 and 8.8 per cent from 1996 to 2003.

The relatively high rate of population increase (7.6 per cent higher in 2003 compared with 2002) combined with the slightly lower percentage increase in GDP (at constant 1995 prices) over the same period (7 per cent) led to a slight (0.6 per cent) reduction in GDP per capita (Dh59,844 in 2003 compared with Dh60,205 in 2002).

Selected Economic Indicators

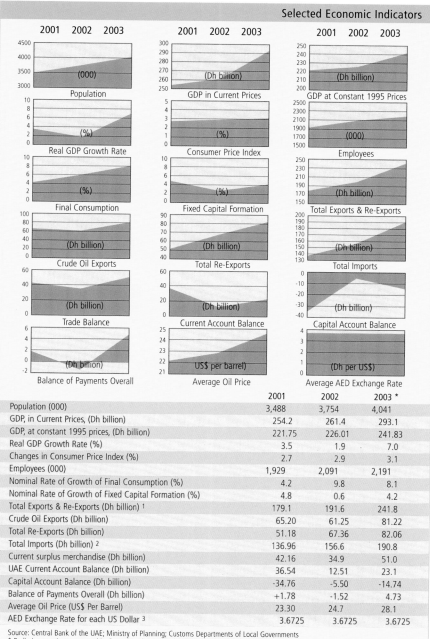

	2001	2002	2003 *
Population (000)	3,488	3,754	4,041
GDP, in Current Prices, (Dh billion)	254.2	261.4	293.1
GDP, at constant 1995 prices, (Dh billion)	221.75	226.01	241.83
Real GDP Growth Rate (%)	3.5	1.9	7.0
Changes in Consumer Price Index (%)	2.7	2.9	3.1
Employees (000)	1,929	2,091	2,191
Nominal Rate of Growth of Final Consumption (%)	4.2	9.8	8.1
Nominal Rate of Growth of Fixed Capital Formation (%)	4.8	0.6	4.2
Total Exports & Re-Exports (Dh billion) [1]	179.1	191.6	241.8
Crude Oil Exports (Dh billion)	65.20	61.25	81.22
Total Re-Exports (Dh billion)	51.18	67.36	82.06
Total Imports (Dh billion) [2]	136.96	156.6	190.8
Current surplus merchandise (Dh billion)	42.16	34.9	51.0
UAE Current Account Balance (Dh billion)	36.54	12.51	23.1
Capital Account Balance (Dh billion)	-34.76	-5.50	-14.74
Balance of Payments Overall (Dh billion)	+1.78	-1.52	4.73
Average Oil Price (US$ Per Barrel)	23.30	24.7	28.1
AED Exchange Rate for each US Dollar [3]	3.6725	3.6725	3.6725

Source: Central Bank of the UAE; Ministry of Planning; Customs Departments of Local Governments
* Preliminary estimates quoted in Central Bank Statistical Bulletin 23/ 4
[1] Including re-exports of Non-Monetary Gold.
[2] Including imports of Non-Monetary Gold. (Ministry of Planning Report 2004).
[3] Effective Nov. 1997, the AED exchange rate has been adjusted to AED 3.6725 for each US dollar.

PUBLIC FINANCE 2003

REVENUES

Total revenues increased by 31.7 per cent in 2003 to reach Dh75.3 billion, up from Dh57.2 billion in 2002, mainly due to the increase in oil and gas earnings.

Tax Revenues

In 2003 tax revenues (customs duties, fees and other charges) dropped by 4.4 per cent from Dh6.9 billion to Dh6.6 billion, accounting for 8.7 per cent of total revenues. The decrease mainly occurred in 'other tax revenues', which fell by Dh946 million (18.1 per cent). Meanwhile, customs revenues rose by Dh640 million to a total figure of Dh2.3 billion following implementation of the new customs tariff that came into force on 1 January 2003.

Non-Tax Revenues

Non-tax revenues rose by 36.6 per cent in 2003, to contribute Dh68.8 billion against Dh50.3 billion in 2002, forming 91.3 per cent of total revenues. This was mainly attributed to an increase of Dh15.6 billion (38.2 per cent) in receipts from oil and gas sales, Dh56.6 billion in 2003 compared with Dh40.9 billion in 2002. Other non-tax revenues also rose by 56.7 per cent contributing Dh9.5 billion in 2003 against Dh6.1 billion in 2002.

EXPENDITURES

Government expenditure increased in 2003 by Dh2.2 billion (2.5 per cent), to Dh88.8 billion against Dh86.6 billion in 2002.

Current Expenditure

Current expenditure constituted 82.5 per cent of total expenditures in 2003, reaching Dh73.2 billion, up from Dh72.6 billion in 2002.

Expenditure on salaries and wages rose by Dh203 million (1.4 per cent) to Dh14.8 billion. Expenditure on goods and services also increased by Dh1.3 billion to Dh23.5 billion. Meanwhile, expenditure on subsidies and transfers dropped by Dh4.4 billion (29.9 per cent) to Dh10.4 billion. Other unclassified current expenditure rose by Dh3.5 billion (16.8 per cent) to Dh24.5 billion.

Development Expenditure

Development expenditure grew by 20.1 per cent to Dh15.0 billion in 2003 against Dh12.5 billion in 2002.

MONETARY AND CREDIT POLICY

Dirham Exchange Rate

Due to its fixed US dollar exchange rate, the dirham depreciated along with a fall in the value of the the US dollar against most major currencies during 2003. The dirham depreciated against the euro (15.6 per cent), the pound sterling (7.6 per cent), the Japanese yen (7.3 per cent), the Swiss franc (13.3 per cent) and the SDR (7.5 per cent). However, the rate of exchange of the dirham remained unchanged against all GCC currencies at the end of 2003, compared with its level in 2002.

The Consolidated Government Finance Account

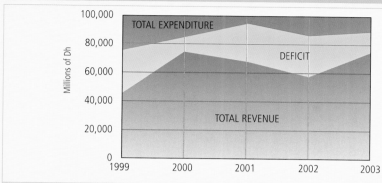

Items — In millions of Dh	2002*	2003**
REVENUES	**57,218**	**75,335**
Tax Revenues	6,881	6,575
Customs	1,663	2,303
Other	5,218	4,272
Non-Tax Revenues	50,337	68,760
Oil and Gas	40,926	56,550
Joint Stock Corporations	3,357	2,721
Other	6,054	9,489
EXPENDITURES	**86,616**	**88,800**
Current Expenditure	76,602	73,234
Salaries and Wages	14,612	14,815
Goods and Services	22,187	23,512
Subsidies and Transfers	14,782	10,360
Other Unclassified	21,021	24,547
Development Expenditure	12,470	14,971
Loans and Equity Participations	1,544	595
Local	592	-1,156
Foreign	952	1,751
Surplus (+) or Deficit (-)	**- 29,398**	**- 13,465**
Financing	29,398	13,465
Changes in net Government Deposits with Banks	-4,339	2,383
Other[1]	33,737	11,082

Source: Central Bank Annual Report 2003 with data drawn from Ministry of Finance and Industry and Local Government Finance Departments
*Adjusted data ** Preliminary data [1] Returns on government's investments.

PUBLIC FINANCE 2003

Dirham Exchange Rate Index

(Foreign Currency Units Per Dirham) (1999=100)

Currency	1999	2000	2001	2002	2003
US Dollar	100.0	100.0	100.0	100.0	100.0
Japanese Yen	100.0	105.0	123.0	121.0	112.9
Euro	100.0	109.4	113.0	106.1	89.5
Pound Sterling	100.0	106.3	112.0	106.8	98.7
Swiss Franc	100.0	106.4	105.6	98.0	85.0
SDR	100.0	104.0	107.8	106.0	98.1

Consumer Price Index Numbers

Data published by the Ministry of Planning on consumer price indices indicate that the general consumer price index (1995 base year) rose from 117.0 in 2002 to 120.6 in 2003 (3.1 per cent). The increment was due to price rises in all major expenditure groups. The index for the medical care and medical services group rose from 150.0 in 2002 to 152.8 in 2003. Likewise, housing and related housing services rose from 104.3 in 2002 to 110.4 in 2003, and transportation and communication services increased from 135.1 in 2002 to 137.9 in 2003. The index numbers for the remaining groups registered only slight rises.

THE BALANCE OF PAYMENTS

The Central Bank Annual Report for 2003 states that amendments have been made to the structure of the balance of payments statement in order to 'meet the requirements of the 5th edition of the *IMF Balance of Payments Manual*'.

The balance of payments recorded an overall surplus of Dh4.7 billion in 2003 against a deficit of Dh1.5 billion in 2002. Both the trade balance and the current account reflected higher surpluses. However, the negative balance of the capital and financial account increased.

The surplus in the trade balance rose by 37.5 per cent in 2003 compared with 2002, to reach Dh73.9 billion against Dh53.7 billion in 2002. This was related to increases in the value of hydrocarbon exports together with rises in other exports and re-exports, despite an increase in total imports. The value of total exports and re-exports was up from Dh191.6 billion in 2002 to Dh241.8 billion in 2003.

The increase in value of hydrocarbon exports was mainly due to increased production volumes resulting from additional refining capacity and gas production capacity and the expanded production of condensates on the one hand, and to increases in oil prices and hence prices of gas, condensates and petroleum products during 2003, compared with 2002, on the other. The weighted average price of oil rose from US$24.7 a barrel in 2002 to US$28.1 a barrel in 2003 (13.8 per cent) causing the value of oil exports (including condensates, which are not included in the country's production quota set by OPEC) to increase from Dh61.3 billion in 2002 to Dh81.2 billion in 2003 (32.6 per cent) and value of exports of gas to increase by 19.4 per cent in 2003, compared with 2002, to reach Dh14.4 billion. Exports of petroleum products also increased in value to Dh13.0 billion in 2003, up from Dh11.9 billion in 2002 (9.1 per cent).

Estimates of UAE Balance of Payments (Dh bn)

	2002	2003
Current Account Balance	12.51	23.09
Trade Balance (FOB)	53.73	73.85
Total Exports of Hydrocarbon	85.18	108.57
Crude Oil Exports	61.25	81.22
Petroleum Products Exports	11.91	12.99
Gas Exports	12.03	14.36
Total of Non Hydrocarbon Exports	39.03	51.06
Free Zone Exports	30.38	41.34
Other Exports [1]	8.65	9.82
Re-Exports [2]	67.36	82.06
Total Exports and Re-Exports (FOB)	191.57	−241.78
Total Imports (FOB)	−137.84	−167.93
Total Imports (CIF)	−156.64	−190.83
Other Imports [3]	−122.80	−147.52
Free Zone Imports	−33.84	−43.31
Services (NET)	−28.36	−33.23
Travel	−8.52	−9.25
Transport	−1.12	−1.19
Government Services	0.08	0.11
Freight and Insurance	−18.80	−22.90
Investment Income (NET)	3.40	−0.42
Banking System [4]	2.48	1.61
Private Non-Banks	0.45	0.19
Enterprises of Public Sector	8.12	7.07
Foreign Hydrocarbon Companies in UAE	−7.66	−9.30
Transfers (NET)	−16.25	−17.12
Public Transfers	−1.05	−1.00
Workers Transfers	−15.20	−16.12
Capital and Financial Account	−5.50	−14.74
Capital Account [5]	—	—
Financial Account	−5.50	−14.74
Enterprise of Private Sector	−7.86	7.61
Direct Investment	−1.27	0.30
Outward	−1.62	0.40
Inward	0.35	0.70
Portfolio Investment	0.92	—
Banks	−13.75	1.05
Securities	−6.77	−6.55
Other Investment	−6.98	7.60
Private Non-Banks	6.25	6.26
Enterprises of Public Sector	2.36	−22.35
Net Errors and Omissions	−8.53	−3.62
Overall Balance: Surplus (+) or Deficit (-)	−1.52	+4.73
Change in Reserves (- indicates an increase)	1.52	−4.73
Net Foreign Assets with Central Bank	1.84	−4.59
Reserve Position with I.M.F.	−0.32	−0.14

1 Including estimates of exports from all emirates.
2 Including re-exports of non-monetary gold.
3 Including imports of non-monetary gold.
4 Central Bank and all banks.
5 Data not available at time of compilation.
* Preliminary Estimates   Source: Central Bank Statistical Bulletin Vol 23 No 4.

PUBLIC FINANCE 2003

The value of commodity exports has continued to rise over the past few years, realising Dh9.8 billion in 2003 against Dh8.7 billion in 2002 (13.5 per cent). Exports from the free zones also increased in value, from Dh30.4 billion in 2002 to Dh41.3 billion in 2003. Moreover, the value of re-exports (including non-monetary gold) rose to Dh82.1 billion in 2003 against Dh67.4 billion in 2002 (21.8 per cent). A substantial portion of the increase in value of re-exports reflects the role of the country's sea ports in the reconstruction of Iraq.

On the other hand, the value of total imports FOB (including free zone imports and imports of non-monetary gold) registered a new record, reaching Dh167.9 billion in 2003 against Dh137.8 billion in 2002 (21.8 per cent). This may be attributed to population increase, the need to meet the requirements of re-exports and a higher propensity to spend among individuals, in addition to the role of commercial festivals held at various times of the year in invigorating commercial activity.

Due to the increase in estimated net imports FOB (minus estimated total value of re-exports and exclusive of imports of free zones) by 21.8 per cent in 2003 compared with 2002, imports per capita rose slightly to reach Dh11,000 in 2003 against Dh10,700 in 2002, despite an increase by 7.6 per cent in population during 2003 compared with 2002.

Data on the structure of imports during 2003 show that consumer goods, capital goods and intermediate goods maintained almost the same shares as those recorded in 2002, at 52.7 per cent, 35.2 per cent and 12.1 per cent of total imports respectively.

Geographical distribution of the total value of imports shows that Europe's share rose from 29.8 per cent in 2002 to 30.1 per cent in 2003. Within this group, Germany had the highest share, despite its decline from 7.8 per cent to 7.5 per cent. Asia's share dropped slightly to 44.1 per cent against 44.6 per cent. Countries in this group almost maintained the same respective shares as those recorded in 2002. Meanwhile, North and South America's share declined from 10.9 per cent in 2002 to 10.5 per cent in 2003.

The current account balance reached Dh23.1 billion, a rise of 84.6 per cent in 2003 compared with 2002. The total negative value of components of 'services' increased from Dh28.4 billion in 2002 to Dh33.2 billion in 2003. The value of freight and insurance, which grew from Dh18.8 billion in 2002 to Dh22.9 billion in 2003, continues to represent more than 66 per cent of the total value of services.

The negative value of the capital and financial account increased from Dh5.5 billion in 2002 to Dh14.7 billion in 2003. This figure, however, reflects development in the financial account only as data on the capital account were not available at the time of writing this *Yearbook*. Those developments were due to the outflow of Dh22.4 billion that occurred in 2003 and appears under the public sector institutions item, against an inflow of Dh2.4 billion in 2002. The private sector institutions figures reflect an inflow of Dh7.6 billion in 2003, compared with an outflow of Dh7.9 billion in 2002.

INFLATION

As a result of external factors, inflation in the UAE surpassed 3 per cent in 2003 for the first time in years. Prices of most consumer items climbed between 1 and 3 per cent, while rents surged by nearly 6 per cent and cost of building materials rose due to a sharp increase in global demand, mainly in China.

INTERNATIONAL MONETARY FUND REPORT

On 28 May 2004 the Executive Board of the International Monetary Fund (IMF) concluded an Article IV consultation with the United Arab Emirates and issued Public Information Notice (PIN) No. 04/66 which reviewed the IMF's economic findings on the UAE. The IMF staff team's independent analysis reinforces economic reporting from the UAE Central Bank, the Ministry of Planning and other Federal and Emirate Government sources that have been used elsewhere in this *Yearbook*. The report, which repeats much of the economic data already outlined, presents a strongly upbeat analysis of the UAE's economic performance and prospects and the main findings are presented *verbatim* below.

The pursuit of a highly liberal, business friendly and market-oriented growth strategy continues to guide the evolution of U.A.E.'s economic development. Consistent with this strategy, each emirate and the federal government conduct economic policies that reflect differences in their natural resource endowments and their respective role within the federation. Openness and a sound record in macroeconomic management have enhanced the role of the private sector and contributed to the diversification of the economy.

In 2003, reflecting favorable developments in the oil market, higher oil production and prices, the U.A.E.'s macroeconomic performance is estimated to have been strong. Non-hydrocarbon real GDP growth is estimated to have remained robust at about 5 percent, one of the highest in the Gulf Cooperation Council area. A number of projects were launched in 2003 in the areas of construction, upstream gas, and downstream oil services. Inflation remained stable at 2.8 percent. Both the external current account and consolidated fiscal balances are estimated to have recorded large surpluses, 8.5 percent and 13.7 percent of GDP, respectively. The non-hydrocarbon deficit (excluding investment income) remained constant as a fraction of non-hydrocarbon GDP, at about 37 percent. The stock market index, which has been rising since 2001, increased sharply in 2003, by about 32 percent, on account of strong economic conditions and optimism regarding the economic outlook. Foreign reserves of the central bank at end-2003 remained steady at about US$15.0 billion, equivalent to about 4.0 months of imports. The broad money stock increased by 16 percent, close to the rates of the previous two years, mainly on account of about 13.5 percent increase in private sector credit. Much of this credit was granted to wholesale trade, construction, and personnel loan sectors.

The financial sector continued to perform well. The U.A.E. banks remained well capitalized and profitable. While the gross nonperforming loan (NPL) ratio at end-2003 remained relatively high at 14 percent, though lower than 2001 and 2002, provisions are considerable, bringing the net NPL ratio below 2 percent. The U.A.E. authorities have undertaken a number of initiatives to improve financial sector supervision and efficiency. Several important steps have been taken to address money laundering and financing of terrorist activities. As a result, U.A.E. is being regarded as a best practice model in this area. Tighter regulations now apply across the entire financial sector. Many Hawala (informal money transfers) dealers have registered and been certified by the U.A.E. central bank and are required to report on a quarterly basis their transactions records on transactions exceeding AED 2,000. As of end-February 2004, the central bank has received 112 applications for registration and 89 certificates have been issued. Considerable progress was made in 2003 in implementing plans to set up the Dubai

International Financial Center (DIFC)—a financial free zone—an initiative of the Government of Dubai, which will deliver a comprehensive set of international financial functions.

Progress in introducing structural reforms has varied among the emirates. Dubai has extended foreign ownership of land and properties to some real estate developments and has also announced the launch of several new free zones. Abu Dhabi is moving ahead with utility privatization, with the objective to privatize its entire water and electricity sector by 2006. Restrictions on foreign ownership of companies and properties, however, remain in place in Abu Dhabi. The federal government has been implementing a series of reforms that include a phased implementation of performance-based budgeting within a newly-introduced three-year medium-term budget framework and corporatization of various supporting services.

In the area of labor policies, to create employment opportunities for U.A.E. nationals in the private sector the authorities have developed at the emirates' level programs to encourage domestic entrepreneurship and small and medium enterprises (SMEs). Key benefits of these programs are simple and streamlined application process, competitive interest rates, and favorable repayment terms. Also, a National Human Resource Development and Employment Authority was created to train nationals to ensure that they have adequate skills to be hired by the private sector.

IMF Executive Board Assessment

Executive Directors agreed with the thrust of the staff appraisal. They commended the United Arab Emirates for pursuing prudent macroeconomic policies, the prudent management of oil resources, and an outward-oriented development strategy, which have resulted in low inflation and high growth, as well as sizeable fiscal and external current account surpluses, a comfortable international reserve position, and the accumulation of foreign assets. Further, they noted that sound policies supported by structural reforms have enhanced the role of the private sector, contributed to growth of the nonhydrocarbon sector and diversification of the economy, and enhanced the economy's resilience to external shocks. Directors agreed that the U.A.E. is in a strong position to take advantage of the global recovery and that the macroeconomic outlook over the medium term remains strong.

The IMF Board of Directors also issued a number of recommendations for further strengthening of fiscal policy and economic structure. They endorsed the pegged exchange rate arrangement, noting that this policy has provided an anchor for price stability, and contributed to low inflation and market confidence. Directors agreed with the thrust of the authorities' monetary policy and supported strengthening the Central Bank's instruments for controlling liquidity.

Directors commended the UAE's open-border foreign labour policy, which has enabled the private sector to recruit expatriate workers at internationally competitive wages, contributed to economic growth, and improved competitiveness of the nonhydrocarbon economy. They endorsed the authorities' long-term labour market strategy to increase employment opportunities for UAE nationals. Directors stressed that such a strategy should continue to rely on raising the skills of nationals through better education and training programs to meet private sector labour demand.

THE ECONOMY IN 2004

For the first time since it began producing oil in the early 1960s, the UAE's oil and gas sector income was expected to exceed Dh100 billion in 2004 as a result of sustained strong oil prices and increased production in line with OPEC quotas. The projected 9.5 per cent growth in this sector should push up its share of GDP to around 32.6 per cent, from nearly 31.7 per cent in 2003. Mid-year projections also predicted that the non-oil sector would grow by around 5.2 per cent in current prices to a record Dh210.2 billion (US$57.2 billion) in 2004.

As a whole, the GDP in current prices is projected to expand by 6.6 per cent to Dh312.4 billion (US$85.1 billion) from Dh293.1 billion (US$79.8 billion), to maintain its position as the third biggest Arab economy after Saudi Arabia and Egypt. While this level of growth is far below the 12 per cent rate recorded for 2003, some experts believe the 2004 growth rate will be significantly ahead of the 6.6 per cent prediction if the annual oil price average exceeds US$30 a barrel.

If the UAE's population reaches 4.32 million by the end of 2004, as is predicted, its per capita income (based on Net National Income) will still show a modest increase to a level of Dh59,700 (US$16,244).

ECONOMIC OUTLOOK FOR 2005

Official government reports, such as the Ministry of Planning document mentioned above, provided economic predictions for 2004 that are based on analysis of partial figures for the year. They do not publish projections for the following year (2005) or beyond. A number of economic 'think-tanks', however, make forward predictions using information currently available. Whilst these may prove imprecise as a result of unforeseen circumstances, they are interesting in so far as they calculate how present performance and economic decisions are likely to impact on future growth. The Economist Intelligence Unit (EIU) is one such 'think-tank' that issues regular updates on projected economic performance of a large number of countries, including the UAE. In mid-2004 it issued a report that suggested the relatively high economic growth rate for 2004 (which it estimated to reach 4.3 per cent (real GDP growth) as against the Ministry of Planning prediction of 4.8 per cent) would increase to around 4.9 per cent in 2005.

LOOKING FURTHER AHEAD

In recent years, the UAE economy has, to a marked extent, become less dependent on oil and gas. Thus, according to Central Bank figures, the contribution of the non-oil sector to GDP has risen from 54 per cent in 1990 to 77.4 per cent in 2003. While the continued upturn in oil prices is likely to impact on the ratio in 2004, the actual value of the non-oil sector continues to show impressive growth, and it is clear that the UAE has achieved considerable success in diversifying its sources of income.

Economic Summary

	2002	2003*	2004**
Population (000)	3,754	4,041	4,320
Workers (000)	2,091	2,191	2,304
GDP in current prices (billion Dh)	261.4	293.1	312.4
GDP Non Oil Sectors (billion Dh)	188.8	199.8	210.2
GDP At Constant 1995 Prices (billion Dh)	226.0	241.8	253.5
Per Capita National Income (Dh)	56.7	59.2	59.7
Gross Fixed Capital Formation (billion Dh)	60.6	63.1	65.2
Final Consumption Expenditure (billion Dh)	174.6	188.7	201.2
Commodity Exports (billion Dh)	191.6	241.8	269.0
Commodity Imports (billion Dh)	156.6	190.9	213.0
Current Surplus Merchandise (billion Dh)	34.9	51.0	56.0
Inflation Rate (%)	2.9	3.1	3.0

*Preliminary Data ** Forecasts Source: Ministry of Planning Report 2004.

Economic Projections*

(per cent unless otherwise indicated)	2004	2005
Real GDP growth	4.8[1]	4.9
Oil production ('000 b/d)	2,180	2,240
Crude oil exports (US$ m)	19,543	16,771
Consumer price inflation (av)	3	2.7
Deposit rate	1.2	3.2
Government balance (per cent of GDP)	-10.7	-13.9
Exports of goods fob (US$ bn)	56	54.4
Imports of goods fob (US$ bn)	39.8	42.7
Current-account balance (US$ bn)	8.7	4.8
Current-account balance (per cent of GDP)	11.3	6.6
External debt (year-end; US$ bn)	22	23.4
Exchange rate Dh:US$ (av)	3.67	3.67

*Source: Economist Intelligence Unit Country Report May 2004, Central Bank Report 2003 and Ministry of Planning Report 2004.
[1.] Ministry of Planning figure. EIU estimated 4.3 per cent.
*Preliminary Data ** Forecasts Source: Ministry of Planning Report 2004.

Diversification of the UAE's economy will continue to play a vital role in maintaining growth and stabilising the impact of oil production or price fluctuations. Continued efforts will be made to attract foreign direct investment, and indications are that these efforts will continue to bear fruit, becoming increasingly significant contributors to economic growth. Dubai, in particular, will concentrate on diversification in order to offset its dwindling oil income. Abu Dhabi's focus on industrial growth will also show positive results. This will not, of course, make oil and gas unimportant, since the revenues they provide are, and will remain, the basic source for the financing of the national economy and for funding the necessary infrastructure in other sectors.

Abu Dhabi, blessed with over 90 per cent of oil and natural gas reserves in the UAE, is likely to maintain its focus on upstream hydrocarbon resources and downstream industrial projects, especially in the petrochemicals sector. It is likely to continue to exert the greatest influence over the Federation's public finances and to remain at the forefront of the privatisation process.

Manufacturing industry will play an increasingly important role in the national economy in future. Among reasons for this are the existing availability of basic essentials such as infrastructure and communications, as well as the availability of resources to fund the acquisition of the appropriate technology. Moreover, in other sectors, there are limited opportunities for investment. In agriculture, for example, the climate and the shortage of water resources plays a part, while the construction sector has finite growth prospects, due to the fact that the basic infrastructure has been completed and most buildings are relatively modern.

FINANCIAL MARKETS

ABU DHABI SECURITIES MARKET

ADSM (which is linked to Dubai Financial Market, DFM) recorded marked growth in all performance indicators during 2003. Trading volume increased by 176.2 per cent, number of traded shares rose by 282.0 per cent and number of executed deals by 126 per cent, compared with 2002. The number and market capitalisation of listed companies also increased. In addition to its main trading floor in Abu Dhabi City, Abu Dhabi Securities Market also operates trading floors in Sharjah and Ra's al-Khaimah and has plans to open a branch in Fujairah.

DUBAI FINANCIAL AND INTERNATIONAL FINANCIAL MARKETS

DFM (which is linked to ADFM) performance indicators rose during 2003. Trading volume increased by 49.3 per cent, traded shares by 120.5 per cent and executed deals by 0.8 per cent.

Abu Dhabi Securities Market

	Number of Traded Shares		Value of Traded Shares		Number of Executed Deals	
	2002	2003	2002	2003	2002	2003
Banking Sector	39,630,979	96,535,497	619,222,435	1,633,280,694	6,822	11,891
Services Sector	7,899,933	24,118,397	368,267,229	1,392,174,040	3,073	9,355
Insurance Sector	3,903,443	102,599,755	75,921,141	264,692,912	94	2,677
Hotels Sector	1,281,182	2,388,776	138,325,783	256,458,801	390	492
Industry Sector	8,860,683	9,559,250	133,313,875	140,356,655	868	1,019
Total	61,576,220	235,201,675	1,335,050,463	3,686,963,102	11,247	25,434

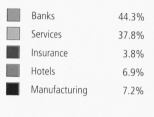

Banks	44.3%
Services	37.8%
Insurance	3.8%
Hotels	6.9%
Manufacturing	7.2%

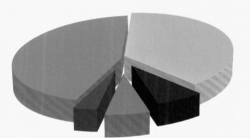

Dubai Financial Market

	Number of Traded Shares		Value of Traded Shares		Number of Executed Deals	
	2002	2003	2002	2003	2002	2003
Banking Sector	26,737,484	28,628,301	928,114,959	1,240,244,799	4,748	5,368
Services Sector	109,788,429	274,975,888	1,523,159,397	2,330,160,204	19,008	17,157
Insurance Sector	171,168	321,185	6,663,810	6,775,238	48	96
Investment Sector	11,253,556	22,310,687	68,356,929	194,310,877	1,268	2,655
Total	147,950,637	326,236,061	2,526,295,095	3,771,491,118	25,072	25,276

Banks	33%
Services	62%
Investment	5%
Insurance	0%

Meanwhile, the Dubai International Financial Centre (DIFC) was given a formal go-ahead in early July 2004 when Federal Decree No. 35 was issued. This was the final federal legislative step enabling the Centre to begin operation. At that stage, among the institutions that had publicly announced their intention to use the DIFC as a base for regional operations were Credit Suisse, Standard Chartered, Julius Baer and Aon. The DIFC concept is a major component of the Dubai government's strategy for accelerating the economic development of the emirate and of the UAE.

Almost simultaneously with the announcement of the enabling legislation, Dow Jones Indexes, a leading global index provider, and the Dubai International Financial Centre, in collaboration with the Dubai-based investment bank SHUAA Capital, launched the Dow Jones DIFC Arabia Titans 50 index, a regional blue-chip index that covers companies in Bahrain, Egypt, Jordan, Kuwait, Lebanon, Morocco, Oman, Qatar, Tunisia and UAE. The new index, based on the stock prices of 50 leading companies in the region, provides a transparent index consistent with the global Dow Jones family. The weighting of each component is determined using 60 per cent market capitalisation, 20 per cent net income and 20 per cent revenue. The new index is quoted on a base value calculated on 31 December 2000. The value at launch of the index in July 2004 was up 70.76 per cent on this base value. A full list of components including weightings and values of the Dow Jones DIFC Arabia Titans 50 is available on www.djindexes.com.

BANKING SECTOR

It is the responsibility of the Central Bank, the country's regulatory authority, to formulate and implement the UAE's banking, credit and monetary policy in order to support the UAE's economic policy objectives, including price stability, and to guarantee the value and stability of the UAE dirham and its free convertibility into all currencies.

There are many aspects to the role the Central Bank plays in supporting the national economy of the United Arab Emirates. In addition to acting as banker to other banking institutions operating in the country, it is also the banker and financial adviser to the government.

Anti-Money Laundering

A key issue for the Central Bank has been to ensure that adequate controls are in place to prevent money laundering. The National Committee for Anti-Money Laundering helps to guide policy in this regard and it participates in meetings of the Financial Action Task Force (FATF–GAFI), an international body concerned with combating money laundering and financial fraud. The task force has stated that the UAE has put in place a comprehensive Anti-Money Laundering System, comprising legislation, regulations and procedures. As such, the UAE is fully cooperative in the internationally declared fight against money laundering.

Selected Monetary and Banking Indicators* (Dh mn)

INDICATOR	2002	2003	2004*
Central Bank of UAE			
Total Assets/Liabilities.................	55,273	54,502	64,130
Foreign Assets and Gold Holdings	55,075	54,221	63,896
Currency issued..........................	13,799	15,969	16,517
Liquidity Indicators			
Money Supply (M1)...................	47,054	58,262	65,381
Private Domestic Liquidity (M2) ..	173,653	200,600	213,272
Overall Domestic Liquidity (M3) ..	220,764	250,942	261,885
Banks [1]			
Total Assets/Liabilities.................	331,550	366,908	377,534
Foreign Assets	110,732	111,727	108,087
Foreign/Total Assets (%).............	33.4	30.5	28.6
Foreign Liabilities	28,247	30,294	31,536
Foreign/Total Liabilities (%)	8.5	8.3	8.4
Deposits [2]	**209,647**	**237,557**	**247,844**
Residents[2].................................	198,244	226,338	236,711
Non-residents.............................	11,403	11,219	11,133
Bank Credit (Net)[3]	**157,810**	**192,675**	**206,013**
Residents	133,723	164,922	175,272
Non-Residents............................	24,087	27,753	30,741
National Banks and Branches [4]	**345**	**367**	**370**
Head Offices................................	21	21	21
Branches	324	346	349
Foreign banks and branches [5]	**112**	**112**	**112**
Head Offices................................	26	25	25
Branches	83	86	87
Number of Workers in UAE banks [6]	**16,080**	**17,229**	**17,544**

[1]. Including the Restricted Licence Bank until 31/5/2003.
[2]. Excluding Inter-Bank Deposits
[3]. Excluding Loans to Banks and Provisions
[4]. Including Pay Offices
[5]. Including a Pay Office
[6]. Excluding Auxiliary Staff.

*Source: Central Bank Statistical Bulletin Vol 23, No. 4.

Money Supply & Domestic Liquidity

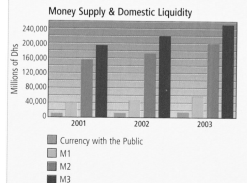

- Currency with the Public
- M1
- M2
- M3

Monetary Survey

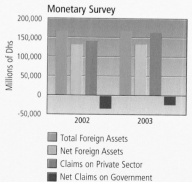

- Total Foreign Assets
- Net Foreign Assets
- Claims on Private Sector
- Net Claims on Government

The UAE's anti-money laundering law has been proposed as a model for adoption by other states. Its efforts and legislation in this regard formed the focus of a US Department of State report at a recent meeting of the Counter Terrorism Action Group of G-8. The international report noted that the UAE's law had clear definitions and criminalised deposits as well as conversion or transfer of funds with the aim of disguising their illegal origin. It also noted that the UAE is a leader in addressing difficulties associated with the *hawala* money transmitting system. The UAE has executed all related UN Security Council Resolutions and the Central Bank has issued orders requesting banks and other financial institutions, to search for and freeze any accounts, deposit or investments, which are in the names of terrorist leaders, terrorist organisations or persons who helped terrorists. Findings of banks are collected and reports presented to the concerned authorities in the UAE.

The Hawala System

Hawala plays a key role in facilitating remittances, especially those of migrant workers and is an integral part of the international finance system. The UAE recently reaffirmed that its stance with regard to *hawala* would continue to be one of regulation and prevention of abuse, rather than a ban on the long established traditional system of financial transfers. It is working with the World Bank and IMF to achieve these objectives.

Hawala predates traditional or 'Western' banking in the Middle East and Asia. Prior to establishment of Asia's first Western bank around 1770, *sarafs* and *potedars*, primarily moneychangers and essentially predecessors of present day *hawaladars*, played a vital role in nearly all commercial and financial transactions.

Today, both *hawala* and Western-style banking systems play vital and frequently intertwined roles in the economies of India, Pakistan and Bangladesh. The UAE's large population of migrant workers from these countries has supported a significant growth in the *hawala* business in the Emirates.

The Central Bank has taken measures to bring the system under control, issuing licences to *hawala* operators in the country so that these dealers can carry on their business within a legal framework. By regulating the *hawala* system, the Central Bank has placed the onus on *hawala* dealers to report any suspicious transactions to the authorities. It was the previous anonymity and scant documentation that made the *hawala* system vulnerable to abuse by individuals and groups transferring funds to finance illegal activities.

Financial institutions

Most of the banks in the UAE performed well in 2003 influenced by factors such as intense property development, high oil prices, rising stock markets and significant investments in private and public sectors. The top ten national banks in the UAE, based on net profits and total assets, were National Bank of Dubai (NBD), National Bank of Abu Dhabi (NBAD), Mashreqbank, Emirates Bank International (EBI), Abu Dhabi Commercial Bank (ADCB), Union National Bank (UNB), Commercial Bank of Dubai (CBD), Dubai Islamic Bank (DIB), First Gulf Bank (FGB) and Bank of Sharjah.

The UAE Central Bank issued five new licences to foreign banks and financial institutions in 2003, bringing to 48 the total number of representative offices of foreign banks in the UAE. The number of branches of the 21 national banks rose to 330 by the end of 2003 compared with 310 at the end of 2002. Two new money exchanging offices of national banks brought the total to 37 in 2003, while one new establishment brought the total number of branches and exchange houses of the 25 foreign banks to 87. Four financial and monetary brokers entered the market in 2003, pushing the total number of licensed brokers to 32 head offices and one branch. The number of finance companies remained unchanged at six by the end of 2003.

THE BUSINESS ENVIRONMENT

Following years of success in promoting diversification of the UAE's economy and creating numerous opportunities for private investment in UAE-based businesses, leading government officials and finance experts are the first to admit that there is still considerable scope for investment growth, both through encouragement of private national investment in the UAE and through further attraction of foreign direct investment (FDI). It is also clear that business opportunities and incentives by themselves are not enough to promote investment. Attention has, therefore, been focused on creating an even more positive business environment that adopts best practice methods, appropriate legal frameworks and is transparent.

Much progress has already been made in this regard. The World Bank has identified the UAE as one of the least cumbersome countries in which to set up a new business. According to a recent report, the World Bank stated that only 29 days is needed to set up a new business in the UAE, whereas the average period for the Middle East and North Africa (MENA) region is 60 days. The report estimates the cost of setting up a new business (as a percentage of gross per capita national income) in the UAE at 24.4 per cent compared with the MENA average of 76.1 per cent. Again, at ten procedures for setting up a new business, the UAE is also lower than the MENA average of 12.

Foreign investment has, to some extent, been affected by legislation that prohibited non-nationals owning more than 49 per cent of registered enterprises. However, 100 per cent ownership by non-nationals is permitted in Free Zones.

The Emirate of Abu Dhabi has made further progress with its long term strategy to diversify its economic base and reduce its dependence on volatile oil and gas revenues. Apart from the emirate's plans to establish five industrial zones and the world's largest complex for service companies in the onshore and offshore oil and gas business, the creation in May 2004 of the Higher Corporation for Specialised Economic Zones (HCSEZ) was the latest step in a series of major measures to promote diversification. The new corporation aims to provide an integrated infrastructure, a suitable business environment and professional services through establishing and managing special zones in Abu Dhabi. The objective is to make the emirate an attractive place for local and international investment. Other objectives include the promotion of local industries and the creation of appropriate opportunities to attract and train UAE nationals so that they may play an active role in business development. The corporation will also seek to develop and encourage small, medium and specialised industries and will encourage the private sector to become involved in the management of the zones. This will be done, in part, through the commissioning of feasibility studies and investment in the appropriate electronic and IT infrastructure.

The Abu Dhabi government has also announced plans to privatise a number of state-owned companies. This is being handled through a newly-established public joint stock company, General Holding Company (GHC), which has taken over the industrial holdings of the General Industries Corporation, which is being wound up. Resolution No. 5 for 2004 provides the legal and organisational framework for the take-over. The new body is undertaking sale of stakes in public utilities to the private sector as part of the emirate's strategy to forge a public-private partnership and stimulate local financial markets. The companies to be privatised include fodder, cement, steel and pipe plants, and flour mills. The privatisation is expected to strengthen the local stock markets as the newly-privatised firms obtain listings. International bank HSBC has been appointed financial consultant for the privatisation process, while Abu Dhabi Investment Co (ADIC) will act as marketing consultant. Simmons & Simmons are the international legal advisors and Hadif Al Daheri & Partners will be local legal advisors.

While Abu Dhabi Department of Economy is now clearly looking to the future, significant results have already been achieved in terms of rationalising and stimulating Abu Dhabi's non-oil industry. According to official figures issued in mid-2004, investment in the Industrial City of Abu Dhabi, at Mussafah, had reached Dh 5.5 billion (US$1.36 billion) with over 30,000 workers employed there by 355 companies. Of these, 36 are in the petrochemicals sector, 28 in foodstuffs, 15 in garments and textiles, 58 in fiberglass, 75 in construction materials, 81 in metal industries and 23 in computers and equipment assembling. The industrial city, initially 14 square kilometres, is being expanded by another 10 square kilometres.

One particular focus of interest, not surprisingly, is the oilfield supply sector, with a major dedicated complex being planned. Nearly 530 companies in Abu Dhabi are already active in this field in various ways, with annual turnover of over US$1 billion. In order to attract the necessary foreign investment, the Abu Dhabi government is planning to revise local economic and investment legislation to ensure that it complies with the requirements of the WTO.

Another initiative expected to assist local and international business is the provision, by the Abu Dhabi Chamber of Commerce and Industry (ADCCI), of an interactive trade map with online access. Launched in collaboration with International Trade Centre (ITC) with a view to rationalise the UAE's imports and promote exports, the trade map is expected to promote UAE exports by increasing the competitiveness of national products in local, regional and international markets. The trade map is being linked to the ADCCI website, with access available for members. The main objective of this initiative is to promote non-oil exports of the UAE with the ultimate aim of progressive reduction of dependence on oil exports. The trade map will provide information on more than 90 per cent of the world trade flows, covering 180 countries and 5000 products. Local importers and exporters will be able to use the map to examine the performance and dynamics of any country's export market for any product.

These and other new initiatives being undertaken by the Department of Economy, with the active participation of the Chamber of Commerce and Industry, should help in a very significant manner to promote the diversification and further growth of the local economy.

FREE ZONES

Following on from the development and steady expansion of the UAE's first free trade zone at Jebel Ali, and the success of other specialised zones that provide attractive facilities for both national and international investors, it has been clearly demonstrated that the free-zone formula is an effective magnet for inward investment, bringing jobs, expertise and a significant boost to the national economy. The basic recipe (100 per cent foreign ownership, corporate tax holidays, no personal taxes, freedom to repatriate capital and profits, no import duties or currency restrictions) differs only slightly among the various zones whose comparative advantages are based more upon individual locations, facilities, areas of specialisation and, last but not least, establishment and operating costs. A list of current free zones and their main areas of activity is given on pages 112–113.

ONLINE MARKETING

Considering the significant focus the UAE Government and private enterprises have given to promotion of modern technology in administration and business development, it is not surprising that the country has taken the lead in certain

Free Zones and Commercial Clusters

FOLLOWING ON FROM the development and steady expansion of the UAE's first free trade zone at Jebel Ali, and the success of other specialised zones that provide attractive facilities for both national and international investors, it has been clearly demonstrated that the free-zone formula is an effective magnet for inward investment, bringing jobs, expertise and a significant boost to the national economy. The basic recipe (100% foreign ownership, corporate tax holidays, no personal taxes, freedom to repatriate capital and profits, no import duties or currency restrictions) differs only slightly among the various zones whose comparative assets are based more upon individual locations, facilities, areas of specialisation and, last but not least, establishment and operating costs. A list of current free zones and their main areas of activity is given below.

JEBEL ALI FREE ZONE

Major Dubai base for warehousing and regional distribution by multinational companies. Features manufacturing, trading and services companies including many global leaders.

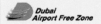

DUBAI AIRPORT FREE ZONE

High tech, IT products, luxury items, jewellery, light industries, aviation industry related businesses.

DUBAI INTERNET CITY

Part of Dubai Technology and Media Free Zone (TECOM). Information technology and telecommunications centre. Internet related businesses.

DUBAI MEDIA CITY

Part of TECOM. Market segments include publishing, broadcasting, film production and post-production, media and marketing services, specialised media services, business and information services, music, new media and multimedia/Internet, leisure and entertainment, media support service and providers, business support and consultancy services.

DUBAI METALS & COMMODITIES CENTRE

Gold, diamond and commodities trading, gold refining, manufacture of gold jewellery, gold trading, diamond exchange.

GOLD & DIAMOND PARK

Dubai located retail and wholesale manufacture and trade in gold and diamond jewellery.

KNOWLEDGE VILLAGE

Part of TECOM in Dubai. Education and training hub, eLearning content/systems/service providers, international academic institutes and programmes, academic services and support providers, professional training centres, management development centres, research and development centres, innovation centres, training and education freelancers.

HAMRIYAH FREE ZONE

Major industrial zone in Sharjah serving companies involved in general industrial development, manufacturing, processing and assembling.

SHARJAH AIRPORT INTERNATIONAL FREE ZONE

Import of raw materials, manufacturing, processing, assembling, packaging and exporting the finished product. General trading and associated services.

AJMAN FREE ZONE

General trading, professional services, industrial production.

AHMED BIN RASHED FREE ZONE

Located in Umm al-Qaiwain, catering for companies involved in general trading, management and consultancy services, light industrial production.

RA'S AL-KHAIMAH FREE TRADE ZONE

Environmentally friendly projects in the service, manufacturing and industrial sectors, with high emphasis placed on attracting technology oriented enterprises. Zone split into business, technology and industrial centres.

FUJAIRAH FREE ZONE

General trading (import, export & re-export of agreed and specified commodities), manufacturing, warehousing.

DUBAI HEALTH CARE CITY

Healthcare industries and services. Healthcare professionals and service providers.

DUBAI CARS & AUTOMOTIVE ZONE

Re-exporting used cars.

Free Zones Under Development

DUBAI AID CITY

Local, regional and international, relief aid community donors, relief aid suppliers and organisations within the humanitarian value chain.

MOHAMMED BIN RASHID FREE ZONE

Dubai located Technology Park. Key areas to include desalination, oil and gas, biotechnology, pharmaceuticals, agrotech and material science, university research and technical services, engineering and R&D projects.

DUBAI AUTO PARTS CITY

Automobile spare parts companies. Tyres, auto batteries, and accessories.

DUBAI TEXTILE CITY

Textile industry companies.

HEAVY EQUIPMENT AND TRUCKS FREE ZONE

A Dubai located zone dealing in re-exports of trucks and heavy equipment.

DUBAI FLOWER CENTRE FREE ZONE

Horticulture industry, global trade in flowers and perishables.

DUBAI CARPET FREE ZONE

Handmade carpet companies.

DUBAI OUTSOURCE ZONE

Will provide comprehensive infrastructure and environment for outsourcing firms to service worldwide market.

aspects of online marketing. The global e-commerce market has been predicted to reach US$7 trillion in 2004, of which 2 per cent is forecasted growth for the Middle East. The figures confirm that the UAE's e-commerce development is likely to continue its growth, provided that the infrastructure and incentives are in place.

The leading e-commerce business-to-business (B2B) web marketing and auctioning company in the Middle East is UAE-based award-winning website www.tejari.com. During 2003, Tejari was awarded 'Gulf Brand of the Decade' (by Gray Business Communications); UAE Superbrand (by the UAE Superbrands Council) and Best e-content (by World Summit Award 2003). One of Tejari's key strengths is that it has focused on government and private sector contracts and tendering procedures, enabling both national and international companies easier access to participation in development projects. In just three years, the Tejari brand has become instantly recognisable as a place for efficient online procurement, throughout the Middle East. By mid-2004, nearly 2500 organisations had used the Tejari trading platform, conducting more than 30,000 online transactions, with a total value of USD$600 million. Use of the Internet among procurement agencies is rapidly increasing with 17 per cent of organisations within the Gulf Cooperation Council (GCC) states engaged in online procurement. The average GCC resident purchases US$1068 worth of goods and services online annually, compared to per capita purchase figures of US$1314 in the United States of America, US$1072 in the UK, and US$875 in Germany.

Another growing e-commerce website in the UAE is www.UAEmall.com. This is similar in format to the global auction website Ebay and provides a 'buy now' or 'make your best offer' option on a wide range of consumer goods. It is especially popular for buying and selling second-hand cars and works by introducing buyers and sellers rather than direct selling. The site has won the Visa award for Best e-Shopping Site in the Middle East. The site, which has over 3500 sellers registered with it from all over the world, including the US, Europe and GCC countries, does not allow card transactions. Sellers and buyers conclude deals through other modes of payment such as bank transfers or cash-on-delivery.

Even the booming property business in the UAE is being facilitated by online marketing and payment solutions. Every real estate developer and broker is dependent upon the Internet for dissemination of up-to-date information on their projects and available properties. Many of them have made virtual offices that showcase fine details of their completed buildings and realistic models or artist's impressions of those that are still on the planning boards. There are also several real estate portals that specialise in the UAE's property market. Ikaar.com and Amlaki.net have search engines to assist in locating different properties throughout the UAE. UAEmall.com also has an online listing of property in Abu Dhabi, Al Ain and Dubai, through its real estate affiliates, Asteco (Dubai), Al Ghanem Real Estate (Abu Dhabi), Atlas Habitat (Abu Dhabi), and Colliers International (Abu Dhabi).

But while investors are thus enabled to make decisions without actually visiting existing properties or new building sites, until recently the documentation and payment facilities were somewhat less streamlined. Eqarat has used its web presence at www.Eqarat.com, in conjunction with Emirates Bank International (EBI), to introduce the region's first online payment service for the rapidly expanding property market. The new facility enables customers to settle online with major credit cards for a range of company-related services, including down-payments on properties.

INDUSTRIAL DEVELOPMENT

The UAE's main industrial manufacturing activities, apart from the oil and gas sector which is covered elsewhere, are in construction, aluminium, chemicals and plastics, metals and heavy equipment, clothing and textiles, and food. As already indicated, each emirate in the UAE has taken steps to nurture the development of these (and other) non-oil industries, both in terms of providing attractive structures and support mechanisms and through development of improved facilities such as industrial zones, business parks and vital energy and transport networks. There has been significant restructuring in the UAE's manufacturing sector in order to meet the challenges it will face when new WTO regulations come into effect in 2005. The main thrust is in establishing projects with production privileges that will enable them to penetrate new markets and increase exports.

The value of the manufacturing sector's contribution to GDP reached just over Dh38 billion (US$10.34 billion) in 2003, second only to the oil sector's value of around Dh54.6 billion (US$14.86 billion). The sector expanded by around 9.7 per cent, compared to the previous year, and accounted for over 15.7 per cent of GDP. Covering mainly light and medium products, this sector is poised for further expansion as the country intensifies its diversification programme.

Promotion of industrial investment depends on satisfactory administrative and legislative environments and considerable efforts have been applied to optimise these important aspects of the economic climate. As noted above, one important step, taken in 2004, was the establishment of the Higher Corporation for Specialised Economic Zones (HCSEZ) in Abu Dhabi. The newly founded body, under chairmanship of the Abu Dhabi Economic Department, has the task of providing support structures for establishment and management of specialised zones in the capital.

The Abu Dhabi Department of Economy has emerged over the last two years as a driving force in the development of non-oil industries in the emirate. It has overseen the formation of GHC, which has recently been assigned the responsibility for privatisation of companies that previously came under the aegis of the General

Industries Corporation (GIC). In collaboration with other bodies like the UAE Offsets Group and the Mubadala Development Company, it is also looking at new areas for economic diversification. Among these are the development of the Industrial City of Abu Dhabi (ICAD) at Mussafah and also drawing up of a tourism strategy for Abu Dhabi. ICAD's range of services include a 'one-stop-shop' for issue of industrial licences; provision of suitable development sites for factories; issue of custom exemption for goods, equipment and machines imported by the factories and solving all obstacles facing industrial projects.

Clusters of industrial projects have been created throughout the UAE at prime locations such as the Industrial City of Abu Dhabi (ICAD), Jebel Ali Free Zone and Hamriyah Free Zone. ICAD is located 30 kilometres from the centre of Abu Dhabi City and 25 kilometres from Abu Dhabi International Airport. It has shown very rapid recent growth with 355 major manufacturing companies employing more than 30,000 workers established there. The City provides all basic services and facilities for a wide range of industrial activities. From over 350 manufacturing units operating in ADIC, 23 per cent are engaged in metallic industries, 21 per cent in construction materials, 16 per cent in fibreglass projects, 10 per cent in the petrochemical sector, 8 per cent in foodstuff manufacture, 6.5 per cent in computers and equipment assembling and 4 per cent in garments and textiles.

Dubai has dramatically stepped up its own drive to attract capital and to expand its manufacturing base to gradually replace its dwindling earnings from oil exports. But, despite its industrial base, Dubai is not a major manufacturer. The vast majority of goods passing through its ports are in transit. The emirate's economic focus has been on development of trade, tourism, communication and finance. Its largest industrial manufacturing venture is Dubai Aluminium Company (Dubal), which has been going through an almost continuous expansion programme over the past few years. This operation has also spawned other connected industries such as Emiroll, which is being set up to manufacture sheet aluminium. Dubai Dry Docks is the emirate's largest service company with four large dry docks, one of which is the largest of its kind worldwide. A Jebel Ali based ship-repair facility adds to the attractiveness of Dubai as a strategically placed maritime centre.

Sharjah's manufacturing sector continues to focus on textiles and light industries and has been involved in modern industrial development for at least three decades, since it started to earn revenues from oil exports. Its deep water harbours at Port Khaled in the Gulf and Khor Fakkan on the East Coast, together with its international airport, provide integrated communication and transport solutions in support of companies operating there. Industrial development is concentrated in two designated areas: Sharjah Airport International Free Zone (SAIFZ) set up in 1996 and the Hamriyah Free Zone (HFZ) created in 1998. On the large industry side, Sharjah has a cement factory that utilises gas from the Saja'a field, and two plants that manufacture steel pipes.

The Northern Emirates have continued their investments in agriculture, ceramics, cement and maritime industries, with an increasing emphasis on creating the necessary infrastructure for tourism, in particular in Fujairah and Ra's al-Khaimah.

THE UAE OFFSETS GROUP

The UAE Offsets Group (UOG) plays a significant role in support of the UAE's diversification plans through the implementation of the UAE Offsets Programme, which has facilitated the creation of innovative and dynamic partnerships between international businesses and local entrepreneurs. Since its inception in 1992, UOG has set up several joint ventures ranging from ship building, aircraft leasing and fish farming to district cooling, agriculture, waste management and energy.

UOG is a commercially-driven entity that focuses on both the macro and microeconomic aspects of the UAE's economy to identify and implement profitable and sustainable businesses. The programme requires defence contractors to fulfil offset obligations by setting up joint ventures in the UAE in partnership with local businesses.

UOG plays the role of a conduit between the joint venture partners. Offsets ventures should yield profits of up to 60 per cent of a contract's value over a period of several years – the typical duration of an offset obligation is seven years – to earn offset credits that are evaluated at several milestones during the life of each offset project. The performance of the joint ventures is closely monitored by UOG and, if defence contractors fail to fulfil obligations, they are required to pay liquidated damages of 8.5 per cent on the unfulfilled portion of the obligation.

For defence contractors with small obligations, UOG has set up the Alfiah Fund. The fund is an investment vehicle for defence contractors who can invest in it rather than setting up independent offsets projects and get credits based on the fund's performance. The Alfiah Fund, managed by the First Gulf Bank (FGB), is capitalised at US$10 million and seeks to maximise returns from a diversified portfolio of investments in civilian ventures under the UAE Offsets Programme. Initial investments of the fund in a single project range from US$500,000 to US$3.5 million.

A recent project supported by UOG is the establishment of a new shipping company, Gulf Energy Maritime (GEM). This is organised as a joint venture between Abu Dhabi's International Petroleum Investment Co. (IPIC), Emirates National Oil Co. (ENOC), the Oman Oil Co. (OOC) and Thales, the international electronics and systems group. The project will have 16 vessels and is being funded by the investors and three local banks: Abu Dhabi Commercial Bank, Emirates Bank International and Mashreqbank. Initially, GEM will have a fleet of two double-hull Panamax vessels and four others that are also Panamax size. They are being built by Hyundai Heavy Industries of Korea and are expected to be delivered by 2005.

MUBADALA DEVELOPMENT COMPANY

Mubadala Development is an investment company which is wholly owned by the Abu Dhabi government. Established under Emiri decree No. 12 of 2002, it has a mandate to form new companies or to acquire stakes in existing companies in the UAE or abroad and to focus on generating sustainable economic benefits for Abu Dhabi Emirate through partnerships with local, regional and international investors. The company intends to invest in a wide range of sectors, including energy, utilities, real estate, public-private partnerships, and basic industries and services, in order to diversify and further develop the economy of Abu Dhabi.

Mubadala's existing investments include a 51 per cent majority stake in Dolphin Energy, the developer of the Dolphin gas project, which involves the creation of the first cross-border gas network in the GCC through the import of Qatari natural gas for the markets of the UAE and Oman. Further details on this project are given below. It also has a 25 per cent stake in the Dutch fleet management giant LeasePlan Corporation and holds shares in ADDAR Real Estate Services, The National District Cooling Company (Tabreed), and Abu Dhabi Ship Building (ADSB).

INVESTMENT IN GLOBAL LEASING

Mubadala Development Company recently acquired a 25 per cent stake in the leading multi-brand vehicle leasing company, LeasePlan. It participated in the purchase alongside the Volkswagen Group, which will hold 50 per cent, and the privately owned Olayan Group. With approximately 1.2 million vehicles under management, total assets of 10.8 billion euro and net earnings of 193 million euro (as at 31 December 2003), LeasePlan is the leading multi-brand fleet management provider in Europe and a major player at worldwide level. The company made a net profit of 193 million euro in 2003 and has over 7000 employees. The acquisition of a stake in LeasePlan is in line with the strategic interests of the government of Abu Dhabi, providing access to global and regional markets and opening up opportunities for further joint ventures with international companies.

Industrial leasing is a major business that provides financing options for many transport, infrastructure and power companies. Another important UAE company operating in this field is the Oasis International Leasing Company (Al Waha), which was set up by the UAE Offsets Group in May 1997 as a Public Joint Stock Company (PJSC). Founding shareholders included BAe Systems, Gulf Investment Corporation (GIC), Abu Dhabi Investment Company (ADIC) and over 50 local institutions and private investors. Oasis Leasing was one of the first companies to be floated and traded on the Abu Dhabi Securities Market (ADSM). An initial public offering (IPO) raised Dh500 million (US$136 million) and resulted in a 55:45 joint venture between UAE nationals and the founding shareholders. Oasis's long-term objective is to identify, structure, manage and invest in high value leasing transactions. Its current asset portfolio includes 20 aircraft, which are all on lease to major regional and international flag carriers. The company hopes to expand its asset and risk profile to US$1.2 billion by 2006 through the acquisition of more aircraft as well as targeted investments in shipping, infrastructure and power plant financing.

The company is currently researching and developing the use of leasing in Abu Dhabi government projects and intends to become involved in public private partnership (PPP) projects in the future. Its Risk Adjusted Lease Book (RALB), which is used as a guide to future earnings based on the lease contracts signed for the assets, stood at Dh714 million (US$194.50 million) at the beginning of 2004, providing a positive indication for sustained profitability in the coming years.

Oasis Leasing already has shareholder and regulatory approval to increase its paid-up capital to Dh700 million (US$190.7 million) through a rights issue of Dh200 million (US$54 million). The proceeds from the rights issue will be used to expand and diversify the company's portfolio.

Recent developments in the UAE's aviation sector, such as the establishment in Abu Dhabi of Etihad Airways and Royal Jet, which are expected to grow at a rapid pace in line with the overall economic growth in the UAE, could offer lucrative business opportunities to Oasis Leasing. Further growth in business through the acquisition of new assets could also see an increase in the company's capital in the near future.

REAL ESTATE, PROPERTY DEVELOPMENT AND SERVICES

Real Estate is a rapidly growing business in the UAE with new residential and commercial units being constructed at a pace that seems to only just keep up with surging demand. The sector is expected to see the total value of developments rise to more than US$50 billion by the year 2010. It is a highly competitive field in which the key words among all the major companies have been quality, reliability and value for money. Some of the biggest operators are ADDAR in Abu Dhabi and Nakheel and Emaar, both based in Dubai.

In mid-2004, ADDAR Real Estate Services was granted a licence to redevelop the site of Abu Dhabi's old souq along Khalifa and Hamdan streets. This landmark site, built in the late 1960s, is to be transformed into a Town Centre with a mixed development of speciality retail outlets, cultural attractions and a traditional Arab souq. It will also become the transport hub for the centre of Abu Dhabi City. Construction work will start in early 2005 and the project will be completed in phases over the next three to four years.

On either side of Khalifa Street, the new souq will be complemented by a retail and entertainment podium complex with mixed-use development above.

The whole development will be linked through bridges and subways. Ample underground parking will be provided to ensure the free flow and ease of pedestrian and vehicular traffic in the area. At the end of the 50 year concession period granted to ADDAR, the development will be handed back to the Abu Dhabi government.

ADDAR is currently working on several other projects in Abu Dhabi and Al Ain, which include residential, commercial and private real estate developments. Established in 1999, ADDAR is an integrated property services company and in early 2004 became the first local property development company to hold both project management and commercial licences. ADDAR's first project was the Al Jimi Mall in Al Ain, developed in conjunction with the Al Ain Municipality and Town Planning Department. The company is owned 40 per cent by the Mubadala Development Company and 15 per cent each by Abu Dhabi Investment Company, Abu Dhabi National Hotels Company, National Corporation for Tourism and Hotels and The National Investor.

Nakheel is one of the key leading companies in Dubai's property sector, with projects worth US$15 billion out of the US$30 billion worth of projects currently being developed in Dubai's new growth corridor. The company, whose Arabic name refers to the date-palm tree and its fruits, is involved in the construction of iconic mega-projects such as The Jumeirah and Jebel Ali 'Palms', 'The World', 'International City', 'The Jumeirah Islands', 'Jumeirah Lake Towers' and the 'Garden Shopping Mall'. The two Palms, Nakheel's signature projects, are the world's largest man-made islands and have effectively doubled the coastline of Dubai and attracted many private purchasers and hotel developers. 'The World', designed in the shape of the map of the world, consists of 300 islands, offering investors an opportunity to develop private or commercial projects. Meanwhile 'The Jumeirah Islands' project has been carved from the desert and comprises a complex of 50 man-made islands, giving investors an opportunity to own unique homes surrounded by seawater pumped in daily from the Arabian Gulf. 'Jumeirah Lake Towers' comprises 69 towers that are being constructed by independent developers for commercial, retail and residential use. They will be surrounded by a vast man-made lake. 'The International City' aims to become a hub for international investors, traders and retailers from across the globe. 'The Gardens Shopping Mall', a massive themed shopping experience, is also attracting investors who are impressed by its location and amenities.

Emaar Properties is a Public Joint Stock Company listed on the Dubai Financial Market. With an asset base of US$7.7 billion (including land) Emaar has grown rapidly since its inception in 1997. In 2003, Emaar reported net profits of Dh676 million (US$184 million), a 31 per cent increase on the previous year. Total sales revenue was Dh3.72 billion (US$1.01 billion), up 179 per cent on 2002. Currently, it has ten major real estate projects under various stages of development. These include 'Dubai Marina', 'Arabian Ranches', 'Emirates Hills', 'The Meadows', 'The Springs', 'The Lakes', 'The Greens' and 'Emaar Towers' in downtown Dubai. The company also owns and manages the Gold and Diamond Park and has begun construction of Burj Dubai – expected to be the tallest skyscraper and largest shopping centre in the world. While Emaar continues to actively pursue expansion in its core business of innovative, high-quality real estate development, it also owns and manages four subsidiaries: Dubai Bank, Amlak Finance, Emrill Services, and Sahm Technologies.

One of the UAE's trading conglomerates, Al Futtaim, also has a real estate arm that was originally established to manage its own property portfolio but which now offers a wide range of services from selection of site and feasibility studies to construction and property management. Al Futtaim's range of properties administered and leased in the UAE includes warehouses, showrooms, workshops, offices, villas and apartment buildings. The massive warehousing complex which it owns and manages at Rashidia in Dubai, measuring 92,900 square metres, is almost certainly the largest of its kind in the Gulf. Al Futtaim recently announced its major investment in a new waterfront development in Dubai to be called Dubai Festival City. The project is described as a 'city within a city' and is being developed by Al Futtaim Investments along Dubai Creek, at the base of the Garhoud Bridge, on a 500 hectare site.

CLIMATE CONTROL FOR BUILDINGS

The National Central Cooling Company (Tabreed) introduced the concept of district cooling to the UAE in 1998 by setting up its first plant at the Zayed Military City in Sweihan, Abu Dhabi. It currently runs 13 plants in Abu Dhabi, Dubai, Al Ain, Ra's al-Khaimah and Fujairah with a combined capacity of 87,000 tonnes daily of chilled water. The company anticipates building seven new plants for the UAE Armed Forces and other customers and expanding two existing ones over the next 30 months, to increase its total installed capacity to over 102,000 tonnes per day.

District cooling technology uses a network of pipes to distribute chilled water produced at a cooling plant to a group of residential and commercial buildings. It cuts air-conditioning costs by minimising the use of electricity consumed by traditional air-conditioners. The energy savings could be up to 50 per cent of the total that consumers spend on traditional air-conditioners. During the summer months, air-conditioning requires up to 70 per cent of the total energy produced. One tonne of chilled water cools up to 20–25 square metres.

Tabreed, listed on the Dubai Financial Market (DFM), has been expanding its operations, revenues and net profits at a rapid pace. The success at home over the last seven years has encouraged the company to set up joint ventures in Saudi

Arabia, Bahrain and Qatar, and it is looking at possible ventures in Kuwait and Oman. When operational, these will make it the largest district cooling company in the world.

In the UAE, Tabreed has more than 20 long-term contracts. Apart from providing the technology, it also provides management services for fees that are much more economical for property owners than making their own arrangements. A number of new contracts signed over the last 18 months in the UAE are a sign of the growing confidence of property owners in district cooling. In Dubai, Tabreed has a contract with the Bin Kharbash Group for its 36-storey Kharbash Tower, a residential building on the Sheikh Zayed Road. Developments such as Shangri-La Hotel, Rotana Towers, Tower Number One Suites and Noor Al Maarif School, also in Dubai, are already using Tabreed's district cooling services. The biggest contract in Dubai so far is the Dh160 million, 20-year agreement signed for the Dh3 billion multi-use Dubai Pearl development, which is currently under construction.

In Abu Dhabi, Tabreed recently signed a 20-year contract with the National Investment Corporation (NIC) to provide district cooling services to the Marina Mall extension and the new Fairmont Sea Resort Hotel that is to be built as part of a 6-square-kilometre, multi-billion-dirham development at the Breakwater. The first phase will see the completion of a 9000-tonne plant by the end of the first quarter of 2005 and the ultimate size of the plant will be 16,000 tonnes. Two cooling plants are already up and running in the capital on the Al Muroor Road and next to Zayed Sports City, catering to the air-conditioning needs of a number of buildings in those areas.

Tabreed has also developed a long-term plan for the emiratisation of its workforce. It is coordinating with several national organisations and authorities, including the National Human Resources Development and Employment Agency (Tanmia), and has introduced a training programme for young UAE national engineers in cooperation with the UAE Armed Forces. The emiratisation programme is to be implemented by 2010 through a step-by-step approach.

CERAMICS

RAK Ceramics has firmly established itself as one of the world's leading producers of high quality ceramic wall and floor tiles, gres porcellanato, and sanitaryware. The company's UAE factories are located 20 kilometres south of Ra's al-Khaimah City, along the highway to Dubai. With a total investment capital of over US$250 million, the company operates from its UAE base but has also established an extensive international network of factories. It was accredited with the ISO 9001 certification by CICS (Ceramic Industry Certification Scheme), UK in 1997.

From its modest beginnings, when it had a single production line producing 5000 square metres per day, the company now exports its products to more than 125 countries across five continents and operates 18 production lines, 14 kilns and 16 large presses engaged in the production of 112,000 square metres per day of ceramic/gres porcellanato tiles. Moreover, two presses and three kilns are being used exclusively to produce special items such as decors and skirtings.

The sanitary-ware factories between them produce 5000 pieces of quality products per day, including complete bathroom sets with toilets, wash-basins, bidets, bathtubs, shower trays, and all related accessories in a wide range of colours and designs. The factories are equipped with five kilns, including one kiln dedicated exclusively for decoration. In May 2002, the company opened new headquarters with 4400 square metres of floor space, including 1600 square metres of showroom.

IRON AND STEEL

UAE steel production presently accounts for about a quarter of the total local demand and the remaining requirements are met through imports. Demand is likely to remain strong as a result of several key factors. Firstly, the high rate of population growth in the GCC states and the subsequent rise in construction-related activities is expected to increase the demand for steel in the near future. Secondly, the rolled steel producers of the UAE are also expecting major demand from reconstruction in Iraq. In June 2004, Abu Dhabi Investment Company (ADIC) announced plans for establishment, in collaboration with local partners, of a steel plant in Fujairah. This will comprise a 1.2 million tons/annum sponge iron unit integrated with an adjacent unit producing steel billets destined primarily for the local market. The plant is likely to form the core of an industrial complex for iron production, with new related projects already under consideration.

TEXTILES AND CLOTHING

Dubai Textile City (DTC) is to be built on approximately 557,000 square metres of land in the emirate's Al-Warsan area and is to be completed by mid-2005. The first phase of the project was pre-allocated to more than 90 investors. Over the past five decades, the emirate's textile industry, valued at 9 billion dirhams (US$2.4 billion) annually, has played a significant economic role and is still Dubai's second largest trade contributor, including both exports and imports. The contract to build the DTC is being carried out by United Engineering Contractors (UNEC).

The structure of the garment industry is presently in a state of flux. A production shift in favour of the woven (non-knitted) category has been accompanied by a general decline in production of both knitted and non-knitted garments and is currently less than 40 per cent of the peak reached in 1997. Woven garments now account for almost three quarters of the production, compared to two thirds in 1997, and have registered successive increases in the last three years.

PHARMACEUTICALS

The UAE has a growing pharmaceuticals industry that serves local, regional and international markets. A new Dh880 million state-of-the-art pharmaceutical plant is to be built in the Industrial City of Abu Dhabi (ICAD). Abu Dhabi International Pharmaceuticals (Abu Dhabi Pharma), as the new company is called, will have two units, one exclusively for antibiotics and the other for general formulations and general drugs. Over a hundred pharmaceutical products, including antibiotics, cardiovascular drugs, anti-cancer drugs, and analgesics, will be manufactured by the company under licence from Novasorel. Initial production will comprise some 60 million vials a year, 1.5 million tablets and capsules and 90,000 kilograms of creams, powders, liquids and formulations.

Another major pharmaceutical company headquartered in the UAE is Ra's al-Khaimah's Julphar, whose sales exceed Dh500 million across 40 countries and four continents. The Julphar group owns six pharmaceutical plants, four in the Emirates, one in Ecuador and one in Germany. It also controls a Gulf-wide infrastructure of distribution and warehousing, pharmacy management, a state-of-the-art printing and packaging house, a plastic dosing cup and aluminum pilfer-proof cap manufacturing unit, an environment-controlled transportation fleet and other service support units.

ALUMINIUM

Dubal is the largest single site aluminium smelter in the region and the largest single non-oil contributor to Dubai's economy. The company's pure grade metal is sold to customers across the world, from Japan and the Pacific Rim, to the US, Europe and the Middle East. It recorded a 5 per cent increase in production in 2003, taking its overall production to 560,000 tonnes. During the same period, the company sold more than 616,000 tonnes of metal alloy products, a 7 per cent increase over the previous year's figures. It also increased overall efficiency, trimming unit costs to place it among the top 20 lowest cost aluminium producers in the world.

There are a number of local companies that take aluminium from Dubal and process it into a wide range of products. One new venture in this category is a new rolling mill for production of sheet aluminium that is being developed by Emiroll. This modern plant will have a capacity of 33,000 tonnes per year and is located close to Dubal in the Dubai Investments Park, near Jebel Ali Free Zone.

Dubal's success with its aluminium smelter at Jebel Ali has led it to seek new opportunities for development close to primary energy sources, and in May 2003 an agreement for a new joint venture was signed between Dubal and Qatar's United Development Company (UDC). According to the agreement, the two sides will enter into a joint venture to build, own and operate a primary aluminium smelter at Ra's Laffan Industrial City in Qatar. The smelter will initially produce

516,000 metric tonnes a year of primary aluminium with the potential to expand in phases to over one million metric tonnes a year.

CABLE MANUFACTURE

Dubai Cable Company (Private) Ltd (Ducab) sales reached Dh530 million, which represents a 22 per cent increase over the preceding year. Ducab has a target of Dh800 million sales by 2006. The company has been successful in acquiring a number of overseas contracts, such as one for supply of cable to the Delhi Metro project. Ducab, which is well-placed to meet local and international demand, was established in 1979 and was the first purpose-built cable manufacturing company in the UAE. Its ownership is split on a 50–50 basis between the governments of Abu Dhabi and Dubai.

In its first major expansion outside Dubai, Ducab has constructed a state-of-the-art factory in Abu Dhabi for manufacturing a wide range of power cables. It has also added capacity at its existing factory in Jebel Ali. The new Abu Dhabi plant, located in the Industrial City of Abu Dhabi at Mussafah, has been designed to increase the combined copper processing capacity of Ducab in the two plants to 60,000 tonnes from the current 35,000 tonnes at Ducab Dubai. The new plant will have a copper processing capacity nearly similar to that of Ducab (Dubai), but will also make complementary products. It will principally produce low voltage electric cables, while the Dubai plant will now cater to the medium and high-end cabling market. Ducab expects the bulk of the new plant's production to be consumed by domestic demand.

JEWELLERY

Exports, imports and re-exports of gold and diamond jewellery through the United Arab Emirates account for about 20 per cent of the global jewellery trade. Dubai is the world's fastest growing diamond market. The UAE's diamond trade was recently reviewed by officials of the Kimberly Process, prior to issuing internationally recognised certification. Diamond trade through Dubai is expected to grow significantly following launch at the Dubai Metals and Commodities Centre (DMCC) of the Arab world's first bourse for the diamond industry – the Dubai Diamond Exchange (DDE).

MARITIME INDUSTRIES

Abu Dhabi Ship Building (ADSB)

Based at the Mussafah industrial area in Abu Dhabi, ADSB is the only ship-building facility in the Arabian Gulf with the capability to build and repair sophisticated naval and commercial vessels. It is building an increasing number of naval vessels for the UAE Navy and commercial boats for a wide range of clients in the shipping and related industries.

ADSB has been working on a major contract to deliver four Baynunah Class corvettes to the UAE Navy as the prime contractor under a project worth more than US$500 million that involves the supply of the 70-metre vessels along with associated training and logistics services. The corvettes, designed by the French shipbuilder Constructions Mecaniques de Normandie (CMN) under a subcontract from ADSB, will be the most sophisticated vessels built by ADSB to date. In addition to the four vessels under contract, ADSB has an option for the delivery of two more identical ships to this same customer.

ADSB has also built Amphibious Transport Boats (ATBs) for the UAE Navy, which in April 2003 inducted the first of the 12 Ghannatha Class boats into its fleet. ADSB is delivering these ATBs under a US$30 million contract in partnership with Sweden's SwedeShip, with the last of the 12 boats to be delivered by the end of 2004. The design of the 24-metre, 45-ton Ghannatha boats is derived from a vessel used extensively by the Swedish Navy. The success of the first contract with the UAE Navy has led to the award of a second contract worth Dh55 million for a 'fast supply' version of Ghannatha. Under this contract, four vessels are scheduled for delivery to the UAE Navy in the next two years.

Refitting and upgrading existing UAE Navy vessels has also been a major activity at ADSB. This capability was further enhanced through a US$50 million expansion at the shipyard completed in June 2002. ADSB concluded its biggest refit and upgrade contract for the UAE Navy in September 2000. Under a Dh300 million deal, the shipyard upgraded the UAE Navy's six 45-metre Baniyas Class patrol boats – increasing their life by between 15 to 20 years and saving the UAE Government millions of dollars. The combat systems of the six vessels are now being upgraded under a separate contract worth more than Dh184 million.

ADSB recently completed repair works on a Qatar Navy vessel and carried out a survey for possible refits. Meanwhile, the UAE Navy has awarded the company another Dh110 million contract for the refit of two 44-metre missile boats and additional naval refit contracts are also expected in the near future. The company has a master agreement with the French Navy to provide maintenance and repair services to vessels of the French Navy fleet serving in the Gulf and also provides repair services to other foreign naval vessels stationed in the region.

The non-military side of ADSB's shipbuilding and repair business has also been expanding at a rapid pace, and it now completes more than 150 commercial ship repair jobs each year. The company is competing for commercial contracts from operators of tugboats, barges and support vessels for the oil and gas industry, including the Abu Dhabi National Oil Company (ADNOC) and its subsidiaries. Under a US$10 million contract, a 50-metre dredger has been recently built and delivered to Dubai-based dredging company Gulf Cobla, and a growing number of local companies are showing interest in ADSB for their repair, refit and new building programmes.

ADSB is a Public Joint Stock Company (PJSC) which is owned 50 per cent by more than 14,000 individual UAE nationals and 50 per cent by the Abu Dhabi government. Set up in 1996 and listed on the Abu Dhabi Securities Market (ADSM), ADSB has a paid-up capital of Dh175.2 million (US$47.7 million) divided into 17,520,000 shares.

Combined Cargo UAE (CCU)

Combined Cargo UAE (CCU) is an Abu Dhabi-based ship investment joint venture set up by the UAE Offsets Group (UOG) in late 1997. CCU has direct or indirect ownership of five vessels. Its dry-bulk operations include the transportation of aggregates from the UAE to other GCC countries, transloading iron ore from large capesize vessels to steel mills in the Arabian Gulf and servicing the regional aluminium industry giants, such as Aluminium Bahrain (Alba).

CCU has set up a ship and contract management joint venture with Klaveness. The new firm, Bulktransfer Inc, is owned 36.15 per cent by CCU and 63.85 per cent by Klaveness. It is responsible for the operation of three specialised panamax vessels that are servicing dry bulk transportation and transloading contracts with regional customers.

During 2003, CCU went through a change in its shareholding structure and became a wholly-owned local company. The Oslo-based Torvald Klaveness Group, which was one of its founding partners, is no longer a direct shareholder in CCU but retains interests in the company's activities through its stake in Bulktransfer Inc. The company is now owned 34.2 per cent by Oman and Emirates Investment Holding Company (OEIHC) and 32.9 per cent each by Mubadala Development Company (MDC) and Abu Dhabi Investment Company (ADIC).

CCU's 2003 net profit went up by 124 per cent to Dh23.49 million in 2003, from Dh10.42 million (US$2.84 million) in the previous year. Total revenues increased by 31 per cent to Dh103.63 million from Dh79.33 million in 2002.

Dubai Maritime City

The new marine-orientated zone Dubai Maritime City will also assist in promoting maritime industries in the Emirates. The project is under construction between Port Rashid and Dubai Dry Docks and will cater to a diverse range of maritime-related businesses in six areas – marine services, management, product marketing, research and education, recreation, ship design and manufacturing. Ship repair and maintenance services will also be headquartered within the zone and marine management services ranging from cargo, vessel and life insurance agencies to legal businesses specialising in consultation, legal advice and marine domain lawyers are also expected to set up offices.

Bunkering

The UAE now ranks among the top locations in the world for bunkering. This, in turn, has spawned a healthy growth in the ship supply business. Around 40 companies operate in this field in the Emirates as a whole, with an annual turnover of around US$300 million. Fujairah is the UAE's main bunkering port and the second largest ship refuelling centre worldwide.

OIL AND GAS

The UAE has invested almost Dh30 billion (US$8.2 billion) in the oil sector over the past four years, with over Dh7 billion (approx US$2 billion) channelled into the sector in 2003. By far the greatest share of this investment is being carried out by the Abu Dhabi National Oil Company, which is implementing an ambitious expansion programme aimed at sharply increasing the UAE's output capacity of oil and gas. OPEC's five largest oil producers, the UAE, Saudi Arabia, Kuwait, Iraq and Iran, control more than 60 per cent of global oil reserves and currently supply world markets with around 16 million barrels per day (mb/d). Total world demand for crude oil in 2004 is estimated at 80.4 mb/d, registering growth at a seven-year high of 2.29 per cent. Expected OPEC supply rate for the whole of 2004 was approximately 30 mb/d. As supplies from the UAE and other major OPEC producers stabilise at somewhat higher than the 2004 rate, supported by strong reserves, other sources are likely to become more seriously depleted. It is against this background that the UAE has committed to major developments in its oil and gas production and supply facilities.

Notwithstanding major progress in its long-standing programme of diversification aimed at reducing dependence on finite oil and gas resources, the UAE's oil and gas sector continues to occupy prime status in the UAE's economic profile — a fact bolstered by confirmed hydrocarbon reserves now standing at 97.8 billion barrels of oil and 212.1 trillion cubic feet of natural gas. On the worldwide stage, these figures rank the UAE in fifth place in terms of the size of its oil reserves and fourth with respect to its natural gas reserves. It has been suggested by oil experts that there could be approximately double the presently discovered reserves in deeper layers, where drilling has so far not taken place. Based on current knowledge the UAE's oil reserves, at 97.8 billion barrels, account for 9.1 per cent of the world's total oil reserves, estimated at 1068 billion barrels. By far the greatest portion of the UAE's oil reserves are located in Abu Dhabi Emirate with 92.2 billion barrels, followed by Dubai with 4 billion barrels, Sharjah with 1.5 billion and Ra's al-Khaimah with 100 million. Natural gas reserves are also concentrated in Abu Dhabi, which has 196.1 trillion cubic feet, followed by Sharjah with 10.7 trillion cubic feet, Dubai with 4.1 trillion cubic feet and Ra's al-Khaimah with 1.2 trillion cubic feet.

Abu Dhabi National Oil Company (ADNOC), one of the biggest oil companies in the world, has been engaged in a major oil and gas expansion capacity programme over the past decade. Oil and gas investments during this period exceed Dh91.75 billion (US$25 billion). A further Dh37 billion (US$10 billion) is being invested to increase sustainable oil production capacity to around 3 mb/d in 2006 and 3.7 mb/d by 2010. A crucial element in this plan is the development of Abu Dhabi's offshore field of Upper Zakum from its present level of 550,000 barrels per day (b/d) to 1.2 mb/d and ADCO's onshore developments at Bab, Al Dabb'iya, Jarn Yaphour, Rumaitha and Shanayel, due to add 200,000 b/d capacity, bringing the combined capacity of these fields to 460,000 b/d. In addition, development work at ADCO's Bu Hasa field, due for completion in 2006, is planned to increase production there from 550,000 b/d to 730,000 b/d, and work at Huwaila and Sahil fields will also enhance their production capabilities. Meanwhile, three more gas development projects are under way, which will boost output of natural gas for domestic consumption and condensate for export.

OIL PRODUCTION AND CRUDE RESERVES

Crude oil production ceilings are set by OPEC members at regular conferences. The UAE production quota at the end of 2003 was 2.138 mb/d. In 2004, the UAE's quota was lowered to 2.051 mb/d. In June 2004, the UAE announced that it would temporarily increase oil output by 400,000 b/d over its OPEC quota in order to help to ease record prices and stabilise the world economy.

Abu Dhabi

The Emirate of Abu Dhabi, with proven crude oil reserves estimated at 92.2 billion barrels, has 94.3 per cent of the UAE's total reserves and 8.6 per cent of the proven world oil reserves (1068 billion barrels). Its largest oilfield, Upper Zakum, contains an estimated 50 billion barrels of reserves in-situ and estimated recoverable reserves of 16 to 20 billion barrels (using extensive water injection).

Oversight of Abu Dhabi's oil and gas industry is provided by the Supreme Petroleum Council, chaired by the Crown Prince, Sheikh Khalifa bin Zayed Al Nahyan. In mid-2004, the Council's membership was reconstituted, with new members including representatives of the Abu Dhabi Investment Authority, as well as Sheikh Mohammed bin Zayed Al Nahyan, Deputy Crown Prince and Sheikh Hamed bin Zayed Al Nahyan, Chairman of the Economy Department.

Output of crude oil in Abu Dhabi during 2003 rose in response to increased OPEC quotas, averaging about 2 mb/d, up from 1.69 mb/d in 2002. This remained well below its installed production capacity of around 2.45 mb/d at the beginning of 2003. The emirate's oil production is split on a roughly 50-50 basis between onshore and offshore fields. Onshore production capacity in 2003 averaged 1.2 mb/d whilst offshore capacity stood at 1.25 mb/d. Actual production figures reversed this relationship, however, with onshore production in 2003 slightly exceeding offshore production. ADCO's onshore facilities produced 1.05 mb/d,

World Proven Crude Oil and Gas Reserves by Region

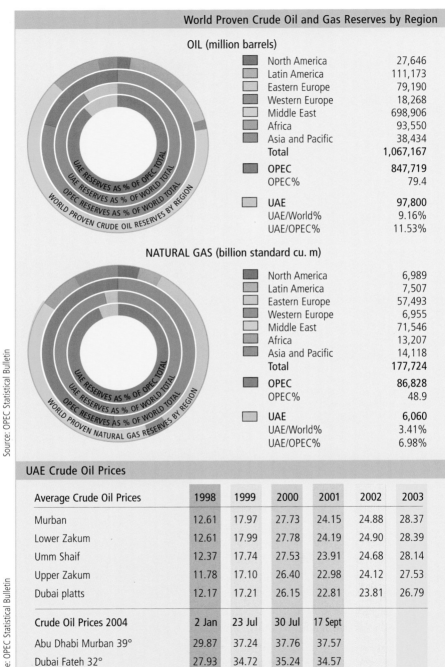

OIL (million barrels)

North America	27,646
Latin America	111,173
Eastern Europe	79,190
Western Europe	18,268
Middle East	698,906
Africa	93,550
Asia and Pacific	38,434
Total	1,067,167
OPEC	847,719
OPEC%	79.4
UAE	97,800
UAE/World%	9.16%
UAE/OPEC%	11.53%

NATURAL GAS (billion standard cu. m)

North America	6,989
Latin America	7,507
Eastern Europe	57,493
Western Europe	6,955
Middle East	71,546
Africa	13,207
Asia and Pacific	14,118
Total	177,724
OPEC	86,828
OPEC%	48.9
UAE	6,060
UAE/World%	3.41%
UAE/OPEC%	6.98%

UAE Crude Oil Prices

Average Crude Oil Prices	1998	1999	2000	2001	2002	2003
Murban	12.61	17.97	27.73	24.15	24.88	28.37
Lower Zakum	12.61	17.99	27.78	24.19	24.90	28.39
Umm Shaif	12.37	17.74	27.53	23.91	24.68	28.14
Upper Zakum	11.78	17.10	26.40	22.98	24.12	27.53
Dubai platts	12.17	17.21	26.15	22.81	23.81	26.79

Crude Oil Prices 2004	2 Jan	23 Jul	30 Jul	17 Sept		
Abu Dhabi Murban 39°	29.87	37.24	37.76	37.57		
Dubai Fateh 32°	27.93	34.72	35.24	34.57		

Oil and Gas Production, Exports, and Prices*

(in millions of barrels per day)	1998	1999	2000	2001	2002	2003	2004*
Crude oil and condensates	2.43	2.26	2.41	2.44	2.27	2.59	2.47
Crude oil	2.26	2.08	2.19	2.12	1.94	2.26	2.24[3]
Abu Dhabi	2.02	1.85	1.99	1.94	1.77	2.10	
Dubai and others[1]	0.24	0.23	0.20	0.18	0.17	0.16	
Condensates	0.17	0.18	0.22	0.32	0.33	0.33	0.33
Refinery output	0.23	0.23	0.30	0.52	0.56	0.56	
Oil and product exports	2.28	2.17	2.33	2.28	2.18	2.50	
Crude oil	2.03	1.90	2.05	1.94	1.85	2.17	
Abu Dhabi	1.83	1.70	1.85	1.80	1.61	1.93	
Dubai and others[1]	0.20	0.20	0.20	0.14	0.14	0.14	
Condensates	0.17	0.18	0.13	0.10	0.10	0.10	
Refined products	0.08	0.09	0.15	0.24	0.33	0.33	
(in billions of cubic metres)							
Natural gas production[2]	33.40	34.60	35.90	45.00	46.00	46.00	49.20
LNG exports	7.41	7.22	7.11	7.46	7.34	7.34	7.60
NGL exports	11.87	11.11	12.30	11.52	11.28	12.75	13.60
NG domestic consumption	30.40	31.40	33.40	38.10	39.30	40.00	
(in millions of US dollars)							
Oil and product exports	10,400	14,200	23,400	19,733	19,727	25,653	
Crude oil	9,200	12,400	20,400	17,612	16,679	22,115	
Abu Dhabi	8,200	11,000	18,500	15,642	14,518	19,801	
Dubai and others[1]	1,000	1,400	1,900	1,166	1,216	1,369	
Condensates		800	1,200	1,300	804	945	945
Refined products		400	600	1,700	2,121	3,048	3,538
LNG, NGL, LPG exports		2,112	2,289	3,668	3,305	3,099	3,912
of which							
LNG	926	782	1,156	1,280	1,172	1,307	
NGL	1,186	1,507	2,512	2,025	1,927	2,605	
Total oil and gas exports	12,512	16,489	27,068	23,038	22,826	29,565	
Average Abu Dhabi oil export price (in US dollars per barrel)	12.34	17.70	27.36	23.81	24.64	28.11	29.50*

*IMF Prediction, June 2004 (See opposite page for subsequent rise in prices)

[1] Sharjah and Ra's al-Khaimah
[2] Net after re-injection into wells
[3] OPEC Monthly Report July 2004

Source: ADNOC and IMF

Source: OPEC Statistical Bulletin

Crude Oil Production by Companies in the UAE

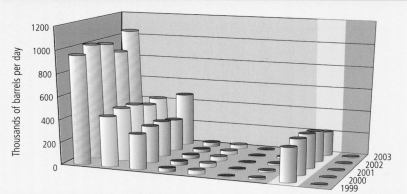

Abu Dhabi	1999	2000	2001	2002	2003*
ADCO	956.2	1014.9	986.7	886.9	1,050
ADMA-OPCO	435.6	462.4	449.5	404.1	420
ZADCO	302.6	321.2	312.2	280.6	470
Abu Dhabi Oil Co.	21.7	23	22.3	20.5	31.5
Total Abu al-Bukhoosh•	27.5	29.2	28.4	25.5	27.5
Mubarraz Oil Co.**	7.0	6.5	6.0	5.5	5
Al-Bunduq Oil Co.**	13.5	13.5	13.5	13.5	13.5
Dubai					
Dubai Petroleum Co.	289.3	307.1	298.5	268.3	212
Sharjah					
Crescent Petroleum	6.4	6.8	6.6	5.9	4.0
Total	2,059.8	2,184.6	2,123.7	1,910.8	2,235

* 2003 figures are estimates and exclude condensates. ** Figures are approximate • these figs include condensates

OPEC Production Quotas for UAE (000s b/d)

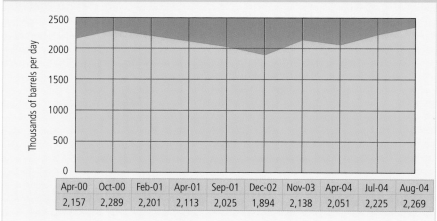

	Apr-00	Oct-00	Feb-01	Apr-01	Sep-01	Dec-02	Nov-03	Apr-04	Jul-04	Aug-04
	2,157	2,289	2,201	2,113	2,025	1,894	2,138	2,051	2,225	2,269

Source: OPEC Statistical Bulletin

Abu Dhabi Oil Fields and Concessions

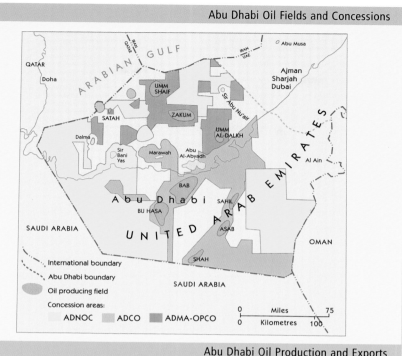

Source: Arab Oil Journal. Note: Boundaries only indicative.

Abu Dhabi Oil Production and Exports

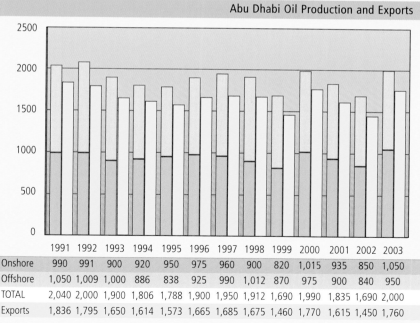

	1991	1992	1993	1994	1995	1996	1997	1998	1999	2000	2001	2002	2003
Onshore	990	991	900	920	950	975	960	900	820	1,015	935	850	1,050
Offshore	1,050	1,009	1,000	886	838	925	990	1,012	870	975	900	840	950
TOTAL	2,040	2,000	1,900	1,806	1,788	1,900	1,950	1,912	1,690	1,990	1,835	1,690	2,000
Exports	1,836	1,795	1,650	1,614	1,573	1,665	1,685	1,675	1,460	1,770	1,615	1,450	1,760

Source: OPEC Statistical Bulletin; Arab Oil & Gas Directory; Abu Dhabi Dept. of Planning

while the offshore operators contributed 950,000 b/d. Meanwhile, ADCO also produced 130,000 b/d of 57.5° API condensate (0.11 per cent sulphur) from the Thamama formation of the Bab field, which started up in 1996. The company's condensate production will increase significantly when the new onshore gas development projects are operational.

Abu Dhabi Company for Onshore Oil Operations (ADCO) thus generates more than half of Abu Dhabi's oil production, and it is one of the ten largest operating oil companies in the world and the largest crude oil producer in the southern Arabian Gulf. The company is engaged in a US$800 million expansion project aimed at adding an extra 400,000 barrels per day to its production capacity.

Offshore, ADMA-OPCO's two fields, Umm Shaif and Lower Zakum, underwent recent expansion to increase their sustainable capacities and produced 420,000 b/d in 2003. Major maintenance work in September and October reduced their combined output to 300,000 b/d for a while. Upper Zakum and the other two fields operated by ZADCO (Umm al-Dalkh and Satah) contributed 470,000 b/d and this figure is likely to increase as a result of ongoing development work on the Upper Zakum field. The remaining offshore fields (Mubarraz/Neewat al-Ghalan, Umm al-Anbar, al-Bunduq and Abu al-Bukhoosh) together continued to produce about 60,000 b/d.

ADCO, ADMA-OPCO and ZADCO are all 60 per cent owned by the Abu Dhabi National Oil Company (ADNOC), and the remaining shares are held by international oil companies.

Dubai

Dubai's proven oil reserves as of 1 January 2004 were officially estimated at 4 billion barrels, but the recoverable portion may be less than half this figure, with industry sources (American Association of Petroleum Geologists) estimating them at 1.6 to 2 billion barrels. Almost all of the emirate's oil reserves are located in the original concession area of the Dubai Petroleum Company (DPC), whose four offshore fields account for its entire output of crude oil and associated gas. Oil output has steadily declined despite a programme of field development, entailing the drilling of infill wells, horizontal production wells and water injectors. The company has installed water and gas injection facilities on a large scale to maximise recovery rates, and all the associated gas produced at its four fields is now re-injected into oil reservoirs. Condensate is also produced from the wholly government-owned onshore Margham field.

Sharjah

Sharjah's oil reserves are put at 1.5 billion barrels of crude oil and condensate. The three onshore gas and condensate fields account for the bulk of the emirate's hydrocarbon reserves, since the Mubarak field contains less than 50 million barrels of oil and 1500 billion cubic feet of associated gas.

The emirate's hydrocarbon production is now declining. In 2003, it consisted of 40,000 b/d of liquids, down from 44,000 b/d in 2002 (48,000 b/d in 2001 and 50,000 b/d in 2000) and around 70,000 b/d in 1996–97. Liquids production was made up of about 4000 b/d of crude and 8000 b/d of condensate from the offshore Mubarak field and 28,000 b/d of condensate from the onshore Saja'a and Moveyeid fields.

Sharjah passes on 20 per cent of its revenues from Mubarak to Umm al-Qaiwain and 10 per cent to Ajman.

Ra's al-Khaimah

Ra's al-Khaimah's liquid hydrocarbon reserves have been estimated at 100 million barrels of crude and condensate, but its only production consists of 500 b/d of condensate from the Saleh field.

There has been a recent surge of exploration activity in Ra's al-Khaimah with three companies active in this field. The Ra's al-Khaimah Oil and Gas Company was granted exploration licences for most of the emirate's land and seabed (with the exception of the area around the Baih field or B structure) in 1996. Its first well, spudded in December 1997, went down as far as 17,850 feet but proved to be dry. Meanwhile, Atlantis Holdings, which was taken over by China National Chemicals Import and Export Corporation (Sinochem) in February 2003 and also holds exploration licences in the emirates of Sharjah, Ajman and Umm al-Qaiwain, has been reassessing a small offshore tract known as B structure, where a non-commercial find was made in the 1970s.

Umm al-Qaiwain

At the present time, Umm al-Qaiwain's sole interest in hydrocarbon production remains its 20 per cent share of the revenues derived from the offshore Mubarak field in Sharjah, part of which lies under its territorial waters.

EXPLORATION AND FIELD DEVELOPMENT

Abu Dhabi

Oil and gas exploration in Abu Dhabi is primarily carried out by companies within the ADNOC group. While most of this is undertaken by the operating companies of ADCO and ADMA-OPCO, ADNOC also has its own 'sole risk' programme. The exploration programme, which began in 1950, has already yielded huge reserves of oil, and the research emphasis has now shifted from finding new fields to a more thorough examination of existing known reserves, along with some high-tech exploration of deep oil and gas prospects. The aim is to maximise the output of each structure through improvements in extraction methods and expansion programmes. It is predicted that efforts currently under way, involving an investment of over US$10 billion, will raise the UAE's sustainable crude output capacity from around 2.5 mb/d at the beginning of 2004 to 3 mb/d in 2006 and 3.7 mb/d by 2010.

DOLPHIN ENERGY

By mid-2004, Dolphin Energy had awarded all major contracts for its Dolphin gas project – which involves the transportation of natural gas from Qatar's North Field to the markets of the UAE and Oman – with the exception of the downstream terminal facilities at Al Taweelah in Abu Dhabi.

The UAE and Oman also signed in early 2004 a pipeline agreement to regulate the transmission of natural gas between the two countries, laying the foundation for a cross-border energy grid to span the southern Gulf that will provide the feedstock for power generation and industrial developments. The UAE-Oman agreement is the first cross-border pipeline accord for refined gas signed in the GCC. Since January 2004, Dolphin Energy has been receiving up to 135 million cubic feet a day (mcf/d) of Omani gas and supplying it to Union Water and Electricity Company (UWEC) in Fujairah. OOC is supplying the gas for up to five years to Al Ain through a link created by Dolphin Energy with OOC's US$120 million, 300-kilometre-long Fahud-Sohar pipeline, inaugurated on 3 January 2004. The gas is being transported from Al Ain to Fujairah to UWEC's 656 MW power generation and 100 million gallons a day (mg/d) plant through Dolphin Energy's 182-kilometre, 24-inch pipeline, also commissioned in January.

Dubai-based Emirates General Petroleum Corporation (Emarat) is responsible for the operations and maintenance of the pipeline under a contract signed with Dolphin Energy on 17 January 2004. Dolphin's long-term gas supplies from Qatar will become available to Oman in subsequent years once the gas starts flowing from Qatar to the UAE, through Dolphin's 3.2 billion cubic feet a day (bcf/d) capacity subsea pipeline.

Work on the UAE-Qatar gas export pipeline has started following the award of a contract worth more than US$350 million to Italy's Saipem. The contract entails the construction of a 48-inch, 372-kilometre subsea pipeline from Dolphin Energy's gas processing and compression plant at Ras Laffan in Qatar – currently under construction – to the onshore receiving terminal at Taweelah. Once the pipeline is commissioned in 2006, Dolphin Energy will start transporting up to 2 bcf/d of natural gas to the UAE.

Dolphin Energy awarded the other major EPC contracts for the project in January 2004. The biggest contract, worth approximately US$1.6 billion, went to Japan's JGC Corporation for the construction of the 2.6 bcf/d capacity gas compression and treatment facility at Ras Laffan. Jebel Ali-based J. Ray McDermott Middle East was awarded a US$190 million contract for the fabrication, installation and hook up of two offshore production platforms in the North Field, while the UK's Rolls Royce won a US$107 million contract for the supply of gas turbines.

Two long-term gas supply contracts have been signed with Abu Dhabi Water and Electricity Authority (ADWEA), and UWEC. Gas supplied to ADWEA will be used by its subsidiaries, Al Taweelah Power Company, Al Arabiya Power Company, Emirates CMS Power Company and Gulf Total Tractebel Power Company. UWEC is already using the gas to run its 656 MW power generation and 100 mg/d water desalination plant at Qidfa in Fujairah, while a major gas supply contract is being negotiated with Dubai.

The Dolphin gas project was initiated by the UAE Offsets Group (UOG) on behalf of the Abu Dhabi government. Dolphin Energy is owned 51 per cent by Mubadala Development Company (MDC), which is wholly-owned by the Abu Dhabi government. Total of France and Occidental Petroleum (Oxy) of the US own 24.5 per cent each.

ADCO

ADCO is continuing its programme of exploration to search for new reserves to offset annual production and maintain reserve levels. Current exploration/appraisal techniques are primarily based on the extensive use of 3D seismic surveys prior to wildcat, appraisal and development drilling. These have recently included a 3D survey of the Qusahwira/Mender and Zarrara/Mashhur areas for the appraisal of known structures and exploration purposes to find new reserves and a 3D survey of the Bab field to improve reservoir characterisation and help optimise development schemes. The main focus on future exploration/ appraisal is in the South East portion of ADCO's concession and undeveloped reservoirs overlying/ underlying or proximate to reservoirs currently on stream.

ADCO is currently undertaking expansion projects to add some 200,000 b/d to its sustainable crude oil production capacity. These include expansion of the onshore Bab field (adding 100,000 b/d of facilities) to achieve a sustainable capacity of 300,000 b/d and full field development of the three north-eastern fields (Al Dabb'iya, Rumaitha and Shanayel) to increase their capacity from 10,000 b/d to 110,000 b/d. The work is scheduled for completion in the first quarter of 2006 and will provide sustainable capacity of 70,000 b/d at the Al Dabb'iya field and 40,000 b/d at Rumaitha/Shanayel fields.

Meanwhile, new work on the Bu Hasa field to replace ageing production facilities and enhance pressure maintenance schemes commenced in September 2003 when ADCO awarded Italy-based Snamprogetti the engineering, procurement and construction (EPC) contract. The project, which also includes gas and water injection facilities with a capacity of 150 million standard cubic feet/day of gas per day and 120,000 barrels water per day, is planned to be completed towards the end of 2006.

Work on Huwaila, located 30 kilometres south of the Bu Hasa field, began in August 2003. The field was discovered many years ago and was being produced on a test basis; it is now being developed as a satellite field to Bu Hasa. Plans are in place to install a production capacity of up to 10,000 b/d of oil by 2006. Veco Engineering, Abu Dhabi, was awarded the front-end engineering and design (FEED) contract for the development of the field. This is an innovative development using multi-phase pumps to pump the fluids (oil/water and gas) to Bu Hasa where they are separated and processed. The second phase of development of the Sahil field will also add 20,000 b/d capacity by 2008. Work also began in late 2003 on further development of Asab with the start of a programme that will add a further 30,000 b/d to capacity by 2008.

Abu Dhabi already applies the most up-to-date production and drilling technology at its oilfields. Both water and gas injection are in wide use at older fields to sustain reservoir pressure and maintain flow rates. Moreover, operators are drilling a growing number of horizontal wells to improve well productivity and boost recovery rates. Many of these, particularly in the Rumaitha and Al Dabb'iya fields, are being drilled as clusters from a relatively small area and the wells deviated to their target zones to minimise the surface footprint. This reduces field congestion and contributes to ADNOC Group's environmental protection programme.

Abu Dhabi's operating companies have acquired considerable expertise in directional drilling methods and utilise short, medium and long radius drilling techniques in conjunction with both oriented and conventional coring. The longest horizontal hole drilled in Abu Dhabi was a 1830-metre section drilled by ADCO.

In addition to its activities in oil field development, ADCO also carries out development of gas fields and undertakes production and processing of gas on behalf of ADNOC. The two gas development projects currently under way are both scheduled for completion in 2007. OGD-3 calls for the expansion of production capacity from the Bab Thamama F reservoir to produce an additional 1.2 billion cubic feet per day (cf/d) of gas, in addition to installation of gas re-injection facilities to recycle some gas into the Thamama F reservoir. It will also increase condensate production by approximately 140,000 b/d. The second project, AGD-2, entails an expansion of the Asab gas plant's processing, sweetening and NGL recovery capacity by 800 million cf/d. The existing Asab gas plant AGD-1 itself was handed over by ADCO to GASCO in early 2004.

Meanwhile, ADCO is tackling increasing corrosion in its onshore fields, awarding a US$70 million contract to a consortium specialising in this area. They are tasked with providing cathodic protection for around 1500 wells and are scheduled to complete the work in 2007–08.

ADMA-OPCO

The Abu Dhabi Marine Operating Company (ADMA-OPCO) is the second biggest oil producer in the UAE after ADCO. The two companies account for more than 80 per cent of Abu Dhabi's total crude oil production. ADMA-OPCO is responsible for development and operation of the Umm Shaif and Lower Zakum offshore fields. With an area of 360 square kilometres, Umm Shaif has 268 producing wells and an output of around 200,000 b/d. It is located about 140 kilometres north-west of Abu Dhabi City. The Zakum field has 321 wells tapping into five productive zones and to date most of the concentration has been on the lower levels (Lower Zakum). It currently produces 220,000 b/d, making it one of the largest offshore oil fields in the world. Water injection was adopted from 1978 to maintain pressure in the reservoir.

Lower Zakum and Umm Shaif have rated capacities of 320,000 b/d and 280,000 b/d respectively, but their sustainable capacities are considered to be approximately 240,000 b/d and 220,000 b/d respectively. As noted above, the company currently produces around 420,000 b/d of oil that is obtained via multiple wells tapping into the productive zones. ADMA-OPCO is focused on maintaining capacity at the current level through the drilling of additional production and injection wells and, in particular, the expansion of gas injection systems.

The Umm Shaif crestal gas injection project entails re-injection of 600 million cf/d of gas from the field's Khuff reservoir into the Arab C and D oil reservoirs and is scheduled for completion in 2006. The project will double the gas injection capacity of the Umm Shaif field.

ADMA-OPCO commissioned a 1500-square-kilometre seismic survey of the seabed in the Zakum field. The aim was to boost productivity of both parts of the Zakum structure through enhanced reservoir definition. In addition, the survey could provide the baseline for a future time-lapse 3D reservoir monitoring programme. Current development of the Zakum field is utilising this data.

The Lower Zakum field has two collecting centres, Zakum West supercomplex and Zakum Central supercomplex. A pilot gas injection project at Lower Zakum was commissioned in October 2002. With a capacity of 100 million cf/d, the high pressure injection system forces gas into the Zakum structures, enhancing the capability to extract oil. The gas required by the project is being drawn from the Khuff gas reservoir under the Umm Shaif field, which is being connected via a gasline to the Zakum West supercomplex, where an additional 200 million cf/d compressor is being installed on the gas injection platform.

Installation of new and improved pumps in 2001 permitted all the associated gas produced at Lower Zakum to be processed and pumped at high pressure to Das Island instead of flaring it off above the rig. The Zakum Central supercomplex was demothballed and recommissioned as part of the Lower Zakum development, enabling easier access to the Thamama IV and V reservoirs. A 10-kilometre, 24-inch pipe was also built linking Zakum Central and Zakum West complexes.

Zakum Development Company (ZADCO)

Upper Zakum, Abu Dhabi's largest oil field, is of considerable significance in relation to Abu Dhabi's intention, supported by a US$10 billion investment, to increase its oil production capacity from a level of 2.5 mb/d in early 2004 to between 2.85 and 3 mb/d in 2006 and 3.7 mb/d by 2010. Upper Zakum's production capacity is set to increase from its present level of 500,000 b/d to 700,000 b/d by 2006. In addition to the Upper Zakum field, ZADCO operates two other small offshore fields: Umm al-Dalkh and Satah. Oil and associated gas from all three fields are piped to Zirku island for final processing, storage and shipping. Facilities on Zirku are being upgraded. Debottlenecking should increase their efficiency and raise capacity from 600,000 b/d to 700,000 b/d by 2005, thus enabling them to handle the increase in ZADCO's production.

The Upper Zakum field contains an estimated 50 billion barrels of crude oil in place but, because of the low pressure and the poor porosity of the rock, the recovery rate is restricted, despite the large-scale use of water injection as well as gas injection. Using gas to inject into oil bearing reservoirs, increasing the pressure and enhancing flow rates is clearly more feasible in the UAE than in countries lacking the UAE's vast reserves of natural gas and oil in close proximity.

Abu Dhabi Oil Company (ADOC)

ADOC operates the Mubarraz field where water and gas injection has been used to increase reservoir pressure. ADOC-GA, a subsidiary of ADOC, operates Neewat al-Ghalan, which has an output of around 5000 b/d of crude piped to ADOC's processing facilities on Mubarraz Island. The latter facility also handles crude from the Umm al-Anbar field (approx 5000 b/d) operated by Mubarraz Oil Company.

Following ADOC's installation of an acid gas injection system at Mubarraz in 2001, the company reported that oil recovery rates had been substantially increased. Furthermore, the project resulted in the elimination of gas flaring, since any recovered associated gas is now re-injected into oil reservoirs. The Mubarraz, West Mubarraz and Neewat al-Ghalan fields presently produce around 31,000–32,000 b/d of crude oil.

Mubarraz Oil Company (MOCO)

MOCO discovered and operates the Umm al-Anbar field, west of Mubarraz Island. It presently produces around 5000 b/d of crude oil, which is piped to ADOC's processing facilities on Mubarraz Island for blending and export. Total reserves within this field are estimated to be 40 million barrels of 35-37°API oil.

Al Bunduq Oil Company (BOC)

The Al Bunduq field straddles the maritime border between Abu Dhabi and Qatar. In May 1969, Abu Dhabi and Qatar agreed to share revenues accruing from the field's oil production on an equal basis. Al Bunduq produces approximately 12,000 to 15,000 b/d for Abu Dhabi.

Total Abu al-Bukhoosh Oil Company (TBK)

Total Abu al-Bukhoosh Oil Company was set up to develop the Abu al-Bukhoosh field discovered by ADMA-OPCO. The field, operated by France's Total, now yields between 12,000 to 15,000 b/d of crude.

Dubai

In 2003, oil contributed only 7 per cent of Dubai's GDP, whereas in 1985 it accounted for just under half, and in 1993, 24 per cent. The government expects that by 2010 it will account for less than 1 per cent. Dubai has installed enhanced recovery systems and other facilities to maximise flow rates at its oilfields in a bid to slow the decline in production. Further development work is taking place at the Margham gas field to stem the fall in gas/condensate output there. Dubai Petroleum Company (DPC), by far the largest producing venture in the emirate, has drilled infill wells and horizontal production wells to boost recovery at four main oilfields, Fateh, Southwest Fateh, Rashid and Falah, which are all located offshore. There have been some impressive successes, for example the tripling of production at Falah D from 10,000 b/d to 30,000 b/d following horizontal drilling at the site. But, despite these development efforts, the seemingly inexorable decline in Dubai's oil production continues. Faced with limited resources within its own territory, Dubai has been looking elsewhere for opportunities in oil exploration and development. One such venture is that of Dragon Oil (an Irish registered company controlled by Emirates National Oil Company (ENOC)), which has an interest in oil production in Turkmenistan, where it produced around 15000 b/d in 2003.

Sharjah

Sharjah's main hydrocarbon production is in natural gas and the emirate's only oil field is the offshore Mubarak field, which has been in production since 1974, two years after its discovery. A continuous fall in production at this field led Crescent Petroleum to embark on a secondary development programme that entailed drilling more wells, including some horizontal wells, tapping into the Thamama formation and development of a new gas processing platform to handle Thamama gas. The platform is equipped for condensate separation and stabilisation, together with gas dehydration and compression. The secondary development programme also had a positive impact on Sharjah's oil production which, after a temporary surge, has levelled out to an estimated 15,000 b/d of liquids (5000 b/d of crude and 10,000 b/d of condensate) and 120 million cf/d of gas.

OIL REFINING

The UAE has a total refining capacity of 708,000 b/d, a figure that includes 400,000 b/d of condensate processing capacity. Its output of refined products in 2002 was 312,200 b/d. Significant growth in the refining sector is attributable to completion of the expansion of Abu Dhabi Oil Refining Company's (Takreer) Ruwais refinery, which has a full production capacity of 420,000 b/d, and Emirates National Oil Company's (ENOC) refinery with its 120,000 b/d condensate processing plant at Jebel Ali Free Zone. Economic conditions for the UAE's refiners were difficult in 2002 and 2003 when high oil prices made feedstock expensive. It was in this somewhat negative climate that the Fujairah refinery temporarily closed and the ENOC facility at Jebel Ali halved its output.

Abu Dhabi

Abu Dhabi Oil Refining Company (Takreer) operates the emirate's two refineries at Ruwais and Umm al-Nar, which have capacities of 420,000 b/d and 88,000 b/d respectively. The Ruwais plant includes two 140,000 b/d condensate processing

Refineries in the UAE and their Respective Capacities

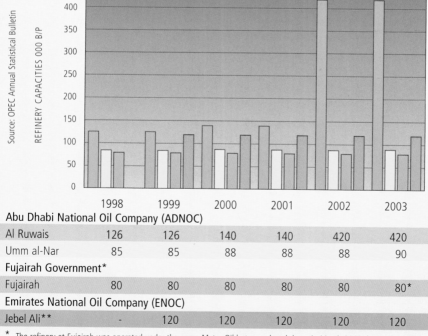

Source: OPEC Annual Statistical Bulletin

REFINERY CAPACITIES 000 B/P

	1998	1999	2000	2001	2002	2003
Abu Dhabi National Oil Company (ADNOC)						
Al Ruwais	126	126	140	140	420	420
Umm al-Nar	85	85	88	88	88	90
Fujairah Government*						
Fujairah	80	80	80	80	80	80*
Emirates National Oil Company (ENOC)						
Jebel Ali**	-	120	120	120	120	120

* The refinery at Fujairah was operated under the name Metro Oil but was closed down in March 2003 due to negative economic factors. It is now fully owned by the Fujairah government which is planning to reopen the plant.

** The Jebel Ail Refinery is a condensate refinery.

trains, which came on stream in 2000, tripling its capacity from 126,000 b/d to 420,000 b/d and increasing Abu Dhabi's total refining capacity from 211,000 b/d to 508,000 b/d. Light products produced at Ruwais are mainly exported to Japan and India, while fuel oil produced there is sold locally and used for domestic power generation.

Unleaded gasoline (ULG) units have been installed at both refineries. The Ruwais facility has also installed a low-sulphur gas-oil (LSGO) plant and expanded its hydrocracker. The other units to be added are central environmental protection facilities (BeeAT) for the processing of toxic waste, a 300,000 tons/year (t/y) base oil refinery (BOR), and additional sulphur loading facilities in the port of Ruwais. This ambitious development programme at Ruwais is being undertaken in a series of stages.

Meanwhile, Takreer's condensate plant at Ruwais, initially comprising two 140,000 b/d units, is to be increased to 360,000 b/d by 2006. This is being done in order to process the extra 135,000 b/d of condensate that will be produced by the expanded onshore Asab field when developments there are completed. Interestingly, the increased capacity has been achieved by debottlenecking the existing splitters to increase their effective capacity by 30 per cent.

Abu Dhabi already produces lubricants at the two oil refineries, as well as at a 30,000 t/y lube oil-blending plant that started up in the late 1980s and a 4000 t/y grease plant in Umm al-Nar. The Ruwais BOR provides a further boost to Abu Dhabi's lubricants production, from 50,000 t/y to 90,000 t/y by 2005–06.

In late 2003, Takreer commenced work on a central Environment Protection Facility for the UAE (BeeAT), awarding an EPIC (engineering, procurement, installation and commissioning) contract worth US$47.4 million. The new facility will comprise several waste treatment units and is scheduled for completion in mid-2006. Its task will be to safely receive, manage, treat and dispose of waste generated by ADNOC and its group of companies.

Abu Dhabi also has direct interests in refining and distribution ventures outside of the UAE. It owns equity in six refineries, with a total capacity of 642,500 b/d, and service station networks totalling 2800 outlets in various countries. These interests are held and managed by the government's foreign investment arm, the International Petroleum Investment Company (IPIC).

Dubai

Whilst Dubai does not have any crude oil refining facilities, it does possess a 120,000 b/d condensate refinery that began operations in 1999. It was developed by state-owned Emirates National Oil Company (ENOC) at a cost of Dh1.3 billion and consists of two 60,000 b/d trains, one for sweet and one for sour condensate. The plant produces a large proportion of the LPG, jet fuel, gas oil and bunker fuel consumed in Dubai, as well as exporting some 66,000 b/d of naphtha. High

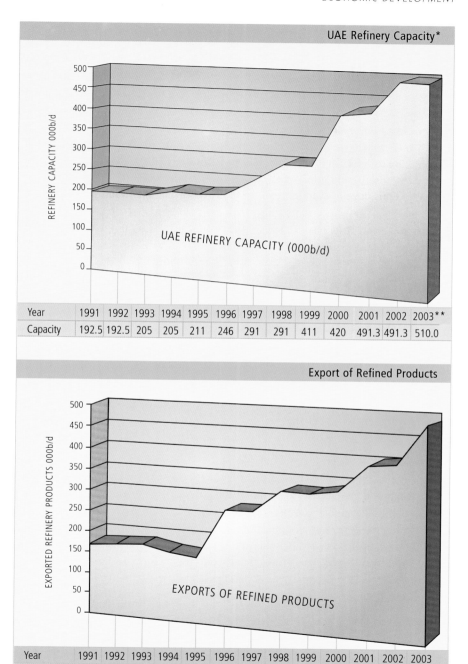

UAE Refinery Capacity*

UAE REFINERY CAPACITY (000b/d)

Year	1991	1992	1993	1994	1995	1996	1997	1998	1999	2000	2001	2002	2003**
Capacity	192.5	192.5	205	205	211	246	291	291	411	420	491.3	491.3	510.0

Export of Refined Products

EXPORTS OF REFINED PRODUCTS

Year	1991	1992	1993	1994	1995	1996	1997	1998	1999	2000	2001	2002	2003
Products	170	173	160	155	269.1	271.9	323.1	319.1	331	391.7	398.2	485.5	502.0

oil prices in 2003 impacted on the profitability of several refineries and ENOC temporarily shut down one of its condensate trains. It is now considering plans to upgrade the refinery to enable it to produce gasoline and naphtha with very low sulphur content.

Several oil reprocessing and lube oil-blending plants are situated at Jebel Ali, including a lube oil blending and packaging plant that can produce 50,000 t/y of lubricants, and its output is marketed throughout the Gulf region as well as in the UAE. An oil processing plant for producing gasoline additives and conditioning products has been developed by Ducham, a subsidiary of Abu Dhabi-based Star Energy Corporation. This has a capacity of 20,000 b/d of unleaded gasoline, 360 ton/day (t/d) of aromatics and 240 t/d of raffinate. Gadgil Western Corporation (GWC) runs a fuel oil reprocessing plant with a capacity of 275,000 t/y. In November 2002, Total gave permission to ENOC to use its Jebel Ali based lube oil blending plant to produce 5 million litres/year of lubricants, with a possible increase to 6.5 million litres/year at some future date.

Sharjah

Fal Oil operates a lubricants plant in Sharjah that started up in 1979 and produces a variety of products for automotive, marine and industrial use. It was the emirate's second lube oil blending plant, following that developed in 1976 by Sharjah National Lube Oil Company (SHARLU).

A bulk oil products storage facility, established at Hamriyah in April 2001, was developed by National Oil Storage Company (NOSCO): a 50-50 per cent joint venture between two Sharjah-based companies, Gulf Energy and Union Energy. It comprises six storage tanks, two of 10,000 tons, two of 6000 tons and two of 5000 tons, for holding diesel oil, fuel oil and bitumen.

Fujairah

Despite the fact that Fujairah has never been a producer of either oil or gas, and no exploration is taking place in the emirate, it does have an 80,000 b/d oil refinery. In addition, the emirate has capitalised on its strategic location on the Gulf of Oman by providing oil storage and bunkering services to shipping. These comprise eight 11,500 ton tanks and three 40,000 ton tanks. In addition, a separate and larger storage and blending facility is owned and operated by a consortium that includes Emirates National Oil Company (ENOC). Fujairah port is the world's second largest ship refuelling centre and has the third largest container terminal in the UAE.

OIL EXPORTS

The UAE earned a record US$29.5 billion from oil and gas sales in 2003, and estimates for 2004 revenues are even higher due to sustained strong oil prices throughout the year. Production of crude oil and condensates peaked at nearly 2.59 million barrels per day in 2003 and natural gas and LNG exports were also at their highest level. Figures for 2003 income included US$25.6 billion in crude and oil products sales, while nearly US$3.9 billion was earned from exports of natural gas, liquefied natural gas (LNG) and natural gas liquids (NGL).

Exports of crude oil and petroleum products totalled 2.50 million bpd, including nearly 2.17 million bpd of crude. Abu Dhabi exported around 1.93 million bpd to Japan, South Korea, the United States, Germany and other key consumers. Gas production peaked at around 46 billion cubic metres, including 7.34 billion cubic metres of LNG exports and 12.75 billion of NGL.

Abu Dhabi

Abu Dhabi's oil exports, affected by the OPEC quota system, increased in 2003 by 310,000 b/d, from 1.45 mb/d in 2002 to 1.76 mb/d in 2003. Japan remained its chief customer and the UAE also retained its position as Japan's main crude oil supplier for most of 2003, accounting for about a quarter of Japan's total crude oil imports. Abu Dhabi sent more than half its crude oil to Japan. Most of Abu Dhabi's crude oil exports, comprising four grades of crude, Murban (39° API), Lower Zakum (30° API), Umm Shaif (37° API) and Upper Zakum (34° API), are sold to the Far East. After Japan, the main importers are South Korea, Taiwan, Thailand, India, Pakistan, Sri Lanka and Bangladesh.

Abu Dhabi condensate exports continued to rise in 2003, reaching almost 400,000 b/d. These exports have no effect on the amount of crude that the emirate can export, since condensate is not covered by OPEC's oil production quota arrangements.

Abu Dhabi's refined products are exported by ADNOC Distribution (ADNOC-FOD), which sells oil products and lubricants both to the Far East and to Arab and African countries. India is the leading export market for Abu Dhabi's refined products, absorbing over half its gas-oil exports as well as substantial volumes of kerosene and LPG. Japan now accounts for about one-third of the emirate's refined product exports, down from 50 per cent in 1993, but remains the largest market for naphtha.

Dubai

Dubai exports all the crude oil it produces, mostly to the Far East. Dubai crude (31° API) is mainly sold on the spot market, and, despite its very limited volume, serves as a price marker for some other Gulf producers. In 2003 the price averaged US$26.85/b, as against US$24.50/b in 2002.

GAS

The UAE's natural gas reserves of 212 trillion cubic feet (tcf) (6.01 tcm) are the world's fourth largest after Russia, Iran, and Qatar. The largest reserves of 196.1 tcf (5.55 tcm) (92.5 per cent of the UAE total) are located in Abu Dhabi with the rest shared by other emirates.

The non-associated Khuff gas reservoirs beneath the Umm Shaif and Abu al-Bukhoosh oil fields in Abu Dhabi rank among the world's largest. Current gas reserves are projected to last for about 150–170 years at present rates of production. Gross production by Abu Dhabi rose to approximately 62 billion cubic metres in 2003. Development of gas production also increases exports of condensates, which are not subject to OPEC quotas. Abu Dhabi Gas Industries Ltd (GASCO) handles associated gas from ADCO's onshore crude production and processes it through three NGL extraction plants at Bab, Bu Hasa and Asab. Offshore, the Abu Dhabi Gas Liquefaction Company (ADGAS) handles associated and non-associated gas from offshore fields at its plant on Das Island. The bulk of the output is sold to Japan.

In addition to the growing volume of gas that is reinjected into oil fields (over 1 billion cf/d in 2003), the country's power stations, desalination plants and other industrial projects depend on burning gas, rather than oil, driving gas consumption to 4 billion cf/d in 2003, a figure that is expected to soar to 5 billion over the next three to four years.

The UAE has been an exporter of natural gas since 1977. Rapid growth in production (from 2.5 billion cf/d in 1995 to 5.8 billion cf/d in 2003) follows a development programme involving three separate projects to enhance recovery of associated and non-associated Khuff gas from onshore reservoirs. The rate of industrial and domestic growth in the UAE is such that national demands for gas are approaching a point where they place severe strains on available supplies. The UAE has, therefore, embarked upon an ambitious project, established by Dolphin Energy, to deliver gas from Qatar's North Dome gas field through an 800-kilometre gasline to Abu Dhabi, from where it will be piped to the centres of use, such as Fujairah's new power and water complex and Jebel Ali's industrial zone. A pipeline to bring gas from Oman has also been completed, and since January 2004 Dolphin Energy has been importing gas from Oman via this route. The gas is used to fuel the UWEC power and desalination plant at Qidfa, in Fujairah.

If confirmation was needed that the UAE sees gas and not oil as the answer to its future energy needs, construction of a new project for natural gas distribution throughout Abu Dhabi should persuade any doubters that this is indeed the way forward. The new pipeline network will deliver clean burning natural gas for commercial and residential purposes. The estimated Dh1 billion initiative comes on the back of increased natural gas availability as several development and expansion projects are under way. In the first phase, the natural gas distribution network will cover 120,000 commercial and residential users in Abu Dhabi, Al Ain and one or two nearby towns. ADNOC Distribution, a subsidiary of ADNOC, is overseeing the project.

Industry sources and government officials share the view that Abu Dhabi will have an abundance of natural gas once major expansions come on stream. The

Onshore Gas Development 2 and 3, Bu Hasa, Bab and others are all being expanded, making more natural gas available. Qatari gas under the mega Dolphin Gas Initiative will also be available in 2006.

Even the UAE's cars are likely to switch to gas as a fuel in the future. ADNOC Distribution has been engaged in a pilot project for use of natural gas by taxis in Abu Dhabi. Initially 48 taxis in the capital have been fitted with gas instead of gasoline. The natural gas filling station is near Mina (Port) Zayed. Future plans include the use of natural gas by all taxis in Abu Dhabi, Al Ain and nearby areas.

Abu Dhabi

The government of Abu Dhabi is sole owner of all natural gas resources on its territory, both onshore and offshore, whether in associated or non-associated form. The Abu Dhabi National Oil Company (ADNOC) is responsible for developing and marketing these resources on the government's behalf and is authorised to form partnerships with foreign companies for that purpose, so long as it retains at least a 51 per cent interest in any venture. Abu Dhabi's proven natural gas reserves were estimated at 5.55 trillion cubic metres (tcm) as at 1 January 2004, representing around 92.5 per cent of the UAE's total gas reserves of 6.01 tcm. Meanwhile, Abu Dhabi's gross gas production reached 62 billion cubic metres (bcm) in 2003.

The impressive production figures are the result of a sustained development programme involving the second and third onshore gas development projects (OGD-2 at the Bab field and AGD-1 at the Asab field). These are operated by the Abu Dhabi Gas Company (GASCO), which also operates the massive gas processing plant at Habshan, built in 1983 to process associated gas from the Thamama C reservoir of the Bab oilfield, and which today also processes non-associated gas from the Thamama B, D and F reservoirs and Thamama Units 6 and 7 at Bab.

Associated gas from oil production at the onshore fields of the Abu Dhabi Company for Onshore Oil Operations (ADCO) is first separated at GASCO facilities at Bab, Bu Hasa and Asab, and is then sent to nearby processing plants. There, the natural gas liquids (NGLs) are extracted and piped to GASCO's main plant for fractionation into liquefied petroleum gas (LPG). The plant has a processing capacity of some 3 bcf/d. Some of the gas is re-injected into the oil reservoirs of ADCO fields, while the rest is supplied to the power and water industries, which account for 80 per cent of Abu Dhabi's gas consumption, as well as to the Umm al-Nar and Ruwais refineries, the Borouge petrochemical complex, the Al Ain cement works, the Fertil fertiliser plant and other industrial plants in the Ruwais industrial zone.

Until late 2000 the 130,000 b/d of condensate output at Habshan was piped to a storage and handling facility at Ruwais, prior to export. Today, however, the 230,000 b/d condensate production is all supplied to the Ruwais refinery for processing into petroleum products.

In addition to the OGD-2 and AGD-1 projects completed in 2001, two more onshore development projects in the Bab and Asab fields, OGD-3 and AGD-2, are under development. OGD-3 will result in production of higher volumes of natural gas liquids (NGL) and condensate and re-injection of gas into oil fields. Wet gas will be extracted from the Thamama reservoirs at Bab, from which condensate will be stripped out and the dry gas re-injected into oil reservoirs to maintain pressure. The project involves the construction of a new gas plant at Habshan to process 1.3 billion cubic feet daily of raw gas and produce 1.2 bcf/d of dry gas, 11,800 tons/day of NGLs and 130,000 b/d of condensate. The Asab-2 project involves setting up two new gas treatment plants, plus two NGL recovery units, to process 743 mcf/d of acid gas into 4700 t/d of NGLs and 1700 t/d of ethane. Project completion is planned for mid-2007. These two projects, being undertaken by GASCO, will yield additional volumes of associated and non-associated gas for supply to the domestic market.

At US$2.3 billion, the OGD-3/AGD-2 project is the biggest single investment in the history of upstream Abu Dhabi gas. Upon commencement of commercial production, towards the end of 2007, the new Habshan plant will comprise a key element of ADNOC's ambitious onshore gas development programme.

Most of Abu Dhabi's gas exports, in the form of LNG and LPG, go to Japan, but there is also a growing market within the UAE. Abu Dhabi began piping natural gas from its onshore fields to Dubai in June 2001, following completion of the OGD-2 project. In 2003 about 900 mcf/d were sent via pipeline to the Dubai Supply Authority.

In October 2003, GASCO awarded an engineering, procurement and construction (EPC) contract worth US$22 million to Fluor Corporation to improve output of the Habshan gas processing plant. Existing facilities are being modified and a new propane refrigeration package and absorber column is being installed. The work will maximise ethane recovery at the site. Upon completion the plant will be able to extract 400 tons of ethane per day. The ethane will be used as feedstock to downstream petrochemical companies related to GASCO and its parent, ADNOC. In January 2004, the Fluor Corporation also received a contract from GASCO for further expansion of the Habshan plant, involving a new processing train and other facilities. This is aimed at boosting the plant's capacity so that it will be able to handle the increased gas to be pumped from the OGD-3 and AGD-2 projects described above.

Offshore gas development is also of crucial importance to Abu Dhabi's economy, with current work being focused on increasing efficiency with regard to extraction rates. Most of the gas produced offshore is supplied to the Abu Dhabi Gas Liquefaction Company (ADGAS) liquefaction plant on Das Island (see below). Following the doubling of the plant's capacity in 1994, the volume delivered to the LNG plant was stepped up to 800 mcf/d.

One major offshore gas development project recently undertaken (due for completion in 2004) entailed further development of the Khuff gas reservoirs under the Abu al-Bukhoosh (ABK) field, 45 kilometres north-west of Das Island. It provides for the volume of gas recovered from the ABK Khuff reservoir to be increased by 240 mcf/d to 540 mcf/d, boosting offshore gas production to 1.44 bcf/d.

Associated gas has been produced at Umm Shaif since 1988, when the existing gas gathering facilities were completed. Two wellhead platforms with a capacity of 150 mcf/d each were installed at the field, as well as two injector/producer platforms. They are all connected to the Umm Shaif Supercomplex, where the Abu Dhabi Marine Operating Company (ADMA-OPCO) recently revamped the gas treatment plant.

ADGAS is responsible for the gas liquefaction plant on Das Island, which began operations in 1977. From the outset, all the plant's LNG and most of its LPG were purchased by Tokyo Electric Power Company (TEPCO) under a 20-year contract that took effect in 1977 and provided for TEPCO to lift 2 million t/y of LNG and 500,000 t/y of LPG. In 1990 the company decided to more than double the capacity of its plant to 5.4 million t/y of LNG, 1.7 million t/y of LPG and 535,000 t/y of pentane-plus. The expansion entailed the installation in 1994 of a third liquefaction train with a capacity of 2.3 million t/y of LNG and 250,000 t/y of LPG. Like the original units, the third liquefaction train has consistently operated in excess of its design capacity.

The plant's LNG capacity was further increased in August 2001, when ADGAS completed the revamp of the propane compressor serving its third liquefaction train, boosting its production capacity from 320 tons/hour to 380 tons/hour. In early 2002, the company signed a FEED contract with the Chiyoda Corporation for an additional LPG train with a capacity of approximately 1 million t/y. Shortly afterwards, in October 2002, ADGAS signed an agreement with BP Gas Marketing Company for the supply of up to 750,000 t/y of LNG. The contract is for an initial period of three years, starting in 2002, and could be extended to five years, depending on BP's requirements. Whilst TEPCO remains ADGAS' major customer, marketing development has considerably broadened the client base in recent years. In addition to the sales to BP mentioned above, the company has sold its gas products to European, American and Asian clients.

As mentioned above, a new pipeline from Oman has been built to link with the new Dolphin pipeline at Al Ain, thus connecting the UAE to Oman's gas network. Omani gas is now flowing to Fujairah and will continue to do so until Dolphin gas from Qatar comes on stream in 2006. Once Dolphin's new pipeline system from Qatar is in operation, Qatar natural gas will flow directly to Fujairah via ADNOC's existing land lines to Al Ain and thereafter the new Dolphin link. The link lays the foundation for a regional gas supply network in the future.

Dubai

Dubai's gas demand is growing by 10–15 per cent per year. Consumption in 2003 averaged 800 mcf/d (not counting gas used for re-injection of oil reservoirs). Peak summer demand can reach 1.5 bcf/d. Dubai's proven natural gas reserves were estimated at 4.1 trillion cubic feet as at 1 January 2004. The only domestic source of natural gas for end users is the onshore Margham field, since all the associated gas produced at the offshore oilfields is now re-injected. Margham's gas production has been declining for some years. After averaging 330 mcf/d in 2000, down from 350 mcf/d in 1999 and 380 mcf/d in 1998, production was reported to be running at no more than 200 mcf/d of natural gas in early 2003, plus 18,000 b/d of condensate. The slump in output led the operator, Dubai Margham Establishment (DME), to embark on a further development programme in 2001 to sustain, if not increase, the field's gas production.

Dubai depends heavily upon imported gas to meet its energy needs. Its power stations, desalination plants and factories could not operate without natural gas as an energy source, and plans are under way to ensure that future needs are met by ambitious and innovative projects such as the Dolphin Energy gas pipeline network linking Qatar, Abu Dhabi, Dubai, Fujairah and Oman. At present, Dubai is importing 300 mcf/d from Sharjah and approximately 900 mcf/d from Abu Dhabi. Once the Dolphin Energy project begins to deliver to Dubai in 2006, the emirate will experience a significant boost in available energy. It is presently planned to draw in 200 to 700 mcf/d of Qatari gas to Dubai Supply Company.

Sharjah

Sharjah's natural gas reserves are estimated at 10,700 billion cubic feet. Production of natural gas in Sharjah has been in steady decline, 600–650 mcf/d in 2003 compared with around 1 bcf/d in 1997–98. The new Zora gas field will provide a small boost to production. As noted above, Sharjah has been exporting natural gas to Dubai since 1986 and presently supplies its neighbour with around 300 mcf/d.

Sharjah LPG Company (SHALCO) operates a gas processing plant in Sharjah. Located in Saja'a, it handles output of the onshore Saja'a and Moveyeid fields and was originally designed to process up to 440 mcf/d of natural gas for the production of 230,000 t/y of propane, 170,000 t/y of butane and 220,000 t/y of condensate. The plant's capacity was increased to 700–800 mcf/d in 1994 to enable it to handle gas from the Kahaif field as well. The propane and butane produced by Shalco are marketed by Itochu and the condensate by BP. Condensate is carried by a 32-kilometre, 12-inch pipeline to Al Hamriyah on the coast, where BP has its own jetty capable of accommodating tankers of up to 83,000 dead weight tonnage (dwt). The terminal includes two storage tanks with a combined capacity of 110,000 cubic metres. The bulk of the condensate is shipped to Japan, although small quantities are exported to Western Europe and North America.

The condensate has low sulphur content (0.01 per cent) and a naphtha yield of almost 80 per cent. BP also exports much of the natural gas it produces, although most is supplied to industrial and household consumers within the emirate.

A new compressed natural gas (CNG) plant has been under development in the Hamriyah Free Zone by a company called Compressed Gas Technology, established in 2003. The plant will produce CNG both for the local market and for export. CGT also designs and assembles CNG filling stations.

Sharjah Electricity and Water Authority (SEWA) has been developing a natural gas distribution network to supply gas direct to residential, commercial and industrial users.

Ra's al-Khaimah

Ra's al-Khaimah is reported to have natural gas reserves of 1.2 trillion cubic feet. Following a number of years in which the Saleh field produced limited quantities of both oil and gas, the field switched to production of just condensate (currently producing 500 b/d). The LPG plant at Khor Khwair in Ra's al-Khaimah now gets its feedstock from the offshore Bukha field in Oman. An Australian company, Novus Petroleum, began exploration work in the second half of 2003, completing a 150 kilometre 2D seismic survey. Novus is hoping that it will discover wet gas on its 600-square-kilometre onshore tract.

Ajman

A petroleum production sharing agreement was signed between Sharjah and Ajman in early July 2002 to jointly develop the Zora field, a gas reservoir located around 40 kilometres off the two coasts. Crescent Petroleum and Atlantis, which hold the concessions from the two respective governments, were also signatories to the agreement. Production is to be shared equally between the parties concerned.

Umm al-Qaiwain

Sinochem, owners of Atlantis Holdings, who hold the offshore concession for Umm al-Qaiwain, are continuing to evaluate options for the development of gas reserves identified in the UAQ3 well. Recoverable reserves are estimated at up to 500 billion cubic feet of gas and 5 million barrels of condensates.

PETROCHEMICALS AND FERTILISERS

Abu Dhabi

Abu Dhabi has two major petrochemical and fertiliser industrial complexes, the Ruwais Fertiliser Industries Company (Fertil) and the Abu Dhabi Polymers Company (Borouge). Fertil was established to utilise lean gas supplied from onshore fields at Bab, Asab and Thamama C to produce fertilisers and market them locally and internationally. It brought its existing nitrogenous fertiliser plant in Ruwais on stream in April 1984. This consists of a 1050 t/d ammonia plant and a 1500 t/d urea plant, but they have operated at over 130 per cent of capacity in recent years (1310 t/d of ammonia and 1850 t/d of urea). The emirate is planning to grow this sector, both as a result of existing facilities expansion and through establishment of new projects that will produce derivatives such as polyethylene (PE), polypropylene, polyvinyl chloride (PVC), vinyl chloride monomer (VCM), linear alpha olefins and aromatics.

Borouge is a joint venture, set up under an agreement signed in April 1998 between ADNOC with 60 per cent and Copenhagen-based Borealis, itself partly owned by the government of Abu Dhabi, with 40 per cent. Its petrochemical complex in Ruwais cost an estimated US$1.2 billion to develop and includes a 600,000 t/y ethane cracker that supplies ethylene feedstock to two 225,000 t/y polyethylene units. Borouge produces up to 450,000 tonnes of Borstar bimodal high-, medium-, and linear low-density polyethylene per year. Combining good processability with excellent mechanical properties, Borouge Borstar products are stronger, lighter, environmentally friendly and more malleable than conventional polyethylene, resulting in material savings of up to 30 per cent. In March 2004, Borouge signed a US$40 million with Tecnimont for debottlenecking the polyethylene units at Ruwais, with the aim of raising capacity to 580,000 t/y by mid-2005. The increased production will be supplied by ethane gas using the new pipeline from the GASCO complex at Habshan.

Borouge's products are used for the manufacture of plastic film and moulding packaging for industries such as pharmaceuticals, food and beverage, cosmetics, and chemicals. Borouge's products are also suitable for the manufacture of high-pressure pipe used in agriculture, mining, water, gas and sewage distribution, as well as coating of steel pipelines.

In addition to promoting its own polyethylene products, Borouge also oversees the distribution and marketing of Borealis' entire range of polyolefins in the Middle East and Asia Pacific. These products include polyethylene for extrusion coating, moulding, and wire and cable, as well as polypropylene for film, moulding, hot water pipes and engineering applications.

Total is to build a melamine plant at Ruwais, the first of its kind in the region. The US$112 million project calls for the construction, by Fertil, of a 50,000 t/y unit. Production, likely to commence in 2006, will primarily be shipped to Europe.

Abu Dhabi Fertiliser Industries Company (ADFERT) commenced production from a plant situated in Mussafah in June 1998. This plant can produce up to 200,000 t/y of water-soluble and granular compound fertilisers. It also produces liquid and suspension fertilisers.

Dubai

Dubai's first fertiliser plant, a joint venture between Kemira Agro Øy of Finland (49 per cent) and the local firm Union Agricultural Group (51 per cent), has the capacity to produce 6000 t/y of water-soluble compound fertilisers. A second and much larger fertiliser plant developed by the same group, and called the Kemira Emirates Fertiliser Company (Kefco), has a capacity of 60,000 t/y and was brought on stream in 2001 in the Jebel Ali Free Zone. Another plant with a capacity to produce 226,000 t/y of ammonia and 400,000 t/y of granular urea came on stream in the first half of 2003. The plant is being supplied with 40,000 million British Thermal Units per day (Btu/day) of natural gas feedstock by Dubai Natural Gas Company (DUGAS) and exports all its output to India. Meanwhile, a 500,000 t/y Methyl Tertiary Butyl Ether (MTBE) plant, established in 1995, utilises the butane isomerisation process of Lummus, the Catofin dehydrogenation process, and CD MTBE synthesis technology for converting butane into MTBE.

Ajman

Ajman has a 600 t/d fertiliser plant that came on stream in December 1987.

TOURISM

The UAE's hotels netted a record Dh5.42 billion (US$1.47 billion) in 2003, including Dh2.78 billion (US$757 million) in lodging revenue. Profits were 11 per cent higher than the previous record earnings of Dh4.87 billion (US$1.32 billion) made by hotels in 2002. Dubai accounted for 75 per cent of 2003 hotel revenues and is expected to generate more of the increased revenues for 2004. Its 271 hotels netted a record Dh4.01 billion (US$1.09 billion), benefiting in September 2003 when more than 20,000 delegates converged on Dubai for the International Monetary Fund and World Bank meetings. Thousands more came for the International Air Show a few weeks later, while large numbers visited the emirate through the year for shopping, business and recreation. Meanwhile, Abu Dhabi hotels earned around Dh996 million (US$271.3 million) and those in Sharjah netted Dh197.3 million (US$53.7 million).

In early 2004, the UAE had 366 hotels, comprising about 38,400 rooms. They included 62 deluxe hotels, 71 first-class, 107 second-class and 126 third-class hotels. The industry is benefiting from a wide range of factors, including the country's development as a financial centre, a leisure zone and a prime shopping location. From an original position of making a negligible contribution to the domestic economy, hotels and restaurants have now become a key component of the country's gross domestic product. In 2004 this sector alone was estimated at around Dh6.34 billion (US$1.72 billion), accounting for around 2.16 per cent of GDP.

Whilst Dubai is clearly at the forefront of the UAE's tourism development, it would be wrong to give the impression that it is the only emirate where tourism developments are taking place. Abu Dhabi, Sharjah, Ra's al-Khaimah, Ajman,

Umm al-Qaiwain and Fujairah have each made significant strides in their tourism programmes. Brand new hotels, and recently renovated ones, can be found throughout the UAE and the visitor is spoilt for choice. The creation, in September 2004, of the new Abu Dhabi Tourism Authority, will provide added impetus to the development of tourism in the Emirate, and will take over the functions of the Al Ain Economic Development and Tourism Promotion Authority, giving an emirate-wide approach to stimulation of this increasingly important aspect of the local economy. The new Emirates Palace Hotel, situated on Abu Dhabi's attractive waterfront, is among the most recent aspects of a steadily improving tourism profile for the Emirate.

Emirates Palace is a most impressive hotel whose sandy coloured structure occupies a magnificent location, its majestic marble walls and ornamented domes visible from afar. Built at a cost of around Dh1.8 billion (US$490 million), the hotel has nearly 440 rooms and suites, 12 restaurants and other entertainment facilities and houses the Middle East's largest auditorium with space for 1200 people.

The capital city is thus building on its natural attributes to attract more visitors and to make the experience of living in the city more enjoyable. It already has magnificent golf courses, many international brand city hotels with beach and resort facilities, new shopping malls, heritage centres and the benefit of an island location with acres of beach. Abu Dhabi National Hotels (ADNH), which is the main hotel developer in Abu Dhabi, announced a net profit of Dh 210.3 million in 2003, a 20 per cent increase over the 2002 figures. The growth in net profit follows a revenue growth of Dh1.049 billion, a 79 per cent increase over 2002 revenues. The company recently completed several renovation projects, including the Sheraton Hotel in Abu Dhabi as well as the Hilton Al Ain, Al Diar Mina and Al Diar Gulf Hotels. ADNH also acquired a new 450-room hotel at the Jumeirah Beach Residence Development in Dubai, due to open in 2007.

Dubai has ambitious plans to attract 15 million visitors by 2010 and 40 million by 2015. It has dozens of hotels under construction with existing properties reporting very high occupancy rates throughout 2004. The emirate has led the way in the UAE's tourism development and continues to announce news, on an almost daily basis, of projects in the travel and tourism field.

Madinat Jumeirah, Jumeirah International's major resort development, is one of the emirate's most attractive developments to have recently come on full stream. Whilst the main hotel has been open since 2003, the entire project, including Al Qasr (The Palace) and the Souq Madinat, welcomed visitors in August 2004. Al Qasr, the centrepiece of the resort, is designed to emulate a Sheikh's summer residence. The boutique hotel features world-class restaurants with enchanting

Hotel Revenues in the UAE*

Emirate	Room	%	Other	%	Total	%
Abu Dhabi	458,761	16.45	537,562	20.42	996,323	18.38
Dubai	2,121,577	76.09	1,894,499	71.95	4,016,076	74.08
Sharjah	119,984	4.30	77,310	2.94	197,294	3.64
Ajman & Umm al-Qaiwain	20,108	0.72	39,144	1.49	59,252	1.09
Ra's al-Khaimah & Fujairah	67,959	2.44	84,629	3.20	152,588	2.81
Total	2,788,389	100	1,633,144	100	5,421,533	100

Source: Ministry of Planning Report 2004. * Figures are for 2003.

terraces, stylish bars and lounges and 292 rooms and suites, all with private balconies, designed and decorated in traditional Arab style.

Dubai has shown its skills for both imaginative developments and worldwide marketing. The world's tallest building, its biggest shopping mall, and one of the fastest growing airlines are just a few of its claims to fame. It already attracts more international travellers than any city in the region. Hotels and business services are also extending their range. While the focus so far has been on high-end hotels, many companies are now building lower-priced properties. Accor Hotels has five new projects under development, including two mid-range Mercures and a budget-range Ibis. The InterContinental Hotels Group is building 20 budget hotels across the region in the next few years, under the Holiday Inn Express brand. But the real focus remains on quality and service. Emirates airline, for example, has been focused on improving its service, offering better value for money, rather than cutting prices. It runs a separate terminal for all passengers flying business or first class, and offers those passengers free limousine service to and from the airport.

The two Palms, at Jumeirah and Jebel Ali, will each accommodate a number of new hotels, residential villas, shoreline apartments, marinas, water theme parks, restaurants, shopping malls, sports facilities, health spas and cinemas. By 2004, all the available properties on The Palm Jumeirah had been sold whilst half those on The Palm Jebel Ali were already taken. Other projects on a grand scale include 'The World', a cluster of man-made islands arranged in the shape of the seven continents and located 4 kilometres off the Jumeirah coastline, between Burj al-Arab and Port Rashid. Each of these islands are being sold to private developers. These marine-based developments not only double the length of Dubai's coastline but also offer pristine white sand beaches and clear warm waters adjacent to hundreds of new plots for hotel and leisure developments that will help to inject a vibrant energy into Dubai's growth for many years to come.

Meanwhile, the biggest terrestrial tourism development in the UAE, the Dh18 billion Dubailand, is also under way. Constructed on a 186 million-square metre area adjacent to Emirates Road, Nad al-Sheba, Al Quoz and Al Barsha, the massive development is expected to attract approximately 200,000 visitors daily and will boast the biggest mall in the world – Mall of Arabia. Other attractions include a sprawling Adventure World, Sports World, Eco Tourism World, Shopping World, Family City World and Kids World. The Dubai government will spend Dh2.6 billion to develop the project's infrastructure and has arranged participation by national and international developers to create the main attractions of the leisure centre. It will be about seven times the size of Disneyland, near Paris, and will house the world's largest indoor ski slope.

But it is not all about high numbers. The UAE cruise market has been encouraged through development of specialised port facilities that enable cruise passengers

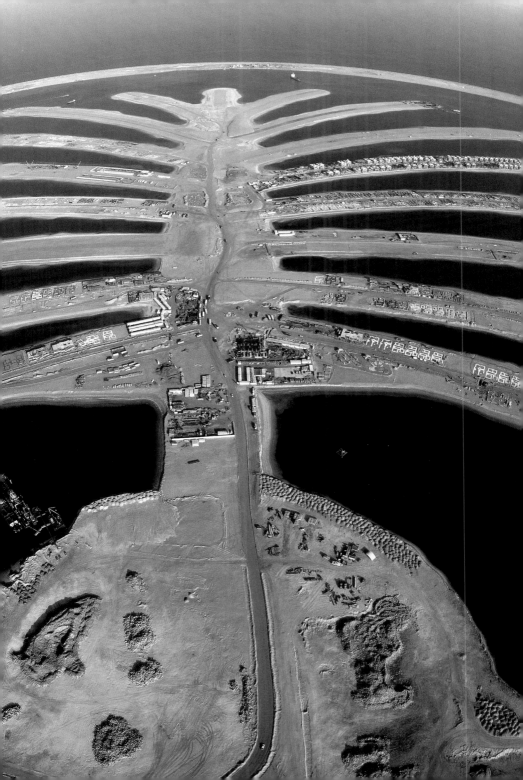

to step ashore close to major attractions and enjoy a hassle free visit to the country. While passenger numbers remain quite modest, Dubai sees these as well worth encouraging. The Dubai Cruise Terminal, which received 12,771 cruise tourists between 2001 and 2003, had around 8000 passengers in 2004. Its ship-shaped building is located on a 335-metre quay at Port Rashid, offering the capacity to berth two ships simultaneously.

Another niche market to receive Dubai's attention in 2004 is that of ecotourism. The emirate aims to attract birdwatchers, scientists, researchers and students from within the country and abroad to visit areas of special natural beauty and interest, such as the Ra's al-Khor Wildlife Sanctuary located at the head of Dubai Creek. Three watchtowers have been provided close to a feeding ground for large numbers of flamingos, other wading birds and a host of migratory species. Other sanctuaries have been created in Hatta, Al Awir and Jebel Ali.

Sharjah has built a reputation for its cultural preservation and its special interest in education, the arts and heritage. Projects such as authentic building and souq preservations, a large number of museums and galleries, together with its special Natural History Museum, Desert Park and Arabian Wildlife Centre have drawn on natural assets and created a unique series of experiences that visitors can enjoy, regardless of where they are staying within the UAE. In addition, Sharjah has recently strengthened efforts to promote tourism. Part of the emirate's attraction is its shopping facilities, with six major shopping malls, including four souqs.

Ra's al-Khaimah, enjoying an attractive location between mountains and deep water, has seven hotels and other leisure facilities, including the recently completed Al Hamra Fort Hotel and Beach Resort. Ajman has four hotels with more than 565 rooms, while Umm al-Qaiwain has some areas of special scientific and historic interest.

Fujairah, situated on the UAE's East Coast, has a number of special attractions, including wonderful beaches and islands. Tourist traffic to the emirate rose by 48 per cent during 2003. The first international hotel to open on the East Coast in over two decades, Le Meridien Al Aqah Beach Resort also won the prestigious Arabian Travel Market silver medal award for the region's best new 5-star hotel. The resort has been very successful in generating renewed interest in Fujairah and is a catalyst for further development of the sector. In 2003, average occupancy at the resort stood at 70 per cent and in 2004 this was expected to reach 82 per cent. On weekends, the resort has 100 per cent occupancy. Agreements were recently signed with local and foreign investors for the construction of a further five hotels in the same area. Preliminary work on land preparation and utilities infrastructure commenced in mid-2004.

Another key engine for growth in tourism is the expansion of local airlines. Emirates airline has led the way in aviation growth. In the first half of 2004

alone it added five destinations, including a direct flight to New York, the first non-stop connection from Dubai to the United States. Gulf Air has also gone through a major renewal and reinvestment programme, while new arrivals Etihad and Air Arabia add significantly to the range of locally-based airline services to and from the UAE.

The Arabian Travel Market, held each year in Dubai, is a focus for all that is happening in the tourism field within the region. The 2004 ATM, opened by Sheikh Abdullah bin Zayed Al Nahyan, Minister of Information and Culture, was eleventh in the annual series and attracted over 1400 exhibitors from 55 countries. Awards are given at the event for tourism projects within Arabia. The UAE scored particularly strongly, with eight platinum medals, eight gold medals, and six silver medals. Award winning projects included the Intercontinental Hotel in Abu Dhabi, Le Meridien Al Aqah Beach Resort in Fujairah and the following Dubai-based projects – Intercontinental Hotel, Le Royal Meridien Beach Resort and Spa, Ritz Carlton, Al Bustan Rotana, Crowne Plaza, Towers Rotana, Jumeirah Rotana, Novotel World Trade Centre Hotel, Dubai Duty Free, The Mongomerie Golf Club, and Cleopatra's Spa. Gulf Air also won an award as the best MENA airline.

AGRICULTURE

The agriculture, fisheries and livestock sector contributed 4 per cent to GDP in 2003 with a value of Dh9.3 billion. The UAE exports dates to Japan, Indonesia and Malaysia, while flowers are sent to other GCC countries, Lebanon, Australia, Britain and Japanese markets. Special focus has been given to biosaline agriculture under the Zayed International Programme for Biosaline Agriculture. By the beginning of 2004, there were 6076 farms in the Central Agricultural Region with 19,000 hectares of new land coming under the plough. Over 2000 farms are using modern irrigation systems to cultivate fruit, fodder and vegetables crops. The region uses tissue culture to grow date palms, and in 2003 13,000 tissue saplings were distributed to farmers to produce high quality date palms: 4000 tons of dates were sold at a value of Dh29.5 million.

Thousands of hectares of palm trees, woodlands and green belts have been planted in the country. Date palm cultivation plays a key role in turning large portions of the desert into green oases. Over 40 million date palms, of which 16 million line the roads, have been grown in the UAE. The date palm is thus playing a very important environmental role.

Despite its extreme climate, the UAE's cultivated areas now extend over 2.7 million donums (891,089 acres). In addition to the date palms mentioned above, this supports production of various types of fruits and vegetables, including mangoes, tomatoes, beans, cucumbers and peppers. The UAE's agricultural research strategic plan has been recently revised in order to focus on integrated and comprehensive research directed at achieving sustainable and significant growth in the sector. Progress to date has been achieved by increasing cultivable land and by enhancing production methods. The timely use of fertilisers, the use of improved seeds, pest and disease control, improvement of the quality of services to producers, especially in the form of agricultural guidance, as well as provision of adequate irrigation facilities and the development of support methods, during both production and marketing stages, contributed to these accomplishments.

By 2003, the UAE produced 30 per cent of its food-grain requirements, while some surplus vegetables and fruits are exported. Significant priority is given to agricultural development in general and sustainable date-palm production in particular. The UAE is 100 per cent self-sufficient in dates and fish and grows 58 per cent of its vegetable needs. Meat and poultry production provide 31 per cent and 17 per cent respectively of requirements. The country produces 83 per cent of its daily consumption of fresh milk and 39 per cent of national demand for eggs.

The challenges and obstacles to successful agriculture in the UAE have been related primarily to the country's extreme aridity, nutrient-poor soil, and high summer temperatures. It is a great tribute to the determination of its President, Sheikh Zayed, that seemingly insurmountable obstacles have been overcome. Support for farmers has come in the form of reclamation and distribution of agricultural land; provision of necessary equipment and training; large scale planting of palm trees to create suitable shaded areas for farming; together with provision of fresh water and seedstock.

The country is striving at all times to optimise productivity through work carried out at agricultural research centres and with agricultural guidance to farmers.

AL WATHBA MARIONNET

Al Wathba Marionnet uses tissue-culture or cloning technology to produce date palms and conducts research on improving their production techniques. The company produces date palms for the UAE at its facilities in the Al Khabisi area of Al Ain and also exports them to several countries.

Al Wathba Marionnet was established in 1997 under the UAE Offsets Group. The company has two greenhouses of 500 square metres each and three shed houses covering a total area of 13,000 square metres. It is currently producing about 300,000 date palms a year, having expanded its shedding area to 6500 square metres in 2003.

Tissue-culture technology has been gaining popularity in the UAE over the last few years as it has resulted in faster growth, uniformity and homogeneity of plants, easier field and plantation management and better overall yields for the farmers.

The total market for tissue-cultured date palms in the UAE stands at more than 200,000 a year and is set to double over the next five years.

In addition to supplying date palms in the UAE, Al Wathba Marionnet is also exporting to Kuwait, Jordan, Yemen, Qatar, Bahrain, Namibia, Somalia, Niger and Colombia under contracts with individual buyers or through the Food and Agricultural Organisation (FAO) of the United Nations. In 2004, it signed two separate deals to export a total of 20,000 date palms a year to Sudan and Yemen. The company also sets up pilot projects in African countries to produce dates and by-products such as wood and dry leaves, which could be used to build huts and houses.

Al Wathba Marionnet is owned 51 per cent by a private UAE investor, 39 per cent by Kranti Developments Limited of France, and 10 per cent by Mubadala Development Company. The company was established after Marionnet GFA – which set up Kranti Developments as a wholly-owned subsidiary to participate in Al Wathba Marionnet – moved its date-palm production facilities from Soings, in Central France, to Al Ain.

POULTRY

The UAE's per capita poultry consumption is the highest in the region. It produces around 400 million eggs and 40 million chickens annually, accounting for 40 per cent of local market consumption.

MUNICIPAL PLANTING

Virtually all cities in the UAE have been greatly enhanced by planting schemes, turning roadsides into gardens and roundabouts into mini-parks. In addition, there are extensive recreation parks where the shade from trees creates a pleasant environment, even in the summer months. The rate of change in the UAE is reflected in these city beautification projects. In 1974, there was only one public park in Abu Dhabi with very little greenery, but today the number has increased to about 40, covering an area of more than 3 million square metres. Seven of these parks have been built exclusively for women and children.

Prior to the annual meetings of the boards of governors of the International Monetary Fund (IMF) and the World Bank Group (Dubai 2003), 300,000 square metres was added to Dubai's greenbelt. The expansion of the green areas in the emirate is in line with the department's goal of planting greenery on 8 per cent of Dubai's total urban area. At present, the planted area amounts to around 3.19 per cent or 2200 hectares.

THREE-YEAR PLAN FOR AGRICULTURE

The Ministry of Agriculture and Fisheries has completed a three-year strategic plan on agricultural research to find practical solutions for obstacles faced by the sector. The comprehensive plan is based on a four-point programme. The

Agricultural Production

'000s of metric tons	1998	1999	2000	2001	2002	2003
Plant products						
Dates and fruits	333	577	798	795	800	822
Vegetables	1554	1722	2622	579	467	453
Other crops	507	584	1495	3176	4308	4436
Animal products						
Meat	22	23	25	26	28	29
Poultry	26	29	27	28	29	30
Eggs (millions)	252	237	266	310	322	340
Milk and dairy products	118	142	163	179	202	215
Fish products	119	115	117	124	141	148

Source: Ministry of Planning and Ministry of Agriculture and Fisheries

first stage consists of research and experiment on palm trees, dates and fruit; the second is research on fodder, pastoral and wild plants; the third is for long-term experiments on agricultural diseases and the fourth is research on protected agriculture, or plants grown in greenhouses.

In the area of palm trees, dates and fruit trees, research activity is divided into two branches: research on improving the growth of palm trees and dates, using the remnants of palm trees, and combating red weevil, and research on improving the growth of fruit trees, similar to parallel studies currently being carried out by one of the Ministry's centres on improving the production of mango and citrus trees. As mentioned above, over 40 million palm trees have been planted in the UAE, and the Ministry is carrying out a project to increase the number of these trees even further, alongside research into palm saplings and the use of high technology. As part of this and other related work, the Ministry has established research centres at Al Hamraniyyah, Dibba and Fujairah.

Meanwhile, the Ministry is also considering the adoption of a sustainable agricultural system for producing different types of fodder that can withstand the country's climatic conditions and can survive on little water. Studies are also under way on combating salinity and the capacity of different types of fodder plants to withstand high salt content in the soil. The plan also aims to encourage further research on use of biological control methods to combat agricultural diseases, rather than resorting to the use of insecticides, which the Ministry is seeking to reduce. The fourth axis of the plan is focusing on producing alternate vegetable products through use of greenhouses.

FISHERIES

The UAE's fishing business has needed to adapt to changing conditions and technologies in recent years. Given the natural limitations on stocks and a steady increase in fishing pressure, it is not surprising that the impact of over-fishing has been felt with reduced catches per unit effort and smaller fish in the landed catches. While considerable efforts have been made to assist UAE fishermen, especially in the provision of suitable boats, engines, equipment and storage facilities, there are limits on what government policy can achieve in this area. An added problem has been that fishing boats have been mainly operated by non-UAE nationals whose concern for stock preservation may be less than that of UAE fishermen. Measures have been taken to address this and other issues in the wild fishery, and it is hoped to achieve sustainable levels of harvesting, together with greater protection of nursery, feeding and breeding grounds.

In order to conserve stocks, the Ministry of Agriculture and Fisheries has issued regulations concerning the fishing gear, fishing areas, seasons and the structure

of the workforce. It is illegal to catch undersize fish; to use less than 2 inch mesh in fish traps or less than one and a half inch mesh in fishing nets; to carry out fishing operations in spawning and nursery areas during the restricted period; and also to fish without the presence of a UAE or GCC citizen on board the vessel. In order to protect the seabed and its demersal fisheries, bottom trawling is not permitted in the territorial waters of the UAE. And whilst a new decree issued in 2004 permits fishermen to carry up to 125 gargours (fish-traps) per vessel, instead of the previous figure of 100, it tightens regulations on how gargours may be used. They must be fitted with escape panels for juvenile fish and may not be retrieved by grapple hooks or anchors which damage the seabed. Every gargour must carry a licence tag, which is not transferable to other fishermen or boats, and it is an offence to be in possession of a gargour without the correct licence tag attached.

But despite these serious efforts to conserve fisheries, there have been dramatic reductions in all key stocks. This appears to be due to a combination of factors including fishing, land reclamation, dredging, and pollution (see section on the Environment).

The Environmental Research and Wildlife Development Agency (ERWDA) recently completed a study of demersal (bottom-living) and pelagic fish resources. The study was based on acoustic surveys backed up by actual fishing operations and was aimed at providing information on stocks that could be applied to fisheries management. It took place throughout the UAE Exclusive Economic Zone (EEZ). Oceanographic data indicated a seawater temperature range off Abu Dhabi of 21°C to 35°C, whilst salinities in excess of 40 ppt were recorded throughout the year. The latter compare with normal oceanic salt levels of 36 ppt. East Coast waters, being more open, have a smaller temperature range and lower salinity levels. The study states that 'There is a close correlation between the abundance and distribution of fish resources on one hand, and oceanographic environmental conditions on the other hand'.

The study encountered 280 species and estimated the total biomass of demersal resources, firstly on the basis of acoustic surveys and secondly based on catch rates. The former gave a result of 20,000 to 100,000 tons, whilst the latter suggested a figure between 22,000 tons and 45,000 tons. These figures lump commercial and non-commercial fish together so that actual biomass of fish caught for consumption is lower. In fact, the study isolated 20 key species that between them constituted 86 per cent of the catch, and fishery surveys of landings suggest that there have been 'major declines in demersal fish abundances since the last survey in 1978'.

The survey also looked at pelagic fish stocks (primarily migratory species) whose populations show significant differences between summer and winter. The biomass of these was estimated at 43,000 tons in summer and 200,000 tons in winter. Around 60 per cent of this mid-water fish stock is composed of anchovies and sardines. Unlike the situation with demersal stocks, the pelagic stocks seem to have held up very well since the 1978 survey with no significant difference in overall size of the biomass noted.

MARICULTURE

Experimental aquaculture in the UAE has been carried on for some years at the Umm al-Qaiwain based Marine Resources Research Centre (MRRC), which produces fingerlings of rabbitfish, seabream and grouper for use in mariculture programmes. In addition, it cultures the shrimp *Penaeus semisulcatus*. But the shift to full-blown commercial fish farming is a more recent occurrence and one that received a strong boost from the UAE Offsets Group, which helped to establish the international fish farming company Asmak – a pioneer and leading aquaculture company in the UAE and Middle East region. The business activities of Asmak span all aspects of the aquaculture industry, including hatcheries, fish farming, processing and packaging, fish feed, fish-farming equipment, marketing, distribution, export and consulting. With associates and subsidiaries in the GCC states and Europe and new ventures on the horizon, Asmak is gradually expanding its operations throughout the Middle East, Arabian Gulf and the Western Indian Ocean.

Asmak's cage farming facilities in Ra's al-Khaimah and Fujairah are producing sea bream, *sobaity,* and other marine fish with a present capacity of 1200 tonnes per year, which will be increased once sufficient hatchery reared seed stock is available and rearing techniques under local conditions have been perfected. Further expansion phases are planned in Ra's al-Khaimah, Fujairah and Abu Dhabi. A new hatchery project is also under construction in Umm al-Qaiwain, while a joint venture hatchery in Kuwait (Gulf International Aquaculture Company LLC) is also producing juveniles of sea bream, *sobaity,* grouper, and other species.

The company has acquired a stake in Feedus S.A. an existing profit-making company in Greece as part of its strategy to invest internationally in successful aquaculture projects. Feedus, as its name suggests, is engaged in manufacturing and supply of fish-feed products.

INFRASTRUCTURE

URBAN DEVELOPMENT

THE PREVIOUS SECTION FEATURED the UAE's dynamic economic environment, highlighting the country's liberal trade and financial policies and the economic diversification strategy that has brought increasing prosperity. None of this would be possible without massive investment in a sophisticated physical infrastructure comprising efficient road networks, excellent telecommunications facilities and freely available electricity and water. In addition, links with the outside world through the UAE's first-class seaports and airports, a vital component of trade and tourism, are constantly being upgraded. At the same time, excellent educational and health facilities and the provision of modern housing required to meet the needs of a rapidly increasing population (from around 250,000 in 1971 to 4.3 million in 2004) guarantees a high quality of life for UAE residents. Today, over 75 per cent of the population live in a handful of cities, many of which are experiencing a new wave of infrastructure development characterised by large-scale ventures, such as huge tourism-related projects, office and residential towers, industrial parks, souqs and shopping malls.

FEDERAL INVESTMENT

Ministry of Planning statistics indicate that the UAE Federal Government invested Dh7.8 billion (US$2.13 billion) in federal development projects in 2003, including new ventures and projects already under construction. Actual spending was Dh1.3 billion (US$354.2 million), higher than the projected allocation of Dh1.2 billion (US$326 million), 85 per cent of which was spent in the Northern Emirates. Dh543 million (US$148 million) was allocated to the Sheikh Zayed Housing Project and the Ministry of Public Works and Housing paid out Dh736.7 million (US$208.7 million) on federal projects in all emirates. New ventures were undertaken in education, health, security, sport and other services, in addition to expansion of the road network linking the emirates and the improvement of electricity and water distribution and storage facilities in the Northern Emirates.

A total of Dh1.9 billion was spent on joint projects serving more than one emirate. The Ministries benefiting from this expenditure included Interior, Petroleum and

Mineral Resources, Foreign Affairs, Education and Youth, Public Works and Housing, and Agriculture and Fisheries. Federal development projects in Abu Dhabi accounted for Dh613 million, Dubai received Dh330 million, Sharjah Dh1.1 billion, Ajman Dh1 billion, Umm al-Qaiwain Dh556 million, while Ra's al-Khaimah and Fujairah were each allocated Dh1.2 billion.

In 2004, the Ministries of Public Works, Communications, Electricity and Water, Agriculture and Fisheries were allocated Dh1.496 billion or 6.26 per cent of the total budget. Of the Dh876 million assigned to the housing sector, Dh640 million was earmarked for The Zayed Housing Project. In addition, Dh357 million was allocated for roads and communications.

ABU DHABI

Abu Dhabi's development budget at the end of 2003 was Dh55.2 billion (US$15 billion). Approved contracts accounted for Dh28.2 billion (US$7.68 billion), while annual allocations were Dh11.1 billion (up from Dh8.4 billion in 2002). Abu Dhabi Municipality and Town Planning Department was awarded 53.7 per cent of total allocations, 26.5 per cent went to the Abu Dhabi Public Works Department, 11.7 per cent to Al Ain Municipality and Town Planning Department, 1 per cent to the Court of the Ruler's Representative in the Eastern Region of Abu Dhabi and 1.2 per cent to Al Ain Agriculture and Animal Wealth Department. Dh229 million (2.06 per cent) was deposited at the general reserve and Dh277 million (2.5 per cent) given to direct work. Actual expenditure for 2003 was Dh9.7 billion US$2.65 billion), compared with Dh7.8 billion (US$2.12 billion) in 2002.

New Urban Areas

At the end of 2003 Abu Dhabi City's inhabitants numbered 552,000, compared with 140,000 in 1980, and this is expected to increase to 1.25 million by 2020. (Population of Abu Dhabi Emirate was 1.6 million at the end of 2003.) The steep rise has led to a high demand for housing, recreational and other facilities. As a result, total developed building space, estimated at 46 million square metres in 2000, is expected to increase to over 95 million square metres by 2020.

In the light of this rapid growth, Vision 2020, which was drawn up with the cooperation of the United Nations Development Programme (UNDP), seeks to lay down a long-term, regional socio-economic strategy as part of a major development plan for Abu Dhabi City, the emirate's Western Region and Abu Dhabi's islands and coastal areas. The plan calls for new residential areas to be developed to meet the needs of the growing population, and hundreds of plots of land have already been distributed to nationals for housing in Khalifa City A and B, situated on the Abu Dhabi–Dubai Road, and Madinat Zayed on the road to Liwa.

In 2004, the Abu Dhabi Executive Council approved an allocation of Dh2.8 billion for housing schemes for Abu Dhabi nationals. Some 2423 nationals will benefit

from the distribution following a comprehensive review of the loan applications that had been received by the Nationals' Housing Authority.

The rise in population has also led to a huge increase in the number of vehicles on Abu Dhabi's roads over the past five years. This is nowhere more evident than in Abu Dhabi City, where the concentration of commercial, educational and health centres in the city centre and traffic to and from Mina (Port) Zayed have contributed to traffic congestion. To meet the challenge that this presents, in addition to the servicing of new residential areas and the provision of recreational facilities for residents and tourists, Abu Dhabi Municipality has updated the transportation element of its 20-year plan, including the widening of existing roads, building of new bypasses, bridges, flyovers, pedestrian underpasses, tunnels, parking lots and expansion of the public transport system. The two-phase Abu Dhabi Master Transportation Plan encompasses Greater Abu Dhabi, which includes Abu Dhabi Island as well as the islands of Saadiyat, Hodairiyat, Mishairib and Lulu and the onshore satellite towns of Bani Yas, Shahama and Al Wathba. One of the main features of the plan is the construction of four new bridges to provide access to the islands.

Major redevelopment of the road network on Abu Dhabi Island, including the Corniche, the Breakwater and Ra's al-Akhdar, and in the surrounding areas is progressing rapidly. Internal roads, such as Hamdan, Khalifa, Falah and Hazza streets, are also being expanded and improved.

Mega-projects

Abu Dhabi's development plan features a number of innovative mega-projects. One of the most obvious is the massive Dh750 million (US$204.35 million) expansion of Abu Dhabi Corniche, which is on schedule to be completed by December 2005. Thousands of square metres have been dredged and filled and most of the basic infrastructure, roads, parking lots and parks, is in place.

A bridge spanning the lagoon near the Sheraton Hotel and another close to Mina Zayed (Port Zayed) are completed, and work has also commenced on a third tunnel and a number of subways along the 6-kilometre new Corniche Road from Al Khaleej al-Arabi (Arabian Gulf) Street to Mina Zayed. Upon completion of the four-lane carriageway, traffic will ease considerably at the Al Khaleej–Al Salam section of the road, while the new bridge will also contribute immensely to reducing congestion on the new Corniche Road.

The spectacular revamped Corniche recreational area will be divided into three themed zones linked by several alternative pedestrian paths. Each of the zones will be provided with a variety of general public facilities and will also contain major features specific to that zone. For example, the Family Zone will include specialised playgrounds and open spaces suitable for children; the Central Zone will have a lakeside park, formal gardens, a refurbished fountain and large plazas;

and the Heritage Zone will feature indigenous cultural elements. Mosques, an amphitheatre, courtyards, pavilions, exhibition spaces and picnic areas will also be part of the Corniche Park. The whole area will be planted with 2500 fully grown date-palm trees and more than 6000 other trees and shrubs.

Extensive land reclamation has been a feature of another impressive project, the multi-billion-dirham extension of the Breakwater and the Marina Mall complex, destined to become a very attractive resort, residential, leisure and retail area. The Breakwater will be joined to the nearby man-made Lulu Island, which is being developed by the Abu Dhabi government-funded General Corporation for Development and Investment of Lulu Island. Plans for the island include a wildlife reserve, Disney-style fun parks, hotels, restaurants, an aquarium and a museum.

Adjacent to the road joining the Breakwater with the Corniche is the magnificent newly-built Emirates Palace Hotel, one of the largest and most luxurious in the region. A number of other new developments are planned for the Corniche, including the Capital Plaza Commercial Development Project, encompassing a 250-room luxury hotel, 220 luxury apartments, a 25,000-square-metre office building located in three towers, along with retail facilities and underground parking.

In 2004, work was completed at the 35-hectare Khalifa Park on the eastern Corniche about 10 kilometres from Abu Dhabi city-centre. The huge park contains an array of landscaped gardens and green parkland, a heritage village, a maritime museum, restaurants, shops and a mosque, in addition to children's playgrounds, a man-made river, paddling pools, a 10,000-seat open-air amphitheatre and a train to transport visitors around the park.

Back in the centre of Abu Dhabi, a two-year project is under way to replace the atmospheric but run-down Abu Dhabi Souq with a new 60,000 square metre air-conditioned bazaar based on traditional Arab design. The first phase of the Dh350 million (US$95.36 million) project necessitated the demolition of the marketplace straddling Hamdan and Khalifa streets, known as the 'old' souq, part of which was destroyed by fire early in 2003. The second stage focuses on the market between Khalifa Street and the Corniche.

ADDAR Real Estate Services, which has been awarded a 50-year concession to redevelop the area into a landmark town centre, plans to start construction in early 2005. The new souq along Hamdan Street will be complimented by a retail and entertainment complex incorporating mixed-use development above. The whole development will be linked through bridges and subways with ample underground parking being provided. This exciting project will add a new dimension to Abu Dhabi's urban landscape.

New Island Crossing

Abu Dhabi Public Works Department continues to work on the Dh900 million (US$245 million) Abu Dhabi Third Crossing project, phase three of which entails the construction of an 850-metre bridge supporting a four-lane highway over the Maqta channel almost parallel to the existing Maqta Bridge (the second crossing is at Mussafah Bridge). An approach bridge over Umm al-Nar Roundabout was built in phase one, whilst phase two involved the construction of approach roads and an interchange; the entire project is due to be completed in 2007.

Work is also progressing on a new 280-metre-long tunnel for one-way traffic from the airport to Mussafah, bypassing the Abu Dhabi Bridges Interchange. Traffic flow from Abu Dhabi City and Mussafah towards the airport and Al Ain will remain unaffected.

Al Ain

Al Ain, Abu Dhabi Emirate's second city, is developing rapidly. Tourism projects in this green oasis, which has a population of 348,000 and numerous heritage sites, are a priority. In particular, the new development on Jebel Hafit featuring hotel, spa, golf and family attractions will help the city capitalise on its considerable tourism potential. New residential areas are also being developed in the Al Ain region and 1000 plots of land and 500 low-cost houses were distributed in the city. Plans have also been approved for the construction of 350 low-cost houses south and north of Na'ama on the Ain Al Faydha–Wagan road and 200 housing units in Mazyad and Al Dhahir.

DUBAI

Dubai City's population of 1.17 million at the end of 2003 is expected to reach 3 million in 2020 and studies indicate that the number of vehicles on Dubai's already congested roads will triple in the near future. All of this necessitates continued investment in transport and other infrastructure.

Dubai Municipality's annual budget exceeds Dh1.28 billion (US$350 million), with approximately 90 per cent allocated to infrastructure development. The emirate plans to invest over Dh22 billion (US$6 billion) in infrastructure related projects in the medium term: Dh16.5 billion (US$4.5 billion) is earmarked for the light rail transit (LRT) development, around Dh 1.83 billion (US$500 million) will be spent on roads and bridges, Dh1.1 billion (US$300 million) on drainage and irrigation and Dh2.56 billion (US$700 million) on general projects. Dubai's road network is under continuous expansion with over 20 major new projects under construction, including an 8-lane tunnel under the airport, due for completion in March 2005, and a new 12-lane bridge across Dubai Creek.

The new bridge, to be built 1.5 kilometres west of Garhoud Bridge, commencing in September 2004, will significantly improve traffic flow. Plans also include a new four-lane approach from the first interchange on Sheikh Zayed Road in the direction of Za'abeel, continuing through the Jadaf area to the new Ra's al-Khor Bridge linking Dubai Festival City to Ra's al-Khor.

Plans for Dubai's Light Rail Transport (LRT) system are intensifying since there is an increased awareness that road widening alone will not solve the city's traffic problem and the rapid rail transit system is seen as a strategic alternative. The first phase of the project, which includes the laying of a 50-kilometre track from Dubai International Airport to Jebel Ali, is scheduled for completion by 2009. The 70-kilometre metro will include two lines, 55 stations, 18 kilometres of tunnel, mainly in the city centre, 51 kilometres of overhead viaduct, more than 100 trains, a major train depot, maintenance workshops and offices. Two transfer stations will be situated at Al Ittihad Square and the BurJuman Mall and it is anticipated that by 2017 nearly 1.2 million people will use the fully-automated trains daily.

New Urban Areas

Dubai's present and projected population increase requires continued investment in housing in both the public and private sectors. Mixed-use developments, such as that planned by Dubai Municipality in the Al Jadaf area, will transform this district from a primarily industrial complex to a waterfront residential, commercial and entertainment area.

Dubai Municipality also plans to develop Deira Corniche by Deira Beach, between Al Hamriyah Port and Port Rashid. Land is being made available for new residential, commercial and entertainment areas. The Corniche will be connected to an artificial island with extensive tourist facilities, including public and private beaches. As part of the project, Al Hamriyah Vegetable and Fruit Market is being shifted to Al Aweer and Al Hamriyah Port will be expanded.

Barsha and Jebel Ali areas are also undergoing renewal. Plans include residential, industrial, tourist and commercial projects, together with an investment park in southern Al Barsha and a new business park west of Jebel Ali.

These and other substantial projects outlined below necessitate considerable investment in basic services, prompting Dubai Municipality to embark on a five-year strategic plan to upgrade the city's drainage and sewerage system and service new urban areas.

Innovative Developments

Dubai's already distinctive skyline and waterfront is evolving at an unprecedented rate and no account of urban development would be complete without mention of some of the impressive mixed-use developments that will change the face of the city and its surrounding waters.

Dubbed the eighth wonder of the world, the visionary Palm resort complexes comprising The Palm Jumeirah and The Palm Jebel Ali are being built on man-made islands south of Dubai City. The shape of both islands was inspired by the much-loved date palm, with the 'trunk 'and 'crown' protected by a sand-fringed, crescent-shaped barrier reef. The two Palm projects will create major residential, leisure and entertainment opportunities.

Following two years of reclamation, The Palm Jumeirah infrastructure is rapidly taking shape. In July 2004, work commenced on phase 2 of the project. A 350-metre-long, 25-metre-wide bridge connecting The Palm Jumeirah to the mainland provides an impressive access route to the Palm's main thoroughfare.

Dubai-government owned Nakheel is also responsible for The World, another imaginative island project involving extensive reclamation. This cluster of artificial islands in the shape of the seven continents is located 4 kilometres off the coast between Burj al-Arab and Port Rashid. Each of the islands is being sold to select private developers for commercial and private use. By May 2004, after less than six months construction, the 17,396-square-metre island representing the UAE had broken the surface.

Meanwhile, back on the mainland, Dubailand, launched by Dubai Tourism Development Company, will have 186 million square metres of world-class facilities, including 45 themed entertainment, retail, and sports parks, double the size of Disneyworld. By June 2004 investors had booked 78 per cent of the space in phase one of the project. The first facility to open was the initial phase of Dubai Autodrome and Business Park with racing facilities approved by the FIA and FIM, as well as a fully equipped media centre and control tower and a world-class racetrack.

Another iconic mixed-use project, including what is likely to be the tallest tower in the world, is being constructed on Sheikh Zayed Road. The Burj Dubai development will combine residential, commercial, hotel, entertainment, shopping and leisure outlets with manicured green spaces, cascading water features, over 3 kilometres of pedestrian boulevard, a reconstructed old town and the adjoining 500,000- square-metre Dubai Mall, one of the world's largest shopping malls.

Further innovative projects under construction include Dubai Marina, described as 'the Nice of the Middle East', which will house 25,000 people in residential towers, shopping and entertainment complexes sited around a man-made marina; Festival City, offering 2.5 million square feet of retail, residential and entertainment space on 1200 acres by Dubai Creek; and dozens of low-rise villa and apartment residential complexes on the outskirts of the city.

Finally, and this is by no means an exhaustive list, Dubai International Financial Centre (DIFC), which, it is hoped, will place Dubai alongside Singapore, Frankfurt and Hong Kong, on the world's financial markets, is being built as an integrated city-centre concept on 110 acres near the Emirates Towers Hotel. Forty-five per cent of DIFC real estate development will be completed by the end of 2006, while the remainder is due for completion by the end of the decade.

NORTHERN EMIRATES

Although they are not experiencing quite the same population pressures as Abu Dhabi and Dubai, the Northern Emirates of Sharjah (population of Sharjah Emirate is 636,000; Sharjah City 519,000), and to a lesser extent Ajman (emirate 225,000;

city 147,000), Umm al-Qaiwain (emirate 62,000; city 38,000), Ra's al-Khaimah (emirate 195,000; city 102,000) and Fujairah (emirate 118,000; city 54,000) are all in the throes of developing and expanding their infrastructure to facilitate residential and tourist development. In addition, as already outlined, the Federal Government continues to invest money on infrastructure projects in the Northern Emirates, especially roads, housing, electricity and telecommunications.

The Sharjah Directorate of Public Works is constructing a new Corniche at Sharjah Creek as part of a major project to transform previous industrial areas for residential and corporate use. This is where most of the government departments will be based. Traffic congestion will be alleviated by the provision of additional parking on the Corniche and the expansion of King Abdul Aziz Road, which will be linked with the new Corniche. A Dh1.3 billion plan (US$355 billion) is also under discussion to upgrade and extend the road network around the emirate. Furthermore, over Dh600 million (US$163.48) in investment is expected in several new projects, including two new shopping malls and six hotel projects in various stages of implementation. This is in addition to Dh2 billion (US$545 million) spent on shopping centres, including the Sahara Centre and the Sharjah Mega Mall.

Work on Ajman's Dh515 million sewerage project is progressing satisfactorily. Over 60 per cent of land-owners will be connected to the system before the end of 2004 and the remaining 40 per cent will be connected over the final 18 months of the project. The new system will assist greatly in future development in Ajman.

Ra's al-Khaimah, sandwiched between mountains and sea, plans to rebuild the old city and reclaim land for housing and tourism projects. In November 2003, it was announced that the emirate had entered the freehold property business with the launch of Noor, a Dh3.67 billion (US$1 billion) tourism project that will develop a new 850-hectare reclaimed area. Noor forms part of the emirate's 2015 structural plan, which also includes development projects such as the Ra's al-Khaimah–Sharjah Ring Road, Al Hamra Fort Resort, Al Murjan Island, Khor al-Qurm (Jazerah al-Hamrah) resort development, Tower Links golf course, Al Shamal area subdivision, Al Khabil area subdivision, Hulayla Island and Ra's al-Khaimah Airport. Work on the massive, beautifully-sited, Dh1 billion Al Hamrah project, which will have 1200 residential units ranging from villas, bungalow-style apartments, an 18-hole golf course and a marina, commenced in 2004.

WATER AND ELECTRICITY

The provision of an adequate supply of water and electricity is the very lifeblood of the UAE's development and a prerequisite for future growth. Vital social services and the tools of economic diversification, such as tourism, agriculture and industry, are all dependent on continued investment in the water and electricity sector.

Electricity production and installed capacity has been growing steadily to meet escalating needs. Total electricity production increased from 45,119 million kilowatts per hour (Kw/h) in 2002 to 48,163 Kw/h in 2003. Approximately 97 per cent of production is fuelled by gas and the remaining 3 per cent is produced by diesel generation or steam turbines. The emirates of Abu Dhabi, Dubai and Sharjah are responsible for 90 per cent of capacity, with federal plants in the smaller Northern Emirates accounting for the remaining 10 per cent. Abu Dhabi, which has the largest capacity and the highest growth in the industry, dominates electricity production in the UAE. Dubai, too, has raised its share of capacity, but it is constrained by lack of gas. Sharjah has increased its capacity considerably since 1996. In addition, projects undertaken by Union Water and Electricity Company (UWEC) have significantly increased capacity in the Northern Emirates.

Historically, all the UAE's water requirements were met from groundwater obtained from shallow, hand-dug wells and the traditional *falaj* system of aquifers. Over the past two decades, rapid economic development, coupled with steep population increases and a push to achieve self-sufficiency in food supplies, have placed ever-increasing pressure on the UAE's precious natural water resources.

Annual water consumption in Abu Dhabi Emirate alone is estimated to be 2.486 billion cubic metres: 1692 million cubic metres or 69 per cent is used for agriculture, 124 million cubic metres or 5 per cent for forestry, 219 million cubic metres or 8 per cent for amenity planting in gardens, parks and roadside plantation and 451 million cubic metres or 18 per cent for domestic consumption. The UAE is now the world's third largest per capita water consumer after the US and Canada, and water consumption in Abu Dhabi is expected to increase to 5.858 billion cubic metres by 2020.

Although groundwater still plays a significant role in meeting demand, a high proportion of the UAE's requirements are being met by an extensive desalination programme. Annual water production was estimated to be 216.4 billion gallons in 2003. The country's capability to produce water touched about 1 million gallons per day (mg/d) in 2003, or 11 per cent of overall output capacity of desalinated water around the world.

In recent years water management initiatives included the construction of more desalination and wastewater treatment plants, restoration of traditional *falaj* systems, the building of delay and recharge dams, well drilling and aquifer testing and exploration. However, with water use now being significantly greater than the renewable water resources of the Emirates, a more coordinated approach is required. To this end the UAE Offset Group-sponsored study completed recently by UK-based Mott Macdonald was designed as a step in developing a comprehensive water resources management plan for Abu Dhabi.

In addition, emirates such as Abu Dhabi are educating the general public about the importance of water conservation. 'Rethink Your Lifestyle – Save Water and

Electricity & Water

	2001	2002	2003
Electricity production (kwh, mn)	42,957	45,628	48,163
Electricity production value (Dh mn)	5,518	6,390	6,745
Water production (bn. gallon)	182.4	204.9	216.4
Water production value (Dh mn)	3,232	3,607	3,810

Source: Ministry of Planning

Regional Power Demand Forecast for Abu Dhabi

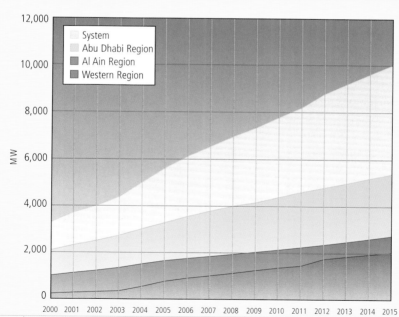

Annual Growth %	6.4	12.7	7.7	9.8	14.1	12.1	8.9	6.8	6.4	5.4	5.9	5.4	7.2	4.8	4.6	4.2

Energy' is the theme of a massive information campaign launched in March 2004 by Abu Dhabi Water and Electricity Authority. The year-long campaign was organised in cooperation with Abu Dhabi and Al Ain Distribution Companies and is designed to encourage residents to develop a responsible attitude towards water and electricity conservation.

ABU DHABI

Spearheaded by Abu Dhabi Water and Electricity Authority (ADWEA), a major restructuring has taken place in Abu Dhabi's water and electricity sector in recent years. Demand for power and water continues to soar, and privatisation of production through the creation of independent water and power projects (IWPPs) remains a consistent feature in ADWEA's strategy to meet these rapidly growing needs. It is expected that privatisation initiatives will dominate the production end of the water and electricity supply chain for the foreseeable future, whilst the distribution and supply chain is set to remain under government ownership.

Established in 1998 to orchestrate the restructuring of the emirate's water and electricity sector and supervise privatisation, ADWEA immediately formed a number of separate companies responsible for production, transmission, distribution and supply. Planning and contracting for new production capacity was assigned to a single buyer, Abu Dhabi Water and Electricity Company (ADWEC). ADWEA's production companies include Al Taweelah Power Company (ATPC), an electricity generation and water desalination company operating the Taweelah B complex where capacity was increased to 1220 megawatts (MW) and 103 mg/d in 2000; Bainounah Power Company (BPC), which has two separate power and desalination stations in Abu Dhabi City (540 MW/16 mg/d) and Al Ain (461 MW); Umm al-Nar Power Company, which runs the 120 MW Baniyas power plant and used to operate the Umm al-Nar complex before it was privatised; and the Al Mirfa Power Company (AMPC), operating the 190 MW/39 mg/d Mirfa combined-cycle plant and the 143 MW Madinat Zayed power plant west of Abu Dhabi City. A number of independent production companies have also emerged from the privatisation process (see below).

ADWEA has assigned transmission and dispatch of electricity and water to Abu Dhabi Transmission and Dispatch Company (TRANSCO). Distribution and supply to customers is divided between Abu Dhabi Distribution Company (ADDC) and Al Ain Distribution Company (AADC), based on the municipality boundaries. Restructuring also created an independent regulator to license companies who wish to produce, transmit or distribute water and electricity in Abu Dhabi Emirate.

Privatisation

The first IWPP undertaken by ADWEA was the Taweelah A2 project situated in the Taweelah complex about 60 kilometres north-east of Abu Dhabi City. This

involved the development of a 710 MW net-capacity, combined-cycle generation plant with 50 mg/d of multi-stage flash desalination capacity. Emirates CMS Power Company (ECPC) was established to build, own and operate the plant, which was commissioned in 2001. As in all IWPP joint ventures, ADWEA holds 60 per cent of the shares of ECPC, and CMS Generation Taweelah Ltd, a wholly owned subsidiary of CMS Generation, has a 40 per cent stake. The Taweelah A2 Operating Company Ltd, also a wholly owned subsidiary of CMS Generation, provides management, operations and maintenance of the facility under the terms of a 20-year agreement.

The pioneering Dh500 million Abu Dhabi Power Bond securing the long-term loan extended to the Taweelah A2 project was launched in June 2004, marking the first time that asset-backed securitisation for an infrastructure-related project had been executed in the Gulf. The bond will be listed initially on the Luxembourg Stock Exchange, to be followed by listings on local and regional markets. National Bank of Abu Dhabi (NBAD) is the lead arranger for the bond, lead managed by Standard Chartered Bank, HSBC and National Bank of Dubai. The bond's launch sets a precedent for subsequent issues related to IWPPs, and it has opened a new avenue for pension funds, insurance companies and other institutional investors to participate in ADWEA's power projects.

Taweelah A1, encompassing the sale, refurbishment and extension of an existing plant that was previously run by the Bainounah Power Company, was the second IWPP formed under ADWEA's stewardship. Commissioned in May 2003 and operated by Gulf Total Tractabel Power Company (GTTPC), Taweelah A1 produces 1350 MW of electricity and 84 mg/d of desalinated water.

The third privatisation focused on the Al Shuweihat project, a brownfield venture whereby Shuweihat CMS International Power (SCIPCO) will produce 1550 MW of electricity and 100 mg/d of desalinated water at Jebel Dhanna, near Shuweihat, 250 kilometres west of Abu Dhabi City. SCIPCO is a joint venture between America's CMS and International Power, the overseas arm of UK-based National Power. ADWEA, as in all privatisations, retains a 60 per cent holding in SCIPCO, with the remaining 40 per cent divided equally between CMS and International Power. Commercial operation is expected to commence in late 2004.

Privatisation of the Umm al-Nar Power Company (UANPC), set in motion in 2003, was the fourth in the series. This time a slightly different corporate structure was put in place. UANPC ran an electricity generation and water desalination plant located 10 kilometres north-east of Abu Dhabi City. This was acquired by the newly-formed Arabian Power Company (APC), 60 per cent of which is controlled by ADWEA's subsidiary, United Arabian Power Company (UAPC); ITM Investment Company Ltd, a joint venture between International Power plc (50 per cent), Tokyo Electric Power Company (TEPCO) (35 per cent), and Mitsui & Co. Ltd (15 per cent), controls the remaining 40 per cent. APC not only took over UANPC's existing capacity (850 MW/162 mg/d) and two recently commissioned units with associated infrastructure, it also assumed responsibility for the development, financing and construction of 1000 MW of new capacity and additional water generation. Commissioning of the first power unit is set for 2005, and full operations will start in summer 2006.

Bids were submitted in July 2004 to develop Abu Dhabi's fifth IWPP Taweelah B involving construction of a new plant and expansion of the existing Taweelah B. The existing plant, which is the only fully government-owned cogeneration plant in the Taweelah complex, already produces 1000 MW of electricity and 90 mg/d of water. The new Taweelah plant will add a power generating capacity of 1000 MW and produce 65 mg/d of water. Plans to privatise Al Mirfa, which was supposed to be the fifth IWPP, have been put on hold.

ADWEA continues to upgrade and expand the emirate's power and distribution network, and in September 2003 awarded two significant contracts to ABB for new substations. One was for the supply of 50 pre-engineered and self-contained 33/11 kV distribution substations, together with 38 medium-voltage switchgear panels and 20 transformers, while the other was for the supply of five 33/11 kV distribution substations incorporating the latest technology in control, protection and monitoring systems, together with 250 air and gas insulated switchgear panels and 25 distribution transformers. The work is scheduled for completion by the middle of 2005.

Wells and Dams

Although, as already outlined, much of the emirate's water is produced by desalination, exploration also plays a significant role in the drive to meet demand. The groundwater exploration and monitoring programme undertaken by two German companies, Deutsche Gesellschaft fur Technische Zusammenarbeit (GTZ) and Dornier Consulting–Daimler Chrysler Services, under the supervision of the Abu Dhabi National Oil Company (ADNOC), has been instrumental in discovering new water wells in Abu Dhabi.

Under the same programme, a major study (Groundwater Assessment Project (GAP)) on groundwater consumption and use in agriculture and forestry will provide precise and reliable data for efficient irrigation management. All data collected by GAP is continuously stored and evaluated in an advanced Groundwater Information System, including an inventory of more than 13,000 wells surveyed by the project in Abu Dhabi. Combined with the application of a countrywide mathematical groundwater model, this tool is seen as one of the most advanced instruments in groundwater resources management in the entire region.

In addition to new wells, over 130 recharge and storage dams have been constructed to utilise an estimated 150 million cubic metres per year of wadi (seasonal river) flow from 15 main catchment areas; 9 major recharge dams have a capacity of 47 million cubic metres, the remainder can hold about 60 million cubic metres. It is estimated that the discovery of groundwater reserves will result in significant saving in future desalination requirements.

DUBAI

The Dubai Electricity and Water Authority (DEWA), which was established in 1992, is continually improving its infrastructure to meet the needs of the emirate's rapidly growing economy and population. Demand for power alone increased by more than 10 per cent in 2003. By early 2004, Dubai had an installed capacity of 4710 MW of electricity and 260 mg/d of desalinated water.

To meet increasing requirements, DEWA's K station power and desalination plants in Jebel Ali were recently commissioned, and a consortium led by Mitsubishi and Toshiba are working under a Dh3 billion contract to develop DEWA's 'L' power and desalination plant, also in Jebel Ali. Construction is split into four phases: the first involves the building of a gas turbine power generation station. A desalination plant will be built during the second phase, a 400 kV transformer station in the third, and the final phase will see the setting up of 400 kV overhead transmission lines to connect the L station to the Dubai electricity grid. Work on phase one is currently in progress. When phase two is completed, the station will have a total capacity of 2050 MW of energy and 120 mg/d of desalinated water.

Early in 2004, DEWA signed a Dh29 million contract with Lahmeyer for engineering consultancy services for the second phase of the 'L' station. DEWA also signed a Dh570 million contract with Areva for the supply, installation, testing and commissioning of two new main 132/400 kV substations at Bukadra-2 and Jebel Ali Free Zone. In addition, Mott MacDonald were granted a Dh16.9 million contract for engineering consultancy services for phase two of the Al Aweer gas turbine power project (Station H). This will be commissioned in stages and be operational in 2006. Station H's production capacity is currently 600 MW and its total capacity will be 1000 MW on completion.

SHARJAH

Sharjah Electricity and Water Authority (SEWA) has initiated a series of projects to ensure that the growth in demand for electricity and water in the emirate is met. Dh19.26 million of SEWA's 2004 budget of Dh1.8 billion was earmarked for water distribution and production in Sharjah and the Eastern Region, in addition to Dh11.8 million for electricity projects in Khor Fakkan and Kalba.

A groundwater exploration project carried out under agreement between SEWA and Boston University is using satellite imagery to identify groundwater resources in Sharjah and the other Northern Emirates. The programme is particularly interested in two unconventional resources: fracture zones and dried river courses.

Geographical Information System (GIS) technology is also being used to establish electricity, water and gas databases and to enhance the coordination between SEWA and local government departments.

OTHER EMIRATES

The Federal Electricity and Water Authority (FEWA) is involved in a number of projects to upgrade the electricity network in the Northern Emirates. Construction work on FEWA's Dh37 million water desalination station at Ghalilah, north of Ra's al-Khaimah, commenced late in 2003. The station will produce 3 mg/d of desalinated seawater by reverse osmosis. Ra's al-Khaimah, at present, enjoys a desalination capacity of 6 mg/d produced by four desalination stations, three of which are based in Al Nakheel while the fourth is in Burairat.

UWEC

The Union Water and Electricity Company (UWEC) is spearheading expansion in the electricity and water sector with the intention of supplying both the Northern Emirates and other parts of the UAE. UWEC, which was set up by the Abu Dhabi government in June 2001 as part of the UAE Offsets programme, has completed a 656 MW power and 100 mg/d desalination plant at Qidfa, Fujairah and a 179-kilometre dual pipeline – capable of transporting up to 200 mg/d of desalinated water – from the plant to Sweihan in Abu Dhabi. An 18-kilometre branch pipeline has also been built to supply the Northern Emirates through Dhaid in Sharjah.

UWEC's desalination plant has the capacity to produce 62.5 mg/d using multi-stage flash (MSF) technology and 37.5 mg/d using a reverse osmosis (RO) process. This makes it the only one of its type in the Middle East and one of the biggest such plants in the world using a combination of the two water desalination technologies. The operations and maintenance (O&M) of the power and water generation plant and the water transmission pipeline are being carried out by Sogex Oman under a five-year contract awarded in late 2003.

UWEC plans to privatise its project in line with the ongoing privatisation of the water and power sector in Abu Dhabi. A foreign partner will be offered up to a 49 per cent stake in the project, a structure similar to the one used by ADWEA. The company also plans to build a second project – an up to 1000 MW power unit and a 100 mg/d desalination plant – at Qidfa. Preliminary work on this second phase is already under way.

UWEC is playing a major role in the Emirates National Grid Project (ENG), to which it will supply up to 500 MW of power from the already commissioned first phase of the project, and up to 1500 MW after implementing phase two by mid-2008. The second phase expansion will also enable the company to export power to neighbouring countries through individual agreements or through the planned GCC power grid.

POWER GRIDS

Contracts worth Dh814 million (US$221.7 million) were signed in May 2004 with seven international and local power companies to commission the Emirates National Grid project (ENG). The two-year project will establish a single national power network for the whole country, thereby ensuring uninterrupted power to all emirates. Set up by the Abu Dhabi government in 2001, the project is being jointly undertaken by UWEC, ADWEA, DEWA, FEWA and SEWA.

The ENG project will also facilitate the UAE's plans to link up with the GCC power grid, further improving performance and reliability throughout the country. In May 2004, the GCC approved a funding plan for the GCC project, which it is estimated will cost US$6 billion. The initial phase, linking grids in Kuwait, Saudi Arabia, Bahrain and Qatar, is expected to be completed by the first quarter of 2008.

The second phase will link grids in Oman and the United Arab Emirates, and the two mega-grids will be joined together in the final phase. In fact, the UAE and Oman have already signed an agreement to link the two countries following the conclusion of a Memorandum of Understanding in December 2001.

TELECOMMUNICATIONS

The UAE has a well-developed, technologically-advanced telecommunications infrastructure and has high mobile telephone and Internet penetration. Since 1976 majority government-owned telecoms company Etisalat, a World Top 500 company in terms of market capitalisation, has operated, maintained and developed the national and international fixed-line network, mobile telephony, Internet access and cable TV services. However, recent government decrees on the reorganisation of the telecoms sector provides for the deregulation of the market.

As a first step, the Ministry of Finance and Industry will supersede the Ministry of Communications as government representative on the Etisalat board. The Minister of Finance and Industry will also head the three-member federal regulatory authority, the Supreme Committee, which will oversee the licensing structure and appoint a five-member Public Committee that will issue guidelines and procedures for compliance with licensing requirements. An Organisational Committee, which will report directly to the Supreme Committee, will also be established with representatives from the Ministry of Communications, Ministry of Information and Culture, Ministry of Interior, the UAE Armed Forces and Internal Security, the Civil Aviation Committee and the Telecoms Public Committee. This committee will be responsible for drawing up a national policy relating to the organisation and distribution of telecommunication frequencies.

Etisalat has been an extremely successful company since its inception in the early days of the UAE. In 2003, it recorded net profits of Dh2.87 billion (US$782

million), 17 per cent higher than in 2002, based on revenues of Dh9.22 billion (US$2.51 billion) against Dh8 billion (US$2.17 billion) in 2002. The company also declared a cash dividend of 2.5 per cent and bonus shares of 10 per cent, and is raising its paid-up capital by 10 per cent to Dh3.3 billion (US$899 million) through a bonus issue. Etisalat's assets grew to Dh17.86 billion (US$4.86 billion) in 2003 (from Dh16.06 billion in 2002). Shareholders' equity was at Dh11.51 billion, up from Dh10.14 billion. Earnings per share rose from Dh8.19 to Dh9.58. Etisalat also announced a 16 per cent growth in net profits to reach Dh 1.71 billion for the half-year period ending 30 June 2004, compared with Dh 1.47 billion for the same period the previous year, and interim dividends of 25 per cent to be distributed to shareholders.

The company's massive investment over the years has ensured that the UAE has one of the most advanced telecom infrastructures in the world, and capital expenditure during 2003 amounting to Dh997 million (US$271.66 million) was mainly used to expand and upgrade the network, to deploy new technology and provide additional buildings and facilities.

By mid-2004, Etisalat's customer base had expanded to 3.308 million mobile phone subscribers, and 1.163 million fixed line subscribers. These numbers, having increased from 2.655 million and 1.113 million, respectively, represent a penetration rate of 81 and 28 lines per 100 residents. Internet connections increased to 332,000 from 297,000 in the corresponding period of the previous year, signifying growth of 12 per cent.

As far as technological developments are concerned, Etisalat is holding trials of a new system that will provide voice, high-speed Internet and broadcast television to consumers through a single cable-based platform. It will be made available to both business and home users, for whom it will represent an increasingly networked environment for the 'Smart Home'. This will represent the next big advance in fixed-line telephony, similar to what 3G services did for GSM. According to the current schedule, it should be commercially available by mid-2005. The system will run on a mix of existing copper cable infrastructure, already in place for Etisalat's fixed-line network, plus the more advanced fibre optic platform. Etisalat has been developing its fibre optic access points in the UAE since 1995.

In late December 2003, Etisalat became the first Middle East operator to launch the 3G service commercially and a sharp rise in 3G usage and subscriber numbers is envisaged, coinciding with the increased availability of 3G-enabled handsets. At the same time, a phased expansion of the 3G network to cover all medium-term requirements is moving forward.

In June 2004, Etisalat announced the launch of its one-stop e-solutions venture 'e-Company', formed from the merger of its online business units Emirates Internet and Multimedia (EIM) and Comtrust. This initiative continues the ongoing process

Transport & Communication

	2001	2002	2003
Paved Highways (km)	3860*	3969*	4030
Vehicles (000s)	745	767	792
International Airports	6	6	6
Air Freight (000s ton)	1186	1289	1525
Passenger Traffic (000s)			
Air Arrivals	8092	9235	9785
Air Departures	8135	9616	10190
Land Arrivals	1215	1326	1572
Land Departures	1332	1435	1548
Commercial Seaports	15	15	15
Sea Freight (mn ton)	88.9*	97	103
Telephones (Exchange) (000s)	1053	1094	1129
Mobile Telephones (000s)	1909	2428	2844
Number of Public Telephones	28,623	28,734	29,000
Internet Subscribers	256,236	290,513	313,750
Total of Minutes (000s)	7,364,141	8,780,544	9,395,670
Total of International Call Minutes (000s)	1,395,726	1,894,205	2,127,800
Number of Pagers	129,438	98,891	90,000
Number of Telegrams sent	161,462	139,199	125,000
Telex Working Lines	1637	1425	1270
Rented Fax Machines**	16,138	15,385	14,850
Number of Land Satellite Stations	23	23	23
No. of Countries Communicating with UAE	258	258	258
Post Boxes (000s)	201	215	238
Air Mail Dispatched	26,271	26,723	26,394
Air Mail Received	50,150	34,314	45,044

*Estimated ** Only rented Facsimile Machines from Etisalat
Source: Ministry of Planning 2004

of streamlining the company to meet the greater challenges of the growing IT market and the more competitive environment. Many of e-Company's solutions will be marketed through partners as part of wider solutions or infrastructure deals.

In addition to separate business divisions like e-Company, Etisalat provides specialised services through subsidiaries such as the cable TV company E-Vision, which services Dubai, Abu Dhabi, Al Ain, Sharjah and Ajman.

E-marine, Etisalat's submarine cable-laying subsidiary, will lay part of the 20,000-kilometre, US$500 million SMW4 (Southeast Asia, Middle East and Western Europe) cable project awarded to e-marine by Alcatel Submarine Networks in 2004. *Niwa*, one of the largest cable-laying vessels in the world, set sail in September 2004 to lay the cable that will carry high-speed telephone, Internet and broadband data streams between 14 countries from Singapore to France through the UAE. The cable will become operational in the third quarter of 2005.

Etisalat has a 34 per cent equity in Zantel (Zanzibar Telecom), a 4.6 per cent stake in Sudatel of Sudan, a 1 per cent stake in Qatar Telecom, a 49 per cent stake in the under-developed Saudi GSM and 3G market, it is the majority shareholder in Thuraya (see below), and it is examining opportunities to take equity in larger markets such as China.

Whatever the scope of the newly-liberalised UAE telecom market, a new operator will probably have to rely on Etisalat's telecommunication backbone, depending on the kind of service in question. In fact, commercial operations that resell telecommunication services to third parties already exist, though the operators are, in effect, government companies, namely Dubai Internet City (DIC) and the real-estate company Emaar. DIC is virtually the telecommunication provider (fixed lines and Internet) for over 1500 companies currently based in DIC, Media City and Knowledge Village. It buys bandwidth from Etisalat and internally handles all related infrastructure and services, including billing and support. Meanwhile, Emaar, which is spearheading mass development of modern residential clusters aimed for expatriate ownership and rental, is in turn buying bandwidth from DIC to cater for the telecommunication needs of what will eventually be tens of thousands of tenants.

THURAYA

Etisalat is a majority shareholder in the Thuraya Satellite Telecommunication Company, and it is Thuraya's service provider in the UAE. Thuraya was founded in January 1997 as a UAE-incorporated, private joint-stock company with an initial capital base of US$25 million. This had increased to US$500 million by August of 1997 as the list of shareholders grew. In December 1998, Thuraya appointed a consortium of four banks to underwrite a loan of US$600 million for the remainder of the project cost.

Country	ICT Use Index	
	End 2002	End 2003
United Arab Emirates	1.40	1.50
Bahrain	1.15	1.26
Kuwait	0.95	1.17
Qatar	0.75	0.92
Saudi Arabia	0.50	0.61
Lebanon	0.52	0.54
Jordan	0.46	0.49
Palestine	0.31	0.40
Tunisia	0.25	0.40
Oman	0.35	0.39
Morocco	0.27	0.30
Egypt	0.21	0.26
Syria	0.15	0.23
Libya	0.16	0.19
Algeria	0.10	0.15
Yemen	0.05	0.09
Iraq	0.04	0.06
Sudan	0.03	0.05
Total	**0.22**	**0.27**

The ICT Use Index covers four ICT parameters: PC installed base and the number of Internet users, mobile phones and fixed lines. The Index is calculated by adding up the values of these four parameters and dividing the sum by the country's population figure. A higher Index score indicates more aggressive ICT adoption in the country under question.

Source: Madar Research Journal, April-May, 2004

Thuraya offers satellite, cellular (GSM) service and a location positioning system (GPS) in a single dual mode lightweight handset that provides voice, data, fax and short messaging services. Remote communities, many of which were previously deprived of all telecommunications services, are serviced by public call offices (PCOs), and subscribers in urban or rural areas can access Thuraya through service providers who are either national GSM network companies or local telecom operators. Thuraya, in effect, complements national GSM networks, allowing subscribers to remain connected to their national mobile networks and to access Thuraya's system whenever their preferred national network is out of reach. Prepaid cards are also available to enable multiple users to maintain independent billing for a single handset.

By mid-2004, more than 2000 public call offices (PCOs) and 250,000 handsets had been sold. Thuraya is also selling version 2 of the Hughes handsets, deliveries of which began in 2004. In addition, agreement has been reached with a Korean company to manufacture Thuraya's second generation handsets.

Thuraya's first satellite, Boeing Satellite Systems Thuraya-1, was successfully launched on board a Sea Launch Zenit-3SL rocket from the equator in the middle of the Pacific Ocean on 21 October 2000. This was also the first satellite initiated from the Middle East and the heaviest satellite to be launched up to that time. Thuraya's second satellite, Thuraya 2, was launched on the 10 June 2003, while a third satellite is being built by Boeing Satellite Systems. Boeing also designed and built the ground system and supplied handsets for the Thuraya network.

The successful launch of the second satellite, followed by a smooth transfer of traffic from Thuraya 1 to the modified Thuraya 2, enabled the company to expand its satellite telecommunications southward in Africa. The expanded service, which is now commercially operational, brings the total number of countries under the new Thuraya footprint to more than 110, spanning Europe, large parts of Africa, the Middle East, central and southern Asia, and from the end of 2004, the whole of Asia.

EMIRATES POST

Emirates Postal Corporation (Emirates Post or EmPost) was formed in 2001 following restructuring of the UAE General Postal Authority to assist in streamlining the existing postal service in line with global developments.

The introduction of automated sorting centres and agreements with international postal authorities improved efficiency and enabled a reduction in postal tariffs. Alliances with world giants such as Western Union and DHL facilitated the introduction of money transfer services and cross-branded products like

'International Express', whereby consignors using Emirates Post packaging can utilise DHL's airway bill system and worldwide network.

As part of Emirates Post strategy to transform UAE post offices into one-stop community services centres, several new non-postal services are being made available at post offices, including consumer banking in alliance with Union National Bank, prepaid telephone cards, payment of utility bills, provision of Internet stations, sale of mobile phones and accessories, prepaid parking cards, stationery items and greeting cards. Some post offices will also offer E-Vision subscriptions. From the first week of August 2004, Emirates Post customers can also purchase Air Arabia tickets by cash or credit card, and Emirates Post offices in Dubai will start taking trade licence registration and payment for renewal applications for the Department of Economic Development from 1 September.

In addition, Emirates Post's new direct marketing service targets national and private sector companies, providing them with a readymade database of consumers for marketing purposes. The service allows clients to dispatch mailers, by traditional methods or through electronic channels, with the aid of Emirate Post's subsidiary, the Electronic Document Centre.

AIRPORTS AND AVIATION

The UAE's aviation industry has expanded steadily over the past few years, a remarkable achievement considering the difficulties faced by aviation worldwide. In 2003 alone, there was a 5 per cent increase in aircraft movements over 2002, passenger throughput increased by 11.2 per cent and cargo traffic exceeded a record 49.5 million metric tonnes at the UAE's six international airports. This impressive pace of development has been facilitated by considerable expenditure on airport expansion, as well as the launching of a number of new airlines. In 2003, five new airlines were licensed, including Etihad Airways, the Abu Dhabi-based airline which is intent on becoming a leading world airline in the shortest possible time-frame. In addition, recent significant aircraft purchases by Etihad Airways and Emirates airline have further underlined the challenge that they pose to the established world aviation hierarchy.

Facilitating this boom is the General Civil Aviation Authority (GCAA), which was established by Federal Law No. 4 of 1996 to provide the enhanced en-route navigation services required by the increasing number of airlines using UAE airspace. GCAA, with headquarters in Abu Dhabi and a regional office in Dubai, also provides registration and licensing services for the aviation industry in the UAE. Since its inception it has modernised the country's air traffic control systems and introduced many new safety features. In recognition of its accomplishments in this field, GCAA won the IATA Eagle Award 2003 and also received commendation from the International Civil Aviation Organisation for its leading role in the implementation of the safety feature known as reduce vertical separation minima in the Middle East region.

GCAA management has developed a strategic plan for 2004–2013 based on the following parameters:

- New and expanding UAE flag carriers and operators will see fleet size expansion of the civil aircraft registry from 109 aircraft in 2003 to 210 aircraft by 2013, an increase of 93 per cent.
- The six UAE international airports are becoming leading hub airports connecting east and west. Local initiatives to diversity the economy, including expansion of tourism, trade and the IT industry, will accelerate this trend.
- Air traffic movements recorded at 276,000 in 2003 will increase to an estimated 426,000 by 2013 using a conservative 4.4 per cent annual growth rate factor.
- Capital growth expenditure by the GCAA for the planning period will be an estimated Dh134 million to ensure that infrastructure and equipment needs remain capable of responding to all expansion forecasts.
- Human resource requirements will increase from 197 in 2003 to a total of 291 by the end of the planning period. The expanded HR requirement will focus heavily on the nationalisation programme.

AIRPORTS

The UAE's six international airports vary considerably in size and capacity. Dubai, the largest, is enjoying considerable success as an aviation hub between east and west. However, Abu Dhabi, the second largest, is making real progress in its efforts to establish itself as an aviation hub; an aspiration that has received considerable impetus from the fact that Etihad Airways is headquartered there.

All UAE airports commenced levying a passenger service charge of Dh30 on 1 September 2004 following a decision taken jointly by all the airport authorities in the UAE. Infants below two years, cabin crew and transit passengers will be exempted from the charge.

Abu Dhabi International Airport

Abu Dhabi International Airport experienced 28 per cent growth in passenger traffic in the first quarter of 2004. The airport expects to handle more than 5 million passengers in 2004, up from 4.3 million in 2003. With Gulf Traveller, Gulf Air's new service, and Etihad Airways, the new national carrier of the UAE, operating from Abu Dhabi, escalating growth is predicted. At present 50 airlines operate from Abu Dhabi, but this is expected to increase in the near future.

Situated 35 kilometres east of Abu Dhabi City, the airport is well equipped with comfortable lounges, a large duty-free area, a hotel and even an adjoining golf course. The airport's Dh1.5 billion three-year expansion is scheduled for

completion by 2006. The facelift, which will effectively double passenger capacity, includes a new 4-kilometre runway, 18 new aircraft stands, a 4000-square-metre transit area, the region's first rapid transit shuttle, and an extensive new duty-free shop overlooking the departure halls. Some modifications to the original plan are being made to accommodate the specific needs of Etihad Airways.

Abu Dhabi Duty Free (ADDF), with its unique promotions and world-renowned raffles, was awarded the Frontier Marketing Award for 'Best Marketing Campaign by a Retailer' in 2003 for the third consecutive year, despite stiff competition from 92 duty-free operators worldwide.

Abu Dhabi Cargo Village

Abu Dhabi Cargo Village, which opened in April 2003, specialises in cargo, storage and re-export operations. The new facility, destined to become one of the biggest cargo hubs in the region, is custom-designed for easy access to bonded warehouses and offices to facilitate cargo airlines, freight forwarders, courier companies, re-exporters, clearing agencies and others. The new facility intends to become one of the biggest cargo hubs in the region.

Al Ain International Airport

Abu Dhabi's second international airport is located on a 600-hectare site, 23 kilometres from Al Ain City, an important agricultural and educational area which is in the process of exploiting its huge tourism potential. Although the airport only commenced operations in 1994, ten airlines, including Gulf Air, are operating out of Al Ain. Plans are already under way to spend Dh75.23 million (US$20.5 million) on doubling the size of the departure lounge and check-in area, and building a VIP lounge, office facilities, dedicated cargo terminal, bonded warehouse and a high-tech inflight catering facility.

Dubai International Airport

A fundamental change in the status of the Department of Civil Aviation was announced in March 2004 in a move to make it financially independent. The department will be renamed the Dubai Civil Aviation Authority, one of its tasks being to raise funds to finance projects such as the airport expansion. Most of the projects tendered to date have been financed by the Dubai government.

Dubai Airport is one of the busiest in the region with over 105 airlines servicing 145 destinations. In 2003, 18 million passengers passed through the airport and 21 million are expected in 2004, positioning the airport sixteenth in the world in terms of international passenger throughput. Projections estimate that 40 million passengers will use Dubai Airport by 2010. This rate of growth has necessitated a massive expansion of the supporting infrastructure to accommodate the ever-increasing volume of passengers and aircraft.

The airport's Dh15 billion (US$4.1 billion) redevelopment programme includes the construction of Terminal 3, Concourse 2 and Concourse 3, all of which will be exclusive to Emirates airline, a huge cargo terminal and a major upgrade of Terminal 2. When the whole project is completed, the airport will have the capacity to handle 70 million passengers a year.

Based on 2003 figures Dubai Duty Free (DDF), which recorded sales of Dh1.39 billion (US$380 million) in 2003, moved up two places and is now the third largest duty free in terms of turnover worldwide, behind London Heathrow and Seoul's Inchon Airport. The award-winning operation is very much on track for annual sales of Dh1.54 billion (US$420 million) in 2004 as the upward trend continues. DDF celebrated its twentieth anniversary in 2003. Sales over that period have grown by 2000 per cent, and on the anniversary day (20 December 2003) sales reached a record US$1.9 million, the proceeds of which were donated to charity.

In 2004, the International Air Transport Association (IATA)/Airport Council International (ACI) voted Dubai International Airport the best airport in three different categories – Best Airport Worldwide, Best in Regional Ratings (Middle East/Africa) and Best Airport Size Ratings (over 15 million passengers), in its latest AETRA Survey (formerly the IATA Global Airport Monitor).

Dubai Cargo Village

In 2004, Dubai Cargo Village (DCV), for the second successive year, was named the Best Airport in the Middle East for its cargo facilities and services. To date, Dubai Cargo Village has won 17 international awards. Almost all the leading regional and international carriers have offices and operations at DCV. However, bulk cargo carried by Emirates Skycargo currently represents about 50 per cent of the total throughput at the airport. DCV is expediting the construction of its mega-terminal in order to, at least, finish part of it ahead of schedule to meet its 1 million tonne target by the end of 2004. In 2003, the Village handled over 956,000 tonnes of cargo, 21 per cent up on the previous year. Imports increased by 18.72 per cent, and exports by 26.33 per cent. Once it is fully operational, probably late in 2004, the Dubai Flower Centre is expected to have significant impact on the DCV's performance in 2005.

Sharjah International Airport

Sharjah has a long association with aviation, beginning back in 1932 when Imperial Airways – the forerunner of British Airways – constructed an airfield in the emirate as a stopover en route to India and Australia. This was the first airport in the country. Today Sharjah Airport provides all the services and facilities that one would expect in a modern first-class, international airport. During 2003 the airport experienced a 13 per cent increase in aircraft movement and a 21.27 per cent increase in passenger movement: a total of 1.25 million passengers used Sharjah Airport in 2003 and there were 9356 scheduled and 4772 non-scheduled passenger flight movements, in addition to 8691 scheduled and 5198 non-scheduled cargo flight operations. An overall increase of 4 to 5 per cent is expected in 2004.

Sharjah Airport's expansion programme is scheduled for completion in 2005. Passenger terminal improvements include 26 new check-in counters, six of which will be dedicated to Air Arabia, the new government-owned airline that operates from Sharjah Airport.

Already a busy air-cargo hub, there are 15 cargo companies working from the airport covering a network of 80 international destinations. Cargo figures showed improvement in 2003. Situated just 10 kilometres from Sharjah City centre and about 15 kilometres from Dubai, the airport has direct road links with the two ports in Sharjah and is easily accessed from all of the main UAE ports, both on the Gulf and East Coast. As a result, Sharjah Airport is a very popular transshipment point, especially for intermodal cargo (cargo arriving by sea and airfreighted onwards).

Ra's al-Khaimah International Airport

Ra's al-Khaimah International Airport, a small modern airport with a daily passenger capacity of 10,000, is located 18 kilometres from Ra's al-Khaimah City. Expansion and modernisation plans for the airport include the construction of an airport hotel, two terminals, expanded runways and taxiways, automated passenger and baggage handling facilities, a cargo collection centre, an aviation academy and an airport free zone.

Fujairah International Airport

Fujairah International Airport, the only East Coast airport and an emerging tourist destination, has spacious lounges and a duty-free shopping complex. In 2003, Fujairah International Airport recorded a 44 per cent increase in aircraft movement (aircraft traffic increased to 14,728 from 10,243), a 22 per cent growth in cargo handling (38,656 tons, up from 31,987 tons) and a 59 per cent rise in passenger throughput (from 65,987 to 104,485) compared with 2002, ensuring that 2003 was the best year in the airport's developing business since it was established in 1987.

Fujairah, which is expecting a boom in tourism in the years to come, is expanding its airport facilities with a second runway, as well as vastly improved facilities and increased capacity in the main passenger terminal. The revamped terminal will be able to handle around 8000 passengers.

Fujairah's strategic location between east and west and the nearby seaport make it a natural choice as an international cargo hub. A 9300-square-metre cargo complex provides flexible options for freight operators who wish to use the airport for transit, sea-air operations or as a regional hub.

AIRLINES

Etihad

Funded by the Abu Dhabi government, the UAE national carrier Etihad Airways was established in July 2003 with a fully subscribed authorised capital of Dh500 million (US$136.24 million). Etihad, which is based at Abu Dhabi Airport, launched its operations with an inaugural flight from Abu Dhabi to Al Ain on 5 November 2003. It subsequently commenced flights from Abu Dhabi to Beirut on 12 November, followed by Damascus and Amman in December.

Etihad did not waste any time in expanding its services worldwide: its first European route (to London) was launched in March 2004, the same month that it commenced flights to Colombo. In June, Etihad opened a route between Abu Dhabi and Geneva with ongoing service to Munich, and announced that it was going to double its flights to London to increase its weekly total to 15. By the end of 2004 Etihad will service 16 destinations, adding new routes on the Indian subcontinent, the Far East and Europe. Cargo operations are already under way and a branded cargo division is to be launched in late 2004.

By mid-2004, Etihad was operating a fleet of six aircraft, including four of the market-leading A330-200s and an Airbus A340-300. At this stage it signed a Memorandum of Understanding (MoU) at the Farnborough Air Show to purchase 24 Airbus aircraft, including 4 of the revolutionary double-decked A380s, 4 ultra-long range A340-500s, 4 A340-600s and 12 A330-200s, an astonishing order for a fledgling airline. The airline has also taken options to purchase 12 additional aircraft, the total value of the agreement being in excess of US$7 billion. Deliveries to Etihad are to begin in 2006 for the A330-200s and A340-500s, and in 2007 for the A340-600s and A380s. The A340-500s and -600s will be powered by Rolls-Royce Trent 500s, the A330 and A380 engines have yet to be announced. Etihad will use the aircraft to further develop its route network within the Middle East and to Europe, Asia, India and to North America.

In the air, Etihad's focus is on doing things differently – reinventing the way an airline works, with the emphasis very much on full customer service and satisfaction. On the ground, complimentary passenger transportation, either coach or limousine, depending on ticketing, is available to and from Dubai and Al Ain to Abu Dhabi Airport.

Gulf Air/Gulf Traveller

Gulf Air, national carrier of the UAE, Bahrain and Oman, celebrated 54 years of successful operations in March 2004. The airline's network stretches from Europe to Asia and Australia, covering more than 45 cities in 34 countries. The fleet, comprising 34 aircraft, is one of the most modern in the Middle East.

Following some difficult trading conditions, the airline is in the second year of its three-year recovery plan to move back to profitability, a strategy affecting every level of operations. Efforts are bearing fruit as figures for 2003, released in May 2004, confirm that the airline had its strongest financial results for four years. Based on a 10.4 per cent increase in passenger numbers to 6,047,447, up from 5,478,556 in 2002, Gulf Air experienced a 12.1 per cent increase in revenues from 343 million Bahrain dinars (US$909.8 million) to 384.6 million dinars (US$1020.2 million). It also cut its net losses from 40.7 million dinars (US$108 million) to 19.9 million dinars (US$52.8 million), a 51.1 per cent reduction. As a result the airline exceeded its 'Project Falcon' turnaround target of halving its losses. The airline has forecast revenues of 500 million dinars in 2004 with a passenger growth of one million, on target with the three-year recovery plan.

This revival of fortunes was underpinned by a series of marketing initiatives, including sponsorship of the Bahrain Grand Prix, more competitive pricing, network and service improvements, and the launch of its subsidiary Gulf Traveller.

In recognition of its efforts, Gulf Air was named winner of the Excellence in Quality Improvement category of the 2004 Skytrax Airline Excellence Awards, the world's largest survey of passenger attitudes towards airlines. Skytrax made the award to Gulf Air in recognition of 'the dramatic changes that have been achieved in the last two years, and the manner with which Gulf Air is now re-establishing as a force across the Middle East.'

Gulf Traveller, the full service, economy subsidiary of Gulf Air (not to be confused with the 'budget, no frills' airlines that operate in the American and European markets) celebrated its successful inaugural year on 1 June 2004. With average loads in excess of 70 per cent, Gulf Traveller has achieved much better results than expected. The airline serves key destinations in Saudi Arabia, the Indian subcontinent and Asia, including exotic leisure destinations like Nepal, Sri Lanka and India. Since its establishment in June 2003, the division has contributed significantly to Gulf Air's strengthened financial position and strong performance.

Emirates

Emirates airline is the world's fastest-growing intercontinental airline, one of the world's five most profitable and among the 20 largest. Emirates, operating from Dubai Airport since 1985, has experienced rapid and consistent growth, on average over 20 per cent a year, and has been profitable for the last 17 years. Emirates carried 10.4 million passengers in the 2003/04 financial year – almost two million more than the year before – and declared a record Dh1.574 billion (US$429 million) profit, an increase of 73.5 per cent over the previous year, on revenues of Dh13.2 billion (US$3.6 billion) – nearly $1 billion more, or 37 per cent better, than the year before.

Emirates' 69-strong, wide-bodied fleet includes five Boeing B747 freighters, and is among the youngest in the skies with an average age of 46 months. The airline plans to increase its fleet to 169 by 2012, having announced the largest order in commercial aviation history at the 2003 Paris Air Show, where it ordered 71 new Airbus and Boeing aircraft worth US$19 billion. Emirates also placed orders for four additional Boeing 777-300ER (extended range) aircraft with nine options at the 2004 Farnborough Air Show.

The airline was the launch carrier for the new ultra long-haul A340-500, which started service on 1 December 2003 on the Sydney route. It was also the first airline to order the revolutionary A380 double-decker in 2001 and will be the main launch carrier for the innovative A340-600 HGW. With 45 A380-800s on order, which it will start receiving in 2006, Emirates is the largest customer of the Airbus super-jumbo. In addition, by late 2007 Emirates will have a total of 51 Boeing 777s, giving it one of the world's largest 777 fleets.

Emirates operates services to 78 cities in 54 countries in Europe, North America, the Middle East, Africa, the Indian subcontinent and Asia-Pacific. Since January 2004 it has begun services to Lagos, Accra, Glasgow, Shanghai, Vienna, New York and Christchurch. To commemorate its new service to New York, its first North American destination, Emirates pieced together a gigantic graphic of the Statue of Liberty on Dubai's 21st Century Tower. Specially built for Emirates, the tower is home to a large number of the airline's staff. The mammoth graphic is 53-storeys and 180 metres in height, 47 metres higher than the original monument, including the pedestal, and 94 metres taller than the statue itself.

Emirates launched its new global electronic ticketing system in May 2004, introducing coupon-free travel and enabling passengers to book and fly at very short notice.

Emirates SkyCargo, the Dubai-based cargo division of Emirates airline, moved more than 660,000 tonnes of freight in 2003–04, an increase of 26 per cent over the previous year, while the division's revenue grew by 42 per cent to Dh2.4 billion (US$653 million), accounting for a record 20 per cent of the airline's operating revenue.

In 2004, Emirates SkyCargo won the award for Best Cargo Airline to the Middle East, for the sixteenth time in a row, and Best Cargo Airline to the subcontinent, for the sixth consecutive time, at the Cargo Airline of the Year Awards held in London. It also won the Air Cargo Carrier of the Year prize at the IFW (*International Freighting Weekly*) Awards held in London in June. Overall Emirates has received more than 250 international awards since its inception.

Emirates also operates a flight training academy (ECFT) in conjunction with the Canadian company CAE, following a Dh477 million (US$130 million) partnership formed in July 2001. ECFT was the first training facility outside the US and Europe to be certified by both the US Federal Aviation Administration and the European Joint Aviation Authority.

Air Arabia

Air Arabia, the Sharjah-government owned airline which bills itself as the Middle East's first low-cost service, commenced operations in October 2003. The airline carried over 160,000 passengers in its first six months. Presently, Air Arabia operates 56 flights a week to 13 destinations in ten countries within the Middle

East and the Indian subcontinent. To cater for continuing expansion of services, Air Arabia's fleet of four A320 aircraft will be augmented by a fifth in 2005. The airline plans to have a fleet of 20 aircraft by 2010.

The budget carrier, which is modelled after leading American and European ticketless, low-cost airlines, operates an online booking service on their website www.airarabia.com, and it has travel shops at centres throughout the Emirates. The airline also provides coach connections to Dubai, Al Ain and Abu Dhabi.

Royal Jet

Just one year after its successful launch on 11 May 2003, Royal Jet, the UAE-based luxury air charter service, purchased two Bombardier Challenger 300 (CL300) super midsize business aircraft and has placed options for two more. It currently operates a fleet of four aircraft, which includes two luxurious Boeing Business Jets, and two Gulfstream G300s, the latest version of the popular G300. Royal Jet's four aircraft fly an average of 100 hours a month to a wide variety of locations.

The new service is already winning accolades such as the UK Institute of Transport Management's 'One to Watch' award (2003–2004) given to new start-up companies that show a significant potential success rate.

Another division of Royal Jet, the Royal Med service, attracts passengers who wish to travel for medical assistance. The Royal Med air ambulance, a dedicated aircraft equipped with state-of the-art medical equipment, was launched in 2003. Royal Med now accounts for almost 45 per cent of Royal Jet business.

Horizon

The first 38 students from the UAE Armed Forces and UAE Interior Ministry graduated from Horizon International Flight Academy in Al Ain in September 2004 as licensed helicopter pilots. The students have completed their UAE General Civil Aviation Authority (GCAA) Commercial Pilot's Licence (CPL) to a standard equivalent to the European Joint Aviation Authority (JAA) standard, which is internationally recognised. Horizon IFA started commercial operations in September 2003.

The Abu Dhabi government-owned Mubadala Development Company (MDC) set up the flight academy to provide world-class helicopter pilot training in the United Arab Emirates. The academy, located at Al Ain International Airport, is currently operating ten Augusta Bell 206-BIII helicopters, and is employing experienced ground and flying instructors from the UK, Australia, New Zealand and South Africa. More staff are being hired to meet demand for pilot training from UAE and regional customers.

Abu Dhabi Aviation

Established in March 1976, Abu Dhabi Aviation, the largest commercial helicopter operator in the region, currently has a fleet of over 40 aircraft – mostly Bell helicopters. In November 2000, the company moved to a 8500-square-metre purpose-built facility at Abu Dhabi International Airport. The bulk of the company's business is in support of Abu Dhabi offshore oil, engineering and construction companies. Abu Dhabi Aviation's specialist skills include such diverse activities as the provision of offshore rescue services and the aerial application of agricultural sprays and fertilisers. The company has expanded its operations in recent years to other countries, including Oman, Yemen, Saudi Arabia, Spain and Iran.

Abu Dhabi Aviation posted a net profit of Dh52.13 million (US$14.2 million) for 2003, an increase of 8.6 per cent over Dh48 million (US$13.07 million) for the previous year. It also announced earnings per share of Dh3.34 for the year, a cash dividend distribution of Dh15.6 million and bonus shares of Dh31.2 million for 2003. Total assets stood at Dh878.72 million, up from Dh735.41 million in 2002.

GAMCO

The Abu Dhabi-based Gulf Aircraft Maintenance Company (GAMCO) commenced operations in 1987 to service Gulf Air, but has since then expanded its customer base to encompass other international airlines and military clients. GAMCO has the maintenance capacity to maintain almost all types of Lockheed and Airbus aircraft and it is equipped to maintain Boeing 737s, 757s and 767s. Moreover, it plans to develop a full maintenance capability for Boeing 747s in 2004.

Growing air traffic in the region has encouraged GAMCO in its plans to double its maintenance capacity in the next five years from nine lines to about 15. While the global aircraft maintenance industry is expected to grow by around 3 per cent in 2004, GAMCO estimates its business will grow by 7 per cent.

Early in 2004 GAMCO's industrial business division announced the signing of a Memorandum of Understanding (MoU) with Rolls Royce Energy to establish a joint venture company to repair and overhaul Rolls Royce Trent industrial gas turbines. Under this agreement, GAMCO will be the approved centre for the maintenance of Trent gas turbines for the Middle East region and North Africa. The Industrial Trent turbine utilises the same core engine as its bigger Aero Trent version. This announcement came at the same time as Rolls Royce Industrial Trent engines were selected for Dolphin Energy's processing plant at Qatar's Ras Laffan.

GAMCO has also taken over maintenance operations from Sharjah Airport Authority. Under the new arrangement, GAMCO will handle all the existing airline and new maintenance services at Sharjah Airport.

SEAPORTS AND SHIPPING

Due to its strategic location on the Arabian Gulf, maritime trade has been a feature of the region now known as the UAE for thousands of years. Today, the country is served by 15 commercial ports (including oil terminals) with a total capacity of over 70 million tons, as well as many smaller harbours. The UAE's ports

export oil, raw materials and finished goods worldwide, import goods and raw materials for local industry and consumers, as well as channelling the country's re-export and redistribution trade to other economies around the Gulf, East Africa and the Indian subcontinent. In addition, the UAE ranks among the top five locations in the world for ship supplies and bunkering and is gaining a strong reputation for its ship-repair facilities.

PORTS

Abu Dhabi

The total volume of Abu Dhabi's foreign trade by sea is more than double its volume by air and land combined. The marine terminals of Jebel Dhanna/Ruwais, Umm al-Nar, Das Island, Zirku and Mubarraz islands handle the vast bulk of the UAE's significant crude oil and gas exports. Mina (Port) Zayed in Abu Dhabi City is the emirate's main general cargo port.

Established in 1972, Mina Zayed's facilities occupy a total area of 510 hectares, including 41 hectares dedicated to container terminals that can handle around 15,000 TEUS (20-foot-equivalent-units). Within the port's boundaries are over a million square metres of paved storage yard, over 100,000 square metres of climatically controlled storage sheds and ample cold storage. There are 21 berths for handling general cargo, including bulk cargo, ro-ro, project cargo, reefer cargo and petroleum products. The port has 17 general cargo berths with a total quay length of 3380 metres and a quayside depth varying from 9 metres to 15 metres.

Expansion plans at Mina Zayed envisage the development of the port in two phases over a period of 15 years, ending in 2013. The first phase, to be completed by 2006, includes rebuilding the docks, constructing a new 650-metre long container depot that will virtually double the port's container handling capacity, and increasing the depth of the access channel from 13 metres to 16 metres. The second stage involves construction of four new docks, a fully computerised quality control system and new fuel storage facilities.

Dubai

Dubai's ports at Port Rashid and Hamriyah in Dubai City and Jebel Ali, south of the city, with over 100 berths between them, play a pivotal role in trade in the UAE. In particular, Jebel Ali, which primarily handles bulk cargo and industrial material for Jebel Ali Free Zone, is the largest port in the country and the largest man-made port in the world. Dubai Ports Authority (DPA), managers of Port Rashid, Jebel Ali and Hamriyah, handled 5.15 million TEUs in 2003, a record growth of 23 per cent in comparison with 2002 throughput.

Dubai's ports are constantly being upgraded and expanded to secure the emirate's pre-eminence as a regional trading hub. For instance, the Dh4.2 billion expansion of Jebel Ali port is proceeding to schedule. DPA has completed the development phase at Berth 11 and added 116,000 square metres to the container yard. Around 120,000 square metres was added to berths 22 and 23, and the first phase of development at berths 18, 19 and 21 commenced in September 2004. The reshaped Quay 4 will add 400 metres of quay length with a draft of 17 metres, and 150,000 square metres of additional yard storage area. Work has also taken place on developing and dredging berths dedicated to general cargo and the construction of an empty container storage area which will provide around 246,000 square metres of extra space.

In addition, Dubai has streamlined much of the paperwork involved in import/export. For example, www.DubaiTrade.ae, Dubai Port Authority's online portal, combines all the services of myDPA, e-Mirsal, e-ATA and myJAFZA into a single bilingual portal. The portal handles inquiries and deals with cargo clearance, as well as manifest and cargo handling services. Registered users can view and pay online.

In 2004, DPA won the Best Port in the Middle East title for the tenth consecutive year at the eighteenth cycle of the Asia Shipping and Imports Prizes held in Shanghai. More than 13,000 readers of *Cargo New Asia* voted for the best port title, one of 34 categories.

Sharjah

Sharjah's busy ports, Mina (Port) Khalid in Sharjah City and Khor Fakkan on the East Coast, have a combined total of 17 berths. Port Khalid's original depth was dredged in the early 1980s to deal with deeper draft vessels, and today the berth and quay configuration is designed to accept most types of vessels. The port handles a wide variety of tonnage, ranging from tankers, container vessels, ro-ro ships, to a multitude of smaller vessels such as coasters, supply boats, tugs, barges and crew boats.

Location plays an important role in Port Khalid's development plans for future growth, especially as Sharjah's industrial base has expanded in recent years, encouraged in no small part by the establishment of Sharjah Airport Free Zone and Hamriyah Free Zone.

Sharjah is the only emirate with a port on both coasts. Its East Coast port, Khor Fakkan Container Terminal (KCT), the only natural deepwater port in the region, is a dedicated container port. KCT has a strategic geographical position in the context of today's huge deepsea container trade, being close to the main east-west shipping lanes and outside the sensitive Straits of Hormuz. A modern highway connects KCT with industrial and urban centres on the UAE's Arabian Gulf coast.

Already one of the top container transshipment hub ports in the country, KCT is being massively expanded. The quay has been lengthened by 400 metres to a total length of 1000 metres, a dredging programme has increased the depth alongside to 15 metres, and the ship turning space has been enlarged to take the largest container vessels envisaged. The container stacking area will be increased by 10,000 square metres, providing an extra 60,000 TEUs ground slots, and 50 additional reefer points will be installed. The port's modern fleet of ancillary equipment is also being enlarged. The new facility will bring the potential annual throughput at Khor Fakkan to over 2 million TEUs and will ensure a suitable berth for the next generation of container ships due to appear in 2005. Facilities at the Inland Container Depot (ICD) are also being developed. Situated between Sharjah and Dubai industrial areas, the depot is expanding its working area to accommodate an eventual 18,000 TEUs on site.

During the first half of 2004 both Sharjah ports recorded traffic increases of 26 per cent and 23 per cent respectively, compared to the same period the previous year. They jointly handled over 1.6 million TEUs in 2003 and are expected by the end of 2004 to record 15 per cent growth.

Ajman

Ajman Port, which also services Ajman Free Zone situated in the port, has eight berths designed to handle both container and general cargo. The port had a depth of 5 metres when it was first built, but this has been dredged to 8 metres. Plans are under way to deepen the port to 10.5 metres, enabling visits by 40,000–50,000 dwt (dead weight tonnage) ships up to 175 metres long. Incoming cargo is stored in large purpose-built warehouses covering an area of 43,200 square metres. There are also special facilities to handle cargoes of chemicals, waste paper and fodder.

The Port Authority has also set up two dry docks to provide maintenance and repair services. One berth is allocated for wooden boats and launches. Maintenance services are provided by firms such as Arab Heavy Industries Company, experts in the field of structural steel fabrication, tank and ship building and marine services.

Umm al-Qaiwain and Ra's al-Khaimah

Umm al-Qaiwain is well served by Ahmed bin Rashid Port and Ra's al-Khaimah by Port Saqr. The latter is located in the Khor Khuwair industrial area 25 kilometres north of Ra's al-Khaimah City. Cement, marble and gravel from the nearby quarries and factories are shipped from the port. In 2004, Ra's al-Khaimah awarded Kuwaiti firm KGL a US$45 million contract to build, operate and manage its container terminal at Port Saqr for the next 21 years. The contract involves investment of Dh55.05 million to build berths 8 and 9, Dh14.68 million to reconstruct berths 1, 2 and 3 and Dh11.01 million to build facilities for the port. Another Dh84.41 million will be spent on equipment.

Fujairah

The number of ships calling at Fujairah Port on the East Coast was down from 1957 in 2002 to 1476 in 2003, although bulk cargo tonnage was up from 6.1

million tons in 2002 to 7.7 million tons in 2003. The port handled around 7.9 million tonnes of oil in 2003, much of it in the form of bunker fuel supplied through the VOPAK terminal and storage tanks just north of the port. Fujairah Port will commission a new 820-metre terminal in early 2005. This new facility will accommodate two vessels up to 180,000 dwt or a Suezmax tanker. New onshore bunker storage facilities are also being built at the port. ENOC Bunkering (Fujairah) LLC (EBFL), a subsidiary of Emirates National Oil Company (ENOC) Ltd, has contracted an additional 150,000 cubic metres of bunker storage capacity to become operational from January 2005. Fujairah now ranks as the second largest bunkering centre in the world.

SOCIAL DEVELOPMENT

Our concern for human development is essential because it is the pivot of any real progress. No matter how many buildings, facilities, schools and hospitals we build and no matter how many projects and bridges we set up, it will remain a lifeless, material entity incapable of survival. The spirit of all this development is man, it is man who is capable with his mind, resources, art and determination to preserve these achievements and push further.

(Sheikh Zayed)

ISLAM, COUPLED WITH A TRIBAL HERITAGE, form the basis of a stable social structure in the United Arab Emirates, enabling its people to meet the human challenges posed by the unprecedented economic transformation that has taken place over the past 30 or so years. A high standard of education, investment in a sophisticated health service, the development of human resources, the empowerment of women and the provision of social welfare to the less well-off have ensured that the UAE continues to be a tolerant, open, caring society that cherishes its traditional roots.

LABOUR AND SOCIAL AFFAIRS

The UAE places considerable emphasis on human resources development to improve its competitiveness through an efficient workforce, higher productivity, fair working conditions and social security.

POPULATION

The demographic structure of UAE society has been altered considerably by the sharp rise in population since the foundation of the state. The upward trend continued in 2003 when the UAE's population increased by 7.6 per cent to 4.04 million. An increase of 4.7 per cent to 4.23 million is expected by the end of 2004. This rapid growth is attributed to an improvement in life expectancy, a sharp cut in infant mortality and a steady influx of expatriate workers.

Ministry of Planning statistics indicated that just over one million people were under 15 years of age at the end of 2003, a rise of nearly 50,000 in one year. Approximately half of the UAE's population, or about 2.2 million, were between

15 and 40 years of age, while 742,000 were aged between 40 and 60. The rest were over 60. Abu Dhabi remains the most populous emirate, with Dubai in second place, while Ajman recorded the highest growth rate and Ra's al-Khaimah the lowest. The figures also showed that the population remained dominated by males who numbered 2.74 million, in contrast to 1.29 million females.

HUMAN RESOURCES

The figures outlined above show that the UAE has a very young and steadily growing population, many of whom will be entering the labour market in the very near future. At present, the majority of nationals work in a public sector that has reached saturation point and is, therefore, incapable of absorbing the 13,361 nationals that are expected to enter the job market in 2004. These figures are expected to rise to 16,187 in 2006, and 19,610 in 2010. UAE nationals account for only 2 per cent of the total workforce in the private sector, while private sector employment accounts for 52.1 per cent of the jobs in the United Arab Emirates. By 2006, 107,087 secondary school graduates, 47,887 HCT graduates and 22,889 university graduates are expected to be in search of jobs. This is a situation that the Government is anxious to address.

According to the Employment and Human Resource Report 2004, released by the National Human Resource Development and Employment Authority (Tanmia) in March 2004, the UAE is, perhaps, the only country in the world where foreigners dominate the private sector, both as employers and employees. This situation, the report states, is in need of 'serious thinking and careful policy-making that sets targets with a long-term vision'. It stresses that in almost all countries that allow immigration the rule is that foreigners are only allowed to take up jobs when suitably-qualified nationals are not available. This provision is also part of the UAE labour law. However, in a country where foreign workers are the rule, not the exception, implementing the law is not easy.

To begin with, the report suggests that in order for nationals to become active participants in the private sector, effort is necessary by both parties. This requires fundamental changes in attitudes, conditions and environment within the private sector as well as among UAE nationals seeking employment.

A common complaint of private sector employers is that nationals have unrealistic expectations regarding their working conditions and never stay long in their jobs. A survey by Tanmia of nationals employed in the private sector found that indeed most national workers do not remain in private sector jobs for more than five years. Tanmia's research indicated that a third of nationals employed in the private sector had taken up their particular employment not by choice but because it was the only job available. These dissatisfied nationals will obviously be more open to a better offer if it comes their way, and they will

Socioeconomic Development Indicators

Indicator		2001	2002	2003
GDP per Capita (000s US $)		19.9	19.0	19.7
Labour Force Size (000s)	Male	1,795	1,948	2,120
	Female	284	321	365
Unemployed Force as % of Labour Force	Male	2.3	2.4	2.6
	Female	3.2	3.4	3.6
	Total	2.4	2.6	2.7
Females as % of Labour Force		13.7	14.1	14.7
Dependency Ratio (Inactive Population/Labour Force)		1.68	1.65	1.63
Population Density (sq. km)		41.7	44.9	45
Sex Ratio (No. of Males per 100 Females)		208.9	210	212
Crude Birth Rate (per 1000 population)		16.1	15.5	–
Life Expectancy at Birth	Male	73.45	75.66	–
	Female	70.43	74.52	–
	Average	72.59	75.25	–
Infant Mortality Rate (per 1000 Live Births)		8.9	7.9	–
Illiterates as % of Total Population	Male	16.1	16.2	–
	Female	9.2	9.0	–
	Total	13.8	13.9	–

most probably look for a job in the public sector, given the lucrative salary package, rather than seek an alternative position within the private sector itself. As little as 20 per cent seemed to be happy with their current jobs in the private sector, these citing good career opportunities as the reason for their satisfaction.

Tanmia commented on the fact that 74 per cent of nationals surveyed expressed their satisfaction with working in a multi-cultural environment. However, 60 per cent of the respondents were of the opinion that nationals suffered from discrimination in a multi-cultural workplace. In particular, there was a perception that nationals were being denied essential training, and, therefore, the chance to be considered for promotion, by foreign employees who feared for their own jobs should a national become capable of replacing them.

In 2003, Tanmia sought the employment of 6563 job-seekers in the private sector, of whom only 12.6 per cent were successful. In order to rectify this situation, the report recommends strong government intervention simply because there is unequal competition in the job market between national workers and a trained and experienced expatriate workforce. Tanmia, although urging a more aggressive approach towards the private sector than has hitherto been the case, clearly recognises that expatriate workers will continue to play a 'vital role' in the country's economy. Nevertheless, Tanmia feels that 'the growth of the private sector and employment of non-nationals cannot be left unregulated' and that choosing the 'carrot policy' as opposed to the 'stick' will simply not work. Hence, Tanmia proposes the establishment of a 2 per cent quota system for nationals in certain job sectors. It cited the example of the banking sector where the 4 per cent quota stipulation was implemented on an experimental basis. Even though the target has not yet been reached, the number of nationals employed in the banking sector has risen from 11.9 per cent to 23.4 per cent between 1998 and 2003. The targeted numbers, says Tanmia, have not been achieved because a penalty system has not been put in place as yet.

The insurance sector is likely to be the next focus of government attention. A report by the Planning and Follow Up Committee for recruiting nationals in the insurance sector showed that from 1997 to the end of 2002 the number of nationals in that sector rose from 1 per cent to 5 per cent. The government would like to see that figure increase to at least 15 per cent. One reason for the reluctance of nationals to work in the private sector is the unsociable working hours encountered. Under consideration, therefore, is the imposition of an eight-hour shift for the insurance industry to replace the current two-shift regime. Along with a five-day week, this would bring the insurance sector in line with the public sector. Such changes, combined with a minimum range of salary packages to be offered to nationals, are expected to enhance the sector's appeal to the career-oriented young national.

Population by Emirate

Emirate	1975*	1980*	1985*	1995*	2003**
Abu Dhabi	211,812	451,848	566,036	942,463	1,591,000
Dubai	183,187	276,301	370,788	689,420	1,204,000
Sharjah	78,790	159,317	228,317	402,792	636,000
Ajman	16,690	36,100	54,546	121,491	235,000
Umm al-Qaiwain	6,908	12,426	19,285	35,361	62,000
Ra's al-Khaimah	43,845	73,918	96,578	143,334	195,000
Fujairah	16,655	32,189	43,753	76,180	118,000
Total	557,887	1,042,099	1,379,303	2,411,041	4,041,00

* Census Data (Dec.) ** Estimated

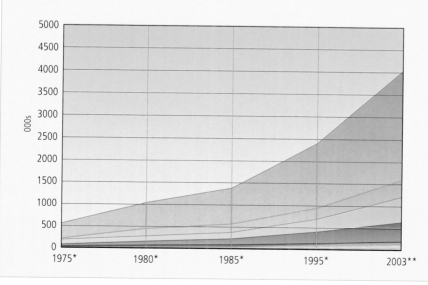

Training is also a key element of a successful emiratisation strategy: a study of skilled labour opportunities for nationals in the private sector by the Centre for Labour Market Research and Information called for increased technical and English language training for nationals, as well as work experience programmes. The training policies of the companies themselves are underdeveloped and worsen with diminishing company size. Fifty per cent of large (over 500 employees), 35 per cent of medium-sized companies (100–499) and 21 per cent of small companies (less than 100) provide regular staff training. Finance companies have the best training record (57 per cent of all firms provide training), while training in education and health is startlingly low, at 15 per cent.

Nationals, on the other hand, in what was one of the key findings of a survey carried out by the Department of Human Resources in Sharjah, have a poor record in matching their qualifications to the demands of the job market, while those who do have relevant degrees are deficient in professional skills and job-oriented training. Tanmia provides pre-employment training for its job-seekers – its statistics indicate that the average cost of pre-employment training offered to its 13,000 registered job seekers (as of the end of 2003) is estimated to be between Dh10,000 and Dh40,000. But it also sought an active role by the country's educational system in assisting nationals to qualify for work in the private sector. 'The country requires a revolution in school curricula. A strong science orientation should be inculcated from the early stages of schooling.' In other words, it seeks a curriculum that is oriented to the job market, keeping in mind that more and more job openings are coming up in the private sector.

NATIONAL IDENTITY CARDS

The Ministry of Interior will start issuing National Identity Cards to UAE nationals and expatriates from 1 December 2004. This will integrate labour and health cards, citizenship documents and driving licences in one card. It can also be used as a travel document for travel in GCC countries. The Ministry is currently setting up a central database to monitor changes in the UAE's demographic structure and to facilitate the project, which is part of the e-government initiative launched on 1 July 2003.

SOCIAL WELFARE

Despite the UAE's economic success, there are, inevitably, individuals who are not in a position to benefit directly from the country's good fortune. Therefore, a welfare system has been put in place to assist those burdened by intractable problems and to help the vulnerable to realise their full potential as productive members of society. In July 1999, the Federal National Council approved new legislation regulating social security benefits. Under the law, those entitled to monthly social benefits include widowed national and divorced women, the disabled and the handicapped, the aged, orphans, single daughters, married students, relatives of jailed dependants, estranged wives and insolvents. Also eligible for social security benefits are widowed and divorced national women previously married to foreigners and the expatriate husbands of UAE women. In 2003, approximately Dh660 million (US$179 million) was distributed among 77,000 beneficiaries of social welfare in the UAE – the elderly accounting for the largest group of recipients (12,000), followed by divorcees (5000). While the number of those receiving assistance has dropped between 1980 and 2003 from 83,076 to the current 77,000, the cost to the government has risen by 16 per cent per head. Sums for social security entitlements amount to between 1 per cent and 2 per cent of GDP.

The Social Security Department at the Ministry of Labour and Social Affairs plans to reduce the number of social welfare recipients by 1800 through assisting suitable recipients to find jobs or to set up small businesses and is inviting charitable and social organisations to contribute to the funding of this innovative project.

The Ministry of Labour and Social Affairs also disbursed a total of Dh1.9 million in domestic relief aid during 2003 compared to about Dh 2.6 million in 2002. The bulk of assistance, about Dh1.567 million or 80.1 per cent of the total, went to victims of fires, followed by boat capsizing incidents at Dh310,194 or 8.58 per cent and other catastrophes at Dh 78,625.

Housing

The rapid rise in population coupled with the demands of modern living has necessitated government intervention at federal level to ensure that the housing needs of nationals are met throughout the Federation. Programmes include the free distribution of houses and land to UAE citizens. Applications for housing are expected to rise to an estimated 33,000 by the year 2005. In 2004, Dh640 million was allocated to the Sheikh Zayed Housing Project to facilitate the process. Islamic banks also offer funding for those nationals with government housing grants and loans who seek Islamic financing to supplement the money that they have available to build their homes.

Social Welfare Associations

Non-government social welfare associations (of which there are more than 100) also assist those in need in the UAE. The UAE Red Crescent Society is prominent among the many charitable organisations that help the needy, covering such areas as medical aid, student sponsorship, disability, special care, health care programmes, prisoner care and lump sum aid programmes. (See Foreign Aid for an account of the Red Crescent Society's work outside the country.)

The Sheikh Zayed bin Sultan Al Nahyan Charitable and Humanitarian Foundation finances projects with precise objectives to benefit large communities both within the UAE and overseas. It does not distribute financial resources to individuals or groups. Within the UAE the charity has spent more than Dh120 million on major projects and about Dh57 million in contributions.

In 2004, the Abu Dhabi-based Zayed Higher Foundation for Humanitarian Welfare of Special Needy People and Minors in Abu Dhabi was formed. Bodies under its auspices include the Authority for Social Welfare and Minors' Affairs, Zayed House for Comprehensive Welfare, Abu Dhabi Elderly Welfare Centre, Centre for Rehabilitation of Special Needy People, and Al Ain Centre and Club for Handicapped.

Eighty per cent of the Mohammed bin Rashid Al Maktoum Charitable and Humanitarian Foundation's budget of Dh25 million in 2003 was allocated to projects within the UAE. The Foundation's domestic programmes concentrate on education, medical treatment, monthly or one-time assistance, food coupons, training courses and housing.

The Bait Al Khair Charity Society, established in 1989, was recently awarded ISO 9001:2000 certification, thereby becoming only the second charitable and humanitarian society to receive this award in the Middle East, the first being the Zayed Charitable Foundation. The Society provides assistance to poor students and emergency aid to those who have been hit by catastrophes. It also works with other charity organisations to ensure that the needy get the best of help.

Other organisations include the women's associations in each emirate, charity associations in Sharjah and Fujairah and Dubai, Ajman Care Society, Sharjah City for Humanitarian Services, the Handicapped Guardians Association and Taryam Omran Establishment for Cultural and Humanitarian Services.

EDUCATION

The UAE invests heavily in education, believing it to be the key to future prosperity in an increasingly globalised economy. Government expenditure on education increased from Dh247 million (US$67.3 million) in 1994 to Dh5.38 billion (US$1.465 billion) in 2003. This increase was due to a large extent to the rising population, with a consequent demand for more educational institutions.

The UAE's educational strategy is based on encouraging the younger generation to play a full and productive role in social and economic development. Today, free education facilitates access for all citizens at every level of the system.

Guiding the educationalists in their efforts to keep up with a rapidly changing cultural and economic environment is Vision 2020, the Ministry of Education's policy document outlining a strategy for further educational development in the UAE up to the year 2020. Education 2020 is a series of five-year plans, designed

Education

	1999/2000	2000/2001	2001/2002	2002/2003
Schools	1137	1167	1167*	1208
Classrooms	23,829	24,114	24,737	25,630
Teachers	36,707	38,097	34,290	40,278
Students				
Kindergarten	65,835	67,752	70,702	74,811
Primary	272,919	280,182	285,473	266,224
Preparatory	120,621	124,875	128,782	153,009
Secondary	86,302	91,068	95,388	98,021
Special Needs Education	1,751	1,772	1,772*	1,632
Religious and Technical	3,304	3,140	3,316	2,975
Literacy and Adult Education	16,553	18,655	19,855	21,330
Secondary School Completed				
Science	7,241	9,029	9,266	9,730
Arts	9,059	12,596	13,333	15,438
Total	16,300	21,625	22,599	25,168
UAE University Students				
Males	3,626	3,540	4,004	3,737
Females	12,820	12,432	13,238	12,391
Total	16,446	15,972	17,242	16,128
Students of Higher Colleges	9,740	11,477	12,236	14,265
Students of Zayed University	1,613	1,866	2,225	2,245
Colleges of Technology and other Institutions	20,715	22,502	23,302	37,134
Scholarship Students	1,348	1,370	1,396	1,422*
Graduates of Colleges & Higher Education				
Males	2,215	1,790	1,910	3,099
Females	4,921	4,484	4,611	7,826
Total	7,136	6,274	6,521	10,925
Government Expenditure on Education (Dh. mn.)	4,858.8	5,133.6	5,095	5,383

* Estimated

to introduce advanced education techniques and improve innovative skills and the self-learning abilities of students. A Planning, Development and Evaluation Office devises the plans and uses model schools to implement them. The National Centre for the Development of Curriculum and Methodology reviews curricula and developments in educational methodology. All developments take place within the strategy's framework.

PRIMARY AND SECONDARY EDUCATION

Primary and secondary education is provided for all UAE citizens in a four-tier process and is compulsory up to ninth grade. In 2002/2003, there was a total of 595,040 students in 1208 public and private schools staffed by 40,278 teachers. Government schools numbered 744, whilst 290,032 students were enrolled at 464 private schools.

Curriculum Changes

The Ministry of Education and Youth (MoE) is initiating a switch from instruction-oriented education to self-education, along with a programme for student care, covering their social, psychological and career needs. The major challenge facing any system undergoing such a fundamental change is how to re-educate a teaching population that has itself been educated and trained under the old regime. A holistic approach that sees the student rather than the teacher as the centre of the educational process requires a total rearrangement of teaching values and methods. Part of the Vision 2020 strategy is to allow the educational zones more autonomy to pursue their own development projects, within set guidelines. Also scheduled was a switch from class teachers to subject teachers at primary level.

An enhanced curriculum for mathematics and integrated science was introduced at first grade level for the 2003/2004 academic year in all government schools. In view of research carried out by the UAE University's College of Education, the curriculum change is timely. The researchers found that a majority of science students at secondary school level lacked the ability to interpret or transform the information contained in graphs, pointing to a need for a shift from a passive culture of rote learning to an active culture of applied learning.

Emiratisation of teaching staff in government schools is scheduled to reach 90 per cent by 2020, making continuous in-service training all the more imperative. Many studies have shown that one of the main barriers to the employment of UAE nationals is a poor grasp of English, and a drive is on to change this by introducing a new English syllabus in all government schools over the next three years. The course, 'The UAE New Parade' developed by Longman, has already been tested in the Abu Dhabi, Dubai and Fujairah educational zones with encouraging results. One of the advantages of the new curriculum is that teachers who may themselves have weak language skills can benefit from its ongoing training.

Student Website

An important initiative by the MoE in activating the process of self-education has been the setting up of an interactive, bilingual website (www.moeya.ae) for school students. Intended to become an authoritative guide for the different disciplines, it includes educational tours, art festivals, science fairs and talent shows; it is also a meeting place for students, where they can access information in privacy about a wide range of topics from science and sports to student welfare. The website runs interscholastic tournaments and quizzes designed to develop a range of skills and abilities, and it is also a channel through which companies and institutions can reach students. Training courses for teachers will help increase their computer and information skills and the site is updated weekly by coordinator teachers.

Computer Training

In a dynamic move to make its schools 'electronically connected, culturally oriented educational institutions of comprehensive quality and regional impact', the Abu Dhabi Educational Zone has entered into an infotech agreement with the UNESCO-backed ICDL UAE to implement the International Computer Driving Licence (ICDL) programme in all faculties of the zone's schools. By 2008 all faculties under the zone will be required to complete the ICDL certification to verify their computer skills.

Another important computer training initiative, the IT Education Project (ITEP) is part of a larger vision to establish the UAE as a major knowledge-based economy. ITEP will ultimately be introduced throughout the UAE. Providing a high quality, industry-relevant IT education, ITEP complements the Ministry of Education's aim of introducing new means of teaching. The IT Academies in Dubai and Abu Dhabi are the vital administrative heart of the project. They are responsible for teacher training and courseware development, Internet-based anytime, anywhere, adaptive learning, project management and quality assurance for all ITEP initiatives.

Dubai Education Council

The establishment of Dubai Education Council, to be funded through the allocation of 5 per cent of the income from The Palm and Jumeirah Residence projects, is an indication of the emirate's commitment to integrate IT into education as the key to maintaining a successful economy. The Council's board, comprising ten top educational and cultural figures, is entrusted with the task of devising an educational strategy that dovetails with the requirements of UAE society and the IT era.

Scholarships and Awards

The Sheikha Latifa Childhood Creativity Awards, organised by Dubai Women's Association, encourages children to explore their creative side. The competition is open to children of all nationalities in the UAE, but is conducted only in Arabic. It is open for any foundation, organisation or centre in the UAE that cares for children, including those with special needs.

The Sheikh Hamdan bin Rashid Al Maktoum Award for Distinguished Academic Performance rewards high achievers, encourages fresh talent and recognises academic excellence. Certificates of recognition, an excellence cup and a financial prize are awarded in several categories covering students, teachers, school social workers, research, project work, schools, administration and educational districts. More than 2000 have been honoured since the award began. In 2003, a prize fund of over Dh7 million was awarded to 335 UAE nationals holding doctorate, masters and postgraduate degrees from various colleges and universities in the country, in addition to outstanding students in the General Secondary School Certificate (GSSC).

The EDAAD scholarship programme was initiated with the ultimate goal of enhancing national skills and accelerating the overall development of the UAE in the new age. Successful candidates have the opportunity to pursue their undergraduate/graduate studies at distinguished universities worldwide.

HIGHER EDUCATION

Admissions to higher education in the UAE continue to rise. Out of 14,151 eligible students, a record 10,459 registered at tertiary level for the academic year 2004/ 2005. A total of 3874 students were approved for admission to UAE University, 5644 to the Higher Colleges of Technology and 941 to Zayed University (ZU). Female students continue to outnumber their male counterparts in higher education in the UAE, comprising 62 per cent of those seeking further education.

UAE University

The twenty-third batch of graduates, comprising 517 students, emerged in May 2004 from the UAE University (UAEU) in Al Ain. UAEU, established in 1976, has nine colleges and is committed to its role as the leading teaching and research institution in the UAE.

A new Dh65 million activity centre exclusively for the female students, who form an overwhelming majority of the student population at the University, was opened in 2004. The activity centre, part of the 'University Town' development, provides a range of modern facilities, including an Internet cafe, games rooms, banks, clinic, theatres and workshops.

Zayed University

Zayed University (ZU) first opened its doors to students in 1998. Popular from its inception, the all-women university, which has campuses in both Abu Dhabi and Dubai, is no longer big enough to cope with demand. Between now and 2017, student numbers at ZU are expected to increase to 7000 (including male students). A major expansion, to encompass a total area of 711,000 square metres and comprising six colleges, departments and laboratories, has been approved by the Minister of Higher Education and Scientific Research. The Dh370 million construction has begun at the Academic City in Al Ruwayyah, Dubai and an inaugural intake of 2000 students is scheduled for 2005. (Construction of as many as 20 colleges and universities is planned on the 1100-hectare University City site.)

The reason for ZU's success lies partly in innovativeness. Smart Square, located in Dubai Internet City (DIC), is an example of the ZU approach. This cooperative venture between ZU and IBM, which was inaugurated in early 2003, aims to establish a new business partner in the UAE for private and public institutions, to create and enhance their e-business and communication activities. The National Human Resources Development and Employment Authority (Tanmia) has agreed to sponsor a section of the graduate on-the-job training for projects undertaken by Smart Square as part of its policy of equipping nationals with the necessary skills for today's demanding work environment.

In 2004, Smart Square and the Air Force signed an agreement for the provision of training as well as administrative and technological consultancy, in line with the federal administration's e-government policy.

Higher Colleges of Technology
In 1988, a system of colleges offering a more technically-oriented education was devised. The four founding HCTs began the new experiment with an enrolment of 239 students. Today, the HCT is a system of 11 single-sex campuses offering over 75 programmes to more than 15,000 UAE students, and by the end of the 2002/03 academic year over 13,000 graduates had received awards through the HCT. New HCTs are constantly being added to the list. A new Higher College of Technology opened in Fujairah in September 2004, and Dubai Men's College, also an HCT, was the first to open the doors of its elegant Dh115 million new campus to students in September 2004 at the new Dubai Academic City.

Crucial links between the HCT and industry are supplied by the Centre of Excellence for Applied Research and Training (CERT), the commercial arm of the HCT established in 1996. The Centre has created strategic alliances with a number of large multinational organisations to develop a diverse range of business and technology solutions. It offers courses in a variety of fields and provides professional development and lifelong learning opportunities for the UAE, the Gulf region, and – through its online training courses – many other parts of the business world. Already operating two technology parks in Abu Dhabi and Dubai, CERT has also opened offices in Dubai Internet City.

A powerful CERT tool is the relationship that it has built up with international partners such as the CERT Thales Institute (CTI) – a partnership between CERT and Thales Université in Paris, delivering short- and long-term programmes through a corporate university structure based in Abu Dhabi; Abu Dhabi Petroleum University

– a consortium of world-class higher education institutions, including the HCT, Texas A&M University, Heriot-Watt University and the University of Oklahoma, providing educational and professional development opportunities for students preparing to enter the industry or for professionals already employed in the sector; CERT Teachers College (CTC) – a high quality teachers college based on the existing programme at HCT. Programme development is carried out in conjunction with the University of Melbourne and the University of Wollongong.

A non-profit professional association, the Emirates Project Management Association (EPMA), is the result of a liaison between CERT and Abu Dhabi Water and Electricity Authority (ADWEA). The new association, located at the CERT Technology Park in Abu Dhabi, provides accredited training courses, seminars and conferences in project management. The EPMA is affiliated with the leading international certification and accrediting bodies, including International Project Management Association (IPMA) and Project Management Institute (PMI). Dovetailing with the association's formation was the launch of a new Masters degree programme in Project and Programme Management.

Another dynamic approach to encouraging entrepreneurs and technological innovation in the student population is the e-biz challenge. Now in its second year, the challenge invites final year HCT and university students from the UAE and GCC to submit a business plan for an e-business or e-service that would benefit the local community by utilising the latest technology and local resources. In groups of three and assisted by a faculty adviser, 73 teams were registered and 43 teams qualified for the second round of the challenge. First prize in 2004 went to Sharjah HCT women's campus. In second place were students of ZU, whilst third place was awarded to Abu Dhabi Men's College.

Other Institutions

Many excellent private institutions offer a wide range of tertiary-level opportunities. Notable institutions include the American Universities of Sharjah and Dubai, Sharjah University and the Ajman University of Science and Technology. The Ministry of Higher Education and Scientific Research is responsible for the accreditation of institutes and degrees and its website (www.uae.gov.ae/mohe/) provides a comprehensive list of recognised institutes and programmes.

A new Ajman University of Science and Technology (AUST) campus, which will be capable of accommodating between 6500 and 7000 students (it currently has the capacity for 3000), was opened in Fujairah at the beginning of 2003, adding to the campuses that already exist in Ajman, Abu Dhabi and Al Ain.

Two new universities are the British University of Dubai (BUD) in Dubai's Knowledge Village and Abu Dhabi University (ADU) located on two campuses – in Abu Dhabi and Al Ain. The former is the only research-based university in the

region. Offering introductory and foundation courses in its initial phase, BUD plans to commence postgraduate studies at Masters and PhD level in September 2004 in association with the University of Edinburgh. ADU, set to be one of the largest private sector universities in the region, will eventually comprise seven colleges. The first three colleges, Business Administration, Education and Computer Science and IT, opened in September 2003.

Tasked with bringing together a select group of international universities, training centres, e-learning and research and development companies under one roof, Knowledge Village (KV), based at Dubai Internet City, has already managed to attract some of the leading institutions of the world to its site.

The UAE's telecoms operator Etisalat, which also invests heavily in education in the UAE, operates the Etisalat College of Engineering, an independent university-status institution educating the national workforce in telecommunications and related technology. Etisalat has also launched the first phase of the Dh120 million Etisalat University being built at University City, Sharjah.

National Research Foundation

In an increasingly global economy where the transfer of technology is a prerequisite for development, research is no longer a luxury but a necessity requiring funding and a sound infrastructure. Therefore, the proposed establishment of a National Research Foundation should enhance the already burgeoning research initiatives evident at the universities and within the colleges of the HCT. The new centre will also forge stronger links between the leading institutions in the UAE and research organisations worldwide.

Studying Abroad

The number of nationals studying abroad with the support of the Ministry of Higher Education and Scientific Research for the year 2003 was 1322. A technical training project, run by the UAE Armed Forces, has been operating since 1993. Under the scheme, UAE nationals undergo a period of training abroad and more than 1500 students are currently studying at 50 colleges and universities in Britain and Ireland. Other institutions like the Abu Dhabi Investment Authority and ERWDA also provide scholarships for UAE nationals to pursue undergraduate and postgraduate courses overseas.

Online Education

The United Nations Development Programme's (UNDP) academic subject review project has highlighted the UAE as the most advanced e-learning country in the region. The project, which studied 15 universities from the Arab world, is part of the UNDP's programme on enhancement of quality assurance and institutional planning at Arab universities and aims to help countries in the region share e-learning more effectively.

e-TQM (www.etqm.net), the world's first online school of total quality management, is based at Dubai Internet City. Another online venture offering flexible learning opportunities is UK eUniversities Worldwide (UKeU). The British government-backed online educational service, which works in partnership with leading UK universities such as Cambridge University, York University and the Open University, has entered into MoUs with the HCT and CERT to provide a variety of purpose-built, quality assured programmes at undergraduate and postgraduate level for students and those seeking further professional development.

Sharjah Institute of Technology
The new Sharjah Institute of Technology, which was opened in September 2003, provides a route to career development for those who did not complete the school curriculum. It is the first vocational institute in the UAE, aiming to teach vocational and professional skills that will meet the market needs of a wide range of industries. Constructed at a cost of Dh80 million, the Institute is run under the supervision of Sharjah Electricity and Water Authority. Students who have completed their ninth grade are eligible for admission. It is open to both nationals and expatriates.

LITERACY

As well as providing free primary and secondary education to national children, the UAE provides free primary and secondary education in the Arab curriculum for those adults who missed out on education during their childhood. Here, too, females have been showing themselves more motivated than males. Recent Ministry of Planning figures show an illiteracy rate of 9 per cent (of total population) for females compared to 16.2 per cent for males. The UAE leads Arab countries in meeting the goals set by UNESCO's 'Education For All' programme, and it is estimated that the nation will achieve full literacy in less than five years.

WOMEN

The UAE Government is committed to promoting the pivotal role of women in the economic, social and political development of UAE society. Much has been accomplished since the founding of the General Women's Union in 1975, the first cohesive force for the self-empowerment of women in the UAE.

THE GENERAL WOMEN'S UNION

Following the formation in 1972 of the Abu Dhabi Women's Society, similar women's groups were rapidly established in almost every emirate, and today the six societies boast 31 branches between them. The General Women's Union (GWU) (originally the UAE Women's Federation) was established in 1975 under the leadership of Sheikha Fatima bint Mubarak, wife of the UAE President, with the aim of bringing together under one umbrella all the women's societies in the country. The GWU since its inception has brought to the fore many inter-related issues of concern for women, children and the family, and it has been instrumental in introducing handicraft, health education and literacy programmes throughout the UAE. It has also provided vocational training, job placement services, family mediation services and religious education.

As the needs of women have developed, so the range and focus of the GWU's concerns and expertise have evolved. The National Strategy for the Advancement of Women, established in 2002, is a joint initiative between the GWU, UNDP, the United Nations Development Fund for Women (UNIFEM), local government agencies and NGOs. The strategy's purpose is 'to activate the role of women and their positive participation in eight major and significant fields, including education, economy, information, social work, health, legislature and environment, in addition to political and executive fields'. The effect of the strategy is to raise the debate on female participation to a new level with a rhetoric that unapologetically assumes gender equality and focuses on the removal of obstacles to that participation.

The GWU was instrumental in ensuring the establishment of the Higher Council for Maternity and Childhood. The Council is responsible for educating public opinion on matters concerning maternity and childhood and for organising research on these topics. It encourages professional organisations to carry out projects targeting mothers and children's educational, health, cultural and social well-being, and is setting up a comprehensive database dealing with these issues. Another important function for the Council is the creation of training programmes to improve the skills of staff in voluntary agencies and foundations.

The GWU also plays a role in women's affairs at a regional and international level. In July 2004, the establishment of The Sheikha Fatima bint Mubarak Fund for Development of Arab Women was announced during the Regional Arab Women's Forum in Beirut. The forum, which was organised by the United Nations Economic and Social Commission for Western Asia (ESCWA) to discuss the achievements made since the convening of the Beijing conference a decade ago, had earlier awarded a certificate of merit to Sheikha Fatima in recognition of her enormous contribution to women's issues in the Arab world.

WOMEN IN EDUCATION

Enrolment rates in pre-university education provide clear evidence of the improvement in educational opportunities for women. A review of registered students in government and private schools at all levels shows that the number of female students increased from 187,069 in the 1990/1991 academic year to 291,213 in 2002/2003. The percentage of female children in primary schools reached 98.7 per cent in 1995/1996, rising to 100.8 per cent in 2002/2003.

In the secondary sector, the percentage of females at school is higher than that of males. In addition, women constitute over 65 per cent of those continuing on to higher education, and they are outperforming males at every educational level. It is clear from the above that the UAE has provided full educational rights to women. This, in turn, will make it possible for women to exercise their right to participate in the labour market and in the decision-making process.

WOMEN AND EMPLOYMENT

As the UAE Government forges ahead with its policy of emiratisation in an economic climate in which knowledge-dependent sectors are of paramount importance, women are seen as being more and more crucial to its success. However, despite the high levels of education achieved by women in the UAE, the ratio of female to male participation in the workforce remains low. Ministry of Planning figures for 2003 show that out of a total labour force of 2.485 million, women comprise only 14.7 per cent, and the bulk of those work in the public sector. There are several reasons for such low percentage figures. Firstly, the male population (2.74 million) far exceeds the female population (1.29 million); secondly, some companies restrict the numbers of females employed; thirdly, UAE society is patriarchal and the changing of traditional views concerning a woman's place in the family is a slow process; fourthly, although women are well-represented at every educational level, it is no longer enough for women to gain a qualification – it is vital that what women choose to do in tertiary education should be relevant to the needs of the ever more technologically challenging workplace. In addition, many UAE women cease working after marriage and bearing children, partly because of an insufficiency of childcare centres and partly because of the well-founded belief that maternal care is likely to be more beneficial for their children.

Nevertheless, UAE women comprise 41.5 per cent of all employees in education, 34.2 per cent in the health sector and 19.7 per cent in social affairs. Women account for nearly 28 per cent of civil servants in 24 Federal Ministries, while women total 57 per cent of nationals working in the banking and financial services sector (and 39.3 per cent of all women employed in the sector). Role models for women are also multiplying in the UAE. Whether her skills lie in finance, IT, the arts, medicine, engineering, police work or the social sciences, the contemporary UAE woman is assured of finding herself following in the footsteps of pioneering predecessors. The formerly unprecedented is gradually becoming the norm. Female police officers throughout the Emirates are working in all aspects of police work from administration and IT to traffic regulation and prison work. The first women to receive full training in cargo and passenger control have graduated from Dubai Civil Aviation Centre's airport security course. A unit of six female firefighters, initially trained for the Dubai Shopping Festival, are set to become a permanent feature of the Civil Defence. Three women have been appointed to the board of the Dubai Chamber of Commerce and Industry, a national woman is Vice President of Distribution at Dubai Bank, another heads the Social Service at the Primary Heath Centre of the Department of Health and Medical Services and the first national endocrinologist is a woman. Amongst 23 new UAE diplomats sworn in by the Minister of State for Foreign Affairs were eight women.

However, gender inequality remains an issue requiring renewed focus to ensure that individual success stories are no longer exceptional but the norm. In particular, there is a need to conduct increasingly targeted and direct interventions to influence policy-makers and legislators and to encourage skilled groups of capable individuals to lend support to and act as advocates for the strategy.

A key recommendation of the National Strategy for the Advancement of Women was for businesswomen's councils to be attached to each of the Chambers of Commerce and Industry throughout the UAE in order to assist women in business and to provide a link with public policy makers   This has been implemented in the larger emirates.

Abu Dhabi Businesswomen Group (ADBW), a network of business, professional and academic women under the umbrella of the National Businesswomen's Committee (NBC), is implementing three major projects in cooperation with trading and educational partners. One is the education and training of potential female entrepreneurs in collaboration with ZU and the HCT. A second – 'Employment Passport' – provides an opportunity for graduates to gain work experience in companies and businesses run by the members of the ADBW.

Dubai Business Women Council (DBWC) is providing women entrepreneurs in the UAE with assistance from feasibility study to consultancy in all areas, including setting up business to availability of finances, for small and medium ventures.

In 2004, a special floor for business transactions for women was opened at the Abu Dhabi Securities Market (ADSM) with the objective of encouraging UAE national women to participate actively in the business activities at the ADSM. Accordingly, the number of UAE women engaged in transactions at the Market is on the rise.

There is some indication that the business community is gradually sitting up and taking notice of the problems that women face in the workplace. The formation of the Professional Women's Sub Group at Dubai Quality Group to create business and professional awareness among women in the UAE through such means as career advisory meetings and the sharing of best practices is a move in the right direction. So too is the sub group's ongoing efforts to establish a crisis centre for working women.

In addition, in an effort to encourage women entrepreneurs, a new and significant measure of excellence, the Emirates Businesswomen Award (EBA), was created by Shell Dubai and Northern Emirates in association with the Dubai Quality Group.

The award honours outstanding women in the professional and business arena through a stringently devised points system based on five parameters: visionary leadership, future goals, professional achievements, career achievements and contribution to the community.

These are just some of the areas whereby a definitive framework is being established to enable women to participate fully in the workforce.

UNESCO CHAIR

The region's first UNESCO Chair in Communication Technology and Journalism for Women (and the first UNESCO Chair devoted solely to women) was inaugurated at Dubai Women's College (DWC) with the mission of promoting professional education and training for journalists, and having a special interest in enabling women to develop careers in the media throughout the Arab region. DWC hopes to organise an annual Women's Documentary Film Festival, a Women's Journalist of the Year Award, and an international conference on women in the media. Linked as it is with UNESCO, the Chair is envisaged as being an 'international centre of excellence in communication' serving 'as a focal point for a pan-Arab network in the field'.

WOMEN IN POLITICS

The door is open under the terms of the UAE Constitution for women to occupy any post, and the women of the UAE are increasingly playing an important part in political and government affairs.

A symposium on 'Parliamentary Performance of Arab Women: Challenges and Future Outlook', was held under the patronage of Sheikha Fatima in May 2004. The seminar examined obstacles facing representation of women in parliament, and also reviewed the experience of female members of parliaments in other Arab countries. A strategy to support women's engagement in parliament was at the top of the agenda.

In a keynote address to the seminar Sheikha Fatima said that 'What has been achieved by UAE women, notably in education and positive participation in the national development and construction, make us look forward with confidence for their entry into the political scene'. 'We are looking forward to the engagement of women in political life, building on the unstinting support of H.H. President Sheikh Zayed bin Sultan Al Nahyan for women's aspirations,' she added. Sheikha Fatima also referred to Sheikh Zayed's support for women's right to take higher positions in decision-making circles and for full participation in the national development process, which also includes political activity.

'Engagement of women in national action is part and parcel of their basic rights guaranteed by Islamic faith and valuable Arab traditions,' Sheikha Fatima stated. She explained that UAE women had taken up their national responsibility on an equal footing with their fellow men and had made remarkable contributions to national development. She went on to say that strengthening the role of GCC women's movements and organisations with the aim of serving local communities is an important way of improving the participation of women in all aspects of national life, including politics. She added that the seminar's recommendations would constitute an important addition to the agenda of the third Arab women's summit, which will be hosted by the UAE early in 2005.

MARRIAGE FUND

Despite the preponderance of males in the UAE, it was recognised in the early 1990s that growing numbers of UAE women were remaining unmarried. One of the main causes of this problem, which had escalating social consequences, was the high cost of marriage. A dowry system is traditional to the UAE and, as the country's wealth soared, dowry expectations rose with equal rapidity, making marriage unviable for many young men and their families. The price of wedding celebrations themselves had spiralled out of control, a further financial disincentive to any couple contemplating marriage. The Marriage Fund was set up in 1992 to combat the problems experienced by nationals wishing to marry. Marriage halls where mass marriages can take place were built to facilitate more economical ceremonies and the Government launched a campaign calling for a reduction in dowry size. Since then, an upper limit of Dh50,000 has been placed on dowry size, and the prohibition on extravagant weddings can be enforced by legal sanctions: a prison sentence or a Dh500,000 fine for the couples concerned.

Young UAE nationals with limited incomes (Dh16,000 per month) wishing to marry can apply to the Fund for a marriage grant of up to Dh60,000, usually paid in two instalments, and the Fund receives between 4500 and 5000 grant applications every year, up substantially from the initial figure of 2036 in 1993. Many couples are participating in mass weddings organised by the Fund to reduce costs. But the Fund's involvement in the marriage process is not confined solely to financial needs. National couples wishing to obtain the marriage grant will first have to undergo a pre-marriage counselling course. In addition, the Marriage Fund plans to hold dispute resolution courses for couples in trouble, and it has developed a hotline for nationals to help solve marital problems.

HEALTH

World Health Organisation (WHO) statistics show the UAE to be in twenty-seventh place in a major analysis of national healthcare systems in 191 member countries. The parameters used for the survey included the overall health of the population, distribution of health care in the population, responsiveness of the healthcare system, including patient satisfaction, opinions of people belonging to different economic strata about the system and how the services were paid for by the population. The finding reflects the success of the UAE's efforts to provide a world-class health service for its population. Advances in medical science and technology and the increasing cost of medical care have created challenges to consolidate these achievements and optimise their technical efficiency, clinical effectiveness, operational economy and quality in the delivery of care.

HEALTH POLICY

Health policy in the UAE seeks to achieve the following:
- To provide the best standard of sustainable health care at primary and secondary levels.
- To reduce mortality rates in general, and disease and accident rates in particular.
- To control and eliminate infectious and parasitic diseases, especially among children and students.
- Early detection and treatment of chronic diseases.
- To provide necessary care to the elderly and the handicapped.

A major focus of UAE health policy has been on the development of maternity and child health care aimed at reducing prenatal and neonatal mortality rates, still birth rates and infant mortality rates. Significant progress has been achieved by:
- Increasing deliveries in hospitals from 98 per cent to 100 per cent, with an emphasis on continuing health care after delivery.
- Developing and promoting the safe motherhood programme, particularly in relation to ante-natal care, healthy nutrition and physical fitness.
- Vaccinating women against infectious diseases, providing pre-marital counselling, including screening for certain diseases and advice on leading a healthy life.
- Reducing child mortality rate for children under five years of age.
- Increasing vaccination of children to ensure that coverage reaches 98 per cent by 2010.
- Controlling diseases by increasing vaccination against all infectious diseases and developing programmes for endemic diseases.

Indicators relating to child mortality reflect positive achievements in decreasing the rate of mortality for children under five by one third. The target set is a rate of 4.8 children per thousand by the year 2015. The same is true of the infant mortality rate, where the target is 3.8 per thousand live births by 2015.

PUBLIC HOSPITALS

In 1970, the health infrastructure in the UAE was limited to 7 hospitals with 700 beds and 21 health centres. By 2000 the Ministry of Health (MoH) was running 30 public hospitals with a total bed capacity of 4473, of which 22 were general. Two psychiatric hospitals are located in Abu Dhabi and Dubai with 157 and 80 beds respectively, while Abu Dhabi also has a 104-bed hospital dedicated to rehabilitation. There is a 40-bed TB hospital in Al Ain. In addition, a number of other government medical establishments exist, including a police hospital and an army hospital.

The MoH is undertaking a Dh450 million programme to provide new health facilities in the seven emirates. Five hospitals are planned – a psychiatric hospital in Dubai (Dh40 million), an obstetric and paediatric hospital in Sharjah (Dh50 million), and general hospitals in Kalba (Dh90 million) in Umm al-Qaiwain and Ra's al-Khaimah (Dh50 million each). In addition, ten medical centres are being built in Jumeirah, Hor al-Anz, Sharjah, Ajman, Ra's al-Khaimah, Umm al-Qaiwain and Fujairah, costing approximately Dh46 million, and four units and clinics will be added to existing health institutions at a cost of Dh67 million. Two hospitals, Rashid and Dubai, are to be enlarged, and construction of the region's first Trauma Centre has commenced adjacent to Rashid Hospital. Staff have already undergone the specialised training required for the running of such a unit.

A new state-of-the-art general hospital, Al Rahba, opened in Abu Dhabi as part of the General Health Authority for the Health Services (GHAS) strategy to upgrade health services in the capital and its outlying areas. The hospital, which has 84 beds (to be increased to 143) and offers a special trauma unit for coping with accident victims, includes as part of its remit the provision of a homecare and home follow-up service, the first of its kind in the UAE. The MoH is also to invest Dh4 million in upgrading research facilities and training medical staff in various medical fields at its government hospitals and medical centres.

The UAE provides a high level of specialised health care at its facilities, including open heart surgery and organ transplantation. In addition, cardiac catheterisation and renal dialysis are available in Abu Dhabi and elsewhere in the Emirates. Comprehensive diagnostic and therapeutic radiological facilities, along with surgical treatment, are offered at oncology departments in Tawam Hospital in Al Ain and Al Mafraq Hospital in Abu Dhabi. Gastrointestinal, renal and ENT units are also available in many general hospitals.

THE PRIVATE SECTOR

The private sector has developed in recent years to become an important partner in providing comprehensive health care to the people of the UAE. It is now contributing effectively to curative, preventive and health awareness services through hospitals, polyclinics, diagnostic and medical centres. Although most of these institutions are found in urban areas, they play a significant role in health provision, which reduces the burden on the government facilities.

As part of its policy to encourage the involvement of the private sector in health care, the MoH has approved the construction of five new private hospitals to be built throughout the UAE (two apiece in Abu Dhabi and Sharjah and one in Al

Ain). Belhoul Apollo Hospital, estimated to have cost Dh120 million and offering advanced tertiary care, was opened in January 2003. The 60-bed complex is part of the Apollo Hospitals Group, the largest corporate hospital chain in Asia and India. In Sharjah, the 160-bed Royal Hospital, estimated to cost Dh110 million, promising affordable care and set to be the largest private hospital in the region, will have two sections – one for the general public, the other for VIPs.

A teaching hospital, specialising in the treatment of chronic and incurable diseases, is to be built adjacent to Dubai Medical College for Girls. The hospital will have three sections – alternative medicine, modern medicine and medical research.

DUBAI HEALTHCARE CITY

Scheduled for completion in 2010, but likely to be finished sooner, Dubai Healthcare City (DHCC) is being built on the 380,000-square-metres former site of the Global Village, in the vicinity of existing hospitals, Al Wasl, Rashid, the American Hospital and Welcare. DHC will have a 300-bed university hospital, medical college (an initial intake of 50 students is planned for 2004), a nursing school for 300 students, a life sciences research centre, 40 fully equipped, ready-to-go clinics (to be offered on both leasehold and freehold terms) and specialised laboratories. The first four buildings in the initial phase will be inaugurated on 15 December 2004.

Such has been the degree of interest in the enterprise that a further site of 929,000 square metres has been proposed to allow for the expansion. Key to the success of the development is the agreement between DHCC and Harvard Medical School to form a joint venture in medical education and training, quality assurance, knowledge management, research and strategic planning. The Harvard Postgraduate Medical Education Programme will start in 2005, initially covering cardiology, oncology, orthopaedics and gastroenterology, while continuing education programmes are expected to begin before the first phase of construction has been completed. In a separate development, the Mayo Clinic has entered into a strategic partnership with DHCC to open a clinic in the complex. Physicians from the Mayo Clinic will provide medical care on site and the partnership will include cooperation in medical care, professional consultancy and research.

PRIMARY HEALTH CARE

Central to the government's strategy of bringing health care to the people are the 115 Primary Healthcare Centres (PHCs). In addition to basic medical care, these health centres provide dental, maternal and child care. The large numbers attending the centres reflect clearly the extent to which the services are utilised.

The MoH School Health Department provides curative, preventive and health awareness services, in addition to supervising the school environment and the nutritional needs of students. The department has created a clinic in every school under the supervision of a nurse, and a physician is allocated for every 3 clinics.

DENTAL HEALTH

Government dental services are provided on three levels: comprehensive dental and oral health at 72 units located in PHC centres and school health clinics; specialised dental services in eight dental centres; specialised hospital dental services. The MoH Dental Department is giving priority to early detection of dental problems, such as prevention of caries by fluoridation, and early detection and treatment of gingivitis. These programmes are implemented through coordinated activities with the Departments of Maternal and Child Health and School Health. Other areas of focus are continuing training, the establishment of standards for dental service performance, in addition to the establishment of specialised centres for facio-maxillary service. There is also a thriving private dentistry sector.

HEALTH EDUCATION

The Ministry of Health has paid particular attention to health education as an effective method for changing unfavourable attitudes and behaviour that negatively influence the health and well-being of individuals and the community at large. To meet this challenge, the Ministry has established a Department of Health Education in the preventive health sector with representation in all medical districts. The Department's responsibility is to develop and implement national plans to raise public awareness. The Department has also organised conferences on cancer prevention, nutrition and chronic diseases, in addition to studies on health topics, including the prevalence of diabetes in the community in collaboration with WHO.

DISEASE CONTROL

In a conservative society like the UAE, AIDS is a rare disease. According to World Health Organisation statistics, the UAE is among countries with the lowest number of reported HIV/AIDS cases in the world. Cultural, social and behavioural Islamic norms have contributed to keeping infection at these very low levels.

The National AIDS Control and Prevention programme, established in 1985, has the ultimate objective of preventing transmission of the disease and the control of its entry into the country, through primary prevention, early detection and effective management.

Prevention is accomplished through early detection and screening, including screening of blood, blood products, organs and tissues before transfusion or transplants and screening of population groups. Budgets have been allocated for testing all expatriates at the time of issuing or of renewing their residence visas. Free treatment is provided to cases, if detected, and the Government provides financial, psychological and social support to patients and their families.

No cases of transmission through blood or blood products provided in UAE facilities have been recorded since 1985, when the AIDS programme was first implemented. This and the very low prevalence of HIV/AIDS in the country indicate the success of the programme. However, as with any programme, it is continually being updated in order to meet the threat that new global patterns of infection may pose to the UAE within the context of the changing social dynamics of the country. The Ministry of Health, in coordination with WHO and the Executive Office of the GCC, is engaged in continuous follow-up of developments in this field.

Thirty-six infectious diseases are included in the control programmes that are jointly organised by the MoH with other relevant ministries and agencies in order to effectively coordinate suitable intervention methods, including vaccination, vector control, health education and chemoprophylaxis. The elimination of polio, measles and neonatal tetanus are examples of the successes achieved in this area.

The Malaria Control Programme has also been successful in eliminating local transmission of the disease. No indigenous cases have been reported in the last few years and it is expected that WHO will declare the UAE free of malaria in the very near future.

The National TB Programme in the UAE was launched as a result of an initiative by WHO in coordination with the Executive Office of the Council of Health Ministers of the GCC countries, taking into consideration the epidemiological factors of the disease and the healthcare system in the country. The death rate resulting from TB decreased from 0.60 per 100,000 population in 1990 to 0.13 in 1995, a reduction of 78.3 per cent. With the re-emergence of the disease worldwide, the death rate increased again in the UAE to reach 0.32 per 100,000 population in 1996 and 0.42 per 100,000 population in 1997. However, due to the country's TB control strategy, including DOTS (Directly Observed Treatment Short Course) and the TB Programme, incidence decreased by 0.1 in 2001 and 2002 consecutively, a reduction of 76.2 per cent since 1997. The incidence rate is expected to decrease to 3 per 100,000 in 2005, the objective being to reduce the incidence rate to less than 1 per 100,000 population by 2010.

BLOOD TRANSFUSION SERVICES

An important factor in the control of disease and the long-term health of the population has been the creation of a state-of-the art blood transfusion service. The UAE ceased the import of blood in 1983 and has relied on local donors ever since. A new mobile blood bank was donated recently to the Blood Transfusion Services by 20 private companies, led by BP. The 40-foot vehicle is being be used to run blood collection campaigns and to provide educational services. The addition of the new bus will greatly expand the capabilities of the existing mobile service.

New laboratories costing Dh15 million were also opened at the Blood Transfusion Services Department based in Sharjah. The Department has the capacity to take blood from 20 donors every five minutes – a rate of extraction which can be increased to 40 in an emergency situation – and provides blood to 22 public and private health institutions in the UAE. It collects in the region of 40,000 units in the UAE annually. The Sharjah facility is one of only ten in the world to utilise gamma radiation for blood sterilisation procedures.

Another pioneering technique being used by the UAE Blood Transfusion Services in Sharjah is the extraction of blood cells from umbilical cords for use in the treatment of patients with leukaemia and thalassemia. Plans are in place to open a cord blood bank in 2006, allowing stem cells from the umbilical cord blood to be stored for future use and research. The bank will share the laboratory, serological testing, equipment and technological facilities of the Sharjah Department, thereby saving 70 per cent of the cost. The service will be available to both private and public sector hospitals in the country.

CAUSES OF DEATH

Cardiovascular disease, followed by accidents and injuries, malignancies and congenital anomalies, are the four leading causes of mortality, accounting for more than half of all deaths reported in the UAE.

Cardiovascular disease is responsible for 28 per cent of total deaths, in comparison with 48 per cent in the industrialised world. The difference in the mortality pattern is attributed to a relatively younger population profile in the UAE. The age-standardised mortality rate of cardiovascular disease in the UAE is estimated to be 82 per 100,000 population per year, compared with age-adjusted mortality of 99 per 100,000 population in the developed world.

The incidence of coronary artery disease in the UAE is estimated to be 3.2 per 100,000, as against 8 per 100,000 in industrialised countries; this variation is also attributable to the UAE's demographic character.

Accidents and injuries constitute the second largest cause of death, accounting for the highest rates of 'Years of of Potential Life Lost (YPLL)', since 60 per cent of YPLL is attributed to fatal traffic accidents among young males between the ages of 15 and 44.

Cancer cases among UAE nationals are estimated at 50 per 100,000 per year, compared with 350 per 100,000 per year in developed countries. These estimates, which are based on the cancer registry in Tawam Hospital, are similar for both genders. The variation in the incidence of neoplastic disease is also attributed to the country's demographic character.

Cancer of the bladder, lung, colorectal region, oesophagus and non-Hodgkin's lymphoma are the five most common forms of cancer reported among males. For females, the five most common types of cancer are breast cancer, cervical, colorectal, non-Hodgkin's lymphoma and acute leukaemia. Breast cancer accounted for 23 per cent of all female cancer cases and 11 per cent of overall registered cancer cases.

A comprehensive plan to reduce the cancer death rate in the country by 40 per cent by the year 2020 and improve curative and survival rates of detected cases by 2010 is in operation The UAE established a Cancer Control and Prevention Department in the early 1980s. This was developed in 1997 into a National Cancer Programme that included a National Cancer Committee. The National Registry of cancer cases will also enhance efforts to assess attributable risk factors and establish trends of morbidity and mortality with special emphasis on indicators pertaining to age, gender, site and geography.

NURSING

The number of nurses in the Ministry of Health has increased from 1902 in 1977 to 6423 in 2000. However, the nursing profession is one area in which UAE nationals are under-represented. Although five new nursing schools have been opened, only a quarter of those enrolled are local women. The UAE's first nursing association, Emirates Nursing Association, has been formed in an attempt to rectify the situation. Nursing salary scales are under review and the profession's first nursing journal, *Abu Dhabi Nurse,* was launched in 2003 by the Abu Dhabi General Authority for Health Services (GAHS).

The UAE was one of 50 countries, and the first in the WHO East Mediterranean Region, to participate in a 'Leadership for Change' programme organised by WHO and the Geneva-based International Council of Nurses (ICN) in cooperation with the UAE's Federal Department of Nursing. The series of workshops is developing the leadership and management skills of nurses and other healthcare professionals.

HEALTH INSURANCE

Since it is generally recognised that free health care cannot continue for all nationals if the country is to keep up its high standards of care, a national health insurance authority has been proposed for the largely public healthcare system to offset the costs of health spending for federal and local authorities.

The insurance scheme (being devised with advice from experts from WHO), which will apply to all residents, regardless of age, nationality or gender, will be managed by the authority acting in coordination with the MoH, and the authority will buy services from public and private health facilities with insurance companies acting as agents for both sides. Premiums will vary, depending on the level of service for which the consumer requires insurance.

ALTERNATIVE MEDICINE

A Federal Law was passed in 1995 to regulate the sale and use of herbal medicines. But with the rapid increase in popularity of herbal remedies in the UAE (the total number of imported herbal medicines increased four-fold between 2000 and

2001, with nationals 17 times more likely to avail of herbal treatments than non-nationals), comprehensive regulation in the field of alternative medicine and the establishment of regional harmonisation of regulations and standards is of prime importance. The MoH has set up an Office of Complementary and Alternative Medicine (OCAM) with two committees – one to draw up rules and conditions governing the licensing of complementary and alternative practitioners, the other to evaluate alternative medicine degrees. Under new regulations, herbal mixtures being sold at herbal medical centres must be prescribed by doctors and registered by the MoH. Pharmacists and assistant pharmacists working in such centres must be licensed to practice by the Ministry.

The Zayed Complex for Herbal Research and Traditional Medicine was created in 1996 and, as well as conducting research on herbs and plants (many of which occur in the UAE), it treats patients suffering from chronic illnesses. In recognition of its success in producing, on a small scale, internationally standardised herbal medicines for the treatment of chronic diseases such as diabetes, hypertension, joint inflammation, and ulcers, WHO named the complex as a regional centre for alternative medicine in the Middle East.

CULTURE AND INFORMATION

CULTURE AND HERITAGE

. . . a people that does not understand its past, and does not draw the correct lessons from it, will not be able to deal with the challenges of the present and the future.

(Sheikh Zayed)

A PROFOUND TRANSFORMATION HAS TAKEN PLACE in UAE society since the formation of the state; today, the cosmopolitan nature of the country is evident at every level. Nevertheless, constants remain, including a renewed appreciation of the culture and traditions of forefathers who capitalised on the limited resources that were available to them. The UAE seeks to guard this precious heritage while laying a base on which to build enduring prosperity. Fortunately, the potential for irreparable cultural loss in the maelstrom of progress was recognised and measures have been taken to conserve and reinvigorate. Consequently, the UAE has managed to preserve many of its unique archaeological and architectural sites, its manuscripts, its literature and its customs, whilst aspects of life which had disappeared have been faithfully reconstructed, through museum displays, the creation of heritage villages, and the rebuilding of vanished monuments from photographs, local memory and documentary evidence. At the same time, the Government continues to encourage its citizens to appreciate the cultural values of other nations.

Playing a central role in guarding the nation's heritage and helping to stimulate cultural awareness are many cultural organisations. Prominent among these are the Cultural Foundation and the Emirates Heritage Club in Abu Dhabi, The Zayed Centre for Heritage and History (a subsidiary of the Emirates Heritage Club) in Al Ain, the newly-established Dubai Cultural Council, the Cultural and Scientific Forum in Dubai, the Department of Culture and Information in Sharjah, the Fujairah Cultural Organisation, the Studies and Archives Centre in Ra's al-Khaimah and the Juma Al Majid Centre for Culture and Heritage, also in Dubai. Other institutions of importance to the cultural well-being of the country include the National Heritage Revival Organisation and the Marriage Fund, while there are also numerous non-governmental organisations that are devoted to promoting cultural activities among the various expatriate communities.

CULTURAL FOUNDATION

Situated in the centre of Abu Dhabi, the Cultural Foundation is at the heart of the capital's cultural life, being used by young and old, UAE citizens and expatriates alike. Surrounded by gardens and with an open courtyard with fountains, the main building is a dramatic white structure of arches and colonnades, within which are lecture halls, libraries and meeting rooms, as well as ample space on its three floors for displays and exhibitions.

Perhaps the most important part of the Foundation is the National Library, which has well over a million books, most in Arabic, although there are also collections in a variety of foreign languages. Most of these are available for consultation by the public, after carrying out a simple registration process, although some of the rarer items, including a fine collection of Qur'ans, can only be examined with special permission.

A special children's area is particularly popular, while there are a number of special events arranged for children, in particular during the school holidays.

An open area occupies much of the ground floor, this being used on a regular basis for exhibitions, which include displays of old photographs of the Emirates, paintings, handicrafts, archaeological artefacts and a wide range of other items, while there are also rooms on the first floor suitable for smaller events.

Along the corridors are a number of small cases displaying a range of items reflecting the UAE's culture and history. These include postage stamps, coinage used in the country before the UAE was established, silver Bedouin jewellery, small carpets and rugs, highly decorated wooden doors and other items.

The two large theatres are used for a range of cultural activities. These include classical music concerts, some staged by the Abu Dhabi Music Foundation, which brings top artists and orchestras from Europe and elsewhere to Abu Dhabi, film shows, including regular film seasons from individual countries or directors, plays and meetings held by external organisations. The Emirates Natural History Group, the UAE's oldest environmental non-governmental organisation, has held its open meetings in the Cultural Foundation on a twice-monthly basis for over 15 years.

Other voluntary groups also make use of the facilities, including a gardening group and chess enthusiasts, while the Foundation's small and tastefully-designed restaurant has become a popular meeting place.

Next to the building, an open area is used each spring for the Abu Dhabi Book Fair. Staged in a large tented compound, this brings dozens of publishers from the UAE and from the rest of the Arab world, as well as from further afield, to promote their titles at a specially-discounted rate.

The Cultural Foundation occupies a whole city block, and within the surrounding walls, besides the Foundation itself, is the Qasr al-Hosn, (often known as 'the Old Fort' or 'the White Fort.') Founded by Sheikh Shakhbut bin Dhiyab, ruler of Abu

Dhabi, in 1795, this is the oldest building on Abu Dhabi Island, although it has been much enlarged over the last couple of centuries. Residence of the rulers of Abu Dhabi until the 1960s, it served for many years as the home of the Government's Centre for Documentation and Research. Surrounded by palm trees, and with old cannon outside its well-fortified door, the Qasr al-Hosn is now scheduled to become a display and exhibition centre.

EMIRATES HERITAGE CLUB

Established in 1993, Emirates Heritage Club (EHC) has as its core objective the preservation and dissemination of the country's heritage to the young generations who would otherwise be unfamiliar with the customs and traditions of their ancestors. EHC organises heritage exhibitions, oversees heritage centres and collaborates with all other UAE institutions sharing the same interests. However, activities organised by the Club for all age groups not only cover traditional sports such as camel racing, boat racing and falconry and traditional skills like tent-building and coffee-making, but also contemporary sailing, equestrian, shooting and other sports. EHC is instrumental in organising competitive events in these fields as well as youth camps on the island of Al Sammaliah, north-east of Abu Dhabi City.

Heritage research is conducted through its affiliate, the Zayed Centre for Heritage and History in Al Ain (see below) and environmental research through the Committee of Environmental Research (CER) on Al Sammaliah. CER is primarily concerned with coastal biodiversity, conservation and sustainable development of coastal habitats. EHC formed the Amateur Astronomers Group (AAG) in May 1998 to spread astronomy awareness among all categories of society. Another affiliate, Emirates Sailing Academy (ESA-ESS), was set up in July 2000.

THE ZAYED CENTRE FOR HERITAGE AND HISTORY

Officially inaugurated in 1999, EHC affiliate the Zayed Centre for Heritage and History pays special attention to the preservation, documentation and publication of the heritage of the UAE. Realising that with the passing of an elderly generation, a wealth of knowledge concerning music, culture and society will be lost, it set out to gather up the memories of those elderly custodians of much of the country's disappearing traditions. The result of those interviews is *An Introduction to UAE Folklores*. The 343-page book in Arabic (an English version is planned) provides a detailed look into the UAE's culture, traditional life and social institutions.

A dictionary of Arabic dialects spoken in the UAE, comprising thousands of entries, both words and phrases, has been completed by a team of ZCHH language experts over a three-year period. The dialects are rich in historical importance to those researching the past as well as those wishing to preserve the rich diversity of language into the future. Finally, the papers of the first International Conference on

UAE Archaeology have been collected into a major new publication, *Archaeology of the United Arab Emirates*, published in English in 2003 and in Arabic in 2004.

THE EMIRATES CENTRE FOR STRATEGIC STUDIES AND RESEARCH

The ECSSR, founded in 1994, is an independent institution dedicated to the promotion of professional research and educational excellence in the UAE and the Gulf area. ECSSR serves as a focal point for scholarship on political, strategic, military, environmental, economic, and social issues pertinent to the UAE, the Gulf, and the greater Middle East through the sponsorship of research and studies conducted by scholars from around the globe. The core of its work lies in identifying and analysing issues of vital significance, predicting future trends and devising management strategies to cope with such issues. As well as maintaining and training its own staff of researchers, it hosts conferences, symposia, workshops and lecture series renowned for the eminence of the participants and the quality of their content and influence. Integral to the success of ECSSR's research programme are the annual Trend Assessment Reports prepared in the Centre's different units which, by providing a survey of major international and domestic developments and their possible implications, become a powerful tool in the task of prioritising the goals for the following year.

The ECSSR's publishing activities have made it a major source of specialised scholarly publications in the region. As well as publishing monographs in its International Studies Series, it also publishes the proceedings of conferences, symposia and lectures in Emirates Occasional Papers (an English series) and Strategic Studies (an Arabic series). In addition to these publications, ECSSR translates into Arabic works of importance to the Centre and its audience.

Of particular significance in 2004 was the lecture by Lawrence Korb in June on 'The Role of the Gulf Region in the Formation of US National Security Policy'; The ECSSR Tenth Annual Energy Conference entitled 'The Gulf Oil and Gas Sector: Potential and Constraints' held on 26–27 September 2004; and the one hundredth issue of the Strategic Studies Series. ECSSR also participated in the Book Expo America 2004, showcasing its broad range of English books. Recent publications include *Human Resource Development in a Knowledge-based Economy*, *Socio-political Security and Communicable Disease and Nuclear Weapons in South Asia*. Forthcoming publications include *Foreign Direct Investment in the UAE: Determinants and Recommendations and Iraq: Reconstruction and Future Role*.

DUBAI CULTURAL COUNCIL

Promotion of cultural activities in Dubai took a major step forward during 2004, with the formation in March of the Dubai Cultural Council. Chaired by prominent UAE writer Mohammed al-Murr, the DCC was established by a decree issued by HH Sheikh Maktoum bin Rashid Al Maktoum, UAE Vice President, Prime

Minister and Ruler of Dubai. The new Council, whose members will serve three year terms, is charged by its articles of association to be responsible for cultural activities throughout Dubai, and to co-ordinate with the federal Ministry of Information and Culture on the promotion of cultural activities.

JUMA AL MAJID CENTRE FOR CULTURE AND HERITAGE

The National Heritage Section at the Juma Al Majid Centre for Culture and Heritage in Dubai contains a substantial collection of books in both Arabic and English about the heritage of the UAE and the Gulf region and a wealth of historical material including documents from the British, American, Russian and Ottoman archives relating to the Arabian Gulf, dating from the European occupation of the Eastern Coast of Arabia up to the finding of oil. It includes reports by British political agents, letters between American ambassadors in the region and the US State Department, Russian books and letters covering topics that range from piracy to politics to oil. In addition, there are copies of the political, economic and military treaties that were signed between the countries in the past. The Centre's Al Qusais workshop is greatly respected for its expertise in manuscript maintenance, treatment and restoration – it has perfected the production of a special kind of paper for use in such work – and it has signed an agreement with the Library of Alexandria to provide special equipment, restoration paper and technical training for the refurbishment of ancient manuscripts and books.

SHEIKH MOHAMMED CENTRE FOR CULTURAL UNDERSTANDING

The Sheikh Mohammed Centre for Cultural Understanding in Dubai aims to be a catalyst for social cohesion through communication and cultural exchange. Interactive programmes introduce expatriates to local culture, traditions and lifestyles. One of its most attractive amenities is the Home Visit Programme through which expatriates are invited to share a meal with a UAE national family. A TV talkshow, 'Open Doors, Open Minds', and numerous cultural events, lectures and seminars form the nucleus of the Centre's work. As well as organising, in partnership with Dubai 2003, an Open Day for those involved with the Annual Meetings of the Boards of Governors of the World Bank Group and the International Monetary Fund, the Centre treated participants to a taste of authentic Arabian culture and traditions by laying on a major exhibition at the Centre. There, visitors who might otherwise not have had the chance to get a feel for life and tradition in the UAE were able to explore everything from Arabic calligraphy, dates and date products, to Iranian carpets and herbalists at work.

SULTAN AL OWAIS CULTURAL FOUNDATION

Dubai gained a major new cultural landmark in 2003 with the opening of the purpose-built premises of the Sultan Al Owais Cultural Foundation. The ten-storey building is the home of the most valuable cultural prize in the Arab world, the Sultan Al Owais Awards, created in 1988 in memory of a prominent local poet and businessman.

At the 2004 awards the US$600,000 prize money was shared by six leading Arab figures, Hasab Al Sheikh Jaafar, from Iraq, playwright and author Mohammed Khudeir, also from Iraq, Mustapha Abdo Nasif from Egypt, for his literary and critical studies, Mahmoud Ameen Al Alim, also from Egypt, for humanitarian studies, and Ali Ahmed Saeed from Syria and Palestinian poet Mahmoud Darwish, for cultural and scientific achievement.

HERITAGE BUILDINGS AND MUSEUMS

Traditional architecture and historic buildings are an important element of the UAE's history and heritage and great efforts are being made to preserve fragile structures for future generations.

Particularly important to the UAE are its forts, many of which have undergone several transformations, eventually ending up as museums. The renovated White Fort or Old Fort (Qasr al-Hosn) in the centre of Abu Dhabi is the oldest building in the capital. The original structure was built around 1795 as the residence of Abu Dhabi's rulers. Major renovations have taken place over the years, but the elegant fort's whitewashed walls, gardens and courtyard retain an old-world charm.

Al Ain has more than its complement of impressive forts and heritage structures, including The Eastern Fort, located within the compound of Al Ain Museum; Murabba Fort, which used to be the police headquarters and a prison; and Jahili Fort, the latter a large restored fort in the city centre that has a distinctive corner turret with four levels or terraces. Going back much further in time is a superb renovation of an important Umm al-Nar tomb from the third millennium BC at Hili Archaeological Park in Al Ain.

An agreement between UNESCO and Al Ain Economic Development and Tourism Promotion Authority now part of the Abu Dhabi Tourist Authority, has initiated a cooperative effort to protect the cultural and historical wealth of the city. Together, they will form a strategic plan which will incorporate all aspects of Al Ain's rich heritage, both man-made and natural with a view to sustainable development of its assets in harmony with the growing value of cultural tourism.

The restored Al Fahidi Fort in Dubai was originally the ruler's residence; it subsequently became an arsenal, then a jail, and is now a thriving interactive museum with a wide range of archaeological and ethnographic exhibits. The underground section of the museum houses lifelike exhibits of an ancient souq, a Qur'an school, typical Arabic households and an oasis. There is also a display of the desert by night with interesting local wildlife.

One of Dubai's more recent heritage renovations has a new function as the editorial office of an Arabic calligraphy magazine, *Huroof Arabiya*, published by

the Culture and Science Association. The building which was constructed in four stages, from 1921 to the late 1960s, is graced with one of the heritage symbols of the UAE, a windtower. Another restored building in the Al Bastakiya heritage district, this time dating from 1939 and adorned with not one but two windtowers, has been handed over to the World Wide Fund for Nature (WWF) to be used as the UAE Project Office. The damaged windtower of a third building was reconstructed by the Historic Buildings Section of Dubai Municipality with the help of historic documents and pictures. This house is now the home of the Sheikh Mohammed Centre for Cultural Understanding.

These renovations are part of Dubai's plan to restore all remaining historic buildings in the Al Bastakiya area to their former glory. Between 1991 and 2008, the authorities hope to have either renovated or reconstructed a total of 230 structures in Dubai Emirate. The Shindagha Heritage Area alone contains around 65 heritage sites of which five have been reconstructed and three are under construction. Of Al Bastakiya Quarter's 55 heritage sites, approximately 20 were completely renovated by the beginning of 2004. Amongst buildings that have been restored are Sheikh Saeed house – an elegant late nineteenth century two-storey building of Arabic design, complete with four windtowers, housing a unique collection of rare coins, photographs, stamps and documents; Bait Al Wakeel – Dubai's first office building dating back to 1934 and now housing a museum devoted to Dubai's fishing and maritime traditions; Al Ahmadiya School, Dubai's first regular school, established in 1912 and now a museum of education.

Sharjah was designated by UNESCO as Cultural Capital of the Arab World for its commitment to art, culture and the preservation of its heritage in 1998. Instrumental in winning this award was Sharjah's renovation and restoration of architecturally acclaimed heritage buildings and an old souq in the Sharjah Arts Area and Sharjah Heritage Area. Many of these fine buildings house art, Islamic and ethnographic museums, including the country's first national art gallery, and one is also home to The Emirates' Fine Arts Society. Nearby is Sharjah Fort or Al Husn. Built by Sheikh Sultan bin Saqr Al Qasimi in 1820, this carefully renovated fort was the residence of the ruling family for 200 years. It was torn down in 1969, but the present ruler, himself a prominent local historian, has restored it with the help of old photographs and documents, his own notes and the assistance of elderly residents. It now houses a museum with exhibits on pearl fishing, education, and trade, as well as jewellery, weapons and old photographs. Al Mahatah Fort at the old airport site right in the centre of Sharjah houses aviation memorabilia relating to the 1930s, 1940s and 1950s.

The eighteenth century fort in Ajman switched in 1970 from being the ruler's palace and office to housing the local police force. In 1981, it changed function once again to become a museum housing an interesting collection of archaeological artefacts, manuscripts, old weapons and reconstructions of traditional life. Another fort which reinvented itself as a police headquarters was that of Umm al-Qaiwain. Subsequently restored as a museum, its upper floor includes a high-ceilinged *majlis* (a meeting room and a place to receive guests) elegantly decorated with carved wooden balconies.

Situated behind the Police Headquarters on Al Hosn Road in the old town, the beautifully renovated Ra's al-Khaimah Fort, residence of the ruling family until the early 1960s, houses an intriguing collection of archaeological and ethnological artefacts, although plans are being drawn up for the construction of a purpose-built museum. An important series of surveys has been undertaken in Ra's al-Khaimah Emirate over the years, documenting mountain villages, towers, mosques, the old houses of the palm gardens of Al Nakheel and Shimal, and now the traditional buildings of Ra's al-Khaimah City. Archaeologists from the Ra's al-Khaimah National Museum are researching and cataloguing all traditional structures and the more important of them are being earmarked for restoration. Already, the museum has begun restoration of the old souq.

The Emirate of Fujairah also has its fair share of historical building, particularly impressive forts and other defensive structures on the coast and traditional routes through the major wadis. Work by the Department of Archaeology and Heritage on restoration of Fujairah Castle, begun in the late 1990s, was completed in 2000, while many of the adjacent buildings, including walled courtyard-houses once occupied by members of the ruling family, have also been restored. The whole area is to be surrounded by a new wall, within which a number of new buildings will be constricted to act as a focus for the heritage of Fujairah. These new buildings are expected to include a three-storey museum, an amphitheatre, a souq, a mosque, a restaurant and a children's play area.

The Department also completed during 2004 the renovation of another major site at Awhala in southern Fujairah, where a Late Islamic fort sits on top of the foundations of a much larger Iron Age fortress. In late 2004, work also began on restoration of the Late Islamic palace and adjacent buildings in Wadi Hayl, around 13 kilometres west of Fujairah City. Once the residence of a junior branch of the ruling family, this is one of the best-preserved sites of its type in the whole of the UAE.

HERITAGE VILLAGES AND CRAFT CENTRES

The renovated forts and buildings described above give a fascinating glimpse into the lifestyle of the UAE's urban inhabitants before the discovery of oil. However, to fully experience the traditions of urban and rural UAE, including its less permanent settlements, it is necessary to visit one of the many excellent reconstructed heritage villages that have been set up throughout the country. Stepping inside the perimeter of these establishments is like stepping back in time when the pace of life was much slower and the tasks of the day centred around artisanal fishing, animal husbandry and date cultivation. These villages are just as instructive for UAE residents as they are for tourists.

Emirates' Heritage Club has chosen a wonderful location for its Heritage Village on the Breakwater near Marina Mall in Abu Dhabi. In addition to bedouin tents, there are reconstructions of palm (*'arish*) and other houses, old fishing villages and traditional souqs. With its spectacular location along the seafront, maritime traditions are a special feature. Of interest also is the reconstructed bedouin encampment behind Abu Dhabi International Exhibition Centre. Here one can also view a more elaborate mudbrick house and a traditional mosque, shop in a traditional souq, take a camel ride and watch a demonstration of the age-old sport of falconry. Traditional handicrafts from woven fabrics and perfumed oils to basketry and pottery are kept alive at Abu Dhabi's Women's Handicraft Centre next to the Royal Stables and at the Women's Craft Centre on Rashid bin Saeed Al Maktoum Street.

In Dubai the Heritage and Diving Village, next to Sheikh Saeed Al Maktoum's House in Al Shindagha, celebrates the many intrepid divers that harvested pearls from the country's lucrative offshore pearl banks. Hatta, the mountain enclave belonging to Dubai, also has a relatively new heritage village near to the town's nineteenth century fort and watchtower.

Near Fujairah Fort, Fujairah's Heritage Village has a good selection of traditional houses (*'arish*) and fishing boats (*shashah*) made from palm fronds, providing an interesting backdrop to its living reconstruction of traditional life on the East Coast.

SHARJAH – CULTURAL CAPITAL

In addition to the large number of forts and heritage buildings that house museums, the UAE has a rich selection of purpose-built, modern museum buildings dedicated to specific subject areas, such as the discovery of petroleum, archaeology, natural history, science, popular medicine, astronomy, numismatics, philately, Islam, traditional jewellery, policing and aviation.

Sharjah takes pride of place, with, besides the museums mentioned above, a number of other world-class displays, not only of local interest but also dealing more broadly with the cultures and science of the Islamic world. The emirate's ruler, HH Dr Sheikh Sultan bin Mohammed Al Qasimi, has devoted much attention to the promotion of this aspect of Sharjah, which has become, as a result, the unquestioned cultural capital of the country.

Located in Majaz near Sharjah Bridge in the centre of Sharjah, the Planetarium specialises in astronomy and celestial navigation. Sharjah Police Museum at the Police Headquarters in the northern suburb of Maysaloun has a good collection of armaments, riot and combat gear and models of old walls and forts.

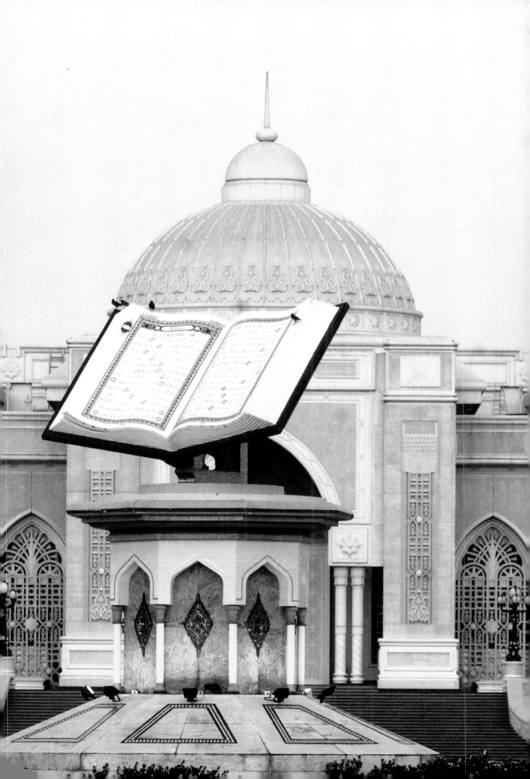

Sited near the very distinctive Cultural (or Qur'an) Roundabout in the northern suburbs, the Archaeological Museum is a modern, lively interactive museum tracing the history of Sharjah from ancient times. A gold halter found with a ritually slaughtered horse in a grave near Mleiha is particularly beautiful. The museum's library houses a range of archaeological and historical books, magazines, periodicals and specialised reports.

Situated in Halwan near Cultural Square, the Science Museum has 50 excellent interactive exhibits covering physics, chemistry, biology and astronomy, whilst the Discovery Centre on the Sharjah–Dhaid Highway opposite the airport, the first interactive 'hands-on' children's museum in the UAE, is a very popular venue.

The grounds of Sharjah Desert Park, 25 kilometres out of town at Junction 8 on the Sharjah–Dhaid Highway, contain the Natural History Museum, a Children's Farm, the Arabian Wildlife Centre and the Breeding Centre for Endangered Arabian Wildlife. The Natural History Museum opened in 1995 and was immediately very popular because of its state-of-the-art exhibits. Lively with light and sound effects as well as interactive video displays, the exhibits deal with local habitats, plant and animal life, geology and marine life. Outside are wildflower gardens as well as formal gardens. The Arabian Wildlife Centre is an impressive modern zoo that displays local wildlife in replicas of their favourite habitats. Most of the displays can be viewed inside an enormous climate-controlled building. Exhibits include a reptile house, a huge aviary with free-flying birds as well as rock-hopping hyrax, a night house with many desert mammals, an 'Ibex Mountain' overlooked by the restaurant, and a corridor with huge windows looking out onto enclosures for hamadryas baboons and large predators such as wolves, cheetahs and the Arabian leopard.

The Breeding Centre is focusing on the breeding of endangered Arabian species with the hope of re-introducing some of the rarer species into the wild. This is where for the first time in the UAE captive breeding of the Arabian leopard was achieved. For obvious reasons, this particular centre is not open to the public.

Over on the East Coast, at Kalba, an enclave of Sharjah, the former house of the local ruling family has been carefully restored, as has a rectangular Islamic fort nearby, while work is also under way on the restoration of a larger fortress at Khor Kalba which may rest on the site of a fort built by the Portuguese in the fifteenth century AD.

Other important displays can be found elsewhere in the country. On Abu Dhabi's Corniche, near Volcano Fountain, the Petroleum Exhibition displays old still photographs, film and interactive features depicting the emirate's oil-fuelled transformation from oasis life to modern, cosmopolitan city. Plans for a completely new exhibition in a purpose-built museum are now being drawn up by companies within the Abu Dhabi National Oil Company (ADNOC) Group, to take account of recent changes in the local oil and gas industry, including technological innovations.

Al Ain Museum, run by the Department of Antiquities and Tourism in Abu Dhabi's Eastern Region, has an extensive archaeological and ethnographical collection, including some spectacular second millennium gold pendants and an important coin collection. Finds from excavations at Umm al-Nar and Qattarah are displayed and the museum also houses a reconstruction of the Great Hili Tomb with its distinctive rock engravings. Reconstructions of a traditional *majlis* and other aspects of life in the pre-oil era are also very interesting. A collection of gifts received by the President from visiting statesmen and royalty is also on display.

Over on the East Coast, Fujairah Museum, south of Fujairah Castle, is a small modern building where many of the artefacts found in archaeological digs at Qidfa, Bithna and other sites in Fujairah are on display.

CULTURAL FESTIVALS

The eighth biennial Gulf Theatrical Festival, back in Abu Dhabi in 2003 after a gap of ten years, was hosted by the Cultural Foundation at the new state-of-the-art 2100-seater Al Raha Theatre, just outside the capital. A fitting venue for many of the plays staged at the Festival, it has a king-size stage with its back wall opening outdoors into an amphitheatre where there is additional seating for 1000.

Twenty-one UAE theatre groups participated in the fourteenth Sharjah Theatre Festival, which was held in 2004. Organised by the Sharjah Culture and Information Department, the event showcased 26 plays for adults and children.

In March 2004, the Emirates Film Competition, an event hosted by the Abu Dhabi Cultural Foundation, screened 170 movies ranging from shorts to documentaries to animation. The competition was divided into two categories – student and professional. The animation section featuring films from around the world included a retrospective on the godfather of animation — Italian Bruno Bozzetto. EFC 2004 also took a look at Iranian cinema and featured Arabic films that would not have been readily available to the public. Films from the well-known Beirut Documentary Film festival were screened as a package, while shorts were picked from the Edinburgh Film Festival. However, the highlight of the festival, as always, was the work produced by local talent.

A feast of films is planned for the first Dubai International Film Festival (DIFF) in December 2004. The inaugural session of the festival will feature 80 films in the main programme, in addition to some sidebars and short films. The festival, a non-competitive event, will showcase a wide selection of contemporary and classic Arabic and global cinema, which will appeal to Dubai's multi-cultural community.

Sharjah International Art Biennial has grown rapidly since it was first held in 1993. The sixth arts biennial, staged in March 2003, was a huge success. In only a decade the Sharjah Biennial has established itself as the single most important artistic event in the UAE – and one of the cultural highspots in the Middle East diary. Curators Hoor Al Qasimi (UAE) and Peter Lewis (Goldsmiths College) worked with a number of other international curators to present installations, video and photography by 117 artists from 25 countries at the new Expo Centre. The seventh biennial will be held in 2005.

MEDIA AND INFORMATION

The windows are open for the free flow of information, and those who would wish to close them again are doomed to fail.
(Minister of Information and Culture Sheikh Abdullah bin Zayed Al Nahyan)

The UAE was quick to recognise the necessity of engaging with the twenty-first century world in which information and entertainment is disseminated so swiftly and so effectively via the Internet, as well as through radio and television satellite services, that the control of information is no longer either feasible or desirable. As a result, the country has readily embraced all aspects of information and communications technology (ICT) both from the point of view of access for its own citizens, as well as capitalising on its location to develop structures that will service not just the region but the rest of the world. Media organisations such as Emirates Media Incorporated (EMI) and facilitators such as Dubai Media and Internet City are playing an important role in new developments.

TV, RADIO AND NEWSPAPERS

The UAE has numerous indigenous satellite TV stations. Some focus on Arab culture and identity, others on business and sport. It also has a number of terrestrial stations broadcasting in Arabic and English, including Abu Dhabi TV, Emirates Channel, Abu Dhabi Sports Channel, Dubai 33, Sharjah Channel 22 and Ajman Channel 4.

Emirates Cable TV and Multimedia (E-Vision), a subsidiary of Etisalat, offers viewers a total of 180 TV entertainment and interactive channels in approximately 14 languages. Plans are in place to raise the number of channels on offer to 200. It also offers a pay-per-view service (pre-paid calling cards were introduced in 2003 to simplify the process further), e-gaming and an interactive electronic programming guide (EPG).

E-Vision was launched in April 2000 with a target of just 20,000 homes and reached around 200,000 subscribers by late 2003. Until then, only certain parts of the UAE were able to access E-Vision via hybrid fibre coaxial cable technology. Following a decision to provide wireless technology through Wireless Broadband Network (WBN), Etisalat is endeavouring to service all the Emirates through wireless, cable or a mix of both. E-vision's services to Al Ain and Ajman are entirely based on the wireless platform, while in Abu Dhabi and Sharjah services will continue to be provided by a mix of cable and wireless. E-Vision launched its wireless services in Dubai in April 2004. It is also considering expansion into the other Northern Emirates where the services are not yet available. E-Vision plans to invest Dh2.5 billion in cable television over the next 15 years.

Radio stations include popular English language stations such as Abu Dhabi Capital Radio, Dubai FM 92, Channel 4 FM, and Emirates 1 and 2 FM, along with UAE Radio Ra's al-Khaimah.

There are nine daily newspapers, six Arabic, *Al Ittihad, Akhbar al-Arab, Al Fajr* and *Al Wahda*, published in Abu Dhabi, *Al Bayan*, published in Dubai, and *Al Khaleej*, published in Sharjah, and three English, *Gulf News* and *Khaleej Times*, published in Dubai and *Gulf Today*, a sister paper of *Al Khaleej*, published in Sharjah. Many overseas newspapers also circulate freely in the country, benefiting from the free-market approach adopted by the Ministry of Information and Culture. At the latest count, there were also more than 160 magazines and journals published by local and national organisations, cultural centres, clubs, chambers of commerce and industry, municipalities and educational institutions, while, again, many international magazines also circulate. During 2004, local editions of the business magazine *Forbes* and the social magazine *Hello* commenced publication in Dubai.

Most prominent of the UAE's own media establishments is the Abu Dhabi-based Emirates Media Incorporated (EMI) (see below).

JOURNALISM IN THE UAE

The profession of journalism in the UAE has continued over the last couple of years to make considerable progress, with a growing number of UAE citizens, both men and women, taking up posts in both the written and the broadcast media.

Besides the experience to be gained in the local media institutions, including overseas reporting stints in places such as Iraq, UAE journalists have also benefited from the emergence of Dubai, in particular, as a regional media centre, both in the Dubai Media City and elsewhere.

The exchange of experiences has been facilitated by the Dubai Press Club (DPC), launched in 1999 to provide a forum for discussion of media issues in the Arab world and with the objective of promoting communication and liaison with the international press. DPC has formed an International Association of Press Clubs in cooperation with 20 other press clubs from around the world and, under the capable management of a UAE woman, Mona Al Marri, DPC was selected by the International Federation for Press Clubs as a key regional centre. DPC organised the Arab Media Summit in October 2003. German Chancellor Gerhard Schroeder was guest of honour at the summit and more than 500 regionally and internationally renowned media experts discussed the theme 'War and the Media'. Plans for a similar club in Abu Dhabi were being developed in late 2004.

In March 2004, the UAE Journalists Association (UJA) held a ceremony to honour pioneers of the UAE press who had completed 25 years of service in the print media in the country, including the Chairman of the Arab Photographers Union (APU), APU previous board members and 48 journalists.

Another major event to be held recently was the 2003 Arab Journalism Awards, the Arab world's most prestigious media honours. This took place at the Dubai Press Club at the conclusion of the Arab Media Summit. Fourteen people from six countries were presented with prizes. In a moving ceremony, the wife and two-year old daughter of Al Jazeera TV correspondent, Tariq Ayoub, collected the Media Personality of the Year Award on his behalf. The journalist died when the Baghdad offices of Al Jazeera were attacked by the US during the Iraq War.

THE EMIRATES NEWS AGENCY

The Emirates News Agency (WAM), managed by the Ministry of Information and Culture, transmits news and picture services, both locally and internationally, in Arabic and English. Its easily navigated revamped website (www.wam.org.ae) also presents news online in both Arabic and English.

During 2004, WAM upgraded its services, both for recipients and for its external offices, and new methods for transmitting and receiving news are now in place. In a cost-effective use of the latest Internet technology, File Transfer Protocol (FTP), is now used to send its services to subscribers, removing the necessity for dedicated telecommunications links, while use is also being made of Virtual Private Network (VPN) facilities for its reporters and offices. Through this means, direct contact can not only be maintained with the WAM Head Office in Abu Dhabi, but the agency's offices elsewhere in the UAE and abroad, as well as travelling correspondents, can also have easy access to other Arabic news agencies through the NEPRAS system.

During 2004, WAM also introduced its new TV news service, transmitting news-clips by fibre-optic cable in the UAE and through satellite and the Internet, at very low cost, to recipient stations overseas.

WAM has a staff of 180 employees within the UAE and 25 reporters widely dispersed outside the country, covering places as far afield as Cairo, Beirut, Washington DC, Islamabad, Sanaa and Brussels. It has cooperation and news exchange agreements with more than 20 Arab countries and is a member of the Group of Gulf Cooperation Council News Agencies, the Federation of the Arab News Agencies (FANA), the Islamic News Agencies Union and the Pool of Non-Aligned News Agencies. Originally set up to cover topics of national interest, WAM has now broadened its remit to cover topical news events worldwide.

EMIRATES MEDIA INCORPORATED (EMI)

EMI was set up under Federal Law No. 5 for 1999 as the legal successor to the Emirates Broadcasting Corporation and Al Ittihad for Press, Publishing and Distribution. As the largest and most diversified media corporation, not only in the UAE but throughout the Arab world, it has interests in all branches of media – television, radio, print, publishing and distribution, and the Internet.

While the government has relinquished formal control over EMI, ownership is still officially vested in the government and the corporation remains partially dependent on government funding. Nevertheless, EMI enjoys administrative and editorial independence and functions very much as a private company. EMI was restructured into eight independent business units in 2002 in order to maximise productivity.

Revenues from its extensive audio-visual interests represent 35 to 40 per cent of Emirates Media's income. The rest come from the print media. Publications such as *Al Ittihad* newspaper and the magazines *Zahrat Al Khaleej* and *Majid* were well established before EMI's reincorporation. EMI's radio division has been developed and expanded to include Abu Dhabi Radio and Holy Qur'an Radio, Emirates FM, the Sound of Music, Urdu Service Station and Emirates FM English stations Radio 1 and 2. Abu Dhabi Television – one of EMI's television stations producing nearly 90 per cent of its own broadcasts – received worldwide exposure during the Iraq crisis and is fast gaining an international reputation. Already covering the Middle East, Europe, and North America, ADTV is scheduled to reach South America and Australia in the near future. Abu Dhabi Sports Channel, a pay channel carried on the Showtime platform, has established itself since its launch in 1996 as a leading channel throughout the Arab world. EMI's Emirates Channel, available through terrestrial and satellite transmission, is aimed at a UAE and Gulf audience, concentrating on cultural issues and issues of identity and heritage, as well as political issues. In February 2000, EMI's Internet service was launched, providing yet another instant medium of contact with the public. Finally, in addition to its commercial operations, EMI has a training and development role to play in media in the UAE, particularly in relation to the fostering of local talent.

Following an agreement between EMI and BBC Arabic, the BBC is broadcasting on two FM stations in the UAE, one based in Abu Dhabi, the other in Dubai (reaching Sharjah, Ajman and Umm al-Qaiwain). BBC Arabic broadcasts news and current affairs programmes to the region as well as several interactive discussion programmes that enable listeners and users of www.bbcarabic.com to take part in the discussions. It also broadcasts throughout the Arab world on short wave and medium wave frequencies.

DUBAI MEDIA CITY

Dubai Media City has become an international centre for media-based operations. It is now a thriving media community whose directory is fast becoming the indispensable reference tool for businesses seeking to utilise its media talent pool. DMC's sophisticated infrastructure hosts broadcasting companies, TV channels and numerous associated media production companies and individual freelancers. Key global companies in DMC include Reuters, CNN, CNBC, MBC, Sony, Bertelsmann, BMG, the Associated Press and McGraw Hill. CNN has launched its Arabic news website and regional news bureau at DMC. Pan-Arabic broadcaster MBC has not only relocated its international headquarters from London to DMC, but has launched an Arabic news channel, Al Arabiya, which is competing with Al Jazeera and the Arab News Network (ANN). CNBC Arabiya, the first regional Arabic-language news channel in the Middle East presenting in-depth economic and business coverage, launched operations from its new studio at DMC in the summer of 2003. Other significant regional companies include Lowe & Partners Middle East North Africa (the main advertising arm of the Lowe Group, ranked fourth among worldwide agency groups), Saudi Research & Publishing Companies (second largest publishers in the world after Time-Warner), Asianet Global, Taj Television Ltd (TEN Sports), Middle East Television (MET), the first Indian satellite channel to broadcast from DMC, Zee Network, the world's largest producer of Hindi language programming, and Al Majd Satellite Broadcasting Star Group, Asia's foremost media company. In addition, the satellite TV network Showtime opened its headquarters and transmission centre at DMC in 2004.

The locating of BMG International's Middle East and North Africa operations at DMC heralds a new development for DMC. BMG Mena controls one of the largest music production libraries, which is used by audio-visual production companies and advertising agencies for content in commercials and corporate presentations.

The Ibda'a Media Student Awards, organised by DMC, are designed to encourage young media talent. In 2003, the awards received a tremendous response, with 1819 entries from 98 universities, representing more than 20 countries. Nine award winners were announced in December 2003 covering categories such as Animation, Journalism, Radio, TV, Film Production, Photography, Graphic Design and two new categories – Print and Television Advertising. Included, for some of the winners, were internships with major media companies represented at DMC.

DUBAI MEDIA INCORPORATED

Dubai Media Incorporated (DMI), incorporated as a commercially independent entity in July 2003, has initiated the first stage of an extensive revamp with the launch of a new-look Dubai TV, its flagship television channel. As part of the changes, Dubai TV has opened a news centre at Dubai Media City. The plan is to further build new facilities to house the entire DMI set-up at the Media City.

In its largest distribution deal to date with a free-to-air Middle East–based broadcaster, Warner Bros. International Television Distribution concluded a multi-year, exclusive deal with DMI, which will bring viewers content from leading global entertainment companies, including Hollywood blockbusters and award-winning television series. Kids Hour, a dedicated slot that offers educational and informative viewing, will complete the list.

INTERNET

The UAE continues to lead the GCC in terms of Internet penetration, according to the International Telecommunications Union (ITU). While the number of actual subscribers in the UAE was 313,750 in 2003, the number of users is much higher – the high penetration rate is due to the country having the highest number of Internet users to PCs among any of the countries in the region, at 2.6 users to every PC. Currently, there are an estimated 1.25 million Internet users, representing 31 per cent of the population. However, it is forecast that by the end of 2008 the UAE will have more than 2.41 million Internet users, over 50 per cent of the population.

The state's focus on e-governance and the prevalence of emerging technologies like cable Internet access, Internet via TV, ISDN LAN, fixed broadband Internet and the iZone wireless network, which will allow users to wirelessly connect to the Internet at broadband speeds from selected public locations (hotspots), will also help boost webuser numbers. The eCompany (formally Emirates Internet and Multimedia), the Internet service arm of the UAE's main telecom provider Etisalat (see section on Telecommunications) has been the instigator of the majority of these developments. Moreover, the fact that Dubai Internet City (part of the TECOM Free Zone) houses a range of leading ICT companies has helped to create a climate where digital accessibility is the norm.

UAE INTERACT

The official website of the UAE Ministry of Information and Culture, UAE Interact (www.uaeinteract.com) was first launched in 1997 and is one of the longest established Internet sites providing news and information on the UAE. UAE Interact is actively managed on a daily basis. During 2004 the website received over 1.7 million distinct visitors (est. 1,715,760) who created over 42 million hits (42,232,690) and over 5.7 million (est. 5,705,680) page views.

The top user locations are the UAE, USA, Saudi Arabia, Germany, France, India, Australia, Hong Kong, Ireland and Canada, in that order. The most frequent referring search engine is Google where UAE Interact is usually listed as the number one website on the UAE. The site contains a substantial database of information that can be searched in a variety of ways. Major sections are as follows: News; Government; Travel Centre; Map Room; Arts Centre; Cultural Centre; The Past; Natural UAE; Educational Centre; Recreational Centre; Shopping and Books. Each of these sections offers comprehensive information sources. The news section, for example, provides a searchable database of over 10,000 news stories together with links to breaking news and information on current and forthcoming events and government websites. The website also presents an art gallery featuring works by UAE artists, a virtual museum, a travel centre packed with information for people visiting the UAE, a fully searchable database on UAE hotels, and a shopping centre with information on what to buy and where to buy it. An online bookshop featuring titles on the UAE that can be purchased via a secure server is another advantage of the website. Past Yearbooks are accessible online. An e-book section is also available, with free access to full texts from major publications on the UAE. The virtual museum displays the UAE's finest artefacts in full 360 degree images that can be revolved on screen with the stroke of a mouse. It also boasts a unique 'ask us' feature, enabling site visitors to post questions to the web team and receive a reply, both posted on the site and emailed to the enquirer.

2005 UAE DVD

In late 2004, the Ministry of Information and Culture released a new state-of-the-art DVD containing a large volume of information on the UAE in interactive format, including the entire 2005 UAE *Yearbook* in English, French and Arabic; and a number of films on the country. The DVD is distributed by the Ministry of Information and Culture as part of its international information service. The DVD format has proved to be exceptionally popular among users and the Ministry has plans to extend use of this platform in future projects.

PROTECTION OF INTELLECTUAL PROPERTY

The UAE operates a strict enforcement policy of its piracy and patent laws, seeing the protection of creativity as a necessity in itself and essential to attracting foreign investment. A member of the World Intellectual Property Organisation (WIPO), the UAE acceded to the Paris Convention for the Protection of Industrial Property in 1996, following the implementation of three intellectual property laws in 1993.

According to the eighth annual Business Software Alliance (BSA) Global Software Piracy Study, the Middle East and Africa region recorded the most significant reduction in piracy rates globally, dropping 31 percentage points from 80 per cent in 1994 to 49 per cent in 2002. The UAE led the region, dropping by 50 points – from 86 to 36 per cent in the period surveyed. This compares with a reduction from 78 to 50 per cent in Saudi Arabia, 96 to 70 per cent in Oman, 92 to 76 per cent in Bahrain, 91 to 76 per cent in Qatar and a worldwide reduction from 49 to 39 per cent for commercial business software. The UAE's record on protecting intellectual property rights has been praised by the Arab Anti-piracy Association (AAA) and by BSA. UAE Federal laws have made it mandatory for companies and end-users to use original software and to maintain evidence of the original software within their IT systems.

Copyright laws – their precise scope and their stringent enforcement – are of particular importance to those involved in any aspect of the media business, and the new Federal Author and Copyrights and Parallel Rights Law No. 7, issued in August 2002, gives copyright protection to authors and artists not only during their lifetime but also for 50 years (an increase from 25) after their death, making the UAE fully compliant with WIPO requirements. Variations exist in the case of joint copyright and community copyright. Works of non-national authors are protected subject to reciprocal treatment by the foreign state or subject to international conventions that the UAE has accepted. The new law lists the works of art entitled to protection, as well as those falling beyond the scope of protection. It defines holders of parallel rights and public performers and stipulates under what circumstances the Court of First Instance may suspend the reproduction, show, display or performance of a work of art, or impound the original work of art together with any copies. The law covers photography (defining the rights of both photographer and person photographed), the misuse of software and their applications, as well as databases. Copyright violations in general attract fines and/or terms of imprisonment varying according to the severity or frequency of the infringement.

The new Patents Law No. 17 came into force in November 2002. It was issued in accordance with the international conventions and treaties to which the UAE is a signatory and, as a result, non-nationals from countries having reciprocal agreements with the UAE will be treated as UAE nationals in terms of protecting their patents and rights. UAE patents law now complies fully with World Trade Organisation (WTO) requirements. The new Patent Law supersedes the previous Federal Law No. 44 of 1992 for the protection of patents, industrial drawings and patterns and their related exploitation rights. Patents will be granted to applicants for any novel invention or creation, or development of an existing one available for industrial exploitation, whether in respect of new industrial products or means. The term of the patent will be 20 years and that of the certificate will be ten years from the date of filing the application. Annual fees will be payable by the patent owner, failing which the patent and relevant certificate will be deemed void. Biological research on reproduction of plants and animals excluding minute organisms, will not be covered by patents. Similarly, diagnosis, treatment of diseases and surgery for human beings and animals, as well as mathematical theories and pure intellectual methods or inventions affecting propriety will not be granted any patents. A patent owner may be deprived of his/her exploitation rights if he/she fails to properly exploit his/her invention within three years.

Sheikh Abdullah bin Zayed Al Nahyan, Minister of Information and Culture, issued a number of ministerial decisions on copyright and related rights in March 2004. The decisions, 131/132/133 and 134 for 2004, regulate the registration, import and distribution, collective management, and mandatory licensing of copyright in line with Federal Law No. 7 of 2002.

Under ministerial decision No. 131 of 2004, works shall be registered at and a copy of the work shall be retained in the UAE registration office so as to safeguard the rights of the owner in the event of any dispute involving copyright. Decision No. 132 governs the import and distribution of copyrighted works and is aimed at preserving the rights of authorised importers and distributors, as well as the rights of copyright owners. The significance of the decision stems from the fact that it regulates the process of circulation of intellectual works in the country in a manner that will make it harder for unauthorised parties to circulate, sale or distribute works without prior permission from the owner.

Decision No. 133 on collective management of rights enables copyright owners – be they authors, artistes, performers, audio-recording producers, radio institutions or otherwise – to authorise other parties to manage their works on the basis of authenticated agreements. These parties shall be responsible for collecting revenues generated by the works. They shall also be entitled to take necessary administrative, legal and arbitrative measures to protect the rights of their clients.

Decision No. 134 regulates the issuing of mandatory licences, specifically for copying and translation of copyright works. The licences shall be issued by the Ministry of Information and Culture as stipulated by Article 21 of the Federal Law.

The Ministry remains the principal enforcer of the law and is absolutely committed to combating all violation of intellectual property rights as is evidenced by their activities in 2004. In March, Abu Dhabi TV cooperated with the Ministry to film an incident of software piracy in a computer store in Abu Dhabi. The raid was conducted following suspicions that it was dealing in pirated software, based on prior information obtained by the AAA.

In May 2004, the Ministry dumped four truck loads of pirated items, including 400,000 DVDs, 200,000 VCDs, 1500 audio CDs, 300 computer applications and games, 2000 music cassettes and 1500 VHS tapes. Duplicating equipment for cassette tapes and discs was also destroyed. Many of the items were seized in raids on apartment units in Dubai. A joint team involving agents from the Dubai Police, Economic Department and the Ports and Customs Department were working with the Ministry.

DEFAMATION

A ruling by the Dubai Court of Cassation in 2003 has confirmed that journalists have the right to publish any material or claim backed by facts so long as it is not intended to defame or malign any person or entity. The court found that the press can publish material if in doing so it is not contravening the Constitution or Articles 372 and 373 of the UAE Penal Code. Article 30 of the UAE Constitution allows the publication of any material, as long as publication does not breach the bounds of responsibility that goes with such freedom. Article 372 of the Penal Code penalises any person who is proved to have published any material that causes someone else moral harm. Article 373 holds that anyone who intentionally and maliciously defames someone else without concrete evidence shall be subject to penalties stipulated in the penal code. According to the Court of Cassation's ruling, accusers must establish that words or phrases of any published or broadcast material actually amount to defamation. The court must also ascertain that the defamation complaints are not a distortion of the facts before issuing a final ruling.

ENVIRONMENT

OVER THE LAST YEAR AND A HALF, the United Arab Emirates has made significant progress in the sphere of environmental protection, with the passing of new environmental legislation, an increase in the number of protected areas across the country and, perhaps most significantly, the commencement of steps to introduce environmental education as an integral part of the curriculum in government schools. A natural history museum is now planned for the capital, captive breeding programmes of threatened wildlife have built on previous years' successes and environmental research is at an all-time high. The importance of conserving the environment for the success of ecotourism initiatives is also firmly acknowledged, while the essential monitoring of compliance with and enforcement of domestic environmental legislation has also become more robust, in particular in pursuit of pollution prevention.

Unleaded fuel was introduced in 2003, the government bearing most of the cost of the overnight switch over, while the oil and gas industry has continued to innovate and introduce cleaner technology impressively faster than anticipated – all good news for the environment. The economic viability of clean renewable energy is also being widely investigated. The Fujairah government is leading the way in developing and marketing wind power. Seven sites have been chosen for evaluation, four of them on inconspicuous, exposed ridges in this predominantly mountain emirate.

An integrated waste management system, with recycling, composting and landfill reduction, has been developed in Abu Dhabi and some of the other emirates. Recycling is now commonplace throughout the country, not least through the continuing concerted efforts of non-governmental bodies such as the Emirates Environmental Group (EEG) and Environment Friends Society (EFS).

A UAE national environmental strategy panel formed under Cabinet Decree No. 17 for 2002 continues to work to fulfil its mandate, with a 'National Committee for Environmental Strategy and Sustainable Development' based at the Federal Environment Agency (FEA). Twenty federal and governmental agencies and other institutions are represented on the Committee.

Problems with drought have, however, continued. Following heavy rainfall in some areas in early 2003 after a four year drought, there was further rainfall in the summer and autumn, mainly in mountain districts. From the beginning of 2004, however, drought set in again, with little rainfall being recorded anywhere in the first few months of the year. Although there were mid-summer 2004 storms in Al Ain, Fujairah and parts of the mountains, these will do little to alleviate the impact of the drought. Desert and mountain vegetation in many areas is now severely stressed, and, in some places, appears to have died altogether, with a consequent impact on native wildlife.

ENVIRONMENT RESEARCH & PROTECTION

The Environmental Research & Wildlife Development Agency (ERWDA) had a budget of Dh85 million (US$23 million) approved for 2003. The different centres of the Agency developed an environmental strategy for Abu Dhabi Emirate, 2003–2007, in collaboration with the relevant local government departments and federal ministries. Resource regulatory and monitoring systems, fisheries and freshwater resource management regimes and wildlife management and rehabilitation programmes are all included in this strategy. In late 2004, work got under way on a review of the strategy, to determine the progress being made towards the set goals.

ERWDA's Environmental Protection Division (EPD) has continued to develop laws, regulations and standards, and to improve processes for permissions, inspections and management systems. Meanwhile, continuing studies by ERWDA of resource management and sustainable development are being supported by the UAE Offsets Group.

Turtle research continues apace in Abu Dhabi, with hatcheries forming part of the conservation effort, while the Wildlife Protection Office of the UAE Defence Minister and Dubai Crown Prince, Sheikh Mohammed bin Rashid Al Maktoum, has also commenced a tagging and satellite-tracking programme. The focus of the work is on hawksbill and green turtles, the species breeding in the UAE's Arabian Gulf waters.

Besides support from government, wildlife research and conservation has also continued to receive assistance from commercial sponsors, the UAE-based West Indian Ocean Marine Turtle Specialist Group having received one such grant late in 2003. Noteworthy for its support for environmental work has been the country's oil and gas sector, including both national companies and foreign firms like Shell, BP and Total.

A major review of the country's extensive afforestation programme was under way in 2004 in Abu Dhabi's Eastern Region, based in Al Ain, with the intention of promoting improved protection of native woodlands, while in Ra's al-Khaimah the Environment Protection and Industrial Development Authority, established in 1999, has now shortlisted a number of sites for protection as nature reserves and has appointed eight new inspectors, five others already being in post.

Concerns have recently arisen over crown of thorns starfish *Acanthaster planci* damaging coral off the UAE's East Coast. The arrival of large numbers of this starfish is reported to be a comparatively recent phenomenon and may be indicative of ecological imbalance. The Emirates Diving Association (EDA) is monitoring and reporting on the situation. Fujairah established three marine reserves in 1995, but although artificial reefs and fish caves have been installed with marked success and fishing banned locally, their integrity is apparently under threat from not only the starfish invasion but also from pollution and violation by fishermen.

Fujairah has now added four mountain reserves to the three marine reserves already designated in the emirate. These, in Wadi Zikt, at Al Ghob, Al Hafya and Ohfurah, have been selected on account of their natural beauty and for the range of wild flora and fauna present, and are to be off-limits to herdsmen and their flocks. A hunting ban is to be strictly enforced and any future development also prohibited in these named areas.

In early 2003, a year-long Fish Resource Assessment Survey of UAE waters was completed, with results being issued later in the year. This concluded that drastic declines in the abundance of both commercial and non-commercial demersal fishes had taken place, but that fishing was not the sole cause. Environmental degradation, resulting from pollution, reclamation and dredging was also blamed. A decline to under a fifth (-81 per cent) of the stock size estimated by a 1978 survey occurred in Arabian Gulf waters, while off the East Coast (Gulf of Oman) during the same period stocks were considered to have fallen by 93 per cent. Pelagic fish stocks, however, appear not to have changed between the two surveys. The study was completed by a consortium under contract to ERWDA.

Abu Dhabi allows the use of fishing with lampara net (*halaaq*), a form of seine-netting widely seen as an alternative to drift netting (*hayali*). Fishing with *hayali* nets, known as the 'web of death', is now formally outlawed. Use of *halaaq* is permitted from November until April inclusive, with a net length limited to a maximum of 700 metres, and mesh size of 7.5 centimetres or greater. Such fishing is permitted in only four specific areas off the Abu Dhabi coast, and possession of a commercial licence is mandatory. Licences are issued by ERWDA. A crack-down on the use of illegal nylon nets continues in all parts of the country.

Also offshore, Abu Dhabi Emirate now has two formally-declared Marine Protected Areas. The island of Qarnein, along with its surrounding waters, was so designated in early 2003, following the designation of the c4250-square-kilometre Marawah-Bu Tina MPA, announced the previous year. Qarnein was also declared by WWF as a 'Gift to the Earth' (see below). Studies of other potential Protected Areas, including both shallow waters and offshore islands, is continuing.

The emplacement of structures for the development of artificial reefs and deposition of cement fish caves that also become rapidly encrusted or support

algal growth is now standard practice both within the Gulf and off the East Coast. Coastal erosion in Dubai is causing worries, however, with more than 50 per cent of the 66-kilometre-long mainland coastline of the emirate eroding. This is being monitored by the local Municipality, with fixed cameras mounted on coastal buildings showing changes in coastal configuration (www.dubaicoast.org). Large-scale engineering projects offshore, of island construction in particular, are believed to be having a particularly adverse impact.

ERWDA has also continued to carry out research on an international scale, with a particular focus on the vast Central Asian range of the houbara bustard. Results announced by ERWDA's National Avian Research Centre (NARC) show that the current population level of the Asian (MacQueen's) houbara will be halved by 2015 and close to extinction by 2027, unless habitat protection increases and hunting and poaching pressure is substantially reduced. Captive breeding of houbara at NARC has, however, enjoyed vastly improved productivity in recent years, with some of these birds to be used in forthcoming release programmes.

CAPTIVE BREEDING

The Breeding Centre for Endangered Arabian Wildlife, which is part of Sharjah's Environment and Protected Areas Authority (EPAA), continues to concentrate much effort on the breeding of Arabian leopards, with continuing success. The Centre also expanded its collection of animals from the region. The majority of the Arabian Peninsula's 23 species of rodent is now held and breeding at the Centre, as well as the region's three native Arabian hedgehogs and some freshwater fishes, including blind cave fish. The Centre boasts the world's largest assembly of Arabian wildlife, and continues to undertake research into physiology, diseases and breeding. Breeding loans regularly take place, with the Centre recently supplying the endemic Gordon's wildcat to institutes in the Czech Republic and Canada, while, to supplement its breeding programme, the World Owl Trust in Britain took receipt of three desert eagle owls from Dubai. An unusual request from the University of Freiburg, Germany, with which the Centre was pleased to be able to assist, was the collection of blood and urine samples from genets housed in the collection for a vital study of enzyme deficiency in humans.

At a regional level, the UAE now hosts the secretariat for the Arabian Oryx Conservation Committee, also currently chaired by the UAE, which comprises representatives of all former range states of the oryx, as well as the World-Wide Fund for Nature (WWF) and the Reintroduction Specialist Group (RSG) of the World Conservation Union (IUCN). The committee has a website at www.whiteoryx.org.

An out-of-town site has been selected for the building of a new US$150 million state-of-the-art Dubai Zoo, while a US$24 million redevelopment of Al Ain Zoological Park, the country's oldest zoo, is well under way. One new feature will be an embryo bank facility.

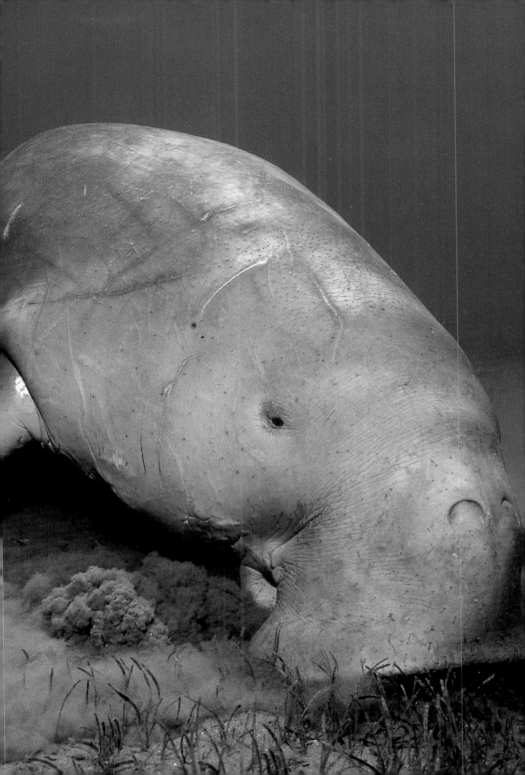

BIRDWATCHING IN THE UAE

In the last decade or so, the UAE has become a well-known and favoured destination for birdwatchers from around the world. This is partly due to the large number of Middle Eastern specialities that occur, but also to the fact that a wealth of information and guides are readily available for them. Although only around 120 different species of bird breed in the UAE, over 420 have been recorded nationally and many are those highly sought after 'target' species, known from pictures in field guides, but otherwise often regarded by birdwatchers as somewhat mythical beasts. For this there is good reason. A number of them occur in parts of the world well off the beaten track and where birdwatching would be regarded as deeply suspicious. Not so in the UAE, although this is not to say that many a bemused eyebrow is not raised at the sight of a binocular-clad 'birder', telescope over their shoulder, out in the midday sun.

Time your visit right and it is in the UAE, and here alone, that a number of species of bird difficult to see anywhere in the world can all be seen in a single trip. Names to conjure with include Socotra cormorant, white-cheeked tern, crab plover, striated scops owl, plain leaf warbler, Hume's wheatear and, a firm favourite in a family or sub-family of its own, the grey hypocolius. All have a justifiable claim to fame.

Of 300 migrant species to visit the UAE, nearly 100 are considered rare or scarce visitors, while some 60 or more occur only by accident, as so-called 'vagrants'. These species often have a particular attraction for enthusiastic birders. The Emirates, located on a migratory crossroads between east and west, is renowned for the frequency of visits by these clearly often lost individuals. Some appear here with regularity, despite their far-off points of origin: great knot, forest wagtail, pale martin, Blyth's pipit and Oriental skylark, to name but a few. Extreme vagrants have included one or two species new even for the Middle East, Pacific swift, Asian house martin, cinnamon bittern and taiga flycatcher being four from the last five years.

Almost every year one or more new species is added to the UAE checklist. This is maintained by the Emirates Bird Records Committee (EBRC) and a resulting Emirates Bird Report is an eagerly awaited publication, now well into its second decade. In the past 20 years, over 60 new species have been recorded nationally for the first time, some having been noted subsequently, but many not recorded again. Amongst the former have been species originating from Asia, crested honey buzzard, Sykes' nightjar, pied stonechat and brown shrike, with others again hailing from Africa or south-western Arabia, lesser flamingo, Kittlitz's sandplover, wattled starling and black bush-robin, for example. Many have been waterfowl or seabirds, such as whooper swan, intermediate egret, sooty shearwater and lesser noddy. A few sites regularly produce records of rare birds, although the increase in greenery has meant that, unless extremely fortunate, it is necessary to work a little harder to find unusual visitors these days. Safa Park, the Emirates Golf Club, Al Wathba camel racetrack, Fujairah National Dairy Farm and Dubai's Wimpey lagoons (Al Warsen Lake) are all well-known venues for the birding fraternity; all continue to turn up unusual species, especially during migration periods, or in colder winters.

New breeding species also continue to be found. For some species breeding has been suspected for some years, and only lacked confirmation. Man-made wetlands have proved to be rewarding in this respect, with recent confirmed breeding by purple gallinule, coot and crested coot. The last-named, which appeared for the first time in UAE only two years previously, constituted the first breeding record in Arabia (and indeed for Asia) of a tropical African species. Clearly these birds found conditions so much to their liking that they decided to stay on.

A two-week holiday can muster around 200 species, which is a good strike rate, although best achieved with a bit of local knowledge. Visitors are advised to contact one of the UAE's few resident birdwatchers, either prior to arriving or when here, to get the latest news and advice on where best to see certain species. Advice is given freely as it provides an opportunity for exchange of news and views between fellow enthusiasts, and because most birdwatchers living in the UAE also work for a living, so they welcome the extra pairs of eyes. Sharp-eyed visitors find many rare and unusual species while out looking for those other species they really came to see and a debt of gratitude is owed to those who report them promptly, and then provide the necessary documentation to the EBRC. New and exciting finds continue to be made, and that adds to the attraction of the UAE for a 'birding' holiday, whether it be for a day or two at the end of a business trip, as a family holiday in five-star luxury, or on an intensive sortie with a car-load of friends.

A detailed summary of the previous week's bird sightings in and around the UAE, the 'Twitchers' Guide', is posted on the UAE Ministry of Information's website (www.uaeinteract.com) each week. Please take the effort to report your sightings for inclusion.

CITES PROGRESS

Enforcement of the CITES convention has been aided by the passing of UAE Federal Law No. 11 for 2002 on 'Regulating and Controlling International Trade in Endangered Species of Wild Fauna and Flora', which prohibits import, transit and transshipment, export, re-export and introduction by sea of any species listed in the CITES appendices, other than in accordance with the provisions of the law. The Abu Dhabi-based programme office of Worldwide Fund for Nature (WWF) (see below), has been actively engaged in the training of customs officers in wildlife recognition and in CITES regulations (see also Conferences & Events below).

Concomitant with the rapid passage and introduction of the federal law, the authorities have seized many illegally imported animals from around the country. Amongst animals confiscated were chimpanzees, large cats, parrots and tortoises, as well as smuggled ivory. An international houbara smuggling ring was cracked in January 2004. Regular inspections take place in registered pet markets, with checks at air and sea entry points now routine.

A falcon registration and 'passport' scheme, run by the Federal Environmental Agency, and Ministry of Agriculture and Fisheries (MAF) and of utmost importance to falconers wishing to legalise their hunting overseas with specific birds, was also initiated as part of the measures to combat illegal movements of wildlife to and from the UAE. While the FEA is the overall management authority, ERWDA has been designated as the UAE scientific authority for CITES. MAF remains the responsible authority in Dubai and the Northern Emirates.

NATIONAL & INTERNATIONAL NGOS

In February 2003, WWF recognised the island of Qarnein, some 160 kilometres from Abu Dhabi, and the UAE's undisputed seabird capital, as a 'Gift to the Earth', congratulating Sheikh Hamdan bin Zayed Al Nahyan, the island's owner, on attaining this internationally prestigious award. Dr Claude Martin, Director General of WWF, conferring this status on Qarnein, said it had been accepted because of the international significance of the site and the considerable effort expended on its conservation. Several seabird species breed, some in large numbers, on Qarnein, while the hawksbill turtle also nests there, one of the UAE's few remaining sites for this globally threatened species. In early 2004, *Mabuya aurata*, a species of skink and a new addition to the reptile checklist of the UAE, was reported from the island, proving the value of continuing research and survey of the country's biodiversity.

WWF works through the local non-governmental organisation, the Emirates Wildlife Society (EWS), which was founded in February 2001 under the patronage of Sheikh Hamdan bin Zayed Al Nahyan. The mandate of EWS is to implement conservation actions for the protection of biodiversity nationally. In February 2003, Dubai Municipality offered WWF premises in the historical Al Bastakiya district of the city, which, together with those already operational under the auspices of ERWDA in Abu Dhabi, have helped the UAE programme of this well-known international NGO to develop its operations locally. WWF-UAE is also working on an education and awareness programme in Abu Dhabi, together with ERWDA.

In addition, WWF and ERWDA have been awarded US$500,000 sponsorship by Dolphin Energy Ltd to complete a major study of coral habitats in Abu Dhabi and Qatar, which will culminate in the first comprehensive coral conservation plan for the region. The three-year project will run, in association with Qatar's Supreme Council for the Environment and Nature Reserves (SCENR), from 2004 to 2006.

FALCON RELEASES

2004 saw yet more saker and peregrine falcons being released back to the wild at the end of winter hunting. A total of 76 individuals were released in what is now the tenth year of the Sheikh Zayed Falcon Release Programme. In total, nearly 860 birds have now been released by the programme. Satellite-tracking of a number of birds continues to add valuable data on the survival and dispersal of these originally wild-caught individuals, following a period of pre-release training and veterinary screening. The programme was instituted by HH Sheikh Zayed bin Sultan Al Nahyan, himself an avid falconer, following concerns regarding the decline of populations of sakers in the wild.

INTERNATIONAL ISSUES

Abu Dhabi National Oil Company (ADNOC) is planning to phase out the use of halon by 2005 (five years ahead of schedule), hitherto used to extinguish chemical fires, large quantities of which are held to protect both onshore and offshore oil installations. This is in compliance with the Montreal Agreement, ratified by the UAE in 1989, to reduce or eliminate emission of ozone-depleting substances.

'UAE Goes Green' was the slogan used to promote the countrywide adoption of unleaded fuel on New Year's Day 2003. This has been reiterated in 2004 and the transition has been achieved without disruption. The cost of the seamless transition was largely borne by the government and prices remained the same at the pumps for more than the a year, before rises in early 2004. The slight increase in consumption with unleaded fuel necessarily means a minor additional expense to motorists.

CONFERENCES & EVENTS

One of the largest events in early 2003, coinciding with the UAE's sixth annual Environment Day, was the 'Environment and Energy Exhibition and Conference 2003'. Over 300 companies from nearly 30 countries participated in this four-day event in early February 2003. The event was organised by Abu Dhabi's General

Exhibitions Corporation in collaboration with ERWDA, together with the Economic and Social Commission for West Asia (ESCWA) and the United Nations Environment Programme (UNEP). ADNOC was the main sponsor. UNEP and ERWDA have since signed an MoU. A further environment conference, also organised by GEC and ERWDA, with sponsorship from the UAE's oil sector and from international oil firms, is planned for early 2005.

A four-day international consultative meeting, hosted by ERWDA, was convened by the CITES Secretariat in Abu Dhabi in May 2004. Forty delegates from 18 countries attended, with a senior representative from *BirdLife International* and from three other international non-governmental organisations present. The primary focus was on measures to control the illegal global trade in falcons for falconry, at the same time as guaranteeing the preservation of regional heritage. Recommendations were issued on enforcement, captive breeding, establishment of quotas and improved cooperation and data sharing.

In May 2004, the fourteenth International Conference on Environmental Protection, held in Alexandria, Egypt, awarded the 'Peace and Environment Prize 2004' to HH Sheikh Maktoum bin Rashid Al Maktoum, UAE Vice President, Prime Minister and Ruler of Dubai, with the UAE Minister for Higher Education and Scientific Research, HE Sheikh Nahyan bin Mubarak Al Nahyan, receiving the 'Environment Prize 2004' for his efforts in environmental protection and development in the UAE.

PUBLICATIONS

Pride of place amongst recent publications on environmental subjects goes to the well-known naturalist, Dr Marijcke Jongbloed, for *The Comprehensive Guide to the Wild Flowers of the United Arab Emirates*. Published by ERWDA, this hardback volume, the first of its kind, runs to 576 pages, and describes some 800 species of plant found in the country to date. It is widely seen as a massive boon to floral research, by both professional and amateur botanists alike.

Feast of Dates by Professor Dan Potts, and published by Trident Press, describes the importance of the date palm and its fruit in prehistory, onward until the modern day, with particular reference to its significance in the UAE. Potts' lucid account was commissioned to complement a technically demanding film covering all aspects of the natural history of the date palm and its cultivation from 7000 years BP to the multi-million dollar industry it has become today.

The Island of Abu Al Abyad, produced by ERWDA, gives an illustrated overview of the geology, archaeology and natural history of the UAE's largest island. ERWDA, meanwhile, continues to produce substantial quantities of educational material for schoolchildren and tours the country in its so-called 'nature bus'.

The Emirates Bird Records Committee (EBRC), which collates all bird records from the country, published a six-year bird report in 2003, *Emirates Bird Report*

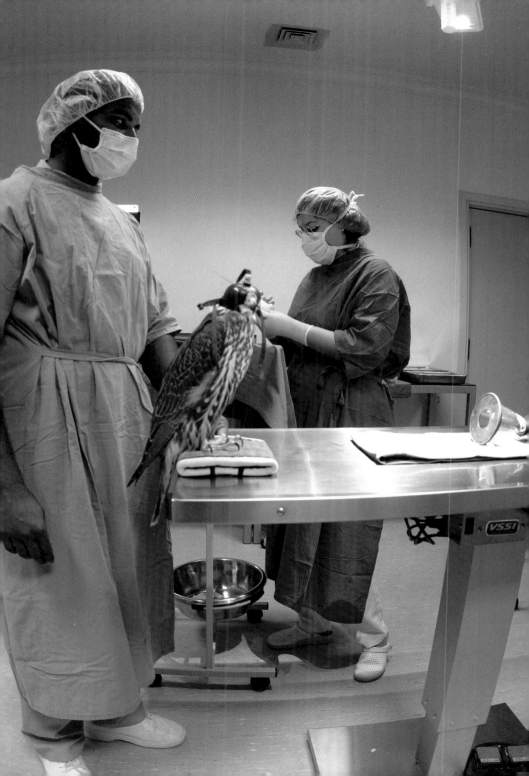

No. 20. Publication was sponsored jointly by the Emirates Natural History Group (ENHG), and by Dubai's Port, Customs & Free Zone Corporation.

Whales and Dolphins of Arabia, by Rob Baldwin, appeared early in 2004 and has proven an extremely popular title. In recent years there have been an increasing number of records of this elusive group in mainly offshore waters around the peninsula, including in UAE waters.

The Emirates Heritage Club (EHC) announced the arrival of its long-awaited coastal zone resource atlas in mid-2004. Separate English and Arabic language editions have been prepared and will be widely distributed.

The Emirates : A Natural History is a sumptious new book on the UAE's wildlife. Published by Trident Press and released in 2005, it provides an all-embracing review of the UAE's natural history, written and edited by experts in their respective fields of interest, from algae to whales and from geology to wildlife traditions. The magnificently illustrated large format book is both a celebration of the UAE's incredible biological diversity and a valuable reference for anyone with an interest in the region's natural environment.

ENVIRONMENT PRIZE

The world's richest environment prize, the Zayed Prize, was presented to the BBC in Dubai in early 2004. The US$500,000 award recognised the BBC for its coverage of issues related to the environment and sustainable development. The judges said the corporation's TV, radio and Internet journalism had put policymakers on the spot, forcing them to justify their positions. The prize was launched to honour the President of the United Arab Emirates, Sheikh Zayed Bin Sultan Al Nahyan, for his campaign to 'green' the UAE through irrigation, desalination and tree-planting, and for his sponsorship of programmes to preserve a number of the region's endangered species. Sian Kevill, editorial director of BBC World, the corporation's commercially funded 24-hour international news channel, accepted the prize on behalf of the BBC.

Two additional prizes worth UN$300,000 each went to the founders of the UN-led Intergovernmental Panel on Climate Change (IPCC) and to two leading environmental activists. The IPCC is the body that has assessed the science behind global warming for world governments. This is only the second time the Zayed Prize has been awarded. The first award ceremony in 2001 honoured the former US President Jimmy Carter for his work on poverty reduction and the environment.

The chairman of the judges for this year's prize was Klaus Toepfer, the executive director of the United Nations Environment Programme (UNEP). Toepfer singled out programmes such as *Earth Report* and *HardTalk* on BBC World for special praise, and paid tribute to David Attenborough's many wildlife series for the corporation. 'This broadcaster has, year in and year out, covered some of the

most pressing environmental and sustainable development issues across the full range of its output,' he said. 'The BBC's reach, not only via television and radio but increasingly through its online Internet service, is matched by its commitment to (42) languages.' The UNEP official said BBC programmes had frequently pushed politicians to reverse poorly thought-out policies. 'Rarely with the BBC are you allowed to duck the question or ignore the real issues,' he said.

The BBC executive was handed the winner's trophy by the patron of the Zayed Prize, Sheikh Mohammed bin Rashid Al Maktoum, the Crown Prince of Dubai and UAE Defence Minister. Sheikh Mohamed said: 'Of course we all care about the environment and we know what's happening around the world now and we recognise these people who did something about it and award them.' The prize-giving ceremony came at the end of the third Dubai International Conference on Atmospheric Pollution, which ran in parallel with the International Exhibition on Environmental Technology, ENVIROTEX2004.

CHELSEA FLOWER SHOW

Sheikh Zayed's exhibit entitled 'Hortus Conclusus' was awarded a gold medal and chosen as the Best Show Garden at the 2004 Chelsea Flower Show in London. Designed by Christopher Bradley-Hole, this was a contemporary work inspired by the traditional enclosed Islamic gardens that brought order and serenity to an otherwise barren environment. Set within the framework of hornbeam hedges and 'green' oak walls was a beautifully proportioned courtyard paved with grey basalt. Dappled shade and structure was provided by a grove of six horizontally pruned plane trees under which were two recessed terraces for contemplation, dining and conversation. Generous beds of planting featured roses among grasses and a palette of perennials.

Additional interest came from glass and oak 'hedges' and, at the end of a vista, a sculptured relief in white marble inspired by the island of Abu Dhabi, the sculptured layers representing the base island, early housing, fishing and contemporary development.

Still pools reflected the trees and lower planting, while at the back of the site a water-wall filled the whole elevation to create a dramatic and lyrical backdrop. Much of the pleasure from the garden was derived from the way that it gradually revealed itself as one moved around the space.

EARTHQUAKES

In a stark reminder of the geological history of the UAE landscape, and although the country is not normally regarded as a seismically active part of the world, several earthquakes hit eastern regions of the UAE in 2002 and 2003, although there were no further quakes in the first half of 2004. In March 2002, a quake measuring 5.0 on the Richter scale was recorded, although, thankfully, those since have all been of lower intensity and deep-seated. That the UAE is susceptible to their occurrence is the result of geological faultlines in the Hajar Mountains. Despite its proximity, the highly active Zagros belt in Iran is not responsible for those quakes experienced in UAE. Remote monitoring stations have now been installed in Masafi and Fujairah, while government and UAE academic institutions are now undertaking studies to permit advance warnings of further quakes to be obtained, as well as on measures to be taken in the event of a serious temblor.

SPORT AND LEISURE

SUPERB FACILITIES AND RELIABLE WEATHER combine to make the UAE a marvellous centre for individual and team sports at all levels. The country is already a top-class destination for sports tourism and it hosts many major international events. Whilst events such as golf, horse racing, cricket and tennis tournaments attract visitors from overseas, they are also a source of inspiration for UAE youth who participate in the many sports programmes on offer in the various sporting disciplines.

Despite the high standards already achieved in tourism-related and other projects, facilities continue to be developed and upgraded. In particular, the General Authority for Youth and Sport Welfare (GAYSW) has undertaken a ten-year programme for the improvement of sporting infrastructure and standards for young people throughout the Emirates. As part of this process, the Al Ghail Youth Centre was opened in Ra's al-Khaimah in June 2004. The Centre provides sports, cultural, artistic and social activities for youths from 12 to 25 years of age. Similar centres are under construction in Ajman and Sharjah.

There is no doubt that planned projects and proposals are ambitious. For example, Dubai has commenced building a Dh7 billion Sports City, the world's first integrated purpose-designed sports complex. Scheduled for completion by 2007, the City will be spread over a 4.6-million-square-metre area as a cornerstone of the massive Dubailand project. It will include a 10,000-seat multi-purpose indoor arena, a 30,000-capacity cricket stadium, a 40,000-capacity multi-purpose outdoor complex and a field hockey stadium that will hold 10,000 spectators. The indoor arena will be able to cater for tennis, basketball, volleyball, netball, handball, wrestling, boxing, judo, gymnastics events and ice hockey, while the outdoor stadium will be suitable for soccer, rugby and track and field. Other sports, such as equestrian, motor racing etc, will also be catered for at this magnificent complex, which will certainly assist Dubai in its bid for the 2016 Olympics.

OLYMPICS GAMES 2004

Whether or not the Olympic Games are held in Dubai in 2016, the Athens Olympics will be etched in the memory of all Emiratis because Sheikh Ahmed bin Hasher Al Maktoum made Olympic history for the country when he won its first ever Olympic gold medal in the men's double trap shooting event on 17 August 2004. In a superb display of marksmanship at the Markopoulo Range, Sheikh Ahmed hit an Olympic record 144 of 150 clay pigeons in qualifying and 45 of 50 in the six-man final to take the gold with a final tally of 189 points. Singh Rajyavardhan Rathore of India took the silver with 179 points and Zheng Wang of China claimed the bronze with 178 points. The victory was particularly sweet since Sheikh Ahmed had missed out on a bronze medal in the trap final by a single point.

Sheikh Saeed bin Maktoum bin Rashid Al Maktoum represented the UAE in skeet shooting. Completing the UAE Olympic squad were athlete Ali Mohammed Murad and swimmer Obaid Ahmed Obaid. Middle-distance runner Ali Mohammed competed in the 800 metres, while Obaid contested the 100-metre freestyle.

Also representing her country in Athens was another UAE national, artist Juwairia Abdul Rahman Al Khaja whose work titled 'Minding Sports' won eighth prize in the Sports and Arts Olympiad 2004, organised by the International Olympics Culture and Educational Committee.

OTHER GAMES

The UAE participated in the Pan Arab Games in Algeria from 24 September to 8 October in athletics, chess, swimming, karate, taekwondo, judo, shooting, wrestling and boxing. The delegation included a team of disabled athletes.

Sheikh Zayed also donated Dh600,000 to assist UAE national teams to take part in the GCC championships scheduled for Qatar from 16 to 28 December. The championships will be held on the sidelines of the GCC football tournaments. National teams are also preparing to participate in the Islamic Solidarity Games in April 2005.

FOOTBALL

Al Ain, the UAE's most successful football team, were the victors in the 2004 first division league title for a record ninth time, beating Al Wasl 2–1. Al Ain are also the only club to win the league title three times in a row. In 2003, they were the first UAE club to win the Asian Football Confederation (AFC) Champions League, the pinnacle of Asian football competition, with a magnificent series of victories over top Asian sides. Al Ain also emerged victorious in the GCC Clubs Championship in 2000, when they hosted the tournament, and they won the President's Cup twice, in 1999 and 2001. The club are hoping to retain the Asian Champions League title in 2004, having won an automatic entry to the quarterfinals.

Al Ain's success can be attributed to the fact that they draw their players from a talented pool of UAE nationals. In fact, the UAE team for the Gulf Cup in Kuwait and the World Cup 2006 qualifiers, where the UAE was top of its group, featured 13 players from Al Ain. In addition, the Club has always signed gifted professionals who have played a significant role in helping the team achieve results, including African Footballer of the Year, Abedi Pele, of Ghana, leading Egyptian goal-scorer

Hussam Hasan, Tunisian Eskander Suwayeh and French defender Amin Afano. The present team includes the talented Brazilian Rodrigo and Ivory Coast striker Abu Bakr Sanogo.

Al Ain Club Honorary Council (HC) President Lt General Sheikh Mohammed bin Zayed Al Nahyan, Deputy Crown Prince of Abu Dhabi and Chief of Staff of the UAE Armed Forces, together with Sheikh Hazza bin Zayed Al Nahyan, vice-president of Al Ain Club HC, closely monitors the club's progress and achievements and seldom misses any of their matches. In recognition of Sheikh Mohammed's support for the highly successful Al Ain and the national football teams, Al Mihwar Sports Channel designated him Arab Football Personality of the Year 2003. He was also given the Best Arab Sports Personality Award 2003 in a poll conducted by Egyptian-based Arabic daily, *Al Ahram* and UAE newspaper *Al Ittihad*'s Sports Personality of the Year Award 2004.

However, the season did not go all Al Ain's way as they lost out in the semi-finals of the coveted President's Cup to Al Shaab following a penalty shoot-out. It was Dubai club Al Ahli who eventually won the title for the sixth time, having defeated the defending champions and record eight-time winners Sharjah in the quarter finals and Al Shaab in the finals at the Mohammed bin Zayed stadium in Abu Dhabi.

Asian Cup Qualifiers

Coached by Dutchman Aad de Mos, the national team were in the toughest group in the Asian Cup Finals, which kicked off in China on 17 July 2004. The UAE lost 3–1 to Kuwait in their first match, and, despite putting up a good performance, were effectively eliminated by a 2–0 defeat to South Korea, even though they still had one match to play. On returning home, they had a short rest before resuming preparations for the Asian qualifiers for the World Cup.

UAE Olympic Football Team

Unfortunately, the UAE national Olympic football team were beaten by Japan 3–0 on the last day of the Group B competition at the Tokyo National Stadium in March 2004 and failed to qualify for the 2004 Athens Olympics. The competition had commenced in Abu Dhabi on 1 March. Japan collected 13 points from six matches; Bahrain finished second with 11, after failing to beat Lebanon in a 1–1 tie; the UAE were fourth with seven points and Lebanon were last with two points.

WATERSPORTS

Most of the emirates have well-established marine clubs that promote a wide range of traditional and contemporary watersports. In addition, Emirates Heritage Club in Abu Dhabi organises traditional sail boat races and Emirates Sailing Academy, an affiliate of EHC, educates and trains UAE youth in the basic principles of contemporary sailing and other marine sports.

DHOW RACES

The competitive sailing season in the UAE runs from October to May, and while modern sailboat races, both local and international, are keenly contested, the dhow, the UAE's magnificent wooden sailing craft with its massive rigs, more than holds its own as a racing boat of choice. The dhow poses a challenge to sailing skills whether it is a 22-, 43-, or 60-footer. The crowning glory of the dhow sailing season has to be the 60-foot Sir Bu Nu'air race from the island of the same name to Dubai, which takes place during May – the third and final race of the 60-foot category and the final race of the watersports season. The 58-nautical-mile race attempts to recapture the traditional resonance of the pearling fleet as it struck for home at the height of the pearling trade. A field of over 90 dhows crossed the starting line in May 2004. *Ghazi*, skippered by Ahmed Saeed Al Rumaithi, battled with varying sea conditions to win the race. *Thaib*, captained by Ahmed Thani Al Rumaithi, was second, with *Atlas*, skippered by Ahmed Rashid Al Suwaidi, taking third place.

Dinghy Races

Optimists and Lasers are the boats of choice for the UAE's young competitive dinghy sailors. Facilities and training are provided by marine clubs in the Emirates and the Marine Sports Federation (UAEMSF) organises international exchange programmes to help the sailors compete at the highest level.

The fifth Dubai International Sailing Week Regatta for Optimist and Laser 4.7 categories, held in January 2004 at the Dubai International Marine Club, provided a welcome opportunity for local sailors to pit themselves against international competition and the elements as strong cross winds blew across Mina Seyahi. South African Justin Onvlee dominated the Laser 4.7 Class against stiff competition from Bahrain's Charlie Hill, his South African team-mate Aaron Larkens and the UAE's Adel Khalid. The Optimist category was heavily contested by Dutch sailor Gijs Pelt and Italians Filippo Rocchini, Sergio Racco and Federico Maccari.

The young UAE Optimist and Laser sailors attended intensive training camps at Lake Garda in summer 2004 in preparation for a further sailing season in their home country.

Emirates Team New Zealand

A UAE-sponsored team, Emirates Team New Zealand, an evolution of the team that was defeated by Swiss-based Alinghi in the thirty-first America's Cup in 2003, will contest the thirty-second America's Cup, the world's greatest sailing spectacle, to be held in Valencia in 2007. Until their defeat, Team New Zealand had completely dominated the event since first winning the Louis Vuitton Cup and the America's Cup in 1995. It is hoped that this relationship between the UAE and the world-class team will help to develop sailing in the UAE, using the

Optimist and Laser sailors as a starting point. The aim will be to train young sailors to participate at international events worldwide, including the 2008 Olympics and, possibly, the America's Cup in 2010.

Swimming

The FINA Marathon Swimming World Cup, organised in association with the UAE Swimming Association, was held for the first time at Dubai Creek in May 2004. As many as 30 of the world's elite long-distance swimmers participated in the 10-kilometre course. Bulgarian Petar Stoychev and Germany's Angela Maurer produced strong performances to win the top prizes in the men's and women's categories. Stoychev paced himself, completing the course between the Al Maktoum and Garhoud bridges in 2 hours, 4.56 minutes. Maurer clocked a time of 2:05.15 and came sixth overall.

FINA also held one of its bi-annual board meetings in Dubai in 2004. This was a significant coup in projecting Dubai as a contender to host future championships at an international level.

Jet Skiing

Heats for the UAE Jet Ski Championships are held throughout the UAE with the seventh and final round staged at Mina Seyahi, Dubai. UAE contestants dominated three of the four categories in the championships in May 2004, while Kuwaiti drivers featured strongly in the fourth. Ahmed Jabir Al Hamli took first place in the Runabout Super Stock 785 cc series, relegating World Champion Nadir bin Hindi to fifth position. USA's Alex Kim maintained his overall title in the Ski Super Stock 800 cc; second and third place went to Khalid Mohsin Ali and Mohammed Al Marri respectively. Kuwaitis Ahmed Al Dawas, Mohammed Khalid Al Sayer and Yousef Rabee'an swept the board in the Runabout Stock 1200 cc series, UAE national Mohammed Saeed Al Hamli coming fourth. But the UAE were back in business for the Runabout Super Stock 786-1200 cc category where the UAE's Mohammed Nasser Al Mansouri (joint first), Saif bin Futais, Thani Atiq Al Qamzi and Rashid Al Tayer were the victors and UAE pilots clinched the first six positions. UAE riders were also victorious in the Super Stock up to 800cc category, Khalid Mohsin finishing first with Othman Falahi in tow and USA's Alex Kim in third place.

Powerboat Races

The final stages of the inshore UIM Formula One World Championship are held in Sharjah and Abu Dhabi waters each winter, while the final rounds of the offshore UIM Class 1 World Championship races are staged off Dubai and Fujairah.

Spirit of Norway duo Bjorn Gjelsten and Steve Curtis won the eighth and final round of the 2003 Class 1 World Championship, the Dubai Grand Prix – the culmination of a triumphant year for the two men. The pair's only mistake of the season came when they not only failed to make pole position ahead of the final round, but did not make it into the top three places at all. This hitch did not prevent them from winning the race; Victory 77, crewed by throttleman and former three-time world champion Saeed Al Tayer and driver Mohammed Al Marri, had to settle for second place, just 28 seconds behind Gjelsten and Curtis.

There was disappointment also in the UIM 2003 Formula One Powerboat World Championship when Scott Gillman, the UAE team's captain and coach, was forced to retire from the Abu Dhabi Grand Prix because of engine trouble, leaving the way open for Italian Guido Cappellini to notch up his eighth championship and a place in the history books. Gillman, who had last won in 2000, had put in an excellent showing in the latter part of the season, winning three races in a row, and had only to beat Cappellini in this final Grand Prix to pick up the title for himself. However the UAE won the team title ahead of Zepter Tamoil Team led by Cappellini, despite the retirement of Thani Al Qamzi due to trim trouble.

The UAE's Victory Team, having spent the winter months in an aggressive training programme, are endeavouring to add a seventh world title to their very impressive CV. The big news for the 2004 season was that throttleman Saeed Humaid Al Tayer, the first Arab and only the second man in history to win three Class 1 World Championships, would not be participating in the 2004 series. Test driver and Victory Team crew chief Jean Marc Sanchez partnered Mohammed Al Marri in Victory 77 for the start of the season in Portugal, where *Spirit of Norway*, driven by Bjorn Gjelsten and Steve Curtis, won the opening round on the River Tagus, Sanchez and Al Marri taking second place with Victory Team's Ali Nasser and Ali Al Qama, the season's favourites, finishing fourth. But the Victory Team soon rallied and Ali Al Qama and Ali Nasser in Victory 7 won an incident-ridden fourth heat in Scandinavia in August to clinch the 2004 European Championship. Victory 77 came third.

EQUESTRIAN SPORTS

Horse Racing

Since the Emirates Racing Association (ERA) was formed early in 1990, horse racing in the UAE has gone from strength to strength. Nevertheless, the inaugural Dubai International Racing Carnival heralded an exciting new era for the sport, nine weeks of prestigious international racing culminating in the Dubai World Cup on 27 March 2004.

The Carnival was conceived to help internationalise horse racing in the UAE. The massive prize money and generous incentives associated with the two-month period were designed to entice leading owners and trainers to Dubai. Horses from England, Ireland, France, Hong Kong, Macau, and India competed with the best in the UAE on Nad Al Sheba's dual surface racetrack. Of the 55 races (20 of which were on turf) held during the Carnival, 16 were run at either Listed or Group level, six of these on turf and the remainder on dirt.

The Carnival encompassed some of the most exciting races in the UAE racing calendar, including the Sheikh Maktoum bin Rashid Al Maktoum Challenge for thoroughbreds and purebred Arabians, the UAE 1000 and 2000 Guineas, the UAE Oaks and the Darley Distaff Series, which included the Cape Verdi Stakes and the Balanchine Stakes. An undoubted highlight of the Carnival was Super Saturday on 6 March 2004. Total prize money on offer during the Carnival was US$21,000,000, with an average of over US$117,000 per race, not counting the World Cup meeting.

UAE-based Syrian trainer Mazin Al Kurdi with stable jockey Ted Durcan won a total of 12 of the Carnival races, while South African De Kock was the best among the visitors with six wins, which secured for him the Trainer's Award. However, Sheikh Mohammed bin Rashid Al Maktoum, Crown Prince of Dubai and UAE Minister of Defence, dominated the Carnival with 16 wins, including the memorable success achieved by *Little Jim* in the UAE 2000 Guineas, *State Shinto* in the first round of the Maktoum Challenge, *Cherry Pickings* in the Burj Nahaar, *Tamaraillo* in the UAE Oaks, and *Van Nistelrooy* in the purebred Arabian version of the Maktoum Challenge.

De Kock's team was led by *Victory Moon*. The 2003 UAE Derby winner landed two legs of the three-race Maktoum Challenge series he contested, including a convincing win in the final round on *Super Saturday*. Turkish-owned *Dinyeper* was second, just over three lengths ahead of Godolphin's *Naheef* under Frankie Dettori.

The US$6 million Dubai World Cup, sponsored by Emirates airline, is the world's richest horse race, one of seven races in the US$15.25 million Dubai World Cup race meeting, the world's richest meet. Out of the seven race cards, five have been accorded Group One status by the International Classification Committee, an acknowledgment of the meet's world status.

The US$2,000,000 Dubai Duty Free proved to be the most dramatic race in the 2004 event with judges declaring a dead heat between Andreas Wohler's *Paolini* and *Right Approach* trained by Mike de Kock. *Lundy's Liability*, ridden by Weichong Marwing, was successful in the US$2 million UAE Derby featuring three-year-old thoroughbreds, supplying Mike de Kock with his second successive win in the race, the final leg of the UAE Triple Crown that includes the UAE 2000 Guineas and the BurJuman Al Bastikiya races. It was a memorable debut for trainer Andre Fabre and jockey Gary Stevens who won the US$2 million Dubai Sheema Classic, their very first race together, when *Polish Summer* beat *American Hard Buck* by just half a length. The US$2 million Dubai Golden Shaheen, sponsored by *Gulf News*, proved to be an exciting race with the 20–1 shot *Our New Recruit*, ridden by Alex Solis, winning by 2.5 lengths. Godolphin trainer Saeed bin Suroor had his seventh success in nine outings when the US$1 million Godolphin Mile was won by defending champion *Firebreak*, ridden by Frankie Dettori. *Kaolino*, owned by Sheikh Hamdan bin Rashid Al Maktoum, Dubai Deputy Ruler and UAE Minister

of Finance and Industry, was the victor in the EMAAR-sponsored, 2000-metre, US$250,000 Dubai Kahayla Classic for purebred Arabian horses.

But all eyes were on the finish line as Gerald Ford's *Pleasantly Perfect* with Panamanian jockey Alex Solis battled it out with favourite American *Medaglia D'Oro* to win the US$6 million Dubai World Cup in a gripping climax, a re-run of the Richard Mandella-trained, *Pleasantly Perfect*'s victory over *Medaglia D'Oro* in the 2003 Breeder's Cup.

Purebred Racing

The world's richest race for purebred Arabian horses was part of a revitalised racing season announced by the newly-formed Abu Dhabi Racing Committee (ADRC), which was constituted by Sheikh Mansour bin Zayed Al Nahyan to run flat-racing at the Abu Dhabi Equestrian Club (ADEC) for the 2003–04 season.

The President's Cup for Arabians, held on 8 February 2004, was said to be the richest race for Arabians in the world with a total prize money of Dh1 million. All in all, ADRC organised 18 race meetings for the 2003–04 season. Increased prize money, a more attractive programme and plenty of prizes for the punters ensured the success of ADRC's endeavours.

Purebred Arabian horse racing is also extremely popular around the world, and this is in no small part due to the efforts of the UAE Equestrian and Racing Federation, which has been organising UAE-sponsored purebred Arabian horse races in Europe for a decade. These races have successfully dispelled the myth that purebred Arabians are not capable of competing in flat racing events.

New venues were added in 2003, including Ireland, Canada and the US, and the inaugural race for the 2004 season was held at Newmarket racecourse in July, featuring the UAE President's Cup (Group I) race and the Abu Dhabi Championship, both run over a distance of 1600 metres each. This was followed by similar races in Deauville, France, Brussels, Belgium, Wilmington, Delaware Park, US, concluding at Newmarket.

Endurance Racing

Over and above its abilities as a flat racer, gruelling endurance races (typically more than 100 kilometres in length) are the undisputed domain of the purebred Arabian horse, and the UAE continues to feature prominently in these events at home and abroad. Commencing annually in October, a host of races and rides are held at Dubai Endurance City in Seih Assalam, Emirates International Endurance Village in Al Wathba, and the new facility at Bu Dheeb, also in Abu Dhabi Emirate, about 80 kilometres from the capital.

A strong team of riders from the UAE challenged their counterparts from the GCC countries in the Second GCC Regional Endurance Competition in January 2004. The CEI-Two star event, organised by the UAE Equestrian and Racing Federation under the patronage of Sheikh Mansour bin Zayed Al Nahyan, was held at the Al Wathba

course. The UAE's Abdul Rahim Helal Al Jenaibi, riding *Super*, took the 120-kilometre seniors' event when stablemate and trainer Ali Khalfan Al Jahouri's horse *Bashaar* was found to be lame and was eliminated, despite finishing first. Mohammed Abdul Aziz Al Hassan from Bahrain riding *Shagra 1* was first in the junior event with the UAE's Layla Abdul Aziz Al Redha on *Misty Reyn* in third place.

An 83-kilometre junior ride, organised by the UAE Equestrian and Racing Federation, was held in April 2004 to inaugurate the Bu Dheeb Endurance Village, which is run by the Emirates Heritage Club. Fourteen-year old Ahmed Mohammed Eisa Bani Hammadi, riding *Kuranda,* took first place in a field of 42. Bani Hammadi continues in the tradition of other UAE riders who have not only featured in rides on the domestic circuit, but have participated in the junior world championships.

Sheikh Hazza bin Zayed Al Nahyan on *Mindari Aenzac* and Sheikh Rashid bin Mohammed Al Maktoum on *Shah* led a strong team of UAE riders in the prestigious President's Cup 160-kilometre ride. This was the first 160-kilometre championship distance of the season. Also joining these two top riders were reigning world champion Sheikh Ahmed bin Mohammed Al Maktoum on *Grafiti du Vermont* and Shareef Mohammed Abdullah Al Baloushi on *Joost*.

Leading the foreign challenge from France, Australia, Spain and the US was two-time world champion from the USA, Valerie Kanavy, who was partnering *In The Cards*, a half-brother to one of the world's best purebred Arabian race horses, *Al Anudd*, a chestnut mare that ran flat races in Sheikh Zayed's colours. She was virtually unbeatable and retired in 2000 after winning a record number of races. European Open Champion General Sheikh Mohammed bin Rashid Al Maktoum, Crown Prince of Dubai and UAE Minister of Defence, did not participate.

In March, a strong field of riders competed in the Omega-sponsored, 140-kilometre, CEI-Three Star Triple Crown Endurance ride, bringing an end to the endurance season for 2003–04. Sheikh Rashid bin Hamdan Al Maktoum emerged overall champion in the series, his first major triumph in endurance racing. Sheikh Rashid extended his run of consistent performances when he finished seventh in the third leg of the Triple Crown, topping the points tally, which took into consideration the individual finish in each leg and the horse ridden.

As the season ended in the UAE, the focus switched to Europe for the summer months with horses and riders from the UAE competing in major events. In June at Newmarket, UK, Sheikh Hamdan bin Mohammed Al Maktoum led a 1–2 finish for the UAE in the CEI-O three-star 160-kilometre endurance ride, while Sheikh Mohammed finished sixth, but his horse failed to clear the final vet check. The Newmarket Race, which attracted some of the world's top riders, also kick-started the final preparations by riders for the World Endurance Championships to be held in Dubai in January 2005. Sheikh Mohammed went on to win the two-day 160-kilometre open endurance championship at the Wicklow Hills Endurance Festival in Ireland in July.

Dubai International Arabian Horse Championship

In the light of the undoubted success of the inaugural Dubai International Arabian Horse Championships (DIAHC), the organising committee has decided to make the Dubai World Trade Centre Complex (DWTC) its official venue until the year 2010. The DIAHC will also be shifting its management office to the DWTC complex. The Championships, which will be held in all eight halls of the sprawling DWTC complex from 27 to 30 March 2005, is the largest and most representative of its kind in the region. Running alongside it will be an exhibition, the Dubai International Horse Fair.

Show Jumping

National, regional and international show-jumping events are held regularly at equestrian clubs in Abu Dhabi, Sharjah and Dubai. A programme for show jumpers is well established and the most promising participants are sent abroad to get wider experience at international level.

Events such as the three-day CSI-B Abu Dhabi Championship, held at Abu Dhabi Equestrian Club under the patronage of Sheikh Mansour bin Zayed Al Nahyan, are helping to put UAE show jumping on the international map. The 2004 CSI Championship featured a star-studded line-up, including reigning world champion, Dermot Lennon. Competing in the team championship for the United Arab Emirates were Mohammed Al Owais, Abdulla Al Sheibi, Adel Khamis and Muftah Al Dhaheri, part of the team that won the previous year. The UAE's Arif Ahmed, winner of the Abu Dhabi Grand Prix, also defended his title.

Lennon, who won the world title in Jerez in 2002, partnered *Impact* to win the International Table A and *Caesar* to win the six bars event. The latter was keenly contested with Lennon, Qatar's Bader Al Darwish and Jordan's Princess Haya participating in three jump-offs. All was not lost for the host country as UAE national Mohammed Al Kumaiti triumphed in the International Two Phases on *Diabolo 244*, whilst Abdulla Ali Al Sheibi on *Elp St. Clair*, Ali Al Kumaiti on *Heros de Sede* and Sheikh Majid Al Qasimi on *Leslie V* clinched the 1–2–3–4 sweep by the UAE.

GOLF

The UAE has become one of the leading golfing destinations in the world. The country now has around a dozen first-class golf clubs, with new courses being added annually throughout the Emirates.

Manicured greens and rich vegetation are a feature of most of the golf courses. However, sand courses like Al Ghazal Golf Course in Abu Dhabi are also popular and landscaping of the newer courses is more in keeping with local conditions, many using salt-tolerant grasses. The 18-hole Tower Links Golf Course, the first grassed golf course to be constructed in Ra's al-Khaimah, is the only one in the UAE to be built around a mangrove reserve, a challenging obstacle for golfers.

Sea Isle *Paspalum* grass, which tolerates saline water and requires lower rates of fertilisation than other grasses, is being used to minimise the environmental impact on the mangroves.

In 2004, it was announced that renowned golfer Greg Norman would be designing three new golf courses for the UAE. One will be an 18-hole 'Signature' course that incorporates the natural movement of the desert. A second 18-hole course, 'The Inspiration', will be a tribute to Norman's career achievements, bringing together distinctive features from holes, courses and regions throughout the world. An additional six-hole par-3 course, 'The Little White,' will feature an assortment of hole lengths, tee placements and pin positions to cater for all ages and abilities.

Innovatively-designed clubhouses are outstanding architectural landmarks in their own right, many of the designs being based on traditional aspects of UAE culture. At Abu Dhabi Golf Club by Sheraton, the clubhouse is in the shape of a falcon swooping down on a golf ball. Emirates Golf Club, although built from thoroughly modern materials such as white concrete and gleaming glass, has managed to create a series of cool, tent-like structures lying low to the ground, redolent of a vanished era. Meanwhile, the clubhouse at Dubai Creek Golf and Yacht Club evokes the gently billowing sails of a stately dhow and that at Jebel Ali Hotel and Golf Resort the prow of a ship overlooking the Arabian Gulf.

Dubai Desert Classic

Ernie Els and Darren Clarke showed individual brilliance en route to winning the nine-hole Challenge Match at the Jebel Ali Golf Resort & Spa, a curtain-raiser for the Dubai Desert Classic. Events like these can usually be relied on to produce top class performances and Els and Clarke, Tiger Woods, Mark O'Meara, Padraig Harrington and Thomas Bjorn thoroughly entertained a 2000-strong crowd of golf fans.

The US$2 million fifteenth Dubai Desert Classic, the biggest since the Desert Classic was first staged in 1989, took place at the Emirates Golf Club's Majlis course at the beginning of March 2004. Spectator figures were at an all-time high, while sponsorship and prize money also set new records. Former US Masters and British Open champion Mark O'Meara took the trophy after an exciting four-day battle against a top-class field that included Ireland's former Ryder Cup hero Paul McGinley, top-ranked Tiger Woods, South African superstar Ernie Els, who won the title in 1994 and 2002, and several European Ryder Cup stars.

A key event on the PGA European Tour calendar, the sixteenth Dubai Desert Classic will be held from 3 to 6 March 2005, once again sponsored by Dubai Aluminium (Dubal). The event is expected to attract leading European Tour players as well as invited world stars.

World Sand Golf Championship

Ireland's Paul McGinley, who narrowly lost the Dubai Desert Classic title to Mark O' Meara, joined other top players in the inaugural Abu Dhabi World Sand Golf

encouraged to administer the grassroots development programme recommended by the International Tennis Federation (ITF).

Meanwhile, the UAE's tennis players participate in regional and international championships, such as the Arab Tennis Championships, Davis Cup and GCC events. In fact, the UAE under-12 team of Faisal Bastaki and Khalid Al Hassaini won the GCC title in the 2003 season. Promising young tennis players were also to the fore at the world ranking under-18 third Abu Dhabi International Airport Tennis Championship held at the Al Ghazal Golf Club and Mafraq Hotel courts in January 2004. Sixty-four players from 28 countries participated in the ITF-sanctioned event in which Morocco's Anas Fattar overcame second seed Ahmad Rabeea in a tense three-setter to emerge as champion. Numerous other events held in the UAE, such as the Marbella Tennis Championships in Sharjah and the Al Yamahi Group Open Tennis Championships in Fujairah, help young and old to hone their skills.

The Dubai Duty Free Tennis Championship is a chance for all enthusiasts to see the best in action, and the 2004 event certainly did not disappoint either the punters or the 160-strong team of young UAE residents who were on ball duty during the tournament.

In the Men's Open, World No 1 and top seed Roger Federer clinched his thirteenth career win with a 4–6, 6–1, 6–2 victory against Spain's Feliciano Lopez, whilst world No.1 Justine Henin-Hardenne also successfully defended her title in the Women's Open with a 7–6 (3), 6–3 victory against Russian teenager Svetlana Kuznetsova. This was the first time in the 12-year-history of the tournament that both top seeds in the men's and women's events retained their titles. Justine Henin-Hardenne, Venus Williams, Capriati and Amelie Mauresmo led a world class field in the women's event comprising 13 of the world's top 20 players.

Meanwhile, the governing body of men's professional tennis (ATP) named the Dubai Duty Free Men's Open 2003 as the top tennis tournament of the year in the International Series Gold category. The award, which is based on votes from the players themselves, was presented at the NASDAQ-100 Open in Miami.

RUGBY

The UAE is the venue for the Dubai Rugby Sevens – one of the Middle East's top sporting and social events. The 2003 Emirates Dubai Rugby 7s confirmed its status as one of the world's leading rugby festivals when a record 1800 players competed in the three-day spectacular from 3 to 5 December 2003. South Africa emerged as final victors, while All Black flyer, Karl Te Nana, entered the International Rugby Board (IRB) series' record books with his one hundred and eighth try, beating previous record holder, Australian Peter Miller. In addition, local teams such the Dubai Dragons, Emirates airline's Flying Muppets and Sharjah Wanderers compete against each other on a regular basis.

CRICKET

The main desire of the UAE's cricketers is to win a berth in the 2007 World Cup in the West Indies, thereby furthering their ambition of winning one-day international status from the International Cricket Council (ICC). The ICC has already put the UAE on the 'high performance programme' (along with Kenya, Holland, Namibia, Scotland and Canada) on the basis of their excellent showing in international tournaments. The UAE last qualified for the World Cup in 1996 (co-hosted by India, Pakistan and Sri Lanka), but failed to do so in either 1999 or 2003.

The national team's victory over Oman by 94 runs in the Asian Cricket Council (ACC) Trophy in Kuala Lumpur on 23 June 2004 will go a long way to furthering their aims at an international level. The UAE played well from the start, beating Singapore by 233 runs in the first match, recording 10-wicket victories over Qatar and Thailand, defeating Malaysia by 61 runs in the quarterfinals and Kuwait by 120 runs in the semifinals. Previously, the UAE had won the ACC Trophy in 2000 in Sharjah, beating Hong Kong by three wickets. They also defended the title in 2002, outplaying Nepal by six wickets in Singapore.

Unfortunately, the team's debut participation in the Asia Cup in mid-July 2004 was not so successful. Home-team Sri Lanka, the Asia Cup winners, coasted to a 116-run victory against the UAE in the first round. India also defeated the UAE by 116 runs. The inexperienced UAE batsmen, many of whom were making their one-day international debut at the event, were no match for some of the world's top players.

Back home, playing facilities are constantly improving. In addition to a 27,000 capacity ICC-approved stadium in Sharjah – the original base of UAE cricket – another top-class venue, the ultra-modern, floodlit Sheikh Zayed Cricket Stadium opened its doors in 2004. Abu Dhabi Cricket Council (ADCC) are confident that the facilities will attract the world's best players to the stadium.

CHESS

Chess is one of the most keenly-followed pursuits throughout the UAE with a thriving junior section in addition to a hugely committed adult following. National and international competitions are organised on a regular basis (see uaechess.org).

The UAE Chess Federation calendar for 2004 revealed 19 different competitions in which UAE chess players are participating, 11 of which are being held on home turf; the remaining 8 are international events like the Pan-Arabic Games and the World Chess Olympiad, staged in such diverse places as Singapore, Yemen, Algeria and Spain. A challenging national series of competitions, such as the Abu Dhabi and Dubai Opens, the UAE League and the UAE President's Cup, produces highly-skilled teams and individuals capable of representing the country admirably at international level.

UAE Taleb Moussa became the first chess player in the UAE to achieve Grand Master status following his results in two tournaments of 29 games played in Alushta, Ukraine from 11 to 31 May 2004. In one he shared first place with 10.5 pts /14 games, while he scored 11 pts/15 games in the second, sharing the first place and raising his rating to 2526 to complete all the requirements for the GM title in line with FIDE regulations. Women's chess in the UAE also has its stars, Mona Al Harmoudi becoming the first woman from the Gulf countries to be awarded the International Masters norm by the World Chess Federation.

CYCLING

Cyclists from the UAE won both the senior and junior competitions on the final day of the 2004 GCC Cycling Championships held in Dubai. Taking top honours in the senior event was Tariq Obaid who covered the distance of 123.2 kilometres in a time of 3 hours, 09.23 minutes. Al Marwi, a young rider from Emarat Club, Ra's al-Khaimah, clinched the junior title in 1 hour, 08.33 minutes. Breaking away at an early stage from the chasing pack, Al Marwi kept a steady pace and went on increasing his lead to finish a clear three minutes from the rest of the riders. Al Marwi's UAE teammates Ahmed Hassan and Essa Abdullah Salim completed the clean sweep.

BOWLING

Bowling in the UAE, already very well served by world-class facilities throughout the Emirates, will receive a major boost with the addition of new alleys. Ra's al-Khaimah is aiming for a larger share of the growing tourism market with the introduction of a 15,000-square-foot bowling alley, which is being launched in collaboration with Brunswick Bowling and Billiards Corporation USA, the world leader in the bowling industry. Plans include a 12-lane Olympic-size facility with a food court, Internet cafe and recreational centre. The facility is scheduled to open during the last quarter of 2004 and competitive events will be held in Ra's al-Khaimah as soon as the alley is established.

The construction of a new US$15–16 million, 56-lane bowling centre, Dubai Millennium Entertainment and Bowling Centre, will facilitate the staging of a proposed US$2.5 million international competition (approved by the World Tenpin Bowling Association), the Dubai World Team Championship. The event will be targeting participation from at least 100 countries with ten different nations hosting as many elimination rounds, the final to be held in Dubai.

Meanwhile, UAE bowling champion Mohammed Khalifa Al Qubaisi was awarded a gold medal at the Moscow World Ranking Masters Championships, having defeated Les Lentila of Finland 2–1 in the final. A total of 24 of the best bowlers in the world (all except Qubaisi were professionals) participated in the championships.

Later in the year, Al Qubaisi announced his decision to retire, due to growing family and professional obligations. However, he was persuaded to rescind the decision and launch an attempt on the Asian title in Thailand in July 2004. Along with Al Qubaisi, the UAE team featured Sultan Al Marzooqi, Naif Oqab, Shaker Ali, Ahmed Attiq and Sayed Ibrahim. Shaker Ali had previously won a gold medal in the singles category of the Asian Championship in 2002 (Qubaisi did not take part in that event). The UAE team is particularly proud of their team result in the 2003 FIQ World Championships in Kuala Lumpur when they won the silver medal. However, success eluded them in the 2004 event.

The UAE youth bowling team gained invaluable experience participating at the eighth WTBA World Tenpin Bowling Youth Championships in Guam from 28 July to 8 August 2004, earning a respectable twentieth place in the Boys 4-Player teams competition with a six-game total of 4380 and an average 182,50.

TABLE TENNIS

Until recently, table tennis was not a serious competitive sport in the Emirates. However, all that changed a few years ago when Hungary's Timar Ferenc was drafted in as the national team coach. In May 2004, a bronze medal was awarded to the UAE junior boys team in the inaugural ITTF Junior Championships organised by the UAE Table Tennis Association, which attracted teams from 21 countries and four continents. Competitions like the international championships are an important aspect of the UAETTA's strategy to achieve excellence in the sport.

The same UAE under-18 squad of Rashid Abdul Hameed, Rashid Mohammad Abdullah, Jassem Mohammad Linjawi and Mansoor Mohammad struck gold in the team event at the 2004 Arab Table Tennis Championships held in Tunisia in August. The boy's under-15 team, consisting of Marwan Mansoor, Hameed Saif, Walid Ahmad, Yousuf Ahmad, Saeed Ali and Ebrahim Al Kook, also came up with a fine display to gain seventh place, and the men's team of Faisal Ahmad Abbas, Mohammad Juma Al Bahar and Mansoor Mohammad did well to end in tenth place in the 17-team competition.

KARATE

Efforts are being made by the UAE Karate and Taekwondo Association (UAE KTA) to improve the profile of these relatively new sports in the UAE. The local clubs have not had much exposure at an international level, so it came as a pleasant surprise when the UAE team, led by Sheikha Maitha bint Mohammad bin Rashid Al Maktoum, won two gold, two silver and three bronze medals on the final day of the first Emirates International Taekwondo Championship on 22 July 2004.

Participating for the very first time in an international Taekwondo championship, Sheikha Maitha was a source of inspiration to the young UAE squad when she

claimed a double in the + 67 kilogram category and the 'Poomsae' (demonstration) competition. UAE teammate Mona Al Gurg took silver in the 'Poomsae', with Wala'a Ebrahim of Bahrain in third place. Bronze medals went to Zainab Ebrahim in the + 67 kilograms and Randa Imam in the -67 kilograms categories.

Abdul Salam bin Deeb was the lone UAE athlete among the male medal winners, picking up a bronze in the –80 kilogram category. But also impressive was teenager Rashid Bilal who went down 6–9 to the World Champion from Iran in the –58 kilogram event.

KITE BUGGYING

The sport of kite buggying, also known as 'parakarting', is relatively new in the UAE. Kite flyers sit on a specially designed, three-wheel, open-frame buggy that is steered using the legs. By adjusting the position of the kite and edging the buggy, the kite flyer can accelerate to significant speeds, climb steep slopes, carve around dune crests, navigate around obstacles, and even travel over water.

The UAE Desert Kite Buggy Challenge, the first ever international kite buggy event in Abu Dhabi, was held in March 2004 under the auspices of Sheikh Ahmed bin Hamdan Al Nahyan, organisation director and UAE team captain. In a weeklong event of thrills and skills, national and international participants covered around 500 kilometres over a combination of terrains across the UAE deserts. The only fuel used in kite buggying is windpower, and the environmental impact on the desert is negligible. Enthusiasts are hoping to attract more people to this unusual sport, which is eminently suitable for the UAE's wide open spaces.

AEROBATICS

Aerobatic experts with their flying machines flew to Al Ain from 15 different nations to take part in the World Grand Prix in January 2004. The event is part of the Federation Aeronautique Internationale (FAI) World Grand Prix Championship, and this was the first time that it was held in the UAE.

OTHER SPORTS

The above is not an exhaustive account of the huge array of competitive and non-competitive sports enjoyed in the UAE. Almost any sport in existence can be played here. Some such as ice hockey, figure skating and skiing seem to be out of place in this desert land. Nevertheless, the facilities for these are excellent. Other more commonplace sports, like basketball, netball, volleyball are also widely played at all levels, while the traditional local sport of camel racing continues to enjoy a wide following.

EXHIBITIONS AND EVENTS

ALMOST EVERY FIELD OF COMMERCIAL, social and leisure activity is served by dedicated exhibitions and conferences in the UAE. Whilst the exhibitions provide valuable points of contact between manufacturers, suppliers and clients, the conferences are forums for exploration of new ideas and wide ranging discussions on various subjects. The country's infrastructure, involving excellent communications, hotels and leisure facilities, has underpinned promotion of the meetings, incentives, and exhibition sector, contributing to economic development. These world-class facilities, combined with a strategic regional and global gateway position, makes it an ideal location for international conferences, conventions and corporate meetings. It has now become a global leader in this field, attracting major events such as the forthcoming International Advertising Association's fortieth world congress in 2006 (unsuccessful bids came from Miami, Bucharest and Sydney) and the 2003 Annual Meetings of the Boards of Governors of the World Bank Group and the International Monetary Fund.

The best source for information on exhibitions and events taking place in the UAE is probably the Internet although, sadly, not all organisers keep their websites up to date. A useful summary matrix and links to forthcoming events is given on the website operated by Abu Dhabi Chamber of Commerce and Industry at http://www.adcci.gov.ae/pls/events/events_statistics.valid.

EXHIBITION CENTRES

Abu Dhabi International Exhibitions Centre (ADIEC), Abu Dhabi's new multi-purpose exhibition area, has greatly facilitated the staging of major exhibitions in the capital. The state-of-the-art centre, owned and operated by the General Exhibitions Corporation, provides 21,500 square metres of flexible interior space with all the services expected from a modern international exhibition centre. Some of the most important international exhibitions in the Gulf are held here, including IDEX, the International Defence Exhibition and Conference; ADIPEC, the Abu Dhabi International Petroleum Exhibition and Conference; POWER-Gen, the International Exhibition and Conference on Power Generation; ROADEX, Abu Dhabi International Exhibition and Conference on Roads; SOFEX, the Special Operation Forces and Law Enforcement Exhibition and Conference; INDUSTRIAL, the International Industrial Exhibition and Conference; IFEX, the International Exhibition of Concepts in Interiors and Furnishings; ADIHEX, Abu Dhabi International Hunting and Equestrian Exhibition; ADIJEX, Abu Dhabi International Jewellery and Watch Show; ENVIRONMENT, the International Exhibition and Conference on the Environment; and Security and Safety, the International Security Exhibition and Conference; the Ramadan and Eid Festival; CONSTRUCT and EDUTECH.

Meanwhile, Abu Dhabi's new seven-star hotel, Emirates Palace, has brought a new dimension to the world of both business and leisure travel in the UAE and will play a key role in creating a new awareness of Abu Dhabi as a destination for major corporate and institutional gatherings. Its state-of-the-art conference centre equipped with the latest communications systems and large seating capacity, combined with the ultra-luxurious guest facilities and beach club, have created another important venue for exhibitions and events in the UAE.

The centrepiece of Dubai World Trade Centre (DWTC) (www.dwtc.com), its 184-metre high office tower, one of the most distinctive buildings on Dubai's skyline, is just part of a complex of large exhibition halls and associated facilities that accommodate approximately 70 exhibitions each year. The Dubai International Convention Centre (DICC), completed in time for the hosting of the 2003 Annual Meetings of the Boards of Governors of the World Bank and International Monetary Fund (IMF), has added to Dubai's exhibition, conference and convention facilities. In addition to its multipurpose auditorium (capacity 600–6000), the DICC, which is large enough overall to accommodate events the size of the World Bank and IMF meetings, is complemented by a variety of onsite accommodation options, including the 412-room Novotel World Trade Centre, the 210-room Ibis World Trade Centre, and the 492-room Dubai International Hotel Apartments. The range and the flexibility of DWTC's interlinked facilities makes it a leading exhibition and conference centre not only in the region, but in the world. New conference facilities were also launched in 2004 at the Madinat al-Jumeriah development where the recently opened Qasr Hotel and Mina a Salam share access to a large new facility for major events.

Dubai's success with hosting the 2003 World Bank and IMF meetings has already led to considerable spin-offs for Dubai's mission to become a chosen location for many other key international events. Dubbed the 'Financial Olympics', the IMF meetings were attended by approximately 15,000 delegates, demanding large-scale infrastructure and logistical organisation.

Dubai also has the real Olympics firmly in its sights, having decided in 2004 to support a UAE bid for the 2016 Olympic Games. The Olympics Committee will start collecting these bids in 2007 and the UAE is likely to be competing against locations in Chile, Belgium, South Korea, India, Germany, Italy, Portugal, Holland, Russia, USA and Israel.

The extensive complex at the Dubai World Trade Centre is frequently home to several different exhibitions at the same time. Many are held each year and have become familiar landmarks in the events calendar of the UAE. These include the Autumn Trade Fair; GITEX, the Gulf Information and Technology Exhibition; Arab Health; CABSAT, the Middle East International Cable, Satellite, Broadcast and Communications Exhibition; ENVIROTEX, an exhibition on the current state of environmental technology and a wide range of related services; Dubai International Boat Show; MOTEXHA Spring and Autumn Fairs, trade shows for the fashion and textile industry; Arabian Travel Market; and the Big Five, which comprises separate exhibitions on Building and Construction; Water Technology and Environment; Air Conditioning and Refrigeration; Glass, Metal, Cleaning and Maintenance; Bathrooms, Ceramics, and Marble.

Sharjah, which pioneered the exhibition industry in the Gulf region with the establishment of an Expo Centre in 1977, continues to expand its capabilities with the construction of the Dh367 million Sharjah World Trade Centre. The 52-storey, 304-metre-high tower is being built on a man-made island and will be connected to the newly-built Sharjah Expo Centre by a bridge. The main block will house the Sharjah Chamber of Commerce and Industry, the exhibition area, conference halls and other commercial representative offices. The exhibition halls will have the capacity to host 7860 people in an exhibition area of up to 20,000 square metres. The Trade Centre will include a mosque, a sailing club and parking spaces for 2500 cars.

The planned structure will complement the 'Expocentre Sharjah', inaugurated in September 2002. This is a versatile venue allowing for the hosting of a range of innovative events. It has its own sophisticated waste water treatment and de-centralised air-conditioning systems, and offers accessible wireless data, Internet and telephone connectivity throughout the complex. Temperature-controlled, column-free halls maximise functionality and flexibility.

Expocentre Sharjah can cope with several exhibitions simultaneously in its four halls of 4000 square metres each, a central boulevard with built-in facilities, including a dedicated press centre, and 6000 square metres of outdoor exhibition area. The centre hosts specialised trade fairs for a number of important trading partners, including Indonesia, Thailand and China. Among its other significant exhibitions are TEXPO, an international trade exhibition for garment machinery, textiles and accessories; the National Careers Exhibition, especially for banking and finance sectors; Gulf Maritime, an international exhibition and conference for the Arab world's commercial, government and military maritime industry; the Middle East Industrial Show, a specialised trade fair for industrial, technology and manufacturing sectors; Consumeexpo Sharjah, a multi-products consumer fair open only to international exhibitors; the Middle East Watch and Jewellery Spring and Autumn Shows, a biannual international exhibition showcasing the

latest designs and trends in watches, jewellery, gold, precious stones, gems and diamonds; the International Food Fair, an international trade fair for food products, supported by the Ministry of Agriculture and Fisheries and the Arab Federation for Food Industries; and the ever-popular Sharjah World Book Fair, organised by Sharjah's Department of Culture and Information, showcasing thousands of titles in Arabic, English and other languages.

Ajman International Exhibition Centre, occupying an area of 22,000 square metres, is designed to carry out complementary activities to those conducted by the other UAE exhibition centres, further supporting rapid economic development in the country and creating facilities for promoting local industries worldwide.

The Ra's al-Khaimah Exhibition Centre (www.rakexpo.co.ae) is a 37,400-square-metre complex located in the Al Nakheel area close to the active business centre. Its calendar for 2004 and 2005 includes the R.A.K. Summer Festival; Indian Products Exhibition; Rehabilitation and Employment of Human Resources Exhibition; the R.A.K. Motor Show; and an International Commercial Exhibition.

Fujairah Exhibition Centre comprises three major exhibition halls, management offices and service utilities in a 1080-square-metre space, as well as an outdoor display area. The Exhibition Centre is centrally located between the International Airport and the Fujairah Trade Centre on one hand and the seaport and Free Zone on the other, and is adjacent to the city's main commercial district. A number of internationally important exhibitions have been held at the Centre since its establishment.

INTERNATIONAL DEFENCE EXHIBITION & CONFERENCE

IDEX is held every second year in Abu Dhabi, with the event occurring in the winter of odd-numbered years (2001, 2003, 2005 etc). It is now acknowledged as the largest tri-services defence and security exhibition in the world. The 2003 event, sixth in the IDEX series, hosted more than 35 national pavilions. The UAE's policy of neutrality and non-alignment facilitated the participation of both India and Pakistan, while 28 American firms set up stall in the 1171-square-metre pavilion organised by the Association of the United States Army (AUSA). Other countries taking part included Russia, the UK, France, Germany and South Africa. First time participants included Malaysia, Romania, Korea and Thailand. Before the close of IDEX 2003, 75 per cent of IDEX 2005's exhibition space was booked out and the UAE itself had concluded defence deals valued at Dh1.6 billion. The second Gulf Defence Conference, organised by the General Exhibitions Corporation in collaboration with the Emirates Centre for Strategic Studies and Research (ECSSR), took place on the sidelines of the exhibition.

Over 70 international official and military delegations are expected to attend IDEX 2005 and the organisers have announced a number of incentives aimed at boosting the 'live' demonstrations segment of the exhibition. All exhibitors are being offered an opportunity to lay on live demonstrations during the event. A 'borrow-back' policy is also being offered to exhibitors whose equipment is stationed in the region. The live demonstrations include tracked and wheeled vehicles over the 100,000 square metres purpose built arena, as well as the demonstration of smaller amphibious naval craft at the marina adjacent to the exhibition site. In addition, live firing during the day and night will take place at the Maqatra Firing Range, which is capable of accommodating weapons with ranges up to 25 kilometres, including artillery and missiles. As always, IDEX '05 will also feature its naval berthing at Mina Zayed Port, where there will be an array of naval vessels of various types and missions that will welcome visitors onboard.

IDEX 2005 also recorded considerable interest in its RotorCraft pavilion, introduced for the first time as a dedicated pavilion. Leading companies, including Agusta Westland, Boeing, Eurocopter, Sikorsky, RDM Schweizer, MIL, Kazan, Kamov, Rosvertol, KAI and Meggitt Defence Systems have all expressed interest in taking part. The RotorCraft pavilion will enable exhibitors to display actual hardware of different maritime, army and police helicopters and will be supported by the UAE Air Force and Air Defence, the Navy and the Special Operations Group.

ROADEX

Emphasising the economic importance of the road industry in the Middle East and to demonstrate the achievements of regional countries in meeting these challenges, the UAE held its first exhibition dedicated to roads, tunnels and bridges, ROADEX 2004, at the Abu Dhabi International Exhibition Centre from 14 to 17 March 2004.

ARAB BUSINESSWOMEN

The first Businesswomen Forum was held in October 2003 at the Beach Rotana Hotel in Abu Dhabi, providing a common platform for Arab businesswomen to share their experiences and develop mutual beneficial business networks. It also contributed towards an enhancement of the role of Arab businesswomen in Arab trade and industry. The event was organised by the Council of Arab Women, the Arab League, the General Women's Union and Abu Dhabi Chamber of Commerce and Industry.

ENVIRONMENT EXHIBITIONS

The third biennial Environmental Conference and Exhibition 2005, held in Abu Dhabi, is focusing on disseminating awareness on the importance of sustainable transportation and its correlation with socio-economic, health and environment issues. It is also designed to achieve consensus on broad principles and guidelines for sustainable transportation. This major international environmental event is expected to draw significant attendance by Arab ministers of transportation, communication, health and environment, as well as their counterparts from the EU, USA, Canada, Japan and several African countries. It is also the chosen forum for issuing of the Abu Dhabi 2005 Declaration on sustainable development.

The theme of the second Environment Exhibition and Conference 2003 was 'Environment and Energy'. The Environmental Research and Wildlife Development Agency (ERWDA), in cooperation with the General Exhibitions Corporation (GEC), were the organisers of the 2003 event, and 250 companies representing 26 countries participated. The UAE alone occupied 11 pavilions (an increase of four over the previous year). Germany was the largest participant with 50 companies, followed by Britain with 30 and France with 20. Major UAE and international companies taking part in the exhibition included ADNOC, Dolphin, Shell, BP, Total, and Aramco. The World Energy Council signalled the importance of the occasion by holding their annual meeting during the conference and an important aspect of the conference's deliberations concerned the development of an integrated environment-energy strategy for the region, building upon and consolidating the provisions of the Abu Dhabi Declaration for achieving sustainable development. Keynote speakers included Barbara McKee, Chairperson of the World Energy Council Fossil Fuel System Committee (CFFS) and Dr Claude Martin, Director of the World Wildlife Fund (WWF). According to World Bank statistics, the UAE will invest more than US$64 billion in environmentally-related projects over the coming ten years.

Envirotex 2004, an exhibition on the current state of environmental technology, was held at the Dubai International Convention Centre in February. The exhibition took place alongside announcements of the Second Zayed International Prize for the Environment (awarded to the BBC), and also the Dubai International Conference on Atmospheric Pollution. These events focused national, regional and global attention on the UAE's approach to environmental issues. Prominent exhibitors included companies from Saudi Arabia, Turkey, Sweden and Belgium. Water resources, air pollution, earth preservation, recycling, waste management and energy regeneration were the main categories of environmental technology on show. The exhibition also targeted prevalent international public health issues, including inadequate or unsafe water and food, microbiological contamination of the environment, and overall poor sanitation and environmental hygiene.

HUNTING AND EQUESTRIAN EXHIBITIONS

The Abu Dhabi International Hunting and Equestrian Exhibition (ADIHEX), held in September 2004, provided a valuable forum for manufacturers of outdoor sports equipment and accessories, guns, hunting vehicles, and suppliers of fishing and falconry resources, to showcase their products and services to a high-profile audience of enthusiasts and practitioners. About 150 companies from 20 countries took part in the exhibition. Equestrian activities were given a high priority, in line

with the government's commitment to promote all types of activities related to equestrian sport. The exhibition catered for both amateurs and professional riders. On the fishing side, the exhibition spread its net beyond the immediate interests of game fishermen to cover a wide range of topics under the general heading of fishing, including aquaculture. Meanwhile, different species of falcons were also exhibited, along with various hunting tools and equipment used in falconry. The International Association for Falconry and Conservation of Birds of Prey (IAF), which currently federates 43 falconry clubs from 34 countries, held its annual meeting during the show.

The fifth International Equine Trade Fair, Al Fares Dubai 2004, was held from 6 to 8 December 2004. It was once again structured around the three Es – Exhibition, Education and Entertainment – of previous events but with several new features. In addition to showcasing the entire range of equine products and services, the exhibition focused on horses and their health. There were 42 horse boxes accommodating stallions and horses of different breeds. A veterinary pavilion displayed medicines, feeds, supplements, breeding techniques and other veterinary services. Other special pavilions focused on equestrian sports, riding for the disabled, equine art, equine infrastructure, lifestyle for horse people, camels and pets.

A number of seminars and demonstrations on total horse management, new products and services, nutrition, horse psychology, injuries, diseases, training and exercising, breeding, breaking, grooming, shoeing, horse examination and visits to Dubai's equine infrastructure were organised.

The exhibition was open to the public and provided entertainment for everyone. Special events included a demonstration by Dubai Mounted Police, a polo match and races, an equine fashion show, show jumping, films and pony carriage rides.

CABSAT

The tenth Middle East International Cable, Satellite, Broadcast and Communications Exhibition (CABSAT 2004), which opened on 9 February 2004, was the largest and most representative edition of the show ever held at the Dubai World Trade Centre (DWTC) Complex. CABSAT is widely acknowledged as the premier platform in the burgeoning Middle East market for the latest technologies and business strategies. The show attracts a wide range of visitors and trade professionals, including major buyer delegations. CABSAT 2004 featured group pavilions from China, Korea, Germany, Taiwan and the UK, and featured over 70 local and 170 overseas exhibitors.

ARABIAN TRAVEL MARKET (ATM)

Arabian Travel Market 2005 will be held at the Dubai World Trade Centre from 3 to 6 May. The eleventh ATM, held in 2004, attracted a record-breaking audience of trade visitors and consumers, featured over 1400 exhibitors from 55 countries and was 30 per cent larger than 2003 in terms of occupied floor space. The growth was described by the show's organisers as 'unprecedented' and a vote of confidence in the industry. ATM 2004 also featured the first official pavilions from Abu Dhabi and Iran. Over 8600 trade visitors (47 per cent up on 2003 figures) from 96 countries attended the show, representing a 25 per cent increase on 2003, while consumer attendance also increased by 85 per cent to 8224.

Speaking at the opening of the event, Sheikh Abdullah bin Zayed Al Nahyan called for a joint meeting between Arab Tourism and Interior Ministers to remove obstacles hampering the smooth flow of inter-Arab tourism. Meanwhile, it was noted that the UAE has become the largest tourist destination in the Arab world with around four million visitors per year.

GULF INFORMATION TECHNOLOGY EXHIBITION

GITEX, the largest and most successful event of its kind in the Middle East, is the premier international exhibition for computing, communications systems and applications dedicated to the Information Technology industry and the entire business environment. The GITEX profile includes IT equipment, hardware systems, telecommunication, wireless and networks, software and applications, banking technology and financial services, and research and development technology. The 2004 event was held from 3 October to 7 October at the World Trade Centre Complex. Digital imaging and telecommunication technology continued to be major growth areas at GITEX Computer Shopper.

DUBAI AIRSHOW

The ninth Dubai Airshow is scheduled to take place from 20 to 24 November 2005. Meanwhile, the eighth show held in December 2003 at the Airport Expo Dubai declared an onsite order book of over US$6 billion. Just over 25,000 industry visitors from 84 countries visited the airshow. The 2005 show will for the first time include a dedicated pavilion for unmanned aerial vehicles.

The biennial show is organised by Fairs & Exhibitions in conjunction with the Department of Civil Aviation, government of Dubai and the UAE Armed Forces. Over 550 exhibitors from 36 countries and 13 country pavilions representing major international companies participated in the 2003 event. Of the 13 pavilions, the US hosted the largest with some 80 companies represented. The exhibition also featured pavilions from Ukraine and Jordan for the first time and its first exhibitor from Kuwait – National Aviation Services. In all, around 140 exhibitors came from the Arab world, which contrasts sharply with the first airshow in 1989 when there were only a handful of regional exhibitors. Eighty-five aircraft were fielded and some 23 took to the skies in the daily flying display. The Helicopter Pavilion proved to be a popular innovation.

Facilities at the Airport Expo, the purpose-built, permanent venue of the exhibition, are to be doubled to cope with the increasing demand. The expanded facilities will be ready for the ninth edition of the show in 2005.

ARAB HEALTH

Now in its thirtieth year, Arab Health, organised by the Institute for International Research, is the largest healthcare event in the Middle East and one of the most important ones in the world. With the Middle East healthcare market valued at US$74 billion annually, the event has been attracting more and more exhibitors and visitors each year. A total of 1422 exhibitors from 50 countries, including 25 national country pavilions, displayed their healthcare products and services to over 30,000 visitors in 2004. The visitors included over 4400 dealers and distributors. Arab Health 2005 is expected to register an increase of 20 per cent over last year's figures. With its impressive growth, the exhibition has now been developed into five distinct segments, i.e. Dentistry, Medlab, Pharma, Hospital Design and Interiors, and International Health Services.

BOOK FAIRS

Approximately 800 publishing houses exhibiting Arabic and foreign titles took part in the fourteenth Abu Dhabi International Book Fair in April 2004, which was opened by Sheikh Abdullah bin Zayed Al Nahyan, the UAE Minister of Information and Culture.

The annual book exhibition in Sharjah, the UAE's longest established and largest book fair, takes place at the Expo Centre Sharjah. Previously known as the 'Sharjah International Book Fair', it is now called the Sharjah World Book Fair. The twenty-first event took place in December 2004 bringing together worldwide publishers and booksellers from 37 participating countries, who display their products to both public buyers and traders. Books at the exhibition are available at discounted prices.

MOTOR SHOWS

There are a number of impressive motor shows held each year in the UAE. The Abu Dhabi Motor Show took place from 28 September to 2 October 2004, while Sharjah held its annual International Car Exhibition, also known as the Sharjah Motor Show, from 23 to 27 November. Whilst these are major events attracting over 50,000 visitors, the largest motor show in the UAE is the Middle East International Motor Show, generally held in December in Dubai. The Middle East is a hugely important market for the automotive industry worldwide. Countries such as the United Arab Emirates, where more than 50 per cent of the national population is still under the driving age, and high-consumption markets, such as Saudi Arabia, where over 100,000 automobile units are sold per year, present valuable opportunities for automobile manufacturers. This was reflected at the seventh

Middle East International Motor Show held in December 2003 at the DWTC complex where over 550 vehicles were on display, a huge increase over previous years. Over 75,000 people attended the show. Buyers, car aficionados and admirers were treated to the single largest display of vehicles in the Middle East, enabling discerning visitors to study, compare and select the latest in design and technology.

The show featured manufacturers such as BMW, Mercedes-Benz, Maybach, Chrysler, General Motors, Ford, Ferrari, Bugatti, Lamborghini, Aston Martin, Bentley, Rolls Royce, Jaguar, Maserati, Porsche, Pagani, Rover, Toyota, Volvo, Audi, Volkswagen, Nissan, Mitsubishi, Suzuki and Peugeot. Many manufacturers unveiled futuristic concept cars and prototype vehicles.

The Motor Show also marked the Middle East debut of the 4x4 off-road-circuit, which provided a one-of-its-kind demonstration circuit covering an area of up to 4000 square metres. The Motor Show also features the Motor Parts, Accessories and Motor Plus as a dedicated section for the automotive aftermarket sector.

SEASONAL FAIRS

Special shopping and trade fairs are held in spring, summer and autumn each year in the UAE. These deal in a very wide range of consumer items, from art and antiques to watches. The profile of the International Spring Trade Fair in Dubai lists a total of 31 different categories of goods that are displayed and within each of these categories there are thousands of different products. The nineteenth edition of the International Autumn Trade Fair (IATF), one of the most effective and enduring trade shows in the Gulf, was held at the Dubai International Exhibition Centre from 12 to 16 December 2004, offering the international business community a strategic launch-pad to access the vibrant MENA market. Over the past 18 years, the Autumn Fair has established itself as a premier trade preview stimulating new customer tastes and trends for the US$200 billion regional consumer market. The Autumn Fair generally attracts no less than 15,000 business visitors and stimulates business deals worth millions of US dollars.

Summer in the UAE heralds a special time for children home from school and seeking something exciting to occupy them. Dubai Summer Surprises, a shopping and family fun extravaganza, was started in order to provide a wide range of interesting options that would keep both children and their parents happy. An initiative by the government of Dubai to boost tourism and shopping in Dubai, with the long-term objective of turning the UAE into a year-round tourism destination, it has evolved into an annual ten-week event, during which time there is seldom a dull moment for young people. DSS unfolds weekly 'Surprises' from June to August under different themes, involving different government departments and the support of key sponsors and other companies from the private sector.

The eighth annual Dubai Summer Surprises (DSS) opened in June 2004. In addition to attractive shopping bargains, the event offered opportunities for thousands of visitors to win prizes and the entire city took on a carnival atmosphere, with plenty of exciting activities and entertainment for the entire family to discover. The 2004 programme included special activities, events and displays in a enticing diary of Surprises involving arts, ice, sweets, cartoons, flowers, heritage, adventure, knowledge, back-2-school and colour.

In addition to Dubai, other emirates also run summer events aimed at keeping young people in healthy activities. Abu Dhabi organises a number of summer courses and special activities for children, while Ra's al-Khaimah has its own summer festival.

DUBAI SHOPPING FESTIVAL (DSF)

The 2005 Dubai Shopping festival takes place from 12 January to 12 February under the same theme as the 2004 festival – One World, One Family, One Festival. It is expected to attract an even bigger audience and spending record than the 2004 event. DSF plays a vital role in the country's innovative plans to promote economic development based, not just on the local population and market, but also on regional and global markets through constantly building on its attractiveness as a place to visit, enjoy and experience some retail therapy.

Dubai Shopping Festival 2004 enjoyed its ninth successful run from 15 January to 15 February. There were record numbers of visitors logged-in at the key DSF attractions such as the Global Village and Night Souq, and the overall number of tourists in Dubai over the period of the festival also increased. The festival registered a total of 3.1 million visitors, a 6 per cent increase on 2003 visitors, while the total visitor spend jumped by 13.28 per cent to Dh5.8 billion, compared with Dh5.12 billion in the previous year.

Dubai Fashion 2004, held as part of DSF, included work by four high profile international designers. Christian Dior, Emanuel Ungaro, Christian Lacroix and Givenchy, all of whom displayed their latest collections at dazzling shows at a beautifully decorated Dubai International Convention Centre.

Events to put Dubai on the international sporting map were the World Wrestling Championships, which held daily matches at a specially erected arena on Al Muraqabbat Street. One of the international sport teams that has set up base in Dubai, having moved from the Czech Republic recently, is the Buggyra Super Truck Racing Team. To celebrate 32 years of the UAE, a Buggyra Truck shattered the existing World Record for land speed.

Meanwhile, the Global Village saw record number of visitors drawn to special features such as the Night Souq, Desert Camp, and the new attraction, Jebel Ali Outlet. Major concerts included Jethro Tull and Pundit Hariprasad Chaurasia in fusion, Indian maestro A.R. Rahman, Bryan Adams, Whitney Houston and Tabla Genius Zakir Hussain. Daily concerts, 'Layali Dubai', featured well-known names in the Arabic music world, who performed to a packed hall every evening.

USEFUL CONTACTS

UAE EMBASSIES WORLDWIDE

COUNTRY	TEL	FAX	E-MAIL
Algeria	00213 21 549 677	00213 21 549 666	emaratesemb@wissal.dz
Australia	00612 6286 8802	00612 6286 8804	uaeembassy@bigpond.com
Austria	0043 1 3681455 56	0043 1 368 4485	emirat.vienna@aon.at
Bahrain	00973 17 748333	00973 17 717724	
Bangladesh	00880 2 9882277	00880 2 8811983	
Belgium	0032 2 640 6000	0032 2 646 2473	
Brazil	0055 61 248 0717	0055 61 248 7543	u.a.e.emb@opengate.com.br
Canada	001 613 5657272	001 613 565 8007	safara@uae-embassy.com
China	008610 653 27561	0086 10 845 14412	info@uaeemb.com
Egypt	0020 2 760 9722	0020 2 570 0844	uae@intouch.com
France	0033 1 443 40200	0033 1 47 55 61 04	ambassade.emirates@wanadoo.fr
Germany (Berlin)	0049 30 516 516	0049 30 516 51900	uae@uae-embassy.de
Germany (Bonn)	0049 228 26 7070	0049 228 26 70775	
Germany (Munich)	0049 89 4120010	0049 89 470 77020	
Hong Kong	00 852 2866 1823	00852 2866 1690	
India (New Delhi)	0091 11 2467 0830	0091 11 2687 3272	emarat@bom8.vsnl.net.in
India (Mumbai)	0091 22 5636 9543	0091 22 5634 0404	
Indonesia	0062 21 520 6518	0062 21 520 6526	uaeemb@rad.net.id
Iran (Bandar Abbas)	0098 761 38712	0098 761 575080	
Iran (Tehran)	0098 21 878 8515	0098 21 878 9084	
Italy	0039 06 3630 61005	0039 06 3630 6155	uaeroma@tin.it
Japan	0081 3 5489 0183	0081 3 5489 0813	info@uaeembassy.jp
Jordan	00962 6 593 4780	00962 6 593 2666	uaeemb@index.com.jo
Jordan (Cultural Attache)	00962 6 569 6634	00962 6 567 6635	
Korea	0082 2 790 3235	0082 2 790 3238	uaeemb@kornet.net
Kuwait	00965 252 6356	00965 252 6382	emarat71@qualitynet.net
Lebanon	00961 1 857000	00961 1 857009	eembassy@uae.org.lb
Libya	0021 821 4832595	0021 821 4832598	libuae@hotmail.com
Malaysia	00603 4253 5221	00603 4253 5220	uaemal@tm.net.my
Mauritania	00222 5251 089	00222 525 0992	
Morocco	00212 37 702035	00212 37 724 145	emirabat@iam.ma
Netherlands	003170 4162636	003170 416 2752	
Oman	00968 600 302	00968 602 584	uaeoman@omantel.net.om
Pakistan (Islamabad)	0092 51 2279 052	0092 51 227 9063	uaeembpk@maktoob.com
Pakistan (Karachi)	0092 21 582 4016	0092 21 582 4015	
Philippines	00632 817 3906	00632 818 3577	
Qatar	00974 4838880	00974 4836186	emarat@qatar.net.qa
Russia	007 095 2374060	007 095 2344070	
Singapore	0065 238 8206	0065 238 0081	emarat@singnet.com.sg
Saudi Arabia (Riyadh)	00966 1 482 6803	00966 1 482 7504	
Saudi Arabia (Jeddah)	00966 2 651 1557	00966 2 651 3246	
South Africa	0027 12 342 7736	0027 12 342 7738	uae@mweb.co.za
Spain	0034 91 570 1001	0034 91 571 5176	uaemadrid@infonegocio.com
Sri Lanka	009411 2565053	009411 2564104	uaeemb@hotmail.com
Sudan	00249 11 471 094	00249 11 471110	
Switzerland	0041 22 9180000	0041 22 734 5562	mission.uae@ties.itu.int
Syria	00963 11333 0308	00963 11 332 7961	emirat-damas@net.sy
Thailand	0066 2 639 9820	0066 2 639 9818	uae_embassy@thai.com
Tunisia	00216 717 88888	00216 717 88777	emirates.embassy@planet.tn
Turkey (Ankara)	0090 312 447 5222	0090 312 447 5545	uaeemb@superonline.com
Turkey (Istanbul)	0090 212 2798062	0090 212 2790500	
Turkmenistan	0099 312 450801	0099 312 450784	uaeembassy@online.tm
United Kingdom	044 207 581 1281	044 207 581 9616	commerce@uaeembassyuk.net
USA, NY.	001 212 371 0480	001 212 371 4923	
USA, WA.	001 202 363 3009	001 202 243 2432	uae-embassy.org
USA, Cultural Division	001 202 243 4444	001 202 243 4422	
Yemen	00967 1 248 778	00967 1 248 779	

USEFUL WEBSITES

FEDERAL
UAE Government (all Ministries)... www.uae.gov.ae
Emirates Media Incorporated.. www.emi.ae
Emirates News Agency... www.wam.org.ae
Federal Environmental Agency.. www.fea.gov.ae
Federal National Council.. www.almajles.gov.ae
Ministry of Education and Youth... www.education.gov.ae
Ministry of Health... www.moh.gov.ae
Ministry of Higher Education and Scientific Research .... www.uae.gov.ae/mohe
Ministry of Information and Culture.. www.uaeinteract.com
Ministry of Planning.. www.uae.gov.ae/mop/e_home.htm
UAE Central Bank... www.cbuae.gov.ae
UAE State Audit Institution... www.saiuae.gov.ae

ABU DHABI
Abu Dhabi Airport and Duty Free... www.dcaauh.gov.ae
Abu Dhabi Chamber of Commerce & Industry............................. www.adcci-uae.com
Abu Dhabi Commercial Directory... www.adcci-uae.com/adcci_database.htm
Abu Dhabi Cultural Foundation.. www.culturalorg.ae
Abu Dhabi Customs Dept.. www.auhcustoms.gov.ae
Abu Dhabi International Exhibitions Centre (ADIEC) .... www.adcci-uae.com/adiecntr
Abu Dhabi Islands Archaeological Survey.................................... www.adias-uae.com
Abu Dhabi Municipality... www.adm.gov.ae
Abu Dhabi National Hotels Company... www.adnh.com
Abu Dhabi National Oil Company.. www.adnoc.com
Abu Dhabi Securities Market... www.adsm.co.ae
Abu Dhabi Water and Electricity Authority................................... www.adwea.gov.ae
Al Ain Municipality.. www.alain.gov.ae
Al Ain Museum... www.aam.gov.ae
British Business Group (Abu Dhabi).. www.bbgauh.ae
Department of Water Resource Studies... www.dwrs.gov.ae
Emirates Internet and Multimedia.. www.eim.ae & www.LearnOnline.ae
ERWDA... www.erwda.com
Gen. Directorate of Abu Dhabi Police... www.adpolice.gov.ae
Gen. Directorate of Civil Defence... www.gdocd.gov.ae
General Exhibitions Corporation... www.gec.co.ae
General Information Authority... www.gia.gov.ae
National Corporation for Tourism & Hotels................................... www.ncth.com
Port Zayed... www.portzayed.gov.ae
TANMIA (National Human Resources & Employment Authority)..... www.tanmia.org.ae
UAE Red Crescent Society... www.uaerc.org
World Trade Centre Abu Dhabi.. www.wtcad.com
Zayed Foundation... www.zayed.org.ae

DUBAI
Al Maktoum Charity Foundation... www.mrmcharity.org
American Business Council.. www.abcdubai.com
British Businessmen's Group Dubai & Northern Emirates.............. www.britbiz-uae.com
Dubai Airport Free Zone.. www.dafza.gov.ae
Dubai Al Awqaf & Islamic Affairs... www.awqafdubai.gov.ae
Dubai Chamber of Commerce & Industry..................................... www.dcci.org
Dubai Civil Defence.. www.dcd.gov.ae
Dubai Department of Information.. www.dubaitv.gov.ae
Dubai Dept of Economic Development.. www.dubaided.gov.ae
Dubai Development & Investment Authority.................................. www.ddia.ae
Dubai Development Board.. www.dubaidb.gov.ae
Dubai Duty Free... www.dubaidutyfree.com
Dubai e-Government Portal.. www.dubai.ae
Dubai Financial Market... www.dfm.co.ae

USEFUL CONTACTS

Dubai International Airport...www.dubaiairport.com
Dubai International Financial Centre..............................www.difc.ae
Dubai Land Department...www.dubailand.gov.ae
Dubai Municipality..www.dm.gov.ae
Dubai Naturalisation & Residency..................................www.dnrd.gov.ae
Dubai Police Headquarters...www.dubaipolice.gov.ae
Dubai Ports and Customs...www.dxbcustoms.gov.ae
                                                           & www.DubaiTrade.ae
Dubai Ports Authority..www.dpa.co.ae
Dubai Tourism & Commerce Marketing...........................www.dubaitourism.co.ae
Dubai Traffic Police...www.dxbtraffic.gov.ae
Dubai Transport...www.dubaitransport.gov.ae
Dubai Water & Electricity Company.................................www.dewa.gov.ae
Dubai World Trade Centre (DWTC)..................................www.dwtc.com

SHARJAH
Hamriyah Free Zone..www.hamriyahfz.com
SAIF Zone, Sharjah..www.saif-zone.com
Sharjah Chamber of Commerce.......................................www.sharjah.gov.ae
Sharjah Commerce & Tourism Development Authority...............www.sharjah-welcome.com
Sharjah Customs Department..www.sharjahcustoms.gov.ae
Sharjah Directorate & Town Planning...............................www.shj-planning.gov.ae
Sharjah Expo Centre...www.expo-centre.co.ae
Sharjah International Airport...www.shj-airport.gov.ae
Sharjah Police...www.shjpolice.gov.ae
Sharjah TV...www.sharjahtv.gov.ae
Sharjah Water & Electricity Department............................www.sewa.gov.ae
Sharjah's Museums ....www.shj.gov.ae

AJMAN
Ajman Chamber of Commerce..www.ajcci.co.ae
Ajman Free Zone...www.ajmanfreezone.gov.ae
Ajman University...www.ajman.ac.ae

RA'S AL-KHAIMAH
Port Saqr...www.saqrport.com
Ra's al-Khaimah Airport..www.rkt-airport.com
Ra's al-Khaimah Exhibition Centre....................................www.rakexpo.co.ae
Ra's al-Khaimah Free Trade Zone......................................www.rakiftz.com
Ra's al-Khaimah Municipality...www.rakmunicipality.com
Ra's al-Khaimah Museum...www.rakmuseum.gov.ae
Ra's al-Khaimah Tourism Department................................www.raktourism.com

FUJAIRAH
Dibba City..www.dibbacity.com
Fujairah Chamber of Commerce & Industry & Agriculture..........www.fujairahchamber-uae.com
Fujairah Exhibition Centre..www.fujairahchamber-uae.com/exhibit.htm
Fujairah Free Trade Zone..www.fujairahfreezone.com
Fujairah International Airport...www.fujairah-airport.com
Fujairah Municipality..www.fujairahmunc.gov.ae (Arabic)
Fujairah Trade Centre...www.fujairahtradecentre.com

GOVERNMENT CONTACTS
UAE FEDERAL GOVERNMENT MINISTRIES IN ABU DHABI

	PO Box	Telephone	E-mail
Agriculture & Fisheries	213	02 6662781	maf@uae.gov.ae
Cabinet Affairs	899	02 6811113	moca@uae.gov.ae
Communications	900	02 6651900	
Defence	46616	02 4461300	
Economy & Planning	901	02 6265000	economy@emirates.net.ae

Education	295	02 6213800	
Energy	59	02 6671999	mopmr@uae.gov.ae
Finance & Industry	433	02 6726000	mofi@uae.gov.ae
Foreign Affairs	1	02 6652200	mofa@uae.gov.ae
Health	848	02 6334716	postmaster@moh.gov.ae
Information & Culture	17	02 4453000	mininfex@emirates.net.ae
			info@extinfo.gov.ae
Interior	398	02 4414666	
Justice, Islamic Affairs & Awqaf	260	02 6814000	moja@gov.ae
Labour & Social Affairs	809	02 6671700	auh@mol.gov.ae
Presidential Affairs			
Public Works & Housing	878	02 6651778	mpwh@uae.gov.ae
Supreme Council and GCC Affairs	545	02 6323900	

GOVERNMENT AND OTHER ORGANISATIONS BY EMIRATE

ABU DHABI	PO Box	Telephone
Abu Dhabi Chamber of Commerce & Industry	662	02 6214000
Abu Dhabi Water & Electricity Authority	6120	02 6943333
Agriculture & Animal Production (Al Ain)	1004	03 7634333
Amiri Flight	689	02 5757777
Civil Aviation	20	02 5757500
Civil Service Commission	2350	02 6268100
Cultural Foundation	2380	02 6215300
Customs	255	02 6730700
Deputy Prime Minister's Office	831	02 6651000
Economics Dept	853	02 6318800
Emirates Media	63	02 4455555
Executive Council	19	02 6666444
Federal Environment Agency	5951	02 6777363
Federal National Council	836	02 6812000
Federation of UAE Chambers of Commerce & Industry	3014	02 6214144
Finance Department	246	02 6651500
General Industry Corporation	4499	02 6214900
General Information Authority (Computer Building)	3870	02 6652110
General Postal Authority Dubai	8888	04 6215415
General Secretariat of UAE Municipalities	3774	02 4444747
Heritage & History Committee	6052	02 6434700
Marriage Fund	44319	02 6311888
Municipality	263	02 6788888
National Consultative Council	933	02 6726555
Organisation & Management Department	371	02 6215990
Planning Department	12	02 6727200
Police, Directorate General	253	02 4461461
Presidential Court	280	02 6652000
Protocol & Guest House	14	02 6652000
Public Works Department	3	02 4434111
Purchasing Department	838	02 6212700
Seaport Authority, Mina Zayed	422	02 6730600
Shari'a Judicial	84	02 4448300
Social Care & Minors Affairs Authority	5853	02 6459500
Social Services & Commercial Bldgs	3564	02 6310000
Supreme Petroleum Council	26555	02 6020000
The Zayed Charitable & Humanitarian Foundation	41355	02 6814700
Town Planning Department	862	02 6780000
UAE Administration Development Institute	779	02 6654665
UAE Armed Forces	3755	02 4414999
UAE Central Bank	854	02 6652220

USEFUL CONTACTS

	PO Box	Telephone
UAE State Audit Institution	3320	02 6448800
UAE University, Al Ain	15551	03 6669422
Water & Electricity Department	219	02 8839280
Zayed University	4783	02 4453300

DUBAI	PO Box	Telephone
Chamber of Commerce & Industry	1457	04 2280000
Dept of Civil Aviation	2525	04 2066333
Dept of HH the Ruler's Affairs & Protocol	207	04 3531060
Dept of Ports and Customs	63	04 3459575
Development Board	4911	04 2216000
DTCM	594	04 2230000
Dubai Duty Free	2525	04 2162453
Dubai Economic Development Dept	3223	04 2020201
Dubai International Airport	252	04 2245555
Dubai Municipality	67	04 2215555
Dubai Naturalisation & Residency Dept	4333	04 3980000
Dubai Police & Traffic Department	1493	04 2292222
Dubai Police Headquarters	1493	04 2229222
Dubai Ports Authority	17000	04 3451545
Dubai Water & Electricity Authority	564	04 3244444
Jebel Ali Free Zone Authority	17000	04 8815000
UAE General Information Authority	13035	04 2940909
UAE Radio and TV	1695	04 3369999
UAE State Audit Institution	5513	04 2286000

AJMAN	PO Box	Telephone
Ajman Free Zone	932	06 7425444
Ajman Museum	2829	06 7423824
Ajman Police	4	06 7430094
Ajman State Prosecutor	1682	06 7452772
Ajman TV	422	06 7465444
Chamber of Commerce & Industry	662	06 7422177
Economic	870	06 7422122
General Postal Authority	760	06 7422257
Land & Property	95	06 7421606
Legal Adviser	415	06 7422122
Management of Private Properties	980	06 7422711
Municipality	3	06 7422331
Petroleum & Mineral Resources	739	06 7424245
Ports & Customs	388	06 7470111

SHARJAH	PO Box	Telephone
Administration and Control Department	201	06 5541999
Airport Authority	8	06 5581111
Chamber of Commerce & Industry	580	06 5688888
Civil Aviation	8	06 5581158
Commerce & Tourism Development Authority	2661	06 5562777
Committee of Administrative & Technical Development	4693	06 5545917
Culture & Information	5119	06 5541116
Customs Department & Ports	510	06 5281666
Economics Department	829	06 5734444
Endowments & Islamic Affairs	1087	06 5727722
Finance & Administration	201	06 5541999
General Postal Authority	4444	06 5722219
Hamriyah Free Zone	1377	06 5263333
International Airport	8	06 5581111
Islamic Centre	1087	06 5727722
Municipality	22	06 5623333

	PO Box	Telephone
Petroleum & Mineral Affairs	188	06 5541888
Real Estate Registration	478	06 5623333
Ruler's Court (Al Diwan Al Amiri)	1	06 5733333
Sharjah Airport Free Zone (SAIF)	8000	06 5570000
Social Services Department	4424	06 5725333
Television	111	06 5661111
Water & Electricity Department	135	06 5288603

UMM AL-QAIWAIN	PO Box	Telephone
Ahmed bin Rashid Port and Free Zone Authority	279	06 7655882
Immigration Dept	461	06 7666419
Ministry of Electricity and Water	792	06 7655111
Ministry of Labour and Social Affairs	6	06 7660159
Municipality	12	06 7656145
Ruler's Court (Al Diwan Al Amiri)	225	06 7656125
UAE General Postal Authority, Dubai	4444	06 7656148
UAE Ports & Customs	279	06 7655882
UAQ Chamber of Commerce and Industry	436	06 7651111
UAQ General Hospital	24	06 7656888

RA'S AL-KHAIMAH	PO Box	Telephone
Civil Aviation Department	5214	07 2448111
Civil Defence	5425	07 2288899
Customs and Ports Department	8	07 2333613
Frontier and Coast Guard	974	07 2276000
General Postal Authority	1900	07 2333517
Lands Dept	221	07 2332610
Law Courts	10	07 2331541
Ministry of Agriculture and Fisheries	60	07 2461666
Ministry of Economy and Commerce	901	07 2278000
Ministry of Electricity and Water	301	07 2288444
Ministry of Labour and Social Affairs	116	07 2337000
Ministry of Planning	887	07 2283480
Ministry of Public Works and Housing	458	07 2332344
Nationality and Immigration	155	07 2273333
Port Saqr	5130	07 2668444
RAK Chamber of Commerce and Industry	87	07 2333511
RAK Free Trade Zone	10055	07 2280889
RAK International Airport	501	07 2448111
RAK Municipality	4	07 2332422
Ruler's Court (Al Diwan Al Amiri)	1	07 2282222
UAE Central Bank	5000	07 2284444

FUJAIRAH	PO Box	Telephone
Civil Aviation	977	09 2226222
Civil Defence	5	09 2222501
Customs	296	09 2224335
Department of Finance	175	09 2222111
Department of Industry & Economy	1	09 2222111
Fujairah Chamber of Commerce, Industry & Agriculture	738	09 2222400
Fujairah Free Zone Authority	1133	09 2228000
Fujairah Municipality	7	09 2227000
Fujairah Tourism Board	829	09 2231436
General Postal Authority	766	09 2222235
Immigration	5	09 2222727
Police	5	09 2224411
Port of Fujairah	787	09 2228800
Ruler's Court (Al Diwan Al Amiri)	1	09 2222111
Traffic Department	5	09 2222748

UNITED ARAB EMIRATES YEARBOOK 2005

UAE AT A GLANCE

UNITED ARAB EMIRATES

Official Name.................. United Arab Emirates
Political Structure........... Federation of seven emirates established in 1971
National Day.................... 2 December
President......................... Sheikh Khalifa bin Zayed Al Nahyan
Capital............................. Abu Dhabi City
Population....................... 4.041 million
   Abu Dhabi.................. 1.591 million
   Dubai......................... 1.204 million
   Sharjah....................... 636,000
   Ajman......................... 235,000
   Umm al-Qaiwain......... 62,000
   Ra's al-Khaimah........... 195,000
   Fujairah...................... 118,000
Religion.......................... Islam
Language........................ Arabic
Dirham Exchange Rate
   (per US Dollar)............. 3.6725

ECONOMIC INDICATORS

Public Finance *

Current Account Balance 2003 (Dh billion)................................. 23.09
Capital Account Balance 2003 (Dh billion).................................. -14.74
Balance of Payments Overall 2003 (Dh billion)........................... +4.73
Nominal Rate of Growth of Final Consumption 2003 (%)............ 8.1
Nominal Rate of Growth of Fixed Capital Formation 2002 (%).... 4.2
Changes in Consumer Price Index 2003 (%)................................ 3.1

* Central Bank figures Annual Report 2003

Gross Domestic Product

GDP per Capita 2003*... Dh 59,844
GDP in Current Prices 2003 (Dh billion)*...................................... 293.1
GDP 2003 at Constant 1995 Prices (Dh billion)*.......................... 241.83
Real GDP Growth Rate 2003 (%)*.. 7
Estimated Real GDP Growth Rate 2004 (%)**............................. 4.8
Estimated GDP in Current Prices 2004 (Dh billion)**.................. 312.4
GDP Non-oil Sectors 2003 (Dh billion)**..................................... 199.8
Estimated GDP Non-Oil Sectors 2004 (Dh billion)**................... 210.2

* Central Bank figures Annual Report 2003
** Ministry of Planning Report issued in 2004

Trade Figures

Total Exports & Re-Exports 2003 (Dh billion)................ 241.8
Crude Oil Exports 2003 (Dh billion)............................81.22
Total Re-Exports 2003 (Dh billion)............................. 82.06
Total Imports 2003 (Dh billion).................................... 190.8
Trade Balance 2003 (Dh billion) 51.0

Oil & Gas

UAE Oil Reserves (billion barrels)................................97.8
Abu Dhabi's Oil Reserves (billion barrels).....................92.2
UAE Natural Gas Reserves (trillion cubic feet).............212.1
Abu Dhabi's Natural Gas Reserves (trillion cubic feet).. 196.1
UAE OPEC Production Quota Aug 2004 (000s b/d)..... 2,269

Fisheries & Agriculture

Cultivated Areas (acres)...891,098
Number of Date Palms (millions)................................... 40
Fishing Fleet 5191
Fishermen 17,264
Estimated Catch (tons)... 97,574

SOCIAL DEVELOPMENT

Employees (000s) 2003.. 2191.3
Literacy (%)..90
Life Expectancy at Birth 75.25
Infant Mortality Rate 2002 (per 1000 live births)............7.9
Crude Birth Rate (2002).. 15.5
Primary & Secondary Students 2003/2004.................... 592,065
Public & Private Schools 2003....................................... 1,208
Higher Education Registrations 2004/2005.................... 10,459
Social Welfare Beneficiaries 2003.................................. 77,000
Government Hospitals... 30
Primary Health Care Centres.. 115
Government Hospital Beds... 4473

INFRASTRUCTURE DEVELOPMENT

Total Electricity Production 2003 (million kW/h)............48,163
Total Water Production 2003 (bn gallons)..................... 216.4
Fixed Line subscribers 2003 (millions)......................... 1.163
Mobile Phone Subscribers (millions)............................3.308
Estimated Internet Users (millions)............................... 1.25
International Airports... 6
Commercial Ports.. 15
Paved Highways (km).. 4030
Vehicles (000s).. 792

INDEX

CAPTIONS AND CREDITS

Page	Subject	Photographer
8	(upper) Camel among sand dunes.	(H&J Eriksen/Trident Press)
8	(lower) Wadi and mountains.	(H&J Eriksen/Trident Press)
9	(upper) Date-palm grove.	(H&J Eriksen/Trident Press)
8	(lower) Crab plovers among mangroves.	(H&J Eriksen/Trident Press)
10	Sheikh Zayed portrait.	(Frank Spooner Agency)
15	10 June 1969, Sheikh Zayed, Ruler of Abu Dhabi, climbs down from a BOAC aircraft at Heathrow Airport, at the start of his first official visit to Britain.	(Tim Graham, Getty Images).
23	Sheikh Zayed, photographed in 2004.	(WAM, Emirates News Agency)
33	(upper) Sheikh Zayed with Sheikh Khalifa and Sheikh Maktoum. (lower) UAE President Sheikh Khalifa with Vice-President Sheikh Maktoum.	
36	The Arabian horse.	(Lucy Monro)
45	Traditional Arabian dhow under sail.	(Ronald Codrai, courtesy of Justin Codrai)
55	Villagers from a small village in the Liwa on their seasonal trek to the coast.	(B.P. plc)
56	Camels and Bedouin encampment.	(Trident Press)
57	Camels.	(H&J Eriksen)
58	*Shashah* and *gargour* fish trap.	(Trident Press)
59	Traditional Arabian dhow under sail.	(Ronald Codrai, courtesy of Justin Codrai)
60 & 61	Pearls collected from the Arabian Gulf.	(Trident Press)
62 & 63	Traditional hunting scene.	(Lucy Monro)
64	Dancer.	(Trident Press)
65	Henna painting.	(Trident Press)
66	UAE flag flies over the capital city.	(Trident Press)
71	(upper) UAE Cabinet Ministers. (lower) UAE President Sheikh Khalifa with Vice-President Sheikh Maktoum.	(WAM, Emirates News Agency) (WAM)
81	(upper) UAE Chief of Staff and Abu Dhabi Deputy Crown Prince, Sheikh Mohammed bin Zayed Al Nahyan, with the Patriarch of the Syrian Orthodox Church of Antioch and All the East. (lower) 27 April 2004, Berlin. Deputy Prime Minister of the UAE, Sheikh Hamdan bin Zayed Al Nahyan, escorted by German Chancellor Gerhard Schroeder, inspects the parade in his honour.	(WAM) (Johannes Eisele, Getty Images).
84	Abu Dhabi Securites Market.	(Trident Press)
97	Small cargo vessels alongside the Creek wharf in Dubai.	(Gulf News)
99	Monument commemorating IMF – World Bank meeting, held between 23–24 September 2004.	(Nasser Younes, Getty Images)
106	(upper) Dubai Financial Market.	(Gulf News).
106	(lower) Steel plant.	(Gulf News)
107	(upper) Dubai World Trade Centre and environs at night.	(Juergen Stumpe)
107	(lower) Street traffic and the amphibious 'Wonder Bus' in Dubai.	(Juergen Stumpe)
115	Bill Gates, CEO of Microsoft, with Sheikha Lubna, CEO of Tejari and now Minister of Economy and Planning.	(Gulf News)
121	New housing in Dubai.	(Trident Press)
138 & 139	Natural gas industry pictures from Dolphin Energy's project.	(Dolphin Energy Press Centre)
145	Refinery pipe lines connect with distribution network.	(Dolphin Energy Press Centre)
158	Madinat Jumeirah Dubai.	(Trident Press)
159	Abu Dhabi	(Trident Press)
161	Looking up from the Lobby of Burj Al Arab Hotel.	(Jumeirah International)